Disabled People and the Right to Life

Disabled People and the Right to Life looks at disabled people's right to life in its wider sense, discussing the right to a life that is not intolerable, a life worth living. This volume uses a human rights perspective to explore debates and challenges around what this means for disabled people.

Human rights has increasingly come to be seen as a significant framework both to aid understanding of the experiences of those who face oppression and to underpin social, legal and political measures to counter it. The most fundamental of human rights is the right to life – a right which is enshrined in international treaties and covenants as well as in domestic law in many countries, but which cannot be taken for granted by disabled people. With perspectives from both developed and developing countries, the book chronicles attitudes and practices, critically analyses changes and explores the extent to which such changes have been driven by social as well as legal developments. Chapters explore issues such as:

- cost-effectiveness analysis and preferences
- disability rights and resuscitation
- assisted dying versus assisted living
- access to care
- the selective non-treatment of disabled babies and young children.

The distinguished panel of contributors includes academics, practitioners, public officials and activists. This truly interdisciplinary book will be of interest to students and researchers of disability, law, social policy and human rights.

Luke Clements is a professor in law at Cardiff University Law School, Wales, and a practising solicitor.

Janet Read is an associate professor and reader at the School of Health and Social Studies, University of Warwick, UK.

Disabled People and the Right to Life

The protection and violation of disabled people's most basic human rights

Edited by Luke Clements and Janet Read

Routledge
Taylor & Francis Group

LONDON AND NEW YORK

First published 2008
by Routledge
2 Park Square, Milton Park, Abingdon, Oxon OX14 4RN

Simultaneously published in the USA and Canada
by Routledge
270 Madison Ave, New York, NY 10016

Routledge is an imprint of the Taylor & Francis Group, an informa business

Typeset in Baskerville by
GreenGate Publishing Services, Tonbridge, Kent
Printed and bound in Great Britain by
Antony Rowe Ltd, Chippenham, Wiltshire

British Library Cataloguing in Publication Data
A catalogue record for this book is available from the British Library

Library of Congress Cataloging in Publication Data
Disabled people and the right to life : the protection and violation of
disabled people's most basic human rights / edited by Luke Clements and
Janet Read.
        p. cm.
      Includes bibliographical references and index.
      ISBN 978-0-415-40713-7 (hardback) – ISBN 978-0-415-40714-4 (pbk.) 1.
People with disabilities–Civil rights. 2. People with disabilities–Civil rights–
Cross-cultural studies. 3. Right to life. 4. Human rights. I. Clements, L. J.
(Luke J.) II. Read, Janet, 1947-
      HV1568.D54 2008
      323.4'3–dc22

ISBN 10: 0–415–40713–3 (hbk)
ISBN 10: 0–415–40714–1 (pbk)
ISBN 10: 0–203–93345–1 (ebk)

ISBN 13: 978–0–415–40713–7 (hbk)
ISBN 13: 978–0–415–40714–4 (pbk)
ISBN 13: 978–0–203–93345–9 (ebk)

This book is dedicated to the memory of Katy Sunman, April 1980 to April 2005.

Her zest for life changed and enhanced the lives of all who knew her.

Contents

Contributors

Shaheen Sardar Ali is a professor in the School of Law at the University of Warwick, England and Professor II at the University of Oslo, Norway. She is a former Professor of Law, University of Peshawar, and a former health minister for the North West Frontier Province, Pakistan. Professor Ali is an expert on women's human rights in Islam, in developing countries, particularly South Asia and in international law. She has published widely in this field.

Adrienne Asch is Edward and Robin Milstein Professor of Bioethics, Yeshiva University, and Director of the Center for Ethics at Yeshiva University. She has published extensively on disability rights and ethics. Recent relevant publications include 'Disability, bioethics and human rights', in G.L. Albrecht, K.D. Seelman and M. Bury (eds) *Handbook of Disability Studies* (Sage, 2001); *The Double-edged Helix: Social Implications of Genetics in a Diverse Society*, with J. Alper, C. Ard, J. Beckwith, P. Conrad and L.N. Geller (eds) (Johns Hopkins University Press, 2002); and *Prenatal Testing and Disability Rights*, with E. Parens (eds) (Georgetown University Press, 2000).

Jerome Bickenbach is a professor in the Department of Philosophy and Faculties of Law and Medicine at Queens University, Kingston, Ontario, Canada. For the past ten years, he has been a consultant with the World Health Organization in the preparation and testing of the international classification of disability, the ICF. He has published extensively on disability, health, ethics and the law. Publications include *Physical Disability and Social Policy* (University of Toronto Press, 1993) and *Introduction to Disability* (W.B. Saunders Ltd., 1998) and co-editor of *Encyclopedia of Disability*.

Baroness Jane Campbell is a disabled activist who has a long history of parliamentary lobbying for disabled people's civil and human rights. She is a Commissioner and Disability Committee Chair on the Equality and Human Rights Commission. She is an independent health and social care policy adviser, and Chair of the Office for Disability Issues (ODI)

Independent Living Review Expert Panel. She has been a commissioner of the Disability Rights Commission (DRC) since its inception in 2000 and is a former chair of the UK Social Care Institute for Excellence. Her published work includes *Disability Politics*, with M. Oliver (Routledge, 1996). In recent years, she has spoken and published on disabled people's right to life, and in her capacity as a disability rights commissioner has taken an active role in relation to several high-profile court cases. She is also a member of the editorial board of the *British Journal of Social Work* and has been awarded two honorary doctorate degrees.

Luke Clements is a professor at Cardiff University Law School, Wales, an associate fellow of the School of Health and Social Studies at the University of Warwick, England and a practising solicitor. He is a member of the Law Society of England and of the Mental Health and Disability Committee of Wales. He has published extensively on human rights and social exclusion.

Christian Courtis is the legal officer for economic, social and cultural rights for the International Commission of Jurists, Geneva. He holds a Bachelor of Law and a law degree from the University of Buenos Aires, Argentina, and an LLM degree from the University of Virginia, USA. He is a law professor at the University of Buenos Aires Law School, and invited professor at ITAM Law School, Mexico City. He was a visiting/invited scholar in several universities in the Americas and Europe, including the universities of Toulouse–Le Mirail (France), Valencia, Castilla–La Mancha, Pablo de Olavide, Deusto and Carlos III (Spain), California–Berkeley (USA), the European Masters Programme on Human Rights and Democratization (Venice, Italy), the International Institute of Sociology of Law (Oñati, Spain), Diego Portales (Chile), Nacional Autónoma de Honduras, among others. He has published books and articles on human rights, constitutional law, legal theory and sociology of law.

Jozef H.H.M. Dorscheidt studied law at the University of Maastricht, the Netherlands. He is a lecturer on health law at the University Medical Center Groningen (UMCG) and the legal faculty of the University of Groningen. He is also a member of the medical-ethical review board of the UMCG. His research focuses on human rights issues in health care, the legal position of care providers and the legal aspects of end of life-decisions regarding incompetent patients. He has a PhD from the University of Groningen on an analysis of the protection of severely disabled neonates with regard to end of life-decisions under international human rights law, with special reference to the principle of legal equality and the prohibition of discrimination on the basis of disability.

Jónína Einarsdóttir is associate professor in anthropology at the University of Iceland. Her main fields of reseach are anthropology of children, medical anthropology and development studies. Einarsdóttir has field-work experience from Guinea-Bissau (1993–98) on which she bases her book *Tired of Weeping: Mother Love, Child Death and Poverty* (University of Wisconsin Press, 2004). Einarsdóttir has conducted research on ethical questions related to treatment of infants born with a birth weight of 1000g or less in Iceland and the implications of their births on the daily lives of their families.

Jan Fiala is Legal Officer of the Mental Disability Advocacy Center, Budapest, Hungary, an international NGO which advances the human rights of children and adults with intellectual disabilities and psychoso-cial (mental health) disabilities. He holds a degree in international relations from the Bratislava Economics University, a degree in law from the Bratislava Comenius University and an LLM in international human rights law from the Central European University in Budapest.

Phillip French is a PhD student researching the international law of dis-ability and human rights in the Faculty of Law at the University of New South Wales, Australia. Phillip has worked for more than 20 years as a disability activist in state and national organizations of persons with disability.

Rosemary Kayess is an adjunct lecturer at the University of New South Wales in international human rights law. She also chairs the manage-ment committee of the NSW Disability Discrimination Legal Centre and was a member of the Australian Government delegation to the General Assembly Ad Hoc Committee on the Convention on the Rights of Persons with Disabilities, in New York.

Oliver Lewis is Executive Director of the Mental Disability Advocacy Center, Budapest, Hungary, an international NGO which advances the human rights of children and adults with intellectual disabilities and psychosocial (mental health) disabilities. He has written widely on mental health and human rights and teaches mental disability law and advocacy at the Central European University.

Janet Read is an associate professor and reader in the School of Health and Social Studies at the University of Warwick, England. Recent relevant publications include *Disabled People and European Human Rights* with Luke Clements (Policy Press, 2003); *Disabled Children and the Law: Research and Good Practice* with Luke Clements and David Ruebain (Jessica Kingsley Publishers, 2006) and *Disability, the Family and Society* (Open University Press, 2000). She is an editor of the journal *Disability and Society*.

Boika Rechel is a clinical academic fellow in public health medicine at the University of East Anglia, UK. She qualified in medicine in Sofia, Bulgaria, and subsequently obtained an MSc in Community Child Health at the University of Warwick, UK, and a Masters in Public Health at Karolinska Institute in Stockholm, Sweden. Previously she worked at the London School of Hygiene & Tropical Medicine, the World Health Organization in Geneva, and has acted as an adviser to the Ministries of Health of Armenia, Azerbaijan, Bulgaria, Russia and Uzbekistan. Her contribution to this book draws on her PhD research on access to child health services in Bulgaria, undertaken at the University of Warwick, UK.

Mirela Saupe is a psychologist working in NGOs in Romania. She studied in Romania and Portugal and has given a number of international conference papers on her rehabilitation work with disabled children in Romanian orphanages. Her research work is focused on abuse, attachment problems and child development.

Tom Shakespeare is a research fellow at Newcastle University. He trained as a sociologist, and has published predominantly in disability studies. In recent years, he has been active in bioethics and in science engagement. His latest book is *Disability Rights and Wrongs* (Routledge, 2006). He is a past member of the Clinical Ethics Advisory Group of the Newcastle Hospitals NHS Trust and has been involved in the disability rights movement for 20 years.

Bryan Vernon is a lecturer in the School of Medical Education Development at Newcastle University, where he is responsible for teaching medical ethics to trainee doctors. He originally trained as a lawyer, and is an ordained priest in the Anglican church. He is a current member of the Clinical Ethics Advisory Group of the Newcastle Hospitals NHS Trust and a member of the governing body of the Institute of Medical Ethics.

David Wasserman is Director of Research at the Center for Ethics at Yeshiva University. His work has focused on the moral underpinnings of legal practice and ethical and policy issues in relation to disability, health care and reproduction. Recent publications include 'Philosophical issues in the definition and social response to disability', in Albrecht *et al.* (eds) *Handbook of Disability Studies* (Sage, 2001).

Acknowledgements

We would like to thank Micheline Mason for permission to print her poem 'Not Dead Yet' (2006) in Chapter 5. Likewise we thank the editors of the *Journal of Law and Society* and Blackwell Publishing, PO Box 805, 9600 Garsington Road, Oxford, for their kind permission to reproduce as Chapter 9, our article 'Demonstrably awful: the right to life and the selective non-treatment of disabled babies and young children' which first appeared in the *Journal of Law and Society*, 31, 4, December 2004, 482–509.

Preface

Luke Clements and Janet Read

This collection of essays is concerned with disabled people's right to life in its wider sense: the right not only to life, but to a life that is not intolerable, a life worth living and all that that connotes. The distinguished contributing authors have been asked to consider this question from a human rights perspective. In relation to the developed and developing world, such an approach has increasingly come to be seen as a significant framework both to aid understanding of the experiences of those who face oppression and to underpin social, legal and political measures to counter it. The concept of human rights is also increasingly being used to provide a unifying and defining paradigm for research on a wide range of topics across the boundaries of different academic disciplines. While the most basic of human rights, the right to life, is enshrined in international treaties and covenants as well as in domestic law in many countries, there is substantial evidence that for disabled people, this most fundamental of human rights can by no means be taken for granted on the same terms as their non-disabled peers. The law is seen as one element of a dynamic set of social, cultural and historical processes impacting on the human rights of disabled people. The book aims to chronicle attitudes and practices, to critically analyse changes that have occurred and to explore the extent to which such changes have been driven by social as well as legal developments.

This preliminary note must, perforce, draw attention to omissions and limitations. Drawing a boundary round the topic and deciding what should be included and what should be left out has not been easy. There is a danger that we shall inevitably appear to offer a partial account or to give only glancing attention to things that appear crucial to individuals or groups for whom the right to life signifies more than an academic debate. Inevitably, too, there are accounts and analyses of experiences that we desperately wished to see documented in the book but which we were unsuccessful in commissioning: an omission, therefore, does not necessarily indicate that an issue is regarded as less important.

It is perhaps inevitable that a book of this nature has 'Western tendencies' since the idea of a legally enforceable right to life for disabled people is more likely to find expression in the literature of developed nations.

Aware of this danger, we have endeavoured to include contributions from as wide a range of countries as possible. In this respect we have been only partially successful and in relation to Africa we have (despite our best efforts) failed. It is of particular concern that the South African experience is absent given its unique situation in history, emerging from the horrors of apartheid and the AIDS disaster. This allied to its relatively enlightened government and an inspirational constitutional court would make for an extraordinary story: a story that must be told – hopefully in a companion publication.

While we took a decision that the prevention or cure of impairment is beyond the scope of this book, it is important to recognize that this has been and continues to be an important area of debate within disability studies and disability rights activism. In many respects, the issues it raises are of course pertinent to, and intersect with, disabled people's right to life.

The essays in this volume represent the work of activists, academics and those involved in some form of practice in relation to disabled people and disability rights. We regard ourselves as fortunate to have worked with those who have made and continue to make such a significant contribution to this field. The contributors were invited to adopt a broadly sociolegal approach and to explore the forces and circumstances in different national contexts which have promoted disabled people's right to life or legitimated its violation. We also asked them to approach the question of disabled people's right to life from the perspectives they considered to be of most importance and relevance to their experience and context. As a consequence, they have offered a broad-ranging, eclectic and stimulating series of essays centring on a number of key themes. The right not to be arbitrarily killed is, of course, crucial and fundamental but it is only one element of right to life issues. Others include the right to *a* life: the right to be valued, to be treated with respect and dignity and to expect the basic life chances, autonomy, aspirations, protections and sustenance that others take for granted.

1 Introduction

Life, disability and the pursuit of human rights

Luke Clements and Janet Read

Introduction

On 13 December 2006 the General Assembly adopted the United Nations Convention on the Rights of Persons with Disabilities. It affirms unequivocally disabled people's right to life. The previous month however, on 6 November, the *Sun*, a British tabloid newspaper, under the headline 'Kill disabled tots, say top docs', reported that the Royal College of Obstetricians and Gynaecologists had asked for a debate on the possibility of introducing active euthanasia in some cases. The *Sun* reported that such practices were intended to spare parents the emotional burden and financial hardship of bringing up sick children. The newspaper invited its readers to contribute to the debate: 'Have your say. Do you think disabled babies should be killed? Tell us what you think.' (*Sun Online*, Monday, 6 November, 2006, p.1). It is difficult to imagine a newspaper inviting its readership to vote on whether any other group of UK citizens should be killed or allowed to live. The fact that the *Sun* saw it as acceptable to do so in relation to disabled infants, together with the issues it highlighted as germane to the debate, offers a telling reminder of the reasons why many disabled people feel that little can be taken for granted in relation to the valuations placed on their lives.

As Shakespeare (2006) indicates, end-of-life issues for disabled children and adults have been given increased public and mass media attention in Western countries in recent years. As well as the issue of active euthanasia in relation to newborn children, there have been debates about the withholding or withdrawing of treatments for babies and for adults for whom such interventions are judged to be futile and too invasive and painful. In addition, there have been proposed changes to the law in relation to physician-assisted suicide. Discussions on matters of principle have often been linked to landmark legal cases; recent examples include: in the US, concerning the withdrawal of a feeding tube from Theresa Marie Schiavo (Lazzarini *et al.* 2006); in Australia the withdrawal of life support (Messiha 2004); in the UK, Oliver Leslie Burke's challenge to maintain life-prolonging treatment (Coggon 2006); before the European Court of Human

Rights, the right to assisted suicide (*Pretty v. UK* 2002) and the failure to make available life-sustaining treatments in South Africa (*Minister of Health and others v. Treatment Action Campaign and others* 2002) and Ecuador (*Mendoza and Ors v. Ministry of Public Health* 2004).

While some end-of-life matters are irrevocably bound up with advanced medicine in developed countries, this is not the key issue for many disabled children and adults across the world who face appalling deprivations without recourse even to the most basic healthcare (see, for example, Ghai 2001). A limited but growing and important literature on disabled children and adults in developing countries indicates the extent to which the lives of many are constantly placed in jeopardy (Priestley 2001a).

This chapter employs a sociolegal approach to explore disabled people's human rights and, in particular, their right to life. In addition to human rights law, our analysis is heavily influenced by a wide-ranging disability rights literature, and we have tried to ensure that the experiences, perspectives and rights of disabled people, insofar as they are known, are the focus of this work. In this paper, we not only explore those things that directly threaten the lives of disabled children and adults and in some cases, arbitrarily bring them to an end, we also consider some of the processes and circumstances which in one way or another, place life in jeopardy. The withholding or restricting of resources that promote and sustain life and health may have a devastating impact on life and life chances. The ways that disabled people are seen or not seen and the degree to which they are subject to carelessness, neglect, disregard or ignorance, all crucially lay the groundwork for and, in turn, may be used to legitimate violations of their right to life.

Understanding disability and the valuation of disabled lives

The ways we define and theorize disability crucially determine how we approach matters bound up with it, including end-of-life issues. But as Asch (2001:300) observes, terms such as 'health', 'normality', 'impairment' and 'disability' are highly contested: 'Their meanings are not clear, objective, and universal across time and space and are contentious even for contemporaries in the same culture, profession and field'.

Until the late 1970s and early 1980s, in published work, the most influential and dominant ways of describing and defining disability were shaped by a Western biomedical paradigm. As Imrie (2004:289) argues, this largely reflected the medical profession's view of the impaired body as an 'object of scientific interest, classification and medical intervention'. The influence of such discourses with their primary focus on impairment, disorder and defect, together with their assumed consequences, went far beyond the profession of medicine. In the quarter of a century following the Second World War, the Western literature associated with all professions with responsibilities towards disabled children and adults had a marked tendency to characterize them, their personal relationships and their wider social functioning as inherently and inevitably pathological. Disabled people and those close to them were frequently problematized and there was little appreciation that disabled people might experience or aspire to things that their non-disabled peers took for granted (Philp and Duckworth 1982; Thomas 1982; Read 2000). It was considered possible by some to predict with accuracy the quality of life that disabled people and those close to them might expect, solely with reference to the type and degree of impairment diagnosed in infancy (Read and Clements this volume). Such predictions could form the basis for crucial treatment decisions with implications for the saving or curtailing of life itself (see, for example, Lorber 1975).

Biomedical understandings of disability have undoubtedly remained highly influential (Asch 2001) but across the past three decades, they have been challenged and shaped by social theories of disability. While a range of work in the late 1970s and 1980s began to acknowledge the social dimensions of disability (e.g. Blaxter 1975; WHO 1980), the major theoretical and ideological corrective to established understandings of disability came from a growing body of politically engaged scholarship which gained ground through the 1980s and 1990s, initially in North America and Western Europe. This wide-ranging work, sometimes identified as 'disability studies', drew variously on social science and the law to reframe disabled people's experience and progress their rights (see, for example, Gliedman and Roth 1980; Fine and Asch 1988; Oliver 1990; Barnes 1991; Bynoe *et al.* 1991; Morris 1991 and 1998; UPIAS 1976). Many of the academics involved were themselves disabled and the interrelationship between the academic endeavour and the political activism of a strengthening disability rights movement was held by some to be a defining feature of the new disability studies (Abberley 1996; Bickenbach *et al.* 1999; Campbell and Oliver 1996).

At the heart of this work lay a central and unifying set of understandings about disability: a conviction, born of experience, that some of the most restricting and debilitating features in the lives of disabled people were not a necessary or inevitable consequence of living with impairment. Rather, it was held that these restrictions were socially and politically constructed and could, therefore, be changed by social and political means. Variants of 'the social model of disability' gained widespread use as an approach to understanding disability. Some differences notwithstanding, there is now, according to Wasserman (2001:225), 'a broad consensus among scholars writing about disability that the limitations associated with impairment are a joint product of biological features, environmental factors and personal goals'. Thus, as a consequence of these developing understandings of disability, it began to be seen as meaningless to consider impairment out of its social context or to use it alone as the primary indicator of present or future life experience, quality of life or life satisfaction.

Over three decades or more, disability rights scholars and activists have identified how arbitrary benchmarks of normality have been used to the detriment of disabled people (Morris 1989). 'Normality' is, of course, not simply a descriptive term indicating the distribution of characteristics within a given population. It is frequently value-laden and there can be disastrous consequences for those whose characteristics are considered abnormal (see for example, Read and Clements this volume). Dominant discourses have been seen to devalue disabled people and at times to define them as exceptions to commonly held notions of people and citizens. In some circumstances, they could be defined as 'other' and excluded from the category of what it is to be human (Shearer 1984). Asch (2001) argues that the esteem attributed to intellect, rationality, self-awareness and self-reliance leads some to question not only the quality of life of those living with cognitive or physical impairment but also their moral status. Such ideologies may be seen powerfully to have shaped civil, economic, cultural, social, legal and personal discourses in ways that ensured that disabled people were either prevented or discouraged from participating in experiences held to constitute important and expected features of the lives of those who did not live with disability. The subordination and relative powerlessness of many disabled people reinforced by damaging characterizations of their lives could be perpetuated by more powerful others, including those in the professions (see, for example, Barnes 1997; French 1994; Morris 1993; Oliver 1990).

Hand in hand with the explication and rejection by disability scholars and activists of damaging features of the social order came an insistence that the perspectives and opinions of disabled people be heard, documented and validated: that they be seen as experts on their own experience. This approach offered one means whereby disabled people could re-define themselves and their lives both publicly and personally and argue for alternatives to the status quo (see, for example, Hannaford 1985; Saxton and Howe 1988; Morris 1989 and 1991). They fought to affirm the authenticity of lives lived with impairment (Abberley 1996), asserting that being disabled was different from (rather than inferior to) being non-disabled. They challenged the dangerous and pervasive notion that disabled people's lives were not worth living (Morris 1989) and offered an alternative vision not only of what was, but also what might be. Changing the social, political and material environment so that it would be more inclusive of disabled people was seen to be the route to reducing the restricting and damaging experiences that had hitherto been assumed by many to be an inevitable consequence of living with impairment.

The development of distinctive, self-defined, disabled identities may be seen as a crucial element in a political and theoretical struggle to resist dominant and damaging orthodoxies and to win rights hitherto withheld. 'Disabled' is, however, a contested term in any context let alone across different cultures (Asch 2001; Hussain 2005) and it is by no means always clear who might regard themselves or be regarded as rightly inside or outside the category (Shakespeare 2006). It has been suggested that it is questionable whether the majority of those who live with impairment, even within a particular national context, adhere to any form of over-arching disabled identity or sense of shared experience (Bickenbach *et al.* 1999; Shakespeare 2006). We know, for example, that many older people in the UK who live with impairment and face considerable restrictions in their lives neither identify themselves as disabled nor appear to have any sense of connectedness with disability politics (Priestley 2003). In addition, if we see disability as 'a socially constructed complex of relationships, some intrinsic to the individual and some part of the social world' (Bickenbach 2001:567), we have to acknowledge that it is not unlikely that there will be considerable variation in the ways that people in very different social worlds view minds, bodies and identities as well as their experience of disability (see, for example, Stone 2001). There may be some commonality of experience between disabled people in different places, some features of the experience in one context and at one time which are redolent of others in a different time and space but it needs to be acknowledged, too, that there are enormous disparities both within and between populations. An easily shared identity cannot be assumed between disabled adults in, say, North America and their counterparts in those regions of the world where widespread, catastrophic poverty is both a primary cause of poor health, impairment and death and a devastating force that shapes the lives of those surviving with impairment and chronic illness (see, for example, Gordon *et al.* 2003; Ghai 2001).

We also need to acknowledge that the larger part of published disability rights scholarship is firmly located within the developed world and is a product of it (Priestley 2001). Some, particularly perhaps the poorest of the poor in developing countries, may experience lives lived with disability in ways that are only just beginning to be documented within the published disability rights literature despite the fact that the majority of disabled people live in developing countries. Attention has been drawn to speculative Western accounts and common misunderstandings perpetuated about the experience of disability in other cultures (Ingstad 2001) as well as the dangers of the 'unthinking export of Western approaches to the majority world' (Stone 2001:61). A lack of internationally available published materials about particular national or regional contexts should not, of course, be taken as a reliable indicator of a lack of development or struggle in relation to disability issues there (Watermeyer and Swartz 2006).

In addition to complexities of shared definitions, identities and heritages within and between disabled populations, the related, often assumed dichotomy between disabled and non-disabled people has also been called into question (Bickenbach *et al.* 1999). Such a dichotomy may of course be seen as important by disabled people as they attempt to progress their rights through establishing a shared identity and politics and by rejecting impositions by those perceived as non-disabled. Nevertheless, Bickenbach (2001), drawing on the work of the American sociologist Zola, argues against an analysis that conceives of disabled people as a distinct and separate group. He puts the case instead for a 'universalist' approach that recognizes disability not as a *minority group* issue, a special category problem or an aberration from the normal, but rather as a part of the general human condition. Thus, a universalist approach, also argued by Albrecht and Bury (2001), sees disability as a much more fluid state which may be experienced at particular times or over time by large proportions of given populations. Re-analysing disability in this way should not be seen as an attempt to neutralize the oppressive experiences of those truly relegated to the margins, through the assertion, for example, that we are all disabled in some way or another. What we are recognizing is first, that disability is not a clearly defined or fixed state and second, that very large numbers of people across the world at some point in their lives may find themselves vulnerable to at least some of those damaging biopsychosocial experiences (including those with relevance to their right to life) that have been so graphically documented and analysed by disability rights scholars and activists. In some regions of the world, this view is powerfully underscored with reference to the AIDS pandemic.

A human rights approach

A number of writers have argued for the use of a human rights paradigm as an appropriate framework for articulating the experiences of disabled people, and progressing their rights and interests (for example, Morris 1998; Bickenbach 2001; Clements and Read 2003). At its most basic, it affirms without qualification that disabled people are not 'other': they are unquestionably included within the category and meaning of what it is to be human, and may therefore expect all the rights derived from that status. By employing such a normative and unifying approach, the things that happen to disabled children and adults, the lives they lead and the goals they aspire to, may be evaluated against norms or benchmarks established by consensus and sometimes by law, as universal *human* rights. As Imrie (2004:300) argues, 'the very point of universalism is to establish an impartial standard between *different* persons and groups'. So, when disabled people's lives and experiences fall short of universal human rights standards in some way, the issue may be understood as a human rights violation rather than something specific to disability and disabled people. One would wish to advocate this position strongly even were disabled people identified as a very discrete minority group within the populations of the world. Adopting an essentially inclusive human rights approach is further reinforced, however, by the recognition that disability is a rather fluid and universal category and experience, involving substantial proportions of populations across the globe at any one time and over time.

Using a human rights framework as the fundamental underpinning approach to disability need not undermine the validity of conceptualizing disability or disabled people's rights and freedoms in other ways that have proved significant to disabled people. Bickenbach (2001) argues, for example, that the social model and a human rights approach are mutually re-enforcing. The limitations of an approach built entirely around special provision or entitlements for disabled people have been argued (Bickenbach *et al.* 1999; Bickenbach 2001): those provisions that entail defining disabled people exclusively in terms of exceptional minority group status and giving assistance accordingly may be seen to confirm their position outside the mainstream and, in some cases, prove demeaning. There is also a danger that special provisions may be construed as an *alternative* to disabled people's perceived inclusion within general human rights provisions. However, there are a number of good reasons why it may not be desirable to call into question the existence of such redistributive entitlements altogether and why they may co-exist with a human rights approach. Apart from the risks attached to giving up hard-won gains that are of some practical benefit, history tells us that disabled children and adults have often been some of the last in line to benefit from general human rights provisions (Clements and Read 2003, 2005). Historically, special provisions for oppressed groups and, sometimes, specific anti-discriminatory measures appear to be precursors to more general equality measures and have been instrumental in combating barriers to inclusion. It also may be important to consider how special entitlements might be reconceptualized positively within a human rights framework: in short, they might sometimes be the *means* by which disabled people are enabled to achieve the human rights accorded to all (see Read *et al.* 2006). Establishing something as a human right is important but is of precious little benefit if there are not a variety of routes in existence that will enable it to be enjoyed in practice.

It has to be recognized that while the application of the principle of distributive justice and its relationship to human rights inevitably raises contentious political issues even within a given familiar domestic economy, it becomes still more challenging when considered in a more global context. While it is outside the scope of this chapter, we need to be aware that any recognition of the global interconnectedness of nations and their economies, together with the relationship between widespread poverty, disease and impairment, make us realize that we may need to conceive of forms of redistributive justice that go beyond our own borders. Stone (2001:61), exploring the links between poverty, development, impairment and disability, argues, 'It requires us to think about poverty at the level of people, their families and their communities; and then to situate this within regional, national and global structures of wealth and power.' As Lister (2007:157) observes, 'In a breathtakingly unequal globalizing condition, who do we recognize and to whom are we prepared to re-distribute?'

Disabled people and the right to life

There is compelling evidence from around the world that in many national contexts, perhaps most, disabled people's right to life cannot be taken for granted. Priestley (2001b) discusses the ways in which both the majority and minority worlds, policies and practices result in decreased life chances and life expectancy for disabled people making disability a life and death issue. Disabled people's vulnerability to violations that put lives in serious jeopardy has been and remains evident across the developed and developing world. The ways that disabled lives are not protected, safeguarded or sustained, and the lower priority frequently accorded to children and adults living with impairment, are and have always been hazardous for disabled children and adults wherever they live (see for example, Campbell this volume; Priestley 2001a; Read and Clements 2003).

The vast majority of the published debates on end-of-life issues or the right to life of disabled people have tended to focus on practices in English-speaking countries and the Netherlands (Cuttini *et al.* 2000). They therefore reflect the dominant concerns in those contexts and are conducted within the professional, political, cultural, historical and academic traditions seen to be most relevant to them. The greatest volume of published material related to end-of-life issues relevant to disabled people is to be found in the literatures dealing with medicine, bioethics, medical law and disability studies. As we have already suggested, debates about end-of-life issues for children and adults have been the focus of a great deal of debate in Western countries in recent years. Almost invariably, disability and its perceived implications are made central to any discussion about, for example, the treatment of low-birth-weight babies, the withdrawing or withholding of medical treatment from adults, or physician-assisted suicide. The likelihood of a child or an adult being or becoming disabled is almost invariably seen to be germane to any professional or public debate or decision-making process.

From the 1960s onwards in developed countries, rapid advances in medical and surgical technologies meant that it was increasingly possible to preserve or extend the lives of children and adults who would have died hitherto, some of whom would survive with impairment. In contexts where such technologies were available, this brought about a shift as Asch (2001:299) suggests, from the essential medical question, 'Can this life be saved?' to the bioethical question, 'Should this life be saved?' It is evident that for a substantial period, decisions about whether to withhold or limit life-sustaining interventions or even actively to end life were made predominantly within the closed boundaries of professional medical discretion (see for example, Duff and Campbell 1976; Weir 1984; Read and Clements this volume). While there was a gradual increase in open debate in medical journals across the 1970s, it was not until the 1980s and beyond that such decision-making was seen to have legal dimensions which took it outside the confines of medicine and to some degree at least, into the public domain (Kennedy 1988). Initially, disabled people had virtually no voice in these debates but, as we have seen, countering the devaluing and asserting the validity of lives lived with impairment became one of the major and highly relevant themes that occupied disability scholars and activists from the 1980s onwards.

Since this time, a large medical and bioethics literature has developed on end-of-life issues in relation to children and adults who are disabled or who are seen to have the potential to be. A great deal of this has been concerned with documenting and analysing decision-making in relation to withdrawing or withholding treatment in, for example, neonatal care units and intensive care units of hospitals (for example, Forde *et al.* 2002; Seale 2006; Tripp and McGregor 2006; Wood and Martin 1995). Attention has also been given to diverse ethical and religious perspectives in relation to professional practice in these circumstances (for example, Boyle *et al.* 2004; Clarfield *et al.* 2003; Lennard-Jones 2000) as well as to comparative analyses of such practices in different (mainly developed) countries (Cuttini *et al.* 2000; Partridge *et al.* 2005; Sprung and Eidelman 1996). In addition, there have been a growing number of publications which consider the procedural, ethical and legal guidance required in relation to such complex decisions (for example, Rocker and Dunbar 2000; Doyal and Larcher 2000; Nuffield Council on Bioethics 2006). From time to time, there has been public debate about the extent to which resources should be devoted to saving and sustaining lives that are or may be lived with impairment (for example, *BBC News Online* 2006; *Sunday Times* 2006).

It is notable that across three decades, the substantial bioethics literature on end-of-life issues relevant to disabled people has grown in parallel with the disability studies literature but with little positive engagement and much tension between the two (Asch 2001; Kuczewski 2001; Parens 2001; Kaufert and Koch 2003; Kuczewski and Kirschner 2003). Asch (2001), drawing on the work of Wendell, argues that the primary way in which bioethics has concerned itself with disability has been to discuss the conditions or degree of impairment that make it permissible to end a life or prevent a birth. She summarizes her concerns in relation to bioethics as follows:

> For the past three decades, scholars and activists in disability have argued that the problem of disability was, indeed, one of a denial of civil, social and economic rights and not one of biology and health. Yet, attitudes towards disability and the assumptions about the impact disabled people have on families and society that abound in medicine and bioethics all compel those scholars and activists to assert that the first right of people with disabilities is to claim life itself, along with the social recognition of the value and validity of the life of someone with a disability.
>
> (Asch, 2001:301 citing D. Wasserman, personal communication)

The quotation from Asch highlights the relationship between the value attributed to disabled people's lives and the ways in which the most fundamental of their human rights may come under attack. As has been repeatedly argued, it is evident that to live with impairment is to live with a body that is accorded less value than one without impairment (Edwards and Imrie 2003). Lives that are not valued, nor indeed understood from the perspective of the disabled person, may sometimes also be construed as not worth sustaining or protecting either (Morris 1989; Read and Clements this volume).

In general, as we have already noted, it is common for non-disabled people, including those in the professions, to underestimate the potential and actual life satisfaction of disabled children and adults. Disability rights academics and activists have consistently questioned, first, the assumed intolerability of life for people who have impairments and second, the way that any difficulty is too often attributed to their impairments rather than the social arrangements in their lives (Asch 2001; Aspis 2003; Campbell this volume). It is argued that people who have not experienced effective personal and social assistance may be unaware of their transformative potential.

Negative and uninformed assumptions may also be used to legitimate or endorse violations in other contexts, such as criminal proceedings. Asch (2001) points to the way in which the stigma and devaluation of life with disability are evidenced in the acquittals or light sentences given to professionals or family members who decide to end the life of a disabled child or adult. The fact that these outcomes would not be countenanced had the victims of the crimes not been disabled might suggest that their lives are seen to be worth less, that they are assumed not to have lives worth living or that their personhood, on a par with others, is somehow being called into question. The violation of the most fundamental human right, the right to life, may not only be regarded by some as an understandable act from the perspective of the perpetrator, but on occasion, it may also be recast as being in the victim's interest: a mercy killing. This may even be the case when a life is taken without the wish, consent or complicity of the disabled person. When there are limited sources of other support and assistance, many family carers undoubtedly cope with alarmingly onerous workloads (see, for example, Howard 2001; Keeley and Clarke 2002; Read *et al.* 2006). The importance of trying to take into account the just but sometimes competing interests and rights of all individuals in complex and frequently under-resourced situations cannot be emphasized too strongly (Nuffield Council on Bioethics 2006). None of this, however, can make it justifiable to allow the wishes of family or the perceived impact on their lives to subvert the individual's right to life.

While the issue of the prevention or cure of impairment is beyond the scope of this chapter, it is important to recognize that this has been and continues to be an important area of debate within disability studies and disability rights activism. In some respects, the issues it raises are pertinent to, and intersect with, disabled people's right to life. Because efforts to establish the authenticity or indeed, ordinariness, of impaired modes of being have been so crucial, they have sometimes (though not invariably) carried with them the conviction that the only logical corollary is to assert, as Abberley (1997:30) does, that the prevention or cure of impairment is undesirable or even 'genocidal'. Cure or prevention has sometimes been seen to go hand in hand with narrowing definitions of acceptable ways of being, a process that may be construed as undermining and dangerous to those who live with impairment (Wolbring 2001). As Kuczewski and Kirschner (2003:456) comment, 'it is unrealistic to expect that persons with disabilities will not see the implications about the value society accords to their lives from work that celebrates the possibility of a society that is dis-ability-free'. While some have strongly resisted the notion of cure, amelioration or prevention per se, others have argued that such develop-ments do not inevitably and in all cases lead to further disrespect or denigration of the lives of disabled people (see, for example, Read 1998; Brock 2005; Shakespeare 2006). Shakespeare argues for a more nuanced engagement by disabled activists and scholars with the new genetics and with interventions which may ameliorate or cure some impairment (1998, 2005, 2006).

While the main emphasis in this chapter is on the challenge to dominant assumptions that disabled lives are not worth living, it is important to rec-ognize that there are undoubtedly situations when some disabled individuals wish their lives to end. As one might expect, radically differing opinions are held about how such wishes should be viewed and acted upon. This has most recently been debated in relation to the question of whether physician-assisted suicide should be made lawful in various countries (see, for example, Campbell this volume; Shakespeare 2006 and this volume). Some disability writers and activists believe that the option of assisted sui-cide might by default become a more mainstream outcome for disabled people rather than an exception; that there would be a reduced imperative to provide assistance, palliative care and other arrangements that offer the potential of life satisfaction; that disabled people might as a result have a reduced opportunity to experience a way of living that might mean that they choose to live rather than to die; that the acknowledgement that death is seen as a preferable option to living might further re-enforce or condone negative attitudes about disability and disabled people's lives (see for exam-ple Aspis 2003; Campbell this volume). Others, for example Shakespeare (2006 and this volume) argue the case for assisted suicide on the grounds of the principle of autonomy and the importance of disabled people and others having ultimate control over their own bodies and own lives. Between disability rights writers who hold a range of views on this matter, however, there exists a consensus concerning the degree to which under-pinning assumptions about disabled children and adults may place them at risk in unacceptable ways and may put their right to life in jeopardy. Those who support assisted suicide in some circumstances are emphatic about the importance of safeguards so that decision-making is not shaped by coercion or the withholding or withdrawal of essential health or social assistance services (Shakespeare 2006).

Irrespective of the assisted suicide debate, the issue of socio-economic rights and access to essential resources, for example health care, is of great significance in relation to disabled people's right to life. Wasserman *et al.* (2005) argue that when it comes to the allocation of scarce resources, the belief that disabled people must lead lives of poorer quality contributes to lower priority being given to the preservation of those lives. Wasserman (2001:235) summarizes the pervasive utilitarian ideology that regards all individuals as mattering mainly insofar as they are bearers and producers of utility:

> The more utility they gain or produce from a resource, the stronger their claim to it. To the extent that impairments reduce utility, the preservation of the lives of people with disabilities has lower priority; to the extent that correction of impairments increases utility, the medical treatment of people with impairments has a higher priority.

While it is recognized that costs of health and other services have to be calculated and that resources are not infinite, there is a fear that dominant assumptions about disability may mean that disabled people's interests are not always well served. In short, without safeguards, when it comes to the allocation of life-saving and other resources that are seen to be scarce, it cannot be assumed that disabled people's claims for equal treatment will override concerns about reduction in utility over all or deeply ingrained perceptions about their presumed quality of life. It is argued that within medicine and bioethics, end-of-life decisions frequently do not take account of how life *could* be lived with particular reference to the social context. Too often the focus is on how life is *currently* lived or how it is *presumed* to continue to be lived in the future (Kaufert and Koch 2003).

In a context where devaluation and misunderstanding of disabled people's experience is so rife and where there is so little appreciation about what can happen when social barriers are removed and positive social arrangements set in place, it is little wonder that disability rights advocates are troubled by the way that treatment decisions and rationing are increasingly shaped by a range of health-related 'quality of life after treatment' measures. Some, it is argued, may give lower ratings to disabled people and thus place them in jeopardy (see, for example, Asch 2001; Wasserman *et al.* 2005). It is not only the use of such metrics that gives rise to concern among disability commentators, however; it is the sense, too, that disabled people's lives and well-being are reliant upon decision-making that frequently may not have their perspectives and best interests at its core or is simply so variable that it cannot be relied upon to be in their interests. For example, in Western countries, there is evidence of discrimination in access to basic, essential health care (see for example, Evans Report 2001; Shakespeare 2005; Sheehan 2003). There is also reported to be considerable variation within and between countries both on the ways doctors in neonatal and intensive care units define prognoses for disabled children and adults and what they regard as futile treatment (Sprung and Eidelman 1996; Cuttini *et al.* 2000). It cannot but cause disquiet among disabled people when in the mass media and elsewhere, the costs of health care for those whose lives are being sustained become a significant focus (*BBC News Online* 2006; Forde *et al.* 2002; *Sunday Times* 2006).

Human rights standards

Confronted by such cost–benefit assessments of worth – essentially the economic 'worth' of a life – it is hardly surprising that many have sought to incorporate a human rights dimension into their analysis. In this section we consider therefore, the extent to which the law has been influenced by, and in turn has influenced, the evolving understanding of disability. In our analysis we take it as axiomatic that these human rights standards encompass principles of non-discrimination (and accordingly domestic and international anti-discrimination instruments), although as Parker (2006) has observed (citing Spenser 2005), in some jurisdictions 'human rights and equality models have traditionally been treated as "almost entirely separate spheres"'.

The challenges over the last three decades to the medical conception of handicap have resulted in a distinctive jurisprudence concerning disability issues. In large measure the law's journey during this period can be characterized as a gradual loss of deference to the biomedical establishment engendered by the intellectual challenges of the emerging social theories of disability and their strong resonance with developing notions of the positive obligations underlying basic human rights standards. This includes the idea, for instance, that a right to life means more than merely not being murdered by the state, but that such a right includes the right to a decent life (or at least one that is not 'intolerable'), the right to have some freedom in relation to the manner in which one lives one's life, the right to be treated equally in relation to those life choices, and so on.

Articulating the experiences of disabled people in the language of human rights law brings to bear a different value system and (for the purposes of this paper) has two additional benefits, namely the advantage of a distinct power base – separate from that of the medical profession, the Treasury, the family and the church – and the expectation of enforceable remedies.

International human rights declarations and treaties, by specifying basic entitlements, create expected norms: benchmarks to which disabled people can refer if their lives and experiences fall short of these. The authority of the drafting institution legitimizes the instruments; building a consensus; transforming debate and practice. These instruments have the potential to empower oppressed communities and give support to those who wish to see an end to such injustice. Their legitimacy ultimately results in a restructuring of the law and in consequence the social and community relationships regulated by the law; as Tribe (1989:8) has observed, 'each legal decision restructures the law itself, as well as the social setting in which law operates, because, like all human activity, the law is inevitably embroiled in the dialectical process whereby society is constantly recreating itself'.

It follows that one must be cautious about conceptualizing human rights standards as distinct or 'separate'. Each and every 'right' that we today consider fundamental has been contested – be it habeas corpus, the prohibition of slavery, women's suffrage or the rights of black people. Human rights principles of this nature are not first formulated by lawyers, but by radicals, social policy activists, scholars and various religious mystics: from Socrates to the many influential and inspirational writers who fill our bibliography and who have contributed to this edition. The principles that have emerged may now be deemed human rights because they are now acknowledged as universal truths – but they have been hard fought for, and during that struggle were seen as anything but self-evident – though we now hold them to be so.

Such rights and freedoms are the outcome of (in its widest sense) political adjustments, where the law and social change move together: sometimes one leads, as arguably the law has done with the enactment of non-discrimination legislation (concerning race, disability, gender, etc.), although most commonly it is social change that goes ahead and the law that lags. We are today living through a period when these social and legal processes are interacting to create structural and intellectual change in the way disability is understood – practically and conceptually. Indeed it is not unreasonable to believe, for example, that before the end of the decade, the majority of the world's national and international courts will recognize an enforceable right to 'independent living'.

The genesis of human rights

An understanding of process is important, the process by which these ideas become recognized by states and become law in its practical professional sense: in effect the initiation ceremony that converts a strapping idea into an accepted – an established – right.

As a matter of law, a right retains the status of 'a good idea' until such time as it has some formal recognition by government. The first stage of its genesis requires the articulation of the idea in clear and simple terms and then for a critical mass of support to develop behind it. In common law jurisdictions, this alone may be sufficient to leapfrog it into an enforceable right: when a court can be persuaded to develop the law that extra ten per cent and concretize an emerging principle. Arguably this is what occurred in relation to the prohibition of slavery in the UK in *Somerset's* case (1772) and the prohibition of racial segregation in schools in the US in *Brown v. Board of Education* (1954).

In legislative terms this process is exemplified, as we have described above, by the politicization of disability issues, the battle for disabled people's rights and the growth of disabled people's movements to force legal change commencing in the US with the Rehabilitation Act 1973. This example and the emerging conceptualization of the social model of disability and the recognition of the impact of discrimination meant that within 25 years a further 38 states had introduced legislation outlawing disability discrimination (Degener 2005) and the UN General Assembly had adopted the Standard Rules on the Equalization of Opportunities for Persons with Disabilities in 1993 (the UN Standard Rules), a non-binding 'soft human rights' instrument. At this stage of the evolutionary process the collection of rights within the UN Standard Rules might be claimed as 'human rights' but they lack enforceability as such: the final stage requires either their presence in a binding human rights treaty or their recognition by a human rights body in the specific context of another treaty obligation – essentially through the process of *rights integration* as discussed below.

We still await a binding treaty that squarely addresses the rights of disabled people. The adoption by the UN of its Convention on the Rights of Persons with Disabilities in 2006 does not of course make the treaty binding. It only comes into effect when it has been ratified by 20 states and even then it is only binding on a state that has so ratified. Indeed, to describe such a treaty as 'binding' is itself a study of semantics: 'aspirational' would be more apt. On ratifying the convention a state is bound only to lodge every four years a report on the measures it has taken 'to give effect to its obligations under the Convention'.

The enforceability of the right to life within human rights treaties

Lawyers are inclined to separate human rights into the somewhat arbitrary categories of social, economic and cultural rights on the one hand and civil and political rights on the other. Civil and political rights embrace what are sometimes known as 'negative' rights. Essentially a defining characteristic of the majority of such rights is that they are concerned with acts that the state should refrain from doing. Examples include the right not to be subjected to ill-treatment, discrimination, arbitrary imprisonment or unreasonable state interference with one's family or private life. On the other hand, economic, social and cultural rights are deemed 'positive' rights since they place an obligation on the state positively to do something, for instance to provide health and education services, social security and employment.

While such categories are helpful in some respects, a neat delineation between these rights is not of course always possible.

Human rights treaties (unlike declarations such as the Universal Declaration on Human Rights (1948) or the UN Standard Rules) place obligations on contracting states. States do not have to ratify them, but if they do, they must generally file routine reports on their progress towards full implementation and/or submit to a complaints regime.

States have been more circumspect about signing human rights treaties and in general terms the greater their specificity and enforceability, the greater state reluctance. The negative characterization of civil and political treaties means that they have been viewed as less demanding of states than socio-economic and cultural treaties: in consequence states have been prepared to sign up to more robust international enforcement mechanisms for the former than the latter.

It follows that the greater the ability to articulate a right in the language of civil political treaties, the greater the potential for enforcing that right. In this context two such treaties warrant particular attention: the International Covenant on Civil and Political Rights (ICCPR) and the European Convention on Human Rights (ECHR). The ICCPR is policed by the Human Rights Committee (HRC) which can in certain situations investigate individual complaints and make findings and recommendations as to remedial action (Hannum 2004). The ECHR is, however, the ultimate in an enforceable human rights convention: its court, based in Strasbourg, hears individual complaints and hands down binding judgement (Clements *et al.* 1999). Findings by the Strasbourg Court or the HRC represent the high point of international human rights enforceability. In relation to the right to life of disabled people, civil and political rights address directly not only the specific right (protected by ICCPR Article 6 and ECHR Article 2) but also the right to personal autonomy (ICCPR Article 17 and ECHR Article 8) and the prohibition of unlawful discrimination (ICCPR Article 26 and ECHR Article 14).

The right to life

The civil and political conceptualization of the right to life is essentially the right not have one's life arbitrarily terminated. It is a right that such treaties hedge with restrictions (not least by making allowance for the death penalty). In socio-economic terms the right to life brings with it connotations of state responsibility for both sustaining life (for instance through the development of a health service) and for the quality of that life (in terms of challenging environmental harms and destitution).

International tribunals concerned with civil and political rights are showing an increasing willingness to envision these rights – such as the right to life – as more than mere negative state obligations. The Strasbourg Court and Commission, for instance, have theorized the possibility of the right requiring the provision of health and other social care support services – but as yet this remains conjecture. In *Öneryildiz v. Turkey* (2005) the Court held that the convention had to be interpreted in such a way as to oblige states to take 'appropriate steps' to safeguard the lives of those within their jurisdiction no matter what the (endangering) activity and in *Osman v. UK* (1998) the Commission speculated as to the extent of these 'appropriate steps' where the risk derived from (amongst other things) disease or environmental factors. In its opinion:

> the extent of the obligation to take preventive steps may however increase in relation to the immediacy of the risk to life. Where there is a real and imminent risk to life to an identified person or group of persons, a failure by State authorities to take appropriate steps may disclose a violation of the right to protection of life by law.

The HRC's approach to the right to life is undoubtedly more progressive than that of the European Court of Human Rights. In its General Comments 6 and 17 (HRC 1994a, 1994b) the committee cautioned against too narrow an interpretation of the right, which in its opinion requires states 'to take all possible measures to reduce infant mortality and to increase life expectancy, especially in adopting measures to eliminate malnutrition and epidemics' – a view it has repeated in relation to the situation in Jordan (HRC 1995) and Romania (HRC 1994c).

Whilst the Strasbourg Court has considered cases concerning the refusal of a state to sanction euthanasia (*Pretty v. UK* 2002) and found this not unreasonable, the HRC has looked through the other end of the telescope and considered whether state-sanctioned euthanasia is compatible with the covenant – and found that it probably is (Joseph *et al.* 2004:193) when in response to a 'voluntary and well-considered request' of an adult in a situation of 'unbearable suffering' offering 'no prospect of improvement' and 'no other reasonable solution' (HRC 2001:5). The HRC suggested that it might consider otherwise where such a law applied to children, considering that it was

> difficult to reconcile a reasoned decision to terminate life with the evolving and maturing capacities of minors. In view of the irreversibility of euthanasia and assisted suicide, the Committee wishes to underline its conviction that minors are in particular need of protection.

In all other respects, notwithstanding the rhetoric and fine intentions of the HRC and Strasbourg Court and despite their preparedness to envision shades of positive obligations beyond the stark negativity of the right not to be arbitrarily killed, in practice they have yet to require states to provide anything of substance – not even a rudimentary health service (Lester and O'Cinneide 2004; Clements and Simmons 2007).

The right to personal autonomy

Both the ECHR and the ICCPR prohibit unlawful state interference in the private lives of individuals. The text of the ECHR however goes further, requiring states to show respect for individual privacy. In consequence the Strasbourg Court has developed (by its standards) a radical and positive jurisprudence as to the scope and enforceability of this right. In *Botta v. Italy* (1998) Commissioner Bratza considered that the positive obligations imposed by Article 8 might 'exceptionally arise in the case of the handicapped' in order to ensure that they are not deprived of the possibility of developing social relations with others and thereby developing their own personalities' and that in this respect there was 'no water-tight division separating the sphere of social and economic rights from the field covered by the Convention'. Such an approach was accepted by Judge Greve in *Price v. UK* (2001) where she argued that the convention required states to take measures to ameliorate and compensate for the impairments faced by disabled people – that these 'form part of the disabled person's bodily integrity'.

The court, in such cases, is attempting to describe what is required by the complex multi-faceted obligation to show 'respect for a person's private life', by using the language of 'dignity': that the 'very essence of the Convention is respect for human dignity and human freedom' (*Pretty v. UK* 2002:65). Such a right is of course fundamental in terms of the relationship between the citizen and the state: encompassing as it does notions such as self-determination, autonomy, 'bodily integrity' and the ability to entertain social relations and to develop one's personality. It is however 'all the more important for people whose freedom of action and choice is curtailed, whether by law or by circumstances such as disability' (Hale 2004).

It is in relation to the Strasbourg Court's conceptualization of the sphere of a person's private life that one can discern the most obvious merger, not only of civil and political rights with socio-economic and cultural rights, but also with the social model of disability: of disabled people having the same choice, control and freedoms as other citizens (De Schutter 2005; Clements and Read 2005).

The right to equality of treatment

The prohibition of unlawful discrimination is contained within all human rights treaties, albeit that these provisions have in practice been of limited benefit to disabled people. In terms of the genesis of a human right the conceptualization of discrimination remains at an early stage. The European Court of Human Rights, for instance, has yet to recognize doctrines first formulated in the US, such as 'indirect discrimination', or the evils of 'separate but equal' policies (*DH and others v. Czech* 2006) or indeed the discriminatory nature of institutionalization (see for instance *Brown v. Board of Education* 1954 and *Olmstead v. L.C.* 1999).

The failure thus far of human rights treaties to have a meaningful impact on such forms of discrimination is a clear example of the limitations of international human rights law. At the point when the issue becomes the permissible extent of indirect discrimination then states become exceedingly hesitant to ratify wide-ranging provisions. In the European context this is evidenced by the failure of any major state (with the exception of the Netherlands) to ratify protocol 12 which is designed to widen materially the reach of the convention's non-discrimination provisions. This is not because European governments are averse to providing enhanced rights for socially excluded groups since most of the non-ratifying states are bound by stringent EU non-discrimination directives and several have domestic non-discrimination provisions of even greater scope. The difference between adopting such domestic/EU provisions and the scope of an international human rights provision (such as protocol 12) lies in the drafting – the former are detailed and matter specific (i.e. limited to employment, housing, etc.): at this level of specificity, a rights provision sits more comfortably within a domestic statute. If discussion of this detail is occurring, then it is almost certainly the case that the right has 'come home' in the sense it has been accepted and is seen as a natural element of national law. Rights of this nature when embodied in domestic law are accessible, enforceable and indeed frequently not seen as 'human rights' at all but merely unexotic and normative. In terms of the goal of creating a human rights culture, this stage is the high point, for at this stage the right has 'gone global by going local, imbedding itself in the soil of cultures and worldviews' (Ignatieff 2001:7).

The socio-economic rights paradox

Civil and political human rights describe concrete rights that can easily be read across into the laws of virtually any state – common law or civil code. They have since the French Revolution become the obligatory norms embedded in most constitutions. Such rights appear to be relatively discrete and simple things: tools that can be handled by professional lawyers; rights that can be described in concrete terms and protected without inordinate (or unascertainable) economic consequences for the state. It is little wonder therefore that any analysis of the reported judgements of most independent supreme courts would show a marked contrast between the abundant references to these fundamental rights (Epp 1998; Hunt 1997) and the paucity of references to general socio-economic and cultural treaties (save where the state's constitution specifically entrenches such rights). Paradoxically such an analysis would reveal not inconsiderable citation of tertiary conventions such as the UN Convention on the Rights of the Child.

The near silence concerning the economic and social treaties is largely attributable to their overly broad aspirational nature which really take professional lawyers nowhere (or at least nowhere with which they are familiar). Legal rights and obligations need to be specific and accompanied by dissuasive and effective sanctions. Fine intentions, generalized well meaning declarations and broad targets are the stuff of policy, not of enforceable law. In this context one merely has to consider the comments of the Committee on Economic, Social and Cultural Rights (CESCR 1994) concerning the especial vulnerability of disabled children warranting their special protection (para. 32) and the obligation to ensure that disabled people have the same level of medical care as other members of society (para. 34) – likewise its comments (CESCR 2000) concerning the importance of health facilities being accessible to all, especially the most vulnerable or marginalized sections of the population, without discrimination on any of the prohibited grounds (para. 12) and the importance of measures to reduce infant mortality and promote the healthy development of infants and children (para. 22). Appeals of this nature contain no hard kernel of an enforceable right, or if one is discernable, it appears better described in the language of civil and political rights – of gross violations leading to degrading treatment, death or disproportionate interferences in private life (Lester and O'Cinneide 2004; Clements and Simmons 2007).

Where, however, socio-economic rights are entrenched within a constitution, as is the case with several 'modern' constitutions, such as in India, South Africa and many South American states, then necessarily these provisions are subjected to considerable analysis. In general however concrete entitlements do not result from such deliberations since such rights are invariably expressed in aspirational terms – a duty on the state to move towards their 'full realization'. It is only where a state has taken a wrong turn or retrograde action that the courts will intervene. In such cases the intervention will generally be limited to annulling the unconstitutional action and to 'declaring' what has gone wrong and the process that the state should follow to make amends. The courts' response where socio-economic rights are engaged is normally therefore negative in nature – leaving it to the executive to decide the form and content of the positive measures that must result (see for example, *Government of RSA and others v. Grootboom and others* 2000). The exception to this rule concerns those constitutional courts that can give relief in response to an individual petition – and in such cases the courts' response may be positive – albeit limited to specific action on the specific wrong disclosed by the petition (see Courtis this volume).

Rights integration and tertiary conventions

In contrast the tertiary conventions such as the UN Convention on the Rights of the Child (UNCRC) and the UN Convention on the Rights of

Persons with Disabilities (UNCRPD) contain sufficient specificities that, when overlain on traditional civil and political rights, have the potential to dramatically advance their reach – a form of legal 'combination therapy'. The integration of these rights arises in large measure by virtue of status. States by having signed up to a tertiary convention of this kind are effectively estopped from arguing against any principle therein. By way of example, in *SP, DP and T v. UK* (1996) the question arose as to whether a lawyer could bring a complaint on behalf of young children in municipal care – even though he had not been formally instructed by them to do so. The European Convention on Human Rights is silent on this question – although the case law on Article 6 (the right to a fair court hearing) suggested that this was not possible. The commission rejected the UK's argument that the lawyer had no such right, relying on the UK's ratification of the UN Convention on the Rights of the Child, since this effectively estopped the UK from denying that children had rights in relation to legal representation (Article 12). The UNCRC has also had an energizing impact on the interpretation of the ICCPR (Joseph *et al.* 2004:625). In the present context an obvious process of rights integration would be the extension of the ICCPR's prohibited grounds for discrimination (articles 2 and 24) to include disabled children (Article 2 UNCRC) and the development of the positive obligations under the ICCPR in relation to private life (Article 17) to embrace the promotion of 'dignity, self-reliance and active participation in the community' (Article 23 UNCRC).

The power of discrete provisions in separate covenants, conventions and indeed constitutions to combine and advance human rights principles is anticipated in many treaties. The UNCRPD Article 4(4) is typical in this respect, stating that the rights it entrenches cannot take precedence over any other provisions which are 'more conducive to the realization of the rights of persons with disabilities and which may be contained in the law of a State Party or international law in force for that State'. Similar caveats are to be found in the ICCPR (articles 46–47) and the ECHR (Article 53). It follows that tertiary conventions such as the UNCRPD can only ratchet up rights – only augment and enhance the protection offered by national law or other international agreements.

The cross-cutting application of rights is a jurisprudential device to which domestic as well as international courts resort. Courtis, in this volume, describes its application by the Columbian Constitutional Court (where it is referred to as the doctrine of interconnection) and it has, with greater or lesser effectiveness been called in aid by many other such courts. In South Africa, for instance, in the *Minister of Health and others v. Treatment Action Campaign and Others* (2002) the constitutional court drew authority from the General Comments made by the UN Committee on Economic, Social and Cultural Rights (CESCR 1990) to bolster a general socio-economic right in the RSA constitution, with the consequence that a state policy restricting the availability of an antiretroviral drug was annulled.

Without specifically acknowledging the inspiration it drew from the UN Covenant on Economic, Social and Cultural Rights the Indian Supreme Court in *Olga Tellis and others v. Bombay Municipal Corporation* (1985) (a case concerning the eviction of pavement dwellers – homeless people living in ramshackle shelters) read up the constitutional right to life to include the right to a livelihood for 'no person can live without the means of living, that is, the means of livelihood'. By a similar process of reasoning the same court subsequently held that the right to life 'implies the right to food, water, decent environment, education, medical care and shelter' (*Chameli Singh v. State of Uttar Pradesh* 1996).

The UNCRPD is likely therefore to be of immense importance in energizing existing civil and political instruments. Its weak enforcement mechanism is likely to encourage early and widespread ratifications enabling its specificities to be seized upon by advocates and courts wishing to extend the scope of civil and political rights. By way of example, the recognition in Article 19 of the right to 'independent living' may well be used to develop the latent *Olmstead v. L.C.* (1999) principles through elision with the private life/non-discrimination rights in the ECHR and ICCPR. In the context of this publication the special recognition given to the rights of disabled children and the right to life (articles 7 and 10) have obvious potential to influence this fast-moving and complex debate.

The increasing sophistication in the way the right to life is articulated in relation to the experiences of disabled people raises at present more questions than it resolves. No longer is it a simple negative right not to have one's life arbitrarily terminated – it now has many powerful dimensions – the right to life; the right to *a* life (to decent care and to dignity) and the right to personal autonomy including respect for all aspects of one's life (which of course inevitably includes the manner of one's dying). In relation to each of these we find ourselves today at a key evolutionary moment – where a powerful dynamic exists between social change and the law. Lord Hoffman in 1993 (*Airedale NHS Trust v. Bland* 1993) referred to this tension in a case concerning the withdrawal of artificial nutrition and hydration from a person in a constant vegetative state. He identified three human rights principles, the sanctity of life, individual autonomy and respect for the dignity of the individual, and then observed that 'what is not always realised, and what is critical in this case, is that they are not always compatible with each other.'

How does one square a right to personal autonomy with the prohibition of assisted suicide? In *Rodriguez v. the Attorney General of Canada* (1994) and *Pretty v. UK* (2002) the Supreme Court of Canada and the European Court of Human Rights respectively heard argument that by criminalizing such action the states were forcing the disabled applicants to endure what for them was unendurable, suffering as they were from degenerative and incurable illnesses. How can states show respect for private life, for individual autonomy, self-determination and 'bodily integrity' (call it what one may) – and yet compel such 'exceedingly distressing and undignified' (*Pretty v. UK* 2002:3) deaths? In Diane Pretty's case, it was argued that her muscles would be so weakened that she would not be able to speak or swallow and would die by choking or (at best) respiratory failure and pneumonia.

How, in a similar vein, can the sanctity of life be accorded fundamental protection when confronted by conjoined twins only one of which can live and only then if severed from the other (*In re A (Children) (Conjoined Twins: Surgical Separation)* 2001)? How can one affirm the right to 'die with dignity' and yet sanction the withdrawal of artificial nutrition and hydration knowing the nature of a death by starvation and dehydration (*Burke v. General Medical Council and others* 2005)?

Through a glass dimly

In this publication we confront these questions and acknowledge that we are witnessing the slow emergence of these rights – shaped by all manner of social and legal forces, with conflict existing within the law as well as with social change. There is the tension created between the established international order and incremental domestic legal movement be it in the Netherlands, India, South Africa, Australia or Canada. Sooner or later international human rights bodies may have to acknowledge these emerging consensuses on the right to a minimum quality of life, on the right to live independently, on the right to palliative health care, on the right to controlled euthanasia – and so on. All these rights lie on the human rights table and all are capable of being articulated in the language of civil and political treaties. What is required, however, is social change and this may or may not occur: for these rights, like all other rights before them will not have any easy birth, raising as they do, controversial issues, not least the fear of eugenics, the fear of slippery slopes, the fear that we are still in a period where disabled people's lives are not seen as worth living, the fear that death may be chosen to ease the plight of the carers. It could however be argued (as is argued in this publication) that if society does move to the point that it delivers decent health and social care support to all in need, then it might still be the choice of some that they do not want to live: that for them non-existence is preferable to existence. If society has moved to that extent – and perhaps it is edging to this situation in the Netherlands, Switzerland and Oregon – then society may be ready to acknowledge the rights of all people to respect for their decisions in relation to that inevitable aspect of their lives – the manner of their dying.

Whatever the uncertainties, something has without doubt changed in the last 50 years, namely that the proper language to articulate these questions is the language of human rights. Decisions concerning the scope of a disabled person's right to life are no longer to be made solely by the church or the medical profession or indeed by the family. What the human rights movement has achieved has been to create a distinct and separate adjudication platform for these questions, and a distinct and separate language – a language that above all affirms the sanctity of life.

References

Abberley, P. (1996) 'Work, utopia and impairment', in L. Barton (ed.) *Disability and Society: Emerging Issues and Insights.* London: Longman.

Abberley, P. (1997) 'The limits of classical social theory in the analysis and transformation of disablement – (Can this really be the end; to be stuck inside of Mobile with the Memphis blues again?)', in L. Barton and M. Oliver (eds) *Disability Studies: Past, Present and Future.* Leeds: The Disability Press.

Airedale NHS Trust v. Bland [1993] 2 WLR 316.

Albrecht, G. and Bury, M. (2001) 'The political economy of the disability marketplace', in G. Albrecht, K. Seelman and M. Bury (eds) *The Handbook of Disability Studies.* Thousand Oaks, CA: Sage.

Asch, A. (2001) 'Disability, bioethics and human rights', in G. Albrecht, K. Seelman and M. Bury (eds) *The Handbook of Disability Studies.* Thousand Oaks, CA: Sage.

Aspis, S. (2003) 'The right to life debate', *Boadicea,* 16. June–July, p.1.

Baldwin, S. and Carlisle, J. (1994) *Social Support for Disabled Children and Their Families: A Review of the Literature.* Edinburgh: HMSO.

Barnes, C. (1991) *Disabled People in Britain and Discrimination.* London: Hurst & Co in association with the British Council of Organisations of Disabled People.

Barnes, C. (1997) 'A legacy of oppression: A history of disability in Western culture', in L. Barton and M. Oliver (eds) *Disability Studies: Past, Present and Future.* Leeds: The Disability Press.

BBC News Online (2006) 'Third birthday for Baby Charlotte'. 21 October. Accessed 21 October 2006.

Bickenbach, J. (2001) 'Disability human rights, law and policy', in G. Albrecht, K. Seelman and M. Bury (eds) *The Handbook of Disability Studies.* Thousand Oaks, CA: Sage.

Bickenbach, J., Chatterji, S., Badley, E. and Ustin, T. (1999) 'Models of disablement, universalism and the international classification of impairments, disabilities and handicaps', *Social Science and Medicine,* 48, 9, 1173–1187.

Blaxter, M. (1975) *The Meaning of Disability.* London: Heineman.

Botta v. Italy (1998) 26 EHRR 241.

Boyle, R., Salter, R. and Arnander, M. (2004) 'Ethics of refusing parental requests to withhold or withdraw treatment from their premature baby', *Journal of Medical Ethics,* 30, 402–405.

Brock, D. (2005) 'Preventing genetically transmitted disabilities while respecting persons with disabilities', in D. Wasserman, J. Bickenbach and R. Wachbroit (eds) *Quality of Life and Human Difference: Genetic Testing, Health Care and Disability.* New York: Cambridge University Press.

Brown v. Board of Education [1954] 347 US 483.

Burke v. General Medical Council and others [2005] EWCA Civ 1003.

Bynoe, L., Oliver, M. and Barnes, C. (1991) *Equal Rights for Disabled People.* London: Institute for Policy Research.

Campbell, J. and Oliver, M. (1996) *Disability Politics: Understanding our Past, Changing our Future*. London: Routledge.

CESCR (Committee on Economic, Social and Cultural Rights) (1990) General Comment 3, The nature of States parties obligations (art. 2, par. 1), 14/12/90, para. 10.

CESCR (Committee on Economic, Social and Cultural Rights) (1994) General Comment 5 concerning the Persons with disabilities UN doc E/C.12/1994/13 (1994).

CESCR (Committee on Economic, Social and Cultural Rights) (2000) General Comment 14, UN Doc. E/C.12/2000/4 (2000).

Chameli Singh v. State of Uttar Pradesh [1996] Indian Supreme Court 2 SCC 549.

Clarfield, A., Gordon, M., Markwell, H. and Alibhai, S. (2003) 'Ethical issues in end-of-life geriatric care: The approach of three monotheistic religions – Judaism, Catholicism and Islam', *Journal of the American Geriatrics Society*, 51, 1149–1154.

Clements, L. and Read, J. (2003) *Disabled People and European Human Rights*. Bristol: Policy Press.

Clements, L. and Read, J. (2005) 'The dog that didn't bark', in A. Lawson and C. Gooding (eds) *Disability Rights in Europe: From Theory to Practice*. Oxford: Hart Publishing.

Clements, L. and Simmons, A. (2007) 'European Court of Human Rights: Sympathetic unease', in M. Langford (ed.) *Socio-Economic Rights*. Cambridge: Cambridge University Press.

Clements, L., Mole, N. and Simmons, A. (1999) *European Human Rights: Taking a Case under the Convention*. London: Sweet & Maxwell.

Coggon, J. (2006) 'Could the right to die with dignity represent a new right to die in English law?' *Medical Law Review*, 14, Summer, 219–237.

Cuttini, M., Nadai, M., Kaminski, M. Hansen, G., de Leeuw, R., Lenoir, S., Persson, J., Rebaliato, M., Reid, M., de Vonderweid, U., Lenard, M., Orzalesi, M., Saracci, M. (2000) 'End-of-life decisions in neonatal intensive care: Physicians' self-reported practices in seven European countries', *Lancet*, 355, 9221, 2112–2118.

De Schutter, O. (2005) 'Reasonable accommodations and positive obligations in the European Convention on Human Rights', in L. Lawson and C. Gooding (eds) *Disability Rights in Europe: From Theory to Practice*. Oxford: Hart Publishing.

Degener, T. (2005) 'Disability discrimination law: A global comparative approach', in L. Lawson and C. Gooding (eds) *Disability Rights in Europe: From Theory to Practice*. Oxford: Hart Publishing.

DH and others v. Czech Republic [2006] European Court of Human Rights (Second Section), 57325/00, 7 February 2006.

Doyal, L. and Larcher, V. (2000) 'Drafting guidelines for the withholding or withdrawing of life sustaining treatment in critically ill children and neonates', *Archives of Diseases in Childhood, Fetal Neonatal Edition*, 83: F60–F63.

Duff, R. and Campbell, A. (1976) 'On deciding the care of severely handicapped or dying persons: With special reference to infants', *Paediatrics*, 57, 487–493.

Edwards, C. and Imrie, R. (2003) 'Disability and bodies as bearers of value', *Sociology*, 37, 2, 239–256.

Epp, C. (1998) *The Rights Revolution*, Chicago: University of Chicago Press.

Evans Report (2001) *The Report of the Independent Inquiries into Paediatric Cardiac Services at the Royal Brompton and Harefield Hospital*. London: Royal Brompton Hospital.

Fine, M. and Asch, A. (1988) 'Disability beyond stigma: Social interaction, discrimination and activism', *Journal of Social Issues*, 44, 1, 3–21.

Forde, R., Aasland, O. and Steen, P. (2002) 'Medical end-of-life decisions in Norway', *Resuscitation*, 55, 235–240.

French, S. (1994) 'Disabled people and professional practice', in S. French (ed.) *On Equal Terms: Working with Disabled People.* Oxford: Butterworth-Heineman.

Ghai, A. (2001) 'Experiences from the Third World', in M. Priestley (ed.) *Disability and the Life Course: Global Perspectives.* Cambridge: Cambridge University Press.

Gliedman, J. and Roth, W. (1980) *The Unexpected Minority: Handicapped Children in America.* New York: Harcourt Brace.

Gordon, D., Nandy, S., Pantazis, C., Pemberton, S. and Townsend, P. (2003) *Child Poverty in the Developing World.* Bristol: The Policy Press.

Government of RSA and others v. Grootboom and others [2000] (CCT11/00) 2001 (1) SA 46; ZACC 19.

Hale (Baroness) (2004) 'What can the human rights act do for my mental health?' The 2004 Paul Sieghart Memorial Lecture. London, British Institute of Human Rights.

Hannaford, S. (1985) *Living on the Outside Inside.* Berkley, CA: Canterbury Press.

Hannum, H. (2004) *Guide to International Human Rights Practice.* New York: Transnational Publishers.

Howard, M. (2001) *Paying the Price: Carers, Poverty and Social Exclusion.* London: Child Poverty Action Group.

HRC (Human Rights Committee) (1994a) General Comment 6, UN doc. HRI\GEN\1\Rev.1 at 6 (1994) para. 5.

HRC (Human Rights Committee) (1994b) General Comment 17, UN doc. HRI\GEN\1\Rev.1 at 23 (1994) para. 3.

HRC (Human Rights Committee) (1994c) UN doc. CCPR/C/79/Add. 30 (concerning Romania) at para. 11.

HRC (Human Rights Committee) (1995) UN doc. CCPR/C/79/Add. 42 (concerning Jordan) at para. 8.

HRC (Human Rights Committee: Netherlands) (2001) 27/08/2001. CCPR/CO/72/NET para. 5.

Hunt, M. (1997) *Using Human Rights Law in English Courts.* Oxford: Hart Publishing.

Hussain, Y. (2005) 'South Asian disabled women: Negotiating identities', *Sociological Review*, 53, 3, 522–538.

Ignatieff, M. (2001) *Human Rights as Politics and Idolatry.* Princeton: Princeton University Press.

Imrie, R. (2004) 'Demystifying disability: A review of the *International Classification of Functioning, Disability and Health*', *Sociology of Health and Illness*, 26, 3, 287–305.

In re A (Children) (Conjoined Twins: Surgical Separation) [2001] 2 WLR 480.

Ingstad, B. (2001) 'Disability in the developing world', in G. Albrecht, K. Seelman and M. Bury (eds) *The Handbook of Disability Studies.* Thousand Oaks, CA: Sage.

Joseph, S., Schultz, J. and Castan, M. (2004) The International Covenant on Civil and Political Rights, Oxford University Press, Oxford.

Kaufert, J. and Koch, T. (2003) 'Disability or end of life? Competing narratives in bioethics', *Theoretical Medicine*, 24, 459–469.

Keeley, B. and Clarke, M. (2002) *Carers Speak Out Project: Report on Findings and Recommendations.* London: Princess Royal Trust for Carers.

Kennedy, I. (1988) *Treat Me Right: Essays in Medical Ethics.* Oxford: Clarendon Press.

Kuczewski, M. (2001) Disability: An agenda for bioethics, *American Journal of Bioethics*, 1, 3, 36–44.

Kuczewski, M. and Kirschner, K. (2003) 'Bioethics and disability: A civil war?' *Theoretical Medicine*, 24, 455–458.

Lazzarini, Z., Arons, S. and Wisniewski, A. (2006) 'Legal and policy lessons from the Schiavo case: Is our right to choose the medical care we want seriously at risk?', *Palliative and Supportive Care*, 4, 145–153.

Lennard-Jones, J. (2000) 'Ethical and legal aspects of clinical hydration and nutritional support', *BJU International*, 85, 398–403.

Lister, R. (2007) '(Mis)recognition, social inequality and social justice: A critical social policy perspective', in T. Lovell (ed.) *Social Inequality and Social Justice*. London: Routledge.

Lorber, J. (1975) 'Ethical problems in the management of myelomeningocele and hydrocephalus', *Journal of the Royal College of Physicians*, 10, 47–60.

Lester (Lord) and O'Cinneide, C. (2004) 'The effective protection of socio-economic rights', in Y. Ghai and J. Cottrell (eds) *Economic and Cultural Rights in Practice*. London: Interights.

Mendoza and Ors v. Ministry of Public Health [2004] Resn No 0749–2003-RA (2004) (Constitutional Court).

Minister of Health and others v. Treatment Action Campaign and others [2002] CCT 8/02 SACC 2002; (2002) AHRLR 189.

Morris, J. (1989) *Able Lives: Women's Experience of Paralysis*. London: The Women's Press.

Morris, J. (1991) *Pride Against Prejudice*. London: The Women's Press.

Morris, J. (1993) *Independent Lives: Community Care and Disabled People*. Basingstoke: Macmillan.

Morris, J. (1998) *Accessing Human Rights: Disabled Children and the Children Act*. Barkingside: Barnardos.

Nuffield Council on Bioethics (2006) *Critical Care Decisions in Fetal and Neonatal Medicine: Ethical issues*. London: Nuffield Council on Bioethics.

Olga Tellis and others v. Bombay Municipal Corporation [1985] Indian Supreme Court 2 Supp SCR 51.

Oliver, M. (1990) *The Politics of Disablement*. London: Macmillan.

Oliver, M. (1996) *Understanding Disability*. London: Macmillan.

Olmstead v. LC [1999] 527 US 581.

Öneryildiz v. Turkey [2005] 41 EHRR 20.

Osman v. UK [1998] EHRR 245 at 305.

Parens, E. (2001) 'How long has this been going on? Disability issues, disability studies and bioethics', *American Journal of Bioethics*, 1, 3, 54–55.

Parker, C. (2006) 'Independent Living and the Commission for Equality and Human Rights', Background paper prepared on behalf of the Disability Rights Commission. London: Disability Rights Commission.

Partridge, C., Martinez, A., Hiroshi, N., Boo, N.-Y., Tan, K., Yeung, C.-Y., Lu, J.-H. and Yu, V. (2005) 'International comparisons of care for very low birth weight infants: Parents' perceptions of counselling and decision-making', *Pediatrics*, 116, 2, 263–271.

Philp, M. and Duckworth, D. (1982) *Children with Disabilities and their Families: A Review of Research*. Windsor: NFER/Nelson.

Pretty v. UK [2002] 35 EHRR 1.

Price v. UK [2001] 34 EHRR 1285.

Priestley, M. (ed.) (2001a) *Disability and the Life Course: Global Perspectives.* Cambridge: Cambridge University Press.

Priestley, M. (2001b) 'Introduction: The global context of disability', in M. Priestley (ed.) *Disability and the Life Course: Global Perspectives.* Cambridge: Cambridge University Press.

Priestley, M. (2003) *Disability: A Life Course Approach.* Cambridge: Polity Press.

Read, J. (1998) 'Conductive education and the politics of disablement', *Disability and Society,* 13, 2, 279–293.

Read, J. (2000) *Disability, the Family and Society: Listening to Mothers.* Buckingham: Open University Press.

Read, J., Clements, L. and Reubain, D. (2006) *Disabled Children and the Law: Research and Good Practice.* London: Jessica Kingsley Publishers.

Rocker, G. and Dunbar, S. (2000) 'Withholding or withdrawal of life support: The Canadian Critical Care Society position paper', *Journal of Palliative Care, 16 Supplement,* October, S53–S62.

Rodriguez v. the Attorney General of Canada [1994] 2 LRC 136.

Saxton M. and Howe, F. (eds) (1988) *With Wings: An Anthology of Literature by Women with Disabilities.* London: Virago.

Seale, C. (2006) 'National survey of end-of-life decisions made by UK medical practitioners', *Palliative Medicine,* 20, 1, 3–10.

Shakespeare, T. (1998) 'Choices and rights: eugenics, genetics and disability equality', *Disability and Society,* 13,5, 665–681.

Shakespeare, T. (2005) 'Disability, genetics and global justice', *Social Policy and Society,* 4, 1, 87–95.

Shakespeare, T. (2006) *Disability Rights and Wrongs.* London: Routledge.

Shearer, A. (1984) *Everybody's Ethics.* London: Campaign for Mentally Handicapped People (CMH).

Sheehan, M. (2003) 'Disabilities and ageing', *Theoretical Medicine,* 24, 525–533.

Somerset's case [1772] *R. v. Knowles, ex parte Somerset* [1772] Lofft 1, 98 ER 499, 20 ST 1.

SP, DP and T v. UK [1996] 22 EHRR CD 148; [1996] EHRLR 526.

Spenser, S. (2005) 'Partner rediscovered: Human rights and equality in the UK', in C. Harvey (ed.) *Human Rights in the Community: Rights as Agents for Change.* Oxford, Hart.

Sprung, C. and Eidelman, L. (1996) 'Worldwide similarities and differences in the forgoing of life-sustaining treatments', *Intensive Care Medicine,* 22, 1003–1005.

Stone, E. (2001) 'A complicated struggle: Disability, survival and social change in the majority world', in M. Priestley (ed.) *Disability and the Life Course: Global Perspectives.* Cambridge: Cambridge University Press.

Sun Online (2006) 'Kill disabled tots, say top docs', Monday, 6 November 2006. Accessed at www.thesun.co.uk/article/0,,2–20006510381,00.html 6 November 2006.

Sunday Times, The (2006) 'Doctors call premature babies "bed blockers"', *TimesOnline,* 26 March 2006. Accessed 26 March 2006.

Thomas, D. (1982) *The Experience of Handicap.* London: Methuen.

Tribe, L. (1989) 'The curvature of constitutional space: What lawyers can learn from modern physics', *Harvard Law Review,* 103, 1.

Tripp, J. and McGregor, D. (2006) 'Withholding and withdrawing of life sustaining treatment in the newborn', *Archives of Diseases in Childhood – Fetal and Neonatal Edition,* 91, F67–71.

UPIAS (Union of the Physically Impaired Against Segregation) (1976) *The Fundamental Principles of Disability*. London: UPIAS.

Wasserman, D. (2001) 'Philosophical issues in the definition and social response to disability', in G. Albrecht, K. Seelman and M. Bury (eds) *The Handbook of Disability Studies*. Thousand Oaks, CA: Sage.

Wasserman, D., Bickenbach, J. and Wachbroit, R. (2005) 'Introduction', in D. Wasserman, J. Bickenbach and R. Wachbroit (eds) *Quality of Life and Human Difference: Genetic Testing, Health Care and Disability*. New York: Cambridge University Press.

Watermeyer, B. and Swartz, L. (2006) 'Introduction and overview', in *Disability and Social Change: A South African Agenda*. Cape Town: HSRC Press.

Weir, R. (1984) *The Selective Nontreatment of Handicapped Newborns*. New York and Oxford: Oxford University Press.

Williams, G. (2001) 'Theorizing disability', in G. Albrecht, K. Seelman and M. Bury (eds) *The Handbook of Disability Studies*. Thousand Oaks, CA: Sage.

Wolbring, G. (2001) 'Where do we draw the line?: Surviving eugenics in a technological world', in M. Priestley (ed.) *Disability and the Life Course: Global Perspectives*. Cambridge: Cambridge University Press.

Wood, G. and Martin, E. (1995) 'Withholding and withdrawing life-sustaining therapy in a Canadian intensive care unit', *Canadian Journal of Anesthesia*, 42, 186–191.

World Health Organization (WHO) (1980) *The International Classification of Impairments, Disabilities and Handicaps (ICIDH)*. Geneva: WHO.

2 Mending, not ending

Cost-effectiveness analysis, preferences and the right to a life with disabilities

David Wasserman, Adrienne Asch and Jerome Bickenbach

Introduction

Far more than perhaps anyone would be comfortable admitting, decisions about who will live and who will die are made in terms of a balance of benefit and cost. In a social environment where scarcity of resources is a given, it would be morally unacceptable for anyone to demand an unending stream of health care resources, irrespective of the benefits he or she received. Even a rough sense of justice insists that it is a waste to use scarce resources on one person when no benefit accrues. On the other hand, the same rough sense of justice insists that the demand for a minimal set of resources when the potential benefits are enormous – say life itself – should always be met, whoever the beneficiary and whatever the circumstances. Between those extremes, however, our sense of justice is less clear.

In the domain of health care, if we grant that health goods and services are scarce and health needs universal, unpredictable, potentially catastrophically great, then the question of fair distribution concerns everyone. Not only does everyone need health resources (not all the time, but sometimes), but the cost of these benefits, although usually expressed financially, is in fact a reduction in their finite supply, a reduction that affects us all. In contrast to the distribution of discretionary consumer goods, the question of how best to distribute health resources concerns everyone, without exception.

For persons with disabilities, however, the balancing of health benefit and health cost has – with little social debate or justification – taken on an additional dimension: people with disabilities are widely believed to have, *ab initio*, a diminished life, one which the provision of health resources may not substantially improve. Pre-existing disabilities, when chronic and severe, are not 'curable' by health interventions that do not specifically target them. Persons with disabilities, like everyone else, require health interventions for acquired injuries, impairments and diseases. Yet, when they need health interventions, it is as if they are already in a health–benefit debt, one which has to be taken into account when we calculate the potential benefits of the health resources they require. Either the person's pre-existing disabilities will shorten their lives or lower their quality of life, or both; but the health resources they need, although they may fix their injuries or cure their diseases, will not change their pre-existing disabilities.

Should our cost–benefit analysis for health resources be affected by whether a person has disabilities, or not? Once again, our intuitions at the extremes are pellucid: suppose because of disabilities a person has only a week to live, in severe and uncontrollable pain. If that person also needs a new kidney, it does not seem to make sense to give it to her rather than a child without disabilities who, with the new kidney, will live for decades. On the other hand, the mere fact that a person is deaf should have absolutely no affect on whether we provide the health services required to save their life after a traffic accident.

In the difficult middle between these extremes, the comparison of costs and benefits is far less clear. In this chapter we briefly examine a variety of attempts to make headway in the application of a highly developed, economic version of cost–benefit analysis, namely cost-effectiveness analysis (CEA) in the area of health resource allocation.[1] These attempts are distinguishable by their shared commitment to evaluate health outcomes in terms of people's preferences for these outcomes. Is it possible to acknowledge that preventing injuries (and therefore impairments) is harm prevention, and so a valuable use of resources, without at the same time assessing the life lived with those impairments as less valuable, or of lower quality of life? Our answer is that it is indeed possible.

The primary purpose behind the various proposals that have been made for measuring and comparing health outcomes, and for clarifying the relationship between health, perceived well-being, and preferences, is to assess the cost-effectiveness of health care interventions and policies designed to improve population health. The standard health economic approach is to compare health states in terms of an individual's preferences between states, and to provide a justifiable method for aggregating these health state preferences into an overall ranking. Most evaluation protocols to elicit preferences would, if successful, provide not merely an ordinal ranking of health states, but interval measurement essential to quantify differences between health states and make CEA feasible. Nearly all health economists assume that only by eliciting and manipulating health state preferences is it possible to provide the quantitative basis for CEA.

These evaluation protocols have, however, been subjected to a disability critique that is both forceful and damning. While not denying a role to expected benefits in allocating scarce health resources, the critique rejects preference-elicitation as a means of assessing those benefits, arguing that its use in standard CEA evaluation protocols systematically undervalues the benefits that accrue from restoring the health and extending the lives of people with disabilities. This critique forms our starting point. What we propose to do is sketch out an approach to assessing the costs of injuries and impairments for the purposes of CEA that does *not* require eliciting preferences.

Approaches to preference elicitation and their problems

Must a determination that one health state is better than another always involve evaluation? If we agree that a health state is a composite of different dimensions of health – such as mobility, cognitive functioning, seeing, pain, mood and so on – then even if comparison along each dimension were purely objective (for example 'being in pain is less healthy than not being in pain'), when multiple dimensions are brought together to form a person's state of health, objective comparisons no longer make much sense. Is a health state of limited mobility, a serious hearing problem, healthier than a health state of severe cognitive impairment but no pain? Moreover, what sense does it make to suggest that a life with cognitive impairment is healthier than one with quadriplegia? Hence, with a few exceptions,[2] most health economists insist that health state comparison requires us to move from 'objectively healthier' to 'better'.

Some philosophers such as Broome and Brocke have insisted that health state evaluation must be directly linked to quality of life;[3] that is, in Derek Parfit's famous phrase, to what makes someone's life go better.[4] Others opt for the 'capabilities' approach of Amaryta Sen and Martha Nussbaum[5] and see dimensions of health implicated, to various degrees, in our assessment of a person's capabilities to function, which capabilities together constitute well-being (a claim that we will return to below). Still the most popular approach, certainly among health economists, is that of eliciting preferences by means of one of several proposed valuation techniques.

Using preferences in this way is popular in part because it seems to ground evaluation in empirical facts, and fits well with a subjectivist account of valuation, commonly used by economists.[6] More plausibly one might argue, following the social choice model, that given the great differences amongst people and their circumstances, an a priori theory of the value of health states seems dubious, and that in any event it is offensive to disregard the evaluations of individuals, however bizarre. Moreover, it is very plausible to link health to well-being, since the former is both a component and a cause of the latter. Without an objective account of well-being, moreover, it is plausible to rely on preferences as either a measure of, or a proxy for, well-being.

Prominent among preference protocols are the following: time trade-off (TTO) – in which a group of respondents are asked to imagine a choice between two health states, say, a) living with a described health condition with a life expectancy of ten years, or b) living in perfect health, but for only five years. By comparing the choices (time trade-offs) made by repondents for a variety of health states, it is possible to identify the number of years of ideal health that is considered to be equivalent to ten years with a given health state. The standard gamble (SG) technique asks respondents to compare living for ten years in a given health state with certainty, with accepting a risky procedure that offers a chance of living ten years in perfect health with the risk of immediate death. By means of iterations of choices, the level of risk at which the uncertain option would be equally attractive as the certain option can be identified. Finally, the person trade-off (PTO) protocol – which seems to be more relevant to the policy arena – asks respondents to imagine themselves as making decisions about resource allocation, and facing a choice between a) a programme that would prevent the deaths of 100 fully healthy individuals (in effect extending their lives for ten years) and b) a programme that would prevent the onset of a given health state for some number of healthy individuals (in effect improving their health expectancy from ten years in sub-optimal health to ten years in ideal health). Once again, by means of iterated choices, we arrive at the number of averted heath problems that this group of respondents feel is equivalent to the prevention of 100 deaths.

Other preference-eliciting protocols – and variations of the above – have been proposed. Although on their face they seem to call upon different preferences, in at least one multi-method investigation it has been claimed that respondents produce highly consistent results regardless of the elicitation method employed, supporting the thesis that 'each different method may be related monotonically to a common set of core values'.[7] There have been several vigorous methodological and ethical critiques of many of these methods, often by those who have employed them in their own work.[8]

Although there is some overlap, the disability critique is different. Without going into the details, this critique highlights the fact that the source of the preferences are people without the impairments at issue, or else health professionals, neither of whom have first-hand experience of what it means to live with an impairment. Typically as well, in order to provide a background to the trade-off exercises, and to satisfy the intuitive requirement that preferences be 'informed', respondents are provided with information that emphasizes the negative life experiences that impairments are thought to create and that virtually requires respondents to base their preferences on the corollary that those lives must be valued less than lives without impairments.

More generally, by their nature, subjective preferences are often based on fallible moral and prudential judgements, which are misleadingly elicited as privileged assertions about an individual's own mental states.[9] Judgements about familiar impairments such as blindness or paraplegia are especially fallible, as these are most susceptible to distortion by fear and social stigma. It is surely true, as disability scholars have long argued, that discrimination, lack of access to opportunities and reasonable accommodation impose a substantial burden on people with these impairments, but it is both conceptually confused, and unfair, to credit this burden to the impairment, rather than the adverse social response to people with disabilities. In addition, as several philosophers have argued, the satisfaction of preferences of itself has little independent moral or prudential value, inasmuch as preferences are a poor proxy for what we have reason to care about: pleasure, happiness, health, autonomy, intimacy, achievement, security, and so on. We do, or should, prefer these goods because they are valuable, not value them because we prefer them.[10] It must be said that health economists themselves are unhappy with preference-elicitation techniques, in part because they yield such unreliable, unaccountably variable numbers, as the Tengs survey[11] reveals.

The alternative approach we describe below would provide a basis for assessing the costs of impairments, and the benefits of preventing them, without eliciting preferences about living with impairments. It could for example ground a claim that preventing certain impairments would result in substantial cost savings, but would do so without the assumption that these impairments are intrinsically bad, or that lives with them are of generally lower quality. Avoiding these assumptions, which inform the preferences elicited by standard techniques, is a considerable virtue of the proposed approach. In relying on those assumptions for public policy recommendations, conventional CEA devalues the life of disabled people, taking the first step in the direction of qualifying their right to life.

'Mend not end'

There are two core issues in the application of CEA to resource allocation for the purpose of reducing injuries and saving lives. The first is whether all numerically equal risks of a given harm are morally equivalent and should be treated as such by policy-makers. This issue is raised, for example, by Tengs,[12] who compared the social cost of saving a life year by means of various interventions and found enormous differences, with environmental toxin reduction by far the most expensive. The dependent variable in that study was reduction in mortality risk, and it found that a given amount of money achieved far more reduction if spent on highway safety than on brown-site clean-up.

The broader issue, though, is whether it makes sense to presume a moral equivalency in risk of death from different causes. For example, it may be morally as well as psychologically more acceptable to incur a much greater risk of death in driving a car, where we have genuine choice about engaging in the activity and some control over the degree of risk while engaging in it, than a much smaller risk of death in breathing the air or drinking water, where we have far less choice and control. Although this issue certainly affects our main concern – the evaluation of lives lived with impairment – we pass on to the second core issue.

That issue concerns the estimation of quality of life for purposes using CEA for injury prevention, by means, for example, of the institution of safety measures. Our suggestion concerns an approach to health outcome valuation that avoids subjective judgements of the quality of life with a given impairment – whether that judgement is made about the risk of the impairment (so-called *ex ante* judgements) or after the injury has been incurred (*ex post*). Our proposal seeks to account for the importance of preventing impairment while recognizing that people who have those impairment can live lives as good as, or on a par with, people without impairments.

We propose a strategy of 'mending, not ending' CEA, one that seeks to estimate the costs of impairments and the benefits of avoiding them without relying on the subjective valuations yielded by techniques of preference-elicitation or contingent valuation. By assigning a dollar value to the costs of 'mending' an impairment, our proposal would assist policy-makers and regulators in assessing the 'cost-effectiveness' of interventions that reduce the risk of injuries, diseases and other conditions that cause impairments. Our proposal firstly attempts to identify those costs in broad terms, and then, more tentatively, to suggest a means for assigning dollar values to them for comparative purposes.

Our proposal departs radically from CEA in one respect: it abandons the metric of life years. As in traditional cost–benefit analysis (CBA), the benefits as well as the costs are expressed in monetary terms. Unlike CBA, however, our approach does not attempt to 'monetize' the value of life or life years in terms of people's preferences for reducing or increasing the risk of death. Rather, we seek to estimate the costs of 'making a person whole' – a notion we introduce in the next section – when that person has experienced injury or impairment (section 6A–C) or when her life has been cut short (section 6D).

Preliminaries of 'mend not end'

In a nutshell, our idea is that rather than estimating what people – disabled or not, expert or lay – would pay, in cash, in longevity, or in risk of death, to avoid a given health condition,[13] we should estimate the cost of making a person with that condition – the injured party – 'as whole in quality of life as possible'. This phrase derives from the basic principle for quantifying the remedy for wrongful injury in tort law, and our approach has a parallel in tort law scholarship, in the attempt to understand 'whole' in terms of an objective and multidimensional conception of human flourishing (a conception associated with, but not limited to, the Sen and Nussbaum capability approach mentioned earlier, which is the most developed contemporary account available). What it means to make a person 'whole' in this sense depends on setting a threshold – the person's pre-injury level, or some population average or other standard. As already noted, the resources required to reach that threshold will depend on a host of factors, some related to the impairment (its onset, chronicity and severity), and some to the character of the physical environment (e.g. climate and topography), the level and extent of accommodation, and the availability of rehabilitative and other technologies to provide alternative means of achieving the same or similar types of flourishing. We will not attempt to do more than outline this approach and consider its practical difficulties, except to say that, as CEA requires us to move beyond individual costing, it should be possible to generalize the costs incurred for specific impairments in ways that are feasible and justifiable.

In understanding 'wholeness' in terms of quality of life or well-being (terms we use synonymously here[14]), and in treating well-being as multidimensional and largely objective, our approach is not committed to a specific theory of well-being. Rather, it draws on what we see as an 'overlapping consensus', broad but by no means complete, among some empirical researchers studying quality of life[15] and some philosophers analysing the concept of well-being (in particular 'objectivists' such as Griffin, and Nussbaum[16]).

That consensus recognizes a number of dimensions in which a human life can go well or poorly (although there is no agreement on that number, or on the value of exhaustiveness), and it resists any weighting of these dimensions to yield a cardinal or even ordinal comparison of overall well-being. Health and functioning are universally accepted as essential dimensions of well-being, but within these are many domains of human functioning, simple and complex (sensory, mobility, cognitive, activities of daily living and so on). Despite classification differences in the number and description of health and functioning domains, there is broad agreement that there is some minimum set of core domains that capture (or are adequate proxies for) the health dimension of well-being. With this core set of domains, it is possible to make rough qualitative judgements about how well a person's life is going, with respect to the dimension of health.

Our claim of consensus acquires threshold plausibility, we believe, in juxtaposing passages from two scholars: one has spent years compiling and comparing instruments that measure health, disease and quality of life; the other has reflected as a philosopher and intellectual historian on understandings of human good across times and cultures.

Ann Bowling, the empirical researcher, argues that her study of 'What things are important in people's lives'

> supports the view that analyses should be based on unaggregated measures, and avoid summing all subscales. This is inconvenient for health care decision making which prefers a simpler approach with a unitary measure of health, but the latter results in the poor integrity of the research instrument. The results of this research support the multidimensionality of quality of life and suggest that questionnaires should independently measure and reflect each construct.[17]

Martha Nussbaum, the philosopher and classicist, asserts that her list of 'central human functional capabilities', which we will discuss further below,

> is, emphatically, a list of separate components. We cannot satisfy the need for one of them by giving people a larger amount of another one. All are of central importance, and all are distinct in quality. The irreducible plurality of the lists limits the trade offs that it will be reasonable to make, and thus limits the applicability of quantitative cost–benefit analysis.[18]

Taking its guidance from these convergent observations, the approach we propose understands well-being to involve an 'irreducible plurality' of valuable goods, activities, and capacities. Far from relying uncritically on the self-appraisal of people with or without impairments, or before or after acquiring impairments, our approach gauges the impact of impairments on activities, relationships, and other components of well-being. With an objective, multidimensional view of well-being (informed by the Sen and Nussbaum capabilities approach), it attempts to assess the impact of impairments on all domains of life quality or central human capabilities and to estimate what it would cost to restore, to some threshold level, functioning in those domains for an individual, in light of his or her social context and life projects.

What is the threshold level of functioning that should be achieved? There are at least three candidate levels: the level of functioning (in a core domain) that the individual possessed prior to the injury that created the impairment; the average level of functioning for some population; the level of functioning that is, based on empirical study, necessary for an adequate level of well-being overall. All three levels are empirically derivable, but the second and third raise far more questions of reliability than the first. The first, however, may achieve reliability at the cost of accepting a morally arbitrary status quo ante: if the individual's pre-onset level of functioning, for whatever reason, was already minimal, why shouldn't the post-injury level be higher, if it can be feasibly raised by restorative services?

Following the discussion and terminology of Menzel *et al.* 2002,[19] our approach assigns little importance to an individual's ability 'to adjust' to an impairment, or to the individual's skills at 'coping', at least as these psychological phenomena function to lower expectations or alter life priorities. The newfound contentment of an adventitiously dismembered violinist or Olympic-level sprinter in simply being alive should not preclude a steep assessment of her loss. Instead, our account assesses the costs of 'adaptation' – the acquisition of the different skills required to achieve the type of flourishing closest to that enjoyed by the individual before the injury, or to achieve goals closest to those foreclosed by the injury.[20] Our account would thus look at the cost of enabling the ex-violinist to make or to facilitate the making of music, or of enabling the ex-sprinter to engage in other forms of participation in athletic competition, either directly or as an organizer or promoter of sports. This would be appropriate to do even if the ex-violinist or ex-sprinter had moved on to different projects and taken a 'sour-grapes' view of her previous pursuits.

Our approach offers a coherent, if still sketchy, resolution of the paradox arising from the disability perspective on impairment: if people with impairments can live as well as, or on a par with, people without impairments, why should society pay anything for prevention? The simple answer is that, given the physical and built environment, and the resources, practices and attitudes of our society, it tends to be more expensive for impaired individuals to achieve a parity of well-being with unimpaired individuals. In seeking to assess how much more expensive it is, we make no claim about the proportion of that expense which results from the failure to provide just accommodation, or about whether that expense should be taken as evidence that impairments are intrinsically bad – contentious issues we do not need to address for this purpose.

With these preliminaries out of the way, things get more complex. Our proposed approach faces significant challenges, some of which we will address below. We are convinced, however, that its difficulties are no worse than those confronted by techniques that attempt to base the value of a health state on the preferences people express concerning that state under controlled circumstances. It should be kept in mind that there is no gold standard in this area – no universal ranking of health states independent of the context in which these states are experienced – so perhaps two bronze standards are better than one.

Sketching out the approach

In this sketch we concentrate on what we call 'substitution' or 'replacement' costs – the costs of restoring or raising an individual to a pre-injury, average, or minimum level of functioning or success in each recognized core domain of health. Obviously, these costs will vary considerably with the threshold or functional baseline that we adopt. In the tort context, the governing principle for most instances is *resititutio ad integrum*, which for the purposes of tort law seems appropriate. The pre-injury baseline is appropriate in the context of corrective justice because, as the law holds, 'the tortfeasor takes his victim as he finds him'. That threshold may not be appropriate, however, for CEA on preventative measures, where most victims and beneficiaries are unknown or unknowable. An average or minimal level may be more appropriate for agency CEA, although the specification of and choice between the two raise difficult theoretical and empirical issues that we will not be able to address here.

Substitution or replacement costs are an important feature of our approach, and we focus on them because they help to illustrate our multidimensional view of life quality and raise interesting issues. But replacement costs by no means exhaust the costs of injury and impairment. There are also costs related to:

- for adventitious impairments, the 'pain and suffering' involved in the loss or disruption of cherished activities, projects and relationships
- for congenital and adventitious impairments, the 'pain and suffering' of stigmatization, exclusion and discrimination
- the increased costs to other people, especially parents, partners and teachers, in helping impaired individuals achieve an average or adequate quality of life
- the lost productivity associated with impairment[21]
- the medical and other health expenses of responding to impairment, at onset and later.

We will have something to say later about the first three; the others are more familiar and have been discussed elsewhere.[22]

Substitution or replacement costs

The contrast between subjective valuation and objective substitution costs parallels that in tort law between prospective or insurance approaches and restorative approaches. Heidi Feldman[23] describes the differences in an article that anticipates some of our suggestions:

> The insurance theory vests authority for identifying tort victims' needs with the counterfactual, hypothetical, fully informed, economically rational actors contemplating her relative desires for pre-accident and post-accident wealth. Tort law locates this authority with a fact finder – usually a jury – concentrating on a particular plaintiff's injuries and comparing his current situation to the one he would have been in if the defendant had not harmed him.

Feldman explains how 'the conception of well-being as flourishing' can structure this determination:

> [T]ortious injury interferes with flourishing; damages restore flourishing or the capacity for it, or both ... Tort compensation can achieve this because an individual can flourish in more than one way. If injury forecloses one possibility, money can open others. Admittedly, different forms of flourishing may not be comparable or commensurable ... Still, we can tell when someone's capacity for flourishing has been impaired, and we can see how to enhance it. Monetary recovery can make a tort victim whole in at least rough terms.

She illustrates such collateral possibilities for flourishing with the example of an amputation:

> With a damages award, the amputee unable to continue playing the violin might start a school for aspiring musicians, or endow the local symphony. Of course, he might succeed in using the money to restore his previous form of flourishing in all respects, but he need not manage this in order to flourish again.

Clearly, for purposes of CEA, since individualized assessment of the costs of collateral ways of flourishing would not be appropriate, some broad generalizations about types of flourishing and their costs would be needed. The challenge is to frame the categories broadly enough so that each encompasses a wide range of similar human activity while maintaining distinctions among types of flourishing essential to the pluralism of the approach. The broader the formulation, the less likely that capabilities are to be precluded by specific impairments. Such generality finds precedent in Nussbaum's revision of her capabilities approach in response to criticism from disability scholars that her initial formulation was too narrow. Thus, Nussbaum has gone from making 'the exercise of the five senses' one condition for human flourishing – which would preclude flourishing for blind or deaf people – to enlarging the capability so that it encompassed the ability 'to use the senses, to imagine, think, and reason'[24] – which makes human flourishing possible for blind and deaf people.

When the relevant capability is framed this broadly, the cost of blindness would be based, *inter alia*, on the costs of maintaining or restoring rich aesthetic experience, by providing the resources for achieving such experience through acoustic and other sensory modalities. Framing the central human goods or capabilities in such general terms does not merely accommodate impairments. By recognizing that people can flourish in a wide variety of ways, and that we are unlikely to achieve an exhaustive enumeration or complete characterization of those ways, the capabilities approach retains an openness to unfamiliar ways of living and social practices that helps to rebut the charge of paternalism.

This expansive approach may be in tension with Norman Daniels'[25] view about the priority of restoring species-typical functioning. Such restoration, as Feldman suggests, will often be practically impossible to achieve even partially (e.g. cumbersome prostheses). But Feldman's example and Nussbaum's reformulation suggest a strategy of substitution rather than incomplete or partial normalization: find the closest feasible substitute capability or functioning, either on the same or a higher order of generality, and estimate the cost of providing or enabling it. This provides an adequate basis for the costing necessary for CEA.

Loss, discrimination, pain and suffering

An entirely prospective approach, which looked only at the costs of substitution, would fail to take account of the significant loss in being denied a cherished pursuit in which the individual may have invested much of her life and energy. If full restoration of function is feasible, this problem will not arise, but it may for even close substitution. The modest cost of teaching a pianist who lost one arm to master the large repertoire of one-armed pieces (as well as to perform all the activities of daily living with one arm) does not cover her loss in no longer being able to play her old repertoire of pieces requiring two arms. Arguably, therefore, a measure of closest-substitution costs should be supplemented in many instances by compensation for 'pain and suffering', however subjective its measure may be and however reductive a view of loss and mourning such compensation presupposes.

But the loss of cherished pursuits is only one part, and not the largest, of the 'pain and suffering' associated with impairment. A generation of disability scholars has argued that the greatest hardships in being impaired lie in facing a relentlessly discriminatory society and a pervasively unaccommodating environment. Of course, a just society would not discriminate, and would build the environment for as wide a range of human variation as was technologically feasible. But we do not live in such a society, and measures to bring us closer to it are, in general, better viewed as the demands of justice than the costs of individual impairments.

For purposes of CEA, then, we need to take society 'as is', with its prevailing attitudes and social practices. Increasing the number of people with various impairments may have only a negligible effect on the costs of discrimination-reduction and environmental modifications for accommodation. But each additional person with an impairment will experience the pain and suffering of existing discrimination and lack of accommodation. Compensation for such pain and suffering may well be the most expensive part of making the person 'whole', and preventing people from having to face those hardships should be treated as saving the cost of such pain and suffering.[26]

There is partial precedent for assessing this cost in the damages awarded plaintiffs for pain and suffering from race and sex discrimination. While there are obvious differences between discrimination on the basis of race, sex and impairment, they all involve the heavy burdens of widespread hostility, contempt and condescension, as well as entrenched social and institutional barriers – 'built-in tailwinds' – to full acceptance and participation.

Because these hardships are faced to one degree or another by all people with impairments, they impose a cost in pain and suffering on individuals who are congenitally as well as adventitiously impaired.[27] In part for this reason, our approach applies to policies for the prevention of impairments across the lifespan, from perinatal to adult onset. We would not, however, apply it to 'prevention' by prenatal or pre-implantation selection, because, as we have argued elsewhere, such selection is morally problematic.[28]

Calculating replacement or substitution costs

Substitution costs, it is apparent, will be assessed differently for congenital and adventitious impairments. Because of the plurality of ways of flourishing, the plasticity of human development, and the countervailing impact of life experience – at once broadening the range of options and entrenching options appropriate to a particular style of living – being born without sight or arm movement will not involve the same kind of adaptation as the loss of sight or arm movement later in life.

For congenital impairments, no re-education or retraining is required, merely the costs of enabling the congenitally impaired individual to construct a fulfilling life from a somewhat smaller or modified set of options. Still, we should be wary of unthinkingly assigning a cost to the reduction of options, at least for the modest truncation involved in many congenital sensory and motor impairments. The mere reduction in the size of an opportunity range or capability set should be treated as a compensable loss, but only to the extent that the congenitally impaired individual has a genuine reduction in a sufficiently wide range of opportunities to make a meaningful choice among reasonable ways of life.[29]

Our approach offers a solution to the vexing problem of estimating the costs of impairments for those too young to have made any significant commitments toward specific pursuits, life projects, or vocations, with congenital impairment being the limiting case. The loss of an arm to a newborn precludes a range of opportunities but frustrates no ongoing pursuits. The same is true of the total loss of limb function. We would not want to treat the former, let alone the latter, as incurring no costs. Still, we should resist adopting an opportunity-metric to assess the loss, or insisting that the child must, at some threshold of reduced opportunity, be compensated for the loss of an 'open future'. We can surely recognize that it is much more expensive in existing society for a child without limb function to fashion any kind of rewarding life, and we would surely take account of the cost of enabling him to do so.[30] Moreover, some congenital impairments may require more costly interventions than similar adventitious ones, because, as already noted, individuals who are congenitally impaired will generally not have had the opportunity to acquire various skills and forms of social support that will facilitate their adoption of pursuits compatible with their impairments.

Again, those costs should not be exaggerated. If a child who is impaired in hearing, sight, or mobility congenitally or from early in life lives in a family with others who do not have impairments, and is fully included in all activities typical for unimpaired children, that child should be able to imagine and achieve continued flourishing at a level comparable to his or her siblings. Many of the costs of raising the child with a disability are of the same kind, if not always the same degree, as the costs of raising a child without a disability. In both cases there are costs in maintaining high expectations and inculcating the belief that many futures are possible. The additional costs incurred in raising a child with a disability are typically those of ensuring that the child gets exposed to all of the ordinary activities of childhood – inclusion in play groups, trick-or-treating, school field trips, neighbourhood games and pranks, and the like.

Costs of inclusion are both material and psychological. The former include the costs of adaptive equipment and other means to facilitate access and participation; the latter are the often greater costs in parental time and effort to persuade anxious or frightened teachers, coaches, activity directors, parents and playmates that the child belongs in the day-care centre, team, camp or party. There may also be additional costs in reinforcing parental resourcefulness and imagination, and in instilling that resourcefulness and imagination in the disabled child him- or herself. Needless to say, these more subtle costs are rarely factored into the costs of raising a child with disabilities.

We now need to turn to two critical issues our approach must address:

1   How, even on an individual level, can we assess closest-substitution costs without a) relying on the individual's own subjective judgements about what would be closest, and b) comparing different dimensions of flourishing, with 'cross-compensation'?
2   How can we generalize about the substitution costs of a given injury, for example, the loss of one arm, or of sight, to a population with very diverse levels and types of flourishing?

In what follows we will sketch out the set of finely grained issues that each question raises, before briefly describing a simpler approach that has already been developed for resolving them. Plainly, both questions raise significant theoretical and practical difficulties; our main purpose here is to suggest the range of ways in which these marginal costs can be assessed.

Averaging the replacement or substitution costs for a sample of individuals

In order to sensibly address question 1a, it is important to understand the variety of ways an individual's actual flourishing may be affected by impairment, and the different implications that has for substitution.

An individual who loses his arm may have been a consummate, avid violin player or baseball pitcher. Assuming that reconstructive surgery cannot reattach his playing or pitching arm, we need a more general characterization of his prior activity in order to assess substitution costs. But in asking what role violin playing or pitching played in the individual's life, we may face uncertainty, ambiguity or conflict. Was he seeking to excel in a specific performance domain, participate in the activity of chamber music or competitive sport, contribute to the production of good music or sport, or carry on a proud family tradition?

Yet different characterizations have different implications for substitution. Do we give the individual the resources to play the violin (and how well, or at what level?) or another instrument. Do we try to get the individual interested in a different sport? Do we give him the resources to play a very different, non-playing role in the same musical activity or sport, say as conductor, coach, manager and producer? Do we give him the resources to carry on some other proud family tradition? Or do we do all of these? And how much of a say do we give the individual in assessing how close any of these alternatives comes to restoring his previous well-being? Obviously, these paths to substitution are not mutually exclusive. The individual may well be uncertain himself about the comparative aptness of these characterizations – which are, to make matters worse, hardly exhaustive. But more to the point, the individual's opinion on this might well be wrong; a sensitive family member, friend, or biographer might provide a better characterization.

Turning to question 1b, the impaired individual might find other forms of flourishing altogether. We could facilitate his becoming a writer, world traveller, or *bon vivant*. But now, clearly, we have moved from one domain of functioning to another, and indeed may be shifting from one dimension of well-being to others. This raises the problem of how to make cross-domain and cross-dimension comparisons without the common metric rejected by strongly pluralistic approaches such as Nussbaum's. Maybe such cross-domain compensation should not be allowed when assessing the savings from injury prevention. But this exclusion would place a heavy burden on what Nussbaum calls the 'individuation' of dimensions of well-being – substitution may be allowed within each dimension but not between dimensions. The more narrowly the dimensions are delineated, the fewer the options for substitution.

The issue of individuation, however, may not pose much of a practical problem. We can assume that the lost arm of the ex-violinist or pitcher contributed to his well-being in more than one dimension, say to include sensory and aesthetic enjoyment or to shared activities with significant others. To make the individual as whole as possible, we would have to restore his functioning across the board. Compensation in the first domain could take a variety of forms, from equipping him to play another instrument to training him as a conductor or coach. Compensation in the second domain could also take a variety of forms; perhaps the injured party and his father could no longer perform together, but could share music-making or baseball in a different way. Or maybe they could share another cherished hobby or pastime, from model trains to backpacking.

How to generalize substitution costs for types of injury or impairment

Our answer to question 2 is in many ways more important to our account since CEA cannot function on a case-by-case approach: some form of generalization is required. Moreover, our approach, unlike Feldman's tort approach, cannot use the prior, pre-injury flourishing of a particular individual as a baseline, since we are concerned with the cost of injuries prevented, not of injuries incurred, and thus with the cost savings for the largely unidentifiable prospective victims – that is, the number of individuals who won't lose limbs in car crashes because of side air-bags, say. The application of a baseline grounded on population average, or on a notion of a minimally adequate level of functioning, must rely on generalizations, often sweeping, about the impact of injuries on a range of life plans. It must generalize over socio-economic status, because we would clearly not want to assign greater savings to safety features on roads traversed by richer people. But the generalization must take as fixed the existing societal resources for, *inter alia*, surgical correction, physical rehabilitation and environmental reconstruction. It must also take as given the discriminatory social attitudes and practices that limit opportunity, damage self-esteem, and cause daily humiliation, among potentially many other factors.

The issues raised by question 1 suggest a highly individualized, labour-intensive assessment. But if we adopt an 'average' baseline for a reformed CEA, what we need is an estimate of society-wide average substitution costs for the various injuries we seek to prevent. We could obtain that estimate by taking a sample – random, representative or stratified – of the population affected. Instead of asking those individuals about their willingness to pay to avoid various injuries and sending them home, we could examine what made their lives go well (to the extent their lives went well). That assessment would not rest on each individual's satisfaction or preference, but would be guided by the individual's account of the roles played by the impairment-affected activities. Admittedly, this too involves subjective judgement, akin to a biographer's assessment of how well her subject is doing in various domains, but it would not demand uncritical deference to the individual's own appraisal of his life. Moreover, as we saw, a sensitive family member, friend or biographer might provide better information about the individual's flourishing.

Next, we could determine what the closest substitute in each domain of the individual's current flourishing would cost, taking resources and costs in current society as given. While we could not make cross-domain substitutions, we could add up the substitution costs for each domain, then average across the sampled individuals. Such averaging may seem less crude if we recall that the average would be used to assess not the cost of actual injuries, but the cost of injuries prevented to unidentified and often unidentifiable individuals. While the sampled individuals would vary widely in how well they were doing in each domain, so that restoration in any individual case might restore or perpetuate inequalities in well-being, averaging across a random or representative sample of individuals would yield de facto egalitarian results – the baseline for restoration would be an average level of functioning in each domain.

In making all of these estimates, the individuals themselves would serve as critical informants; but their views would lack the privileged, authoritative status they enjoy in preference-based contingent valuation. Thus, we would not take as gospel an individual's declaration that nothing could replace his violin playing or pitching. We would instead assess his other skills and enthusiasms, and draw on the rehabilitation literature to learn what sorts of substitutions have been, or might be, affected, and how successful they have been.[31] Obviously, this exercise would take a lot more time and effort than a relatively simplistic willingness-to-pay survey or some other preference-elicitation protocol. But our approach is far more sensitive to the nuances of flourishing, and has the virtue of being directly linked to an objective understanding of what makes a life go well.

Comparing the costs of living well with and without an impairment

We remarked above that there is a considerably simpler methodology than the one just outlined, one that is far less finely grained and individualized, but would satisfy the need for generalization. We can merely compare the average cost of living in core domains by unimpaired individuals, or a subset of such individuals (e.g. those above the poverty line) with an estimate of the costs of living just as well in these domains by individuals with representative impairments.

A recent study in the UK,[32] funded by the Joseph Rowntree Foundation, has estimated the latter sum. The study entitled *Disabled People's Costs of Living: More Than You Would Think* employed focus groups of individuals with varying levels of impairments both to delineate the areas of need and to estimate the costs of meeting those needs. The groups were given hypothetical cases of individuals at different levels of impairment. The report summarizes the key feature of the methodology as follows:

> [The] budget standards 'experts' in this study are disabled people themselves, as they, better than anyone else, understand the needs and priorities that are associated with disability. It was they who, in groups, drew up, debated, negotiated, and agreed [upon] the lists of items and resources needed to maintain a minimum standard of living.

Although the categories of need varied slightly among groups, they included food, clothing, housing, health and personal care, household goods, transport, communication, recreation and social engagement, as well as personal assistance. The main purpose of the study was to show how little of the costs in these areas were covered by government provisions for people with disabilities in the UK. A similar methodology, however, might be used to estimate the costs of reaching a minimum standard of living for non-disabled people. The differences between the costs assessed by disabled and non-disabled people would provide a rough but quick and easy means of estimating the additional costs of achieving a minimum level of well-being for people with various levels of impairment.

As our description of possible procedures for estimating the costs of impairments makes clear, our approach addresses, as it must, the challenges of finding an appropriate baseline and maintaining objectivity in judging 'closest substitutions'. Obviously, this approach faces other significant objections and challenges as well. Perhaps the most obvious is the difficulty of assessing the costs of fatal injuries. But we are hardly unique in having to confront issues of discontinuity between the treatment of mortality and 'morbidity'/level of impairment. Preference approaches rely, problematically, on the willingness of individuals to trade off years of life or risk of death against reductions in quality of life. Clearly, our approach must integrate death in a different manner, one that does not open the door to the substantial objection many have made to preference approaches, namely that they limit or qualify the basic right to life of people with disabilities.

Replacement costs for lost life – extending the approach to mortality

Our approach departs significantly from standard CEA in not treating death as an end point for damages and compensation. In a word, in our account, it will not necessarily be the case that saving someone from death will involve a greater saving than saving someone from certain kinds of injury.

More profound outcomes of injuries, of which death is the extreme, will often leave few if any alternative forms of flourishing. The attempt to find appropriate compensation with few or no proximate replacements may push the approach to an uncomfortably high level of generality. The limit to generality is the abstract notion of utility or welfare familiar to economists. But to generalize that far would be to forfeit the objectivity and particularity of a pluralistic approach.

A similar problem confronts the valuation of death in tort law. In one obvious sense, the dead cannot flourish, so there are no substitute types of flourishing to pay for. Feldman recognizes this problem as it applies to 'wrongful death' cases, and she addresses it by focusing on aspects of flourishing that do not require continued experience or existence, for example, providing for one's children, promoting one's causes, and completing one's projects. One can set up generous trust funds for the children, contribute lavishly to famine relief and commission the best writers to complete the decedent's unfinished novel. Of course, what Sen calls 'agency well-being' is noncompensable: someone else, not the decedent, will provide for his children, help relieve famines and complete the 'Great American Novel'. Although these forms of vicarious agency would be closely informed and directed by the actual agency of the deceased, they would provide only a very partial substitute for it. True enough, but all that this or any approach can hope for is rough substitution. Moreover, without compensation for agency losses, it may well be cheaper in general to provide vicarious alternatives for the deceased than to provide close substitutes for the living. This awkward consequence is reflected in the lawyer's blackly humorous advice that if you are going to have an accident, make sure you kill rather than wound your victim. While this may be a broader problem, it is one that should concern disability advocates.

The costs of death should also include the pain and suffering of loved ones, as well as the loss of income and other tangible goods. And these costs will (or certainly should) be greater for death than impairment. Again, these costs will be society-wide averages, not victim-specific. These costs may vary with the type or characteristics of the (ultimately) fatal injury – was death sudden and immediate, or gradual with steady deterioration or remitting–relapsing features?; or did the injury result in reduced life expectancy with no specific intervening morbidity (by, for example, compromising the immune system so that common diseases become life-threatening)?

There may be other ways to capture the loss of death under our substitution-plus-pain-and-suffering approach. To be sure, some possibilities are manifestly inappropriate, such as spousal- or child-replacement costs (reminiscent of God's 'compensation' to Job for his lost family). More promising is some measure of the costs of realizing the deceased's 'potential' as fully as possible, even if he or she was unlikely to have done so while alive. Moving in this direction would raise the costs of death if one presumes that the deceased would have flourished to the maximum extent possible, had he or she survived (an assumption that seems morally if not empirically defensible, since the injurer should bear the burden of uncertainty about how well the deceased would have done). Estimating the costs of lost potential can apply to early as well as late deaths, although we leave it open whether 'lost potential' costs should be age-indexed. But in any case, we would look at the maximum potential of an average individual, not of a Leonardo da Vinci or a Stephen Hawking. Admittedly, this treatment of the costs of death is not, and could hardly be, a straightforward matter of 'making whole'. Rather, it suggests that in assessing the costs of fatal injury, we should be assessing the costs of achieving the maximum potential of a life cut short.

One final concern about cost under estimation is raised by measures that prevent injury and further impairment to individuals who already have serious impairments, for example, the provision of safety features in group homes or assisted-living facilities. Many of the marginal costs incurred by injury and impairment may be smaller for already-impaired individuals. In a society with limited accommodation, they will already be much less productive economically on average than unimpaired individuals,[33] and they will already suffer the effects of stigmatization and discrimination, which may increase only slightly, if at all, with further impairment. They may have few relatives and friends to share their additional losses, and they are all-too-likely to have been socialized to develop very modest projects and goals, whose closest replacement might be relatively cheap. All of this would lead to cost estimates that were morally inadequate.

At the same time, two other considerations work against this tendency to underestimate the costs of further impairment. First, impairment of additional functions may well make the restoration of previous levels of functioning, however modest, extremely difficult and expensive, even on a highly pluralistic view of well-being. The loss of sensory and motor functions may not be additive in its impact on well-being: while it may be fairly easy for a person who is blind, deaf or paraplegic to live well in our society, it may be quite hard to fashion a rewarding life when one lacks sight, hearing *and* limb function.

Second, the failure to provide the same level of safety to already-impaired individuals that others enjoy would itself deny them a critical aspect of well-being, which Nussbaum (2001), following John Rawls, calls 'the social bases of self-respect'. The disparity in protection would involve profound insult even in the absence of injury, since it would reflect the view that the physical and mental integrity of already-impaired individuals had lesser value or importance. In other words, even if less protection were justified in terms of lower marginal costs, assigning lesser value to further impairments would devalue the already-impaired individuals.

Is the rejection of preferences paternalistic and anti-democratic?

As mentioned, perhaps the strongest argument in favour of using elicited preferences for valuation as input for cost-effectiveness analysis (one acknowledged even by critics of standard methods of preference-elicitation) is that the use of preferences along the general lines of social choice theory is both non-paternalistic and democratic in spirit and consequences. Our alternative of using an 'objective list' account of quality of life for CEA in particular and policy-making in general would, therefore, be open to the objection that it is both paternalistic and anti-democratic.

One response to this charge is that, while objective accounts are vulnerable to paternalism, they can avoid it to the extent that i) their domains are framed in very general terms and subject to a broad consensus,[34] and ii) they emphasize the capacity for, rather than the actual performance of, activities in each domain.[35] One could also insist that the more appealing forms of preference-elicitation, and the accounts of well-being that inform them, may be no less paternalistic since they assess 'rational, informed' preferences rather than the actual 'raw' preferences of the population.

The response to the claim that objective theories of well-being are anti-democratic is straightforward. This objection simply confuses the content of a theory of well-being with the mechanism by which collective decisions may be made. Even if preferences were elicited in a manner that was not elitist, and did not exclude marginalized groups, their elicitation would have little to do with democratic governance. Democracy is about the exercise of choice, not the elicitation of preferences, raw or informed. No method of assessing quality-of-life or the costs of injury is inherently demo-cratic; its democratic character depends upon the transparency of the methods it uses, and the uses to which its results are put. However it is accomplished, CEA can be more or less democratic, depending upon the role it plays in the collective decision-making process.

It might also be objected that our approach is not objective enough, and in particular that our uncertainty about the appropriate baseline for restoration – average or minimally adequate level in each domain – casts doubt on the claimed objectivity of our approach. In the face of this uncer-tainty, who is to decide how well someone has done in a given domain, or what counts as doing minimally or adequately well? Though clearly there will be disagreement, within a single society a rough consensus may well be achieved by public deliberation. And it is possible to exaggerate the background disagreement in a given society. Even without public deliber-ation, we can agree, for example, that the funds provided by most transit and para-transit systems to enable people with mobility impairments to get around are woefully inadequate, and that much more money is required. We may not agree on precisely how much more, but we can agree on a range.

Finally, our approach to assessing the costs of injuries and impairments might seem hopelessly expensive or time-consuming to put into practice. Although implementing our proposal for estimating the costs of impair-ments, sketchy as it is, would surely be labour-intensive, it need not be prohibitively so. Our approach, moreover, is merely one of several similar methods, some of which are far less time- and labour-intensive. We have described one of these, a radically simpler method that has been adopted in the recent UK study of the costs of impairment. On the other hand, stan-dard preference-based approaches achieve economy only by sacrificing reliability, transparency and both policy and moral relevance.

Even with these remaining challenges, we believe that it is important for those with the requisite expertise to explore alternative methods for doing CEA when the lives of people are at stake. This need not require preference-based approaches to be abandoned altogether, but rather, sup-plementing and qualifying them with other ways of assessing the cost of injury, impairment and death. Pluralism in methods more fully respects the values at stake, in particular, the fundamental right to life itself.

Conclusion

We have offered the broad outlines of an approach to assessing the costs of impairments without recourse to preferences, and responses to some of the problems it will face if it is to be a contender for use with CEA in health or other policy domains. Our goal has been to offer a constructive alternative to subjective judgements of the badness of impairments, an alternative which recognizes that impairments can make it more difficult and costly to live well, even in a partially accommodating society. Assessing the cost of alternative forms of flourishing, and of pain and suffering from discrimination and exclusion, provides critical input, however rough and incomplete, for determining the cost-effectiveness of preventive measures. And it does so without devaluing the lives of people living with impairments, forestalling the judgement that some lives are simply too costly in health and other resources to maintain. It is our hope that our approach avoids measures that, in light of an increasing strain on health care resources, would lead to the further erosion of the enjoyment of the basic right to life, and to live with disabilities.

Our approach differs from most of the alternatives primarily because it relies on an objective approach to quality of life. To take a prominent example, it departs in this respect from the approach developed by Erik Nord who, in various places, has insisted that quality-of-life judgements must be subjective if they are to avoid the danger of cultural and other forms of bias.[36] We believe that embracing purely subjective judgement is the wrong response to that very real risk. Rather, we need an appropriately flexible, pluralistic understanding of human flourishing, one which the capabilities approach may have the potential to provide, and we need to look closely at how individuals with atypical functioning fare in their physical and social environments. We would not judge the well-being of Tiny Tim by his brave assurances, or even his genuinely sunny disposition, but by how he, and others with (severe or progressive) mobility impairments, were able to live in Victorian England. Their extremely limited options for flourishing in that social context might make the costs of the impairments that they incurred very high, and place a premium on prevention (perhaps a lot more than in affluent post-industrial nations).

Our approach also diverges from Nord's in making no attempt to build distributional judgements into our cost assessments. It's not that we think distribution is unimportant; on the contrary, we think that it's important enough to be judged separately from the costs of impairment.

What we are presenting here is only the bare bones of an alternative form of costing for the purposes of CEA. To flesh it out in practical terms, our approach would require expertise in a wide variety of specialties: surgery, psychology, employment economics, rehabilitation, architecture, to name a few. We are encouraged by the fact that our approach has parallels to that used, and used successfully for many decades, in Anglo-American tort law for the assessment of damages. For that purpose, complex protocols for lost productivity, pain and suffering and other kinds of damage have been developed and, to the extent feasible within the legal system, tested against intuition and economic expertise.

Ultimately, we begin with the common recognition that there are conceptual, methodological and ethical problems with CEA based on preference-elicitation, especially when CEA is used within the health care and public health arenas, where questions about who will receive scarce resources and live, and who will not and die, are not theoretical but highly practical questions. In light of that consensus, it is essential that we explore other forms of valuation as input into CEA, if it is ever to become a useful, appropriate and ethically sound tool for policy analysis. We have sketched out such an alternative here.

As we mentioned at the outset, our approach actually replaces CEA with a form of CBA. It does not use life years as a metric; costs and benefits are both expressed in monetary terms. What those dollar figures represent, however, is entirely different from that in traditional CBA. We do not attempt to 'monetize' the value of a human life; rather, we estimate the cost of making a person whole when his life has been cut short. Expressing costs and benefits in dollars may appear to give our approach broader comparability than CEA. That appearance is deceptive, however. Traditional CBA monetizes the value of human lives, wilderness areas and art alike by the use of preference-elicitation in willingness-to-pay or contingent valuation protocols. It would be both meaningless and misleading to compare the numbers yielded by our approach for the costs and benefits of a highway safety programme to those yielded by contingent value techniques for a wetlands preservation programme. But our approach (if it could be made practicable) would facilitate the comparison of different health and safety measures competing for scarce dollars.

Yet we face a significant dilemma in the application of our approach to those policy domains. We have aspired to comprehensiveness, in the sense of trying to take account of all the costs involved in making a person whole in the face of injury or impairment. Yet we would balk at two obvious uses of those cost figures: 1) to reduce the estimated benefits for saving or extending the life of an already-impaired person, or 2) to reduce the estimated benefits for saving or extending a life while not preventing an impairment. As we have argued, the death of an average person with a given impairment results in a greater cost savings than the death of an otherwise similar person without that impairment. Yet to take that difference into account would be, in effect, to treat the death of a disabled person as the removal of an economic burden.

We do not believe that the value of extending a life with a disability should be discounted by the concomitant increase in the various costs of impairment we have described in previous sections. In saving the lives of people with disabilities we continue to incur those costs, but those costs must not enter the calculation of the value of saving those lives. To take those costs into account in assessing the benefit of preventative measures is to recognize the expense of living as well in our society with various impairments as without them; in contracts, to take those costs into account in assessing the value of lives saved is, effectively, to treat the lives of people with disabilities as having less value than those of people without them. Excluding the marginal costs of living well with impairment from the calculation of the value of saving the lives of people with impairments may seem *ad hoc* and unprincipled from an accounting perspective. But we believe that exclusion is essential to preserve the moral equality of lives with disabilities. It would be a hollow victory if we merely succeeded in replacing the devaluation of disabled lives based on their supposedly lesser quality with the devaluation of disabled lives based on their estimated greater expense.

Notes

1 It is worth remarking that some studies suggest that, left to themselves, physicians do not always take into account costing information, or even cost-effectiveness, when they prescribe potentially life-saving treatment, preferring to rely on medical protocols alone, see Ubel, P.A., Jepsond, C., Barone, J., Hershey, J.C. and Asch D.A. (2003) 'The influence of cost-effectiveness information on physicians' cancer screening recommendations', *Social Science and Medicine,* 56, 1727–1736.

2 Murray, C., Salomon, J., Mathers, C. and Lopez, A. (2002) 'Summary measures of population health: Conclusions and recommendations', in C. Murray, J. Salomon, C. Mathers and A. Lopez (eds) *Summary Measures of Population Health: Concepts, Ethics, Measurement and Applications.* Geneva: World Health Organization, pp.731–756.

3 Broome, J. (2002) 'Measuring the burden of disease by aggregating well-being', in *Summary Measures of Population Health,* pp.91–113. Brock, D. (1995) 'Justice and the ADA: Does prioritizing and rationing health care discriminate against the disabled?', *Social Philosophy and Policy,* 12, 159–185.

4 Parfit, D. (1984) *Reasons and Persons.* Oxford: Clarendon Press.

5 Sen, A. (1991) *Inequality Reexamined.* Cambridge, Mass.: Harvard University Press; Nussbaum, M. (2006) *Frontiers of Justice: Disability, Nationality, Species Membership (The Tanner Lectures on Human Values).* Cambridge, MA: Belknap Press.

6 Hausman, D.M. (2006) 'Valuing health', *Philosophy & Public Affairs,* 34, 246–274.

7 Salomon, J.A. and Murray, C.J.L. (2004) 'A multi-method approach to measuring health-state valuations', *Health Economics,* 13, 281–290.

8 Nord, E., Pinto, J.L., Richardson, J., Menzel, P. and Ubel, P. (1999) 'Incorporating societal concerns for fairness in numerical valuations of health programmes', *Health Economics,* 8, 25–39.

9 D.M. Hausman (2006) op.cit.

10 Scanlon, T. (1991) 'The moral basis of interpersonal comparison', in J. Elster and J.E. Roemer (eds) *Interpersonal Comparisons of Well-being.* New York: University of Cambridge Press, pp.17–44; Griffin, J. (1991) 'Against the taste model', in J. Elster and J.E. Roemer (eds) (1991) op. cit. pp.45–69.

11 Tengs, T. and Wallace, A. (2000) 'One thousand health-related quality-of-life estimates', *Medical Care,* 38, 583–637.

12 Tengs, T., Adams, M., Pliskin, J., Safran, D., Siegel, J., Weinstein, M. and Graham, J. (1995) 'Five hundred life-saving interventions and their cost-effectiveness', *Risk Analysis*, 15, 369–390.

13 Although we use the term 'health condition' here and throughout, it is not without problems of its own. In particular, is a health condition merely an injury, disease, disorder that resides, so to speak, entirely 'under the skin' of the individual, or is it that contextualized to a specific physical and social environment? Since, clearly, the same injury will manifest itself differently in different physical, social and attitudinal environments, the resulting costs of returning the person to 'wholeness', as we are proposing, will vary considerably. For our purposes, we propose to use a narrow definition of 'health condition' and presume that the costing exercise will be highly dependent on features of the person's environment and social context. This is a complication, but not one that does not already affect the costing enterprise: preventing injuries in cities has different cost consequences from doing so in rural areas, costs in developed countries are very different from developing countries, and so on.

14 We do this fully recognizing that in other contexts and for other purposes these terms may be used differently.

15 Bowling, A. (1995) 'What things are really important in people's lives?: A survey of the public's judgments to inform scales of health-related quality of life', *Social Science and Medicine*, 41, 1447–1462.

16 Griffin, J. (1986) *Well-Being: Its Meaning, Measurement, and Moral Importance*. Oxford: Clarendon Press, 1986; Nussbaum, M. (2001) 'Humanities and human capabilities', *Liberal Education*, 87, 38–45.

17 Bowling, A. (1995) op. cit. p.1460.

18 Nussbaum, M. (2001) op. cit. pp.3–4.

19 Menzel, P., Dolan, P., Richardson, J. and Olsen, J.A. (2002) 'The role of adaptation to disability and disease in health state valuation: A preliminary normative analysis', *Social Science and Medicine*, 55, 2149–2158.

20 Arguably, our account should also take notice of 'adjustment' in the more restricted sense in which the skills that an individual once possessed, but which after the injury are now more in demand, are either preserved or re-acquired.

21 Frick, K. and Foster, A. (2003) 'The magnitude and cost of global blindess: An increasing problem that can be alleviated', *American Journal of Ophthalmology*, 135, 471–476.

22 Ibid.

23 Feldman, H., (1997) 'Harm and money: Against the insurance theory of tort law', *Texas Law Review*, 75, 1567–1604.

24 Nussbaum, M. (2001) op. cit.

25 Norman Daniels (1985) *Just Health Care*. Cambridge University Press.

26 But is not the entire agenda of 'prevention' of impairment complicit in this discrimination? Prevention of impairment, arguably, avoids the difficulty of confronting the discrimination directly and so contributes to it. This is a concern about prevention (whether primary or secondary in the public health sense) that we can do no more than raise here.

27 Pain and suffering costs will vary with the onset of impairment, but the difference may go in either direction: people with congenital impairments may learn to deal more effectively with discrimination, and so be inured to it, but people with adult-onset impairments may have developed social networks that cushion some of the impact of discrimination.

28 Asch, A. (2001) 'Disability, bioethics, and human rights', in G.L. Albrecht, K.D. Seelman and M. Bury (eds) *Handbook of Disability Studies*, Thousand Oaks, CA: Sage Publications, pp.297–326.

29 For example, the loss of certain physiological functions used only in esoteric pursuits, as opposed to common or everyday activities and vocations (or what are usually called 'activities of daily living', or ADLs), should not be assigned much of a cost. The calculation might be that of the cost of the nearest substitute for someone who engages in the esoteric pursuit, discounted by the low probability of the injured individual being such a person, and perhaps augmented by some small loss for the marginally shrunken horizons for those who imagined that pursuit as a possible alternative to their current projects. We would also place significant value on a reduction in opportunities or capabilities so large that it limited meaningful choice – some comprehensive motor, sensory and cognitive impairments might so truncate opportunity as to represent a compensable loss even to those not currently engaged in the activities precluded. But such truncation would not be typical of more common sensory and motor impairments, as opposed to the preclusion of the specific activities that impaired individuals had actually been engaged in. See Dworkin, G. (1982) 'Is more choice better than less?', *Midwest Studies in Philosophy*, 7, 47–61; Wasserman, D. (1998) 'Distributive justice' in A. Silvers, D. Wasserman and M. Mahowald *Disability, Difference, Discrimination*. Lanham, MD: Rowman & Littlefield.

30 But we would *not* compensate parents for thwarted expectations, e.g. the disappointment of having a child who, as a result of injury, cannot carry on the proud family tradition of excellence in a particular musical instrument. Parents should not have such expectations about their children, expectations that can easily be frustrated in a myriad of non-compensable ways, and we would be reluctant to treat their frustration as a compensable damage.

31 But in judging the success of these rehabilitative interventions, would we not have at some stage to rely on the expressed satisfaction of the individuals who had undergone rehabilitation? Of course we would, but their satisfaction would be only one of several indices of success, others of which would be more objective. The science of rehabilitation has its own standards of success, namely performance outcome measures, developed as generalizations from countless cases of increased flourishing across domains.

32 Smith, N., Middleton, S., Ashton-Brooks, K., Cox, L., and Dobson, B. with Reith, L. (2004) *Disabled People's Costs of Living: More Than You Would Think.* York: Joseph Rowntree Foundation/York Publishing Services.

33 Frick, K. and Foster, A. (2003) op. cit.

34 Scanlon, T. (1991) op. cit.

35 Sen, A. (1991) op. cit; Nussbaum, M. (2001) op. cit; Nussbaum, M. (2003) op. cit.

36 Nord, E. *et al.* (1999) op. cit.

This chapter develops/draws on 'Mending, Not Ending, Cost Effectiveness Analysis (CEA): A Proposal for Conducting Agency CEA of Health Benefits Without Eliciting Preferences'. Background paper prepared for the Institute of Medicine, Committee to Evaluate Measures of Health Benefits for Environmental, Health, and Safety Regulation, November 29, 2004.

Bibliography

Cummins, R. (1996) 'The domains of life satisfaction: An attempt to order chaos', *Social Indicators Research*, 38, 303–328.

Kessler, R. and Stang, P. (eds) (2006) *Health and Work Productivity*. Chicago: University of Chicago Press.

McDowell, I. and Newell, C. (1996) *Measuring Health: A Guide to Rating Scales and Questionnaires.* New York: Oxford University Press.

Murray, C. (1996) 'Rethinking DALYs' in C. Murray and A. Lopez (eds) *The Global Burden of Disease: A Comprehensive Assessment of Mortality and Disability From Diseases, Injuries, and Risk Factors in 1990 and Projected to 2020.* Geneva: World Health Organization.

Nord, E. (2006) 'Values for health states in QALYS and DALYS: Desirability versus well-being and worth', in D. Wasserman, R. Wachbroit and J. Bickenbach (eds) *Quality of Life and Human Difference: Genetic Testing, Health-Care, and Disability.* New York: Cambridge University Press, pp.125–141.

Nussbaum, M. (2000) *Women and Economic Development.* New York: Cambridge University Press.

3 Deadly currents beneath calm waters

Persons with disability and the right to life in Australia

Phillip French and Rosemary Kayess

Introduction

Australia has traditionally considered itself at the forefront of nations committed to the recognition and respect of human rights, including the right to life of all human beings.[1] Australia has signed and ratified the International Covenant on Civil and Political Rights (ICCPR), which codifies the right to life in international law.[2] Australia has also signed and ratified the Convention on the Rights of the Child (CRC), which codifies both the right to life, and a related right to survival and development, for all children and young persons.[3] Recently, Australia has actively participated in the development of, and has been among the first to sign,[4] the Convention on the Rights of Persons with Disabilities (CRPD), which again codifies the right to life, and extends the right of survival to situations of risk and humanitarian emergency for both children and adults, specifically referenced to persons with disability. By world standards, Australia also has in place progressive domestic disability legislation and policy, which affirm the human rights of persons with disability, and promote their participation in society. Additionally, Australia is a wealthy country with relatively well developed health and social security systems, which include a wide range of specialist services targeted specifically at persons with disability and their families. Together, these factors would appear to provide a strong foundation for securing the rights to life and survival of Australians with disability. However, beneath these calm waters lie deadly currents.

This chapter analyses the degree to which Australians with disability effectively enjoy the rights to life and survival, as they are understood in international law. We adopt an expansive understanding of the right to life, noting the Human Rights Committee's view that '[t]he expression "inherent right to life" cannot be properly understood in a restrictive manner'.[5] This expansive understanding views the right to life as far more than an obligation on states to merely prevent and punish arbitrary deprivation of life, as important as this is. Instead, we argue that the right to life requires states to pursue a range of positive legal, social and economic measures to ensure that this right is fully realized, especially in a disability context. This approach will no doubt generate debate in relation to the delimitation of the right to life, as a civil and political right, from economic, social and cultural rights. However, it is our contention that this distinction is artificial in a disability context and is reflective of the disablism that infects traditional human rights paradigms. We argue that the rights to life and survival for persons with disability cannot be effectively secured without some transformation of traditional understandings of these rights, and we examine the potential for the CRPD to effect such a transformation. Our overall theoretical approach is based in a social relational understanding of impairment and disability – one that views the primary threats to the lives of persons with impairments as products of a hostile social environment rather than as immutable incidents of individual pathology.

The rights of life and survival

In the post-war era the United Nations has formulated seven so-called 'core' human rights treaties. Although these treaties are universal in application they have provided little effective protection of the human rights of persons with disability. Latent within the traditional formulation of civil and political rights, of which the right to life is an example, has been an able-bodied right-bearer perceived as capable of life and survival merely under conditions of state non-interference with life and prohibition against arbitrary killing. This traditional 'negative' formulation of the right to life fails to encompass the positive measures – such as the provision of health and social services (economic and social rights) – that will often be required by persons with disability in order that they may effectively realize their rights to life and survival.

Although the mandate under which the CRPD was developed stipulated that it was merely to apply existing rights to the circumstances of persons with disability, the CRPD has modified and transformed traditional human rights concepts, including in relation to the right to life, in key respects. The CRPD does, in fact, contain entirely new formulations of human rights,[6] as well as highly disability-specific interpretations of existing human rights, which transform formerly essentially 'negative' rights into 'positive' state obligations.[7] In these and other respects, the CRPD blends civil and political rights with economic, social and cultural rights, not only within its overall structure, but also within its individual articles. Additionally, the CRPD integrates so-called third-generation rights and concepts, such as the right to development, and international cooperation, which are woven extensively through the fabric of its interpretive, substantive and implementation articles. The CRPD also incorporates a number of other concepts and priorities from the field of social development, such as poverty reduction, and an expansive new concept of social protection. Broader discussion of these developments is beyond the scope of this chapter, but they are deliberately noted here for their implications for the way in which the rights to life and survival of persons with disability are now to be interpreted and understood.

The right to life in the CRPD is stated in the following terms: 'States Parties reaffirm that every human being has the inherent right to life and shall take all necessary measures to ensure its effective enjoyment by persons with disabilities on an equal basis with others'.[8]

The article reflects the substantive transformation of existing rights concepts effected by the CRPD. The first limb of the article seeks to merely 'reaffirm' that every human being has an inherent right to life. If left there, the article would arguably confine the operation of the right to its traditional 'negative' or 'non-interference'-based formulation. However, the second limb of the article requires states to 'take all necessary measures' to ensure the effective enjoyment of the right by persons with disability on an equal basis with others. The second limb transforms the right into a positive state obligation to secure the conditions under which persons with disability may effectively realize their rights to life and survival. Both on its face, and particularly when read in the context of the CRPD as a whole, this formulation of the right of life clearly adverts to action in the economic, social and cultural spheres. In this respect the CRPD solidifies and extends the Human Rights Committee's somewhat tentative jurisprudence on the positive dimension of the right to life, and elevates this jurisprudence to the level of statute. The CRPD therefore has much greater potential to penetrate to social, economic and culturally based threats to the lives of persons with disability.[9]

The right to life in Australian law

Article 6(1) of the ICCPR states that 'every human being has an inherent right to life'. These words are repeated in both Article 6 of the CRC and Article 10 of the CRPD. A number of commentators have suggested that the use of the adjective 'inherent' and the present tense 'has' reflect a belief by the framers in a superordinate natural law basis of the right, or alternatively or additionally, that the right to life formed part of customary international law prior to the formulation of the International Bill of Rights. According to this analysis, the right to life enunciated in Article 6(1) of the ICCPR is merely declaratory in nature.[10]

Australian law does not appear to recognize or incorporate any natural law or customary basis to the right to life. In the only case that appears to have dealt with the issue, the Supreme Court of the Northern Territory declined to strike down an Act of Parliament of the Northern Territory that permitted active voluntary euthanasia.[11] In doing so, the majority rejected the plaintiff's claim that the parliament's exercise of legislative power was constrained by an obligation to protect an inalienable right to life 'deeply rooted in the Australian democratic system and common law'. The court held that in the absence of a constitutionally enshrined Bill of Rights the issue was 'ethical, moral or political', rather than legal, and the parliament has legislative power to abrogate any 'fundamental rights, freedoms or immunities' of its citizens.[12]

Australia is a federation of six states. The Australian Constitution contains a series of 'enumerated powers', which circumscribe the limits of commonwealth legislative competence. Those powers that are not enumerated remain within the legislative competence of the states, which is plenary in nature, limited only by what is necessary for 'peace, order and good government'. Australia also has three self-governing territories, each of which also has plenary power; however, the source of their self-government is commonwealth legislation rather than municipal constitutional power. Most international human rights treaties, including the ICCPR, the CRC and the CRPD, require state signatories to adopt legislative and other measures to give effect to the obligations they enunciate. Section 51(xxix) of the Australian Constitution, the so-called 'external affairs power', provides the Commonwealth Government with power to enter into international obligations and to pass domestic legislation to give effect to those obligations. It permits the Commonwealth to legislate in areas outside its enumerated powers, and traditionally the province state power, where it has entered into a relevant international obligation.

International law is binding upon Australia in its relationship with the community of nations. However, this does not mean that an international obligation entered into by the Australian Government, or recognized in customary international law, automatically becomes part of Australian municipal law. For that to occur, with very limited exceptions, the Australian Parliament must legislate specifically to incorporate the obligation.[13] In spite of its obligation to do so, Australia has not comprehensively enacted into municipal 'hard law' those international human rights treaties to which it is a signatory.[14] Australia does not have a national bill of rights, and at the commonwealth level, there remains significant political resistance to such a bill. As one senior judicial commentator has recently noted:

> Putting it bluntly, we have so far largely ignored, or rejected, the relevance for our own legal system of the great change that came about in the protection of basic rights, following the Second World War and the creation of the United Nations.[15]

Particular human rights instruments are, however, attached as schedules to the Human Rights and Equal Opportunity Commission Act, 1986 (Cth), an Act which constitutes the (Australian) Human Rights and Equal Opportunity Commission. This includes the ICCPR, the CRC, the Declaration on the Rights of Mentally Retarded Persons (1971) and the Declaration on the Rights of the Disabled (1975). In the absence of direct incorporation of a specific obligation by other means, these obligations have an essentially 'soft law', or policy status in municipal Australian law. The Human Rights and Equal Opportunity Commission has conciliation, public education and policy functions, but no determinative powers. It may receive a complaint in relation to an alleged breach of an international instrument incorporated as a schedule to its constituting Act by a commonwealth agency (but not a state or territory or non-state actor), but may only respond to it within its limited functions. If it is not capable of conciliation, apart from taking up the matter in its general policy and education functions, the commission's only alternative is to refer the matter to parliament for attention through the Attorney General.

Due to its federal character, and in the absence of any unifying national bill of rights, the task of assessing Australia's compliance with its international obligations with respect to the rights to life and survival is a complex one, requiring examination of laws, policies and institutional arrangements that do not necessarily have a human rights focus, and which may be situated in different tiers of government, resulting in significant differences of approach and outcome across the country.

The Australian Government enacted disability services legislation in 1986 and non-discrimination legislation in the area of disability in 1992, obviously well in advance of the CRPD. By world standards both are progressive, even visionary, pieces of legislation that assert the dignity, worth and human rights of persons with disability. This legislation underpins Australia's national action plan on disability, the Commonwealth Disability Strategy, and the Disability Services Act, 1986 (Cth) also provides the underlying policy platform of the national specialist service delivery framework for persons with disability – the Commonwealth, State and Territory Disability Agreement. Although this legislation does not deal directly with the right to life, it does bear upon the services and supports that are essential for persons with disability to effectively enjoy these rights, and the Disability Services Act, 1986 (Cth) places major emphasis on the right to development.

The Disability Services Act, 1986 (Cth) applies to generic and specialist services utilized by persons with disability and is underpinned by a set of principles and objectives that effectively operate as a charter of service user rights. In the specialist service area these principles and objectives have been translated into a set of standards according to which services are regulated. Services that fail to meet the relevant standards are ineligible for commonwealth funding. However, these standards are not directly enforceable by persons with disability or their associates. They also operate in relation to discretionary and budget-capped programmes, which are historically grossly under funded, and subject to intense unmet demand. Many disability services are institutionally based and of poor quality, yet they have proved very resistant to change. In part, this is because government as both the principal contributor of funding and regulator of these services is subject to a conflict of interest that operates as a disincentive to the enforcement of standards (enforcement of standards may produce greater cost for government). Consequently, in spite of its aspirations, Australian disability services legislation has proved a relatively weak mechanism for securing the human rights of persons with disability, including some of the essential foundations for the realization of the rights to life and survival.

The Disability Discrimination Act, 1992 (Cth) prohibits discrimination on the ground of disability in enumerated areas, including the provision of goods and services that also have direct bearing on the rights to life and survival. The legislation has a number of major strengths, including a very broad definition of disability,[16] application to state and non-state entities, structural as well as individual complaint-based mechanisms to eliminate discrimination,[17] and it is enforceable by persons with disability and their associates.[18] It is, however, framed within a formal equality model and focuses only on the elimination of unreasonable barriers to the participation of persons with disability in Australian society. Consequently, it has failed to penetrate to some specific human rights violations impacting on the rights of life and survival that can only be effectively addressed by positive measures designed to achieve substantial equality. For example, the legislation cannot compel government to provide specialist health or social services necessary for the survival of persons with disability, and it has very limited capacity to ensure that specialist services are delivered at a standard that would be acceptable to non-disabled persons.

The deprivation of life

Article 6(1) of the ICCPR operates essentially as a restraint on state interference with life, and as an obligation on states to prohibit homicide. This latter aspect of the right to life is incorporated into Australian criminal law. Under the Australian Federation, the criminal law is principally the responsibility of state and territory governments, and consequently provisions vary somewhat across jurisdictions. Intentional killing of another person attracts the strongest sanctions in Australian criminal law. A person who commits homicide may be sentenced to life imprisonment, while a person who commits the lesser crime of manslaughter may also be sentenced to imprisonment for life in Queensland, South Australia and the Northern Territory and up to 26 years in other jurisdictions.

Where criminal penalties are not mandatory, the sentencing officer has discretion to take into account matters that may aggravate or mitigate the offender's culpability. In New South Wales, this discretion is structured by statute. A sentencing officer may take into account as a matter aggravating the culpability of the offender, evidence that the crime was motivated by hatred for, or prejudice against, a group of people to which the offender believed the victim belonged, which includes persons living with a particular impairment or disability.[19] The sentencing officer may also take into account as an aggravating factor any special vulnerability of the victim, such as impairment and disability,[20] and any evidence that the offender abused a position of trust or authority in relation to the victim, which would be the case if, for example, the offender was responsible for the care and support of a victim living with impairment or disability.[21] In some other jurisdictions, the sentencing officer may take into account as a matter aggravating the offender's culpability any relevant personal circumstances of the victim.[22] This might also potentially include a victim's impairment and disability. To some extent these represent positive measures to deter crimes against persons with disability, including those that threaten life. However, we are not aware of any reported case where these principles have been applied with their intended effect in relation to the intentional killing of a person with disability.

In 2003, Daniela Dawes suffocated her ten-year-old autistic son, Jason, by holding her hand over his nose and mouth until he died. Ms Dawes then attempted suicide, but was discovered and revived. She was initially charged with murder, but the charge was subsequently reduced to manslaughter when the prosecution accepted that she was subject to severe depression at the time of the offence.[23] Ms Dawes entered a plea of guilty and was sentenced to a good behaviour bond for a period of five years. There was a public outcry about the leniency of the sentence. Although it had failed to seek a custodial sentence at first instance, the prosecution appealed, arguing that the seriousness of the offence required the imposition of a custodial sentence.

This was a complex and genuinely tragic case. As the Court of Criminal Appeal observed:

> This was not merely a case of a mother killing her severely disabled son, but of a mother suffering from major depression occasioned not only by the need to care for her son and the devotion she gave to that task, but overwhelmed by a number of other stressors all impacting upon her at about the same time ...

However, there can be little doubt that it was the perceived burden of caring for Jason, and the direct and indirect consequences of his impairment and disability on Ms Dawes, that resulted in the leniency of the sentence imposed. At first instance, the trial judge constructed Jason as suffering, dependent and incapable and as constituting an intolerable and unimaginable burden on Ms Dawes:

> Jason was a profoundly handicapped autistic child suffering from ... [Jason's autistic characteristics are then interrogated in detail].

> The practical reality is that the care in terms of daily responsibility to feed, toilet, bathe, educate, entertain and love fell to his mother, this offender. There is no doubt that this was an unrelenting, tiring, frustrating and never-ending task that very few people have ever experienced or are even capable of fully comprehending.[24]

Jason was portrayed as a principal cause of Ms Dawes' depression, and of other stressors to which Ms Dawes was subject, such as his father's emotional breakdown, suicidal ideation and resort to alcohol (which in turn resulted in Ms Dawes being subject to domestic violence). Jason was also portrayed as the cause of the breakdown of his parents' marriage and his parents' loss of community ties as a result of their moving from a country town to the city in an effort to obtain services for him. The appellate court specifically approved of this construction of Jason by the trial judge.[25]

Both at first instance and on appeal, the courts appear to focus on Jason's victim characteristics not as matters aggravating the seriousness of the offence, even though the relevant provisions are formally adverted to, but as matters mitigating its seriousness.[26] Neither court does so in any explicit way, but their detailed interrogation of Jason's impairment and disability-related characteristics and behaviour, and the impact of this on Ms Dawes, her husband and daughter, can lead to no other conclusion. This discussion does not resolve into any definitive statement about Jason's value or humanness, but its effect is to construct him as demonic 'other', and by implication, to offer a degree of excuse for his killing. This is particularly evident from the courts' specific reliance on evidence such as the following passage from Ms Dawes' husband's statement:

> He was getting older. He had started to grow pubic hair. We began to ask ourselves how we were going to shave his face, and we were concerned that he may start masturbating in public. Daniela and I were frightened, concerned and stressed by Jason getting older and the things that went along with this.[27]

In Australia, the 'principles' or 'purposes' of sentencing vary in detail across jurisdictions, but are generally directed to: punishment of the offender; general deterrence of members of the community from committing similar crimes; specific deterrence of the offender from committing crime; denunciation of the conduct of the offender; and, recognition of the harm done to the victim and the community. In the Dawes case, the court at first instance determined that general and specific deterrence ought to be given 'very little weight'. It also determined that: '[i]n all the circumstances of this case, [Ms Dawes'] moral culpability was very low. Accordingly, the need to denounce her conduct and make her accountable for her actions does not have the significance it might otherwise have had'.[28]

The explicit factors relied upon by the court in reaching these determinations were Ms Dawes' mental illness and consequent diminished responsibility for the offence, and her frank admissions and early plea of guilty.[29] However, implicitly, Jason's victim characteristics also appear to have strongly influenced the court's approach. These determinations were criticized by the Court of Criminal Appeal for their failure to give appropriate weight to the objective seriousness of the offence, the 'courts' responsibility to uphold the sanctity of human life', to 'denounc[e] the conduct of the offender, mak[e] the offender accountable for her actions and ensur[e] adequate punishment for the offence'. The appeal court concluded that the judge at first instance allowed these factors to be outweighed by Ms Dawes' 'strong subjective case', and thus fall into error. However, the appeal was, in effect, unsuccessful. While the majority held that the trial judge had erred in not imposing a custodial sentence, it nevertheless exercised its discretion to dismiss the appeal having regard to the principle of double jeopardy; the Crown's failure to seek a custodial sentence at first instance; and Ms Dawes' progress in rehabilitation since the sentence was first imposed.[30]

In another recent case, the parents of Matthew Sutton, a 28-year-old man with severe multiple impairments, pleaded guilty to his manslaughter,[31] after initially reporting to police that they had found him dead in his bed. They were each sentenced to a good behaviour bond for a period of five years.[32] Matthew's parents submitted to the court that Matthew's murder was precipitated by the necessity of surgery to correct chronic ear pain and prevent meningitis. This would have resulted in his total hearing loss for a period of at least three months, and a significant risk of permanent hearing loss. Faced with this risk, Matthew's parents claim to have formed the view that he would not have had 'quality of life', and that he should be spared further 'suffering' by euthanasia.[33]

As it did with Jason in the Dawes case, the court undertakes an extensive interrogation of the nature and degree of Matthew's impairment and disability, and the perceived impact of this on his parents. It also reviews the abuse and neglect Matthew experienced in supported accommodation. Matthew is constructed as a suffering, living tragedy, as 'other than human', and a source of profound grief, shame and burden to his parents. The court explicitly approves of the following passage of expert testimony submitted on behalf of the parents by a treating psychiatrist:

> This poor woman has suffered the terrible and indescribable horror of having a son who had the most serious deprivation of senses imaginable and then having the remaining senses having to be removed. She and her husband fully realized the horror this meant for their son with a mental age of three years. Both she and her husband have been stressed to the limit ... It seems that she was of the opinion that they were not acting to kill their son but the primary aim was to stop the suffering that he had had at the hands of fate, genetics and the NSW government instrumentalities.[34]

Matthew is portrayed as the cause of both his parents' depressive illnesses, stress disorders and suicidal ideation, their relationship difficulties, their social withdrawal and his father's alcoholism. Matthew's victim characteristics, and the position of trust and authority occupied by his parents, are not dealt with as matters aggravating the offence. Again, the court appears to treat these as factors mitigating, and as even excusing, the offence.

In its discussion of how the statutory sentencing principles are to be applied in the case, the court concludes in relation to the principle of general deterrence: 'Nobody in the community suffering under the burden that weighed on the offenders is likely to give consideration to sentences imposed on others and thereby be deterred from committing similar offences.'

Predictably, in response to the court's decision, Australia's leading euthanasia advocate immediately contradicted this view, claiming that the case demonstrated that 'not all taking of human life is bad', and that the case would encourage others to make similar 'courageous' decisions.[35] He and others claimed the case should never have been prosecuted.[36]

In relation to the role of the criminal justice system in denouncing the conduct of the offenders, the court concludes:

> [36] ... Their criminal conduct may be summarized thus. The law entrusted them with the responsibility to care for a severely disabled and vulnerable person ... The offenders decided that the only thing they could do was protect Matthew from a future life without sensation by bringing his life to an end. They decided to breach their trust because they loved him and could not bear to contemplate his suffering any more. [38] ... It seems to me that nothing that the Court can do by way of sentence can add to the offenders' suffering. The need for further punishment is spent.[37]

In light of these and other similar passages in its judgement, it is difficult to resist the impression that the court certainly empathized with, and even implicitly approved of Mr and Mrs Sutton's conduct.

The Dawes and Sutton cases would thus appear to provide strong evidence of a great disparity between even the limited text of the criminal law in relation to prohibition of homicide and the reality of its application with respect to persons with disability in Australia. The sentencing outcomes in these cases are not reflective of the inherent dignity and value of Jason and Matthew's lives, or of their equality with others. In both cases the courts were obviously deeply repelled by Jason and Matthew's impairment and disability, acquiesced or colluded in their construction as other than human, and appear to have strongly identified with those responsible for depriving them of life. Implicitly, both courts appear to consider Jason and Matthew's impairment and disability a powerful excuse, if not complete justification, for their homicide. In the Sutton case particularly, the court implicitly countenances the view that Matthew was better off dead, and even the view that Matthew somehow *himself* sought death as a 'reward' for his suffering. This is evident from the following passage of Mrs Sutton's statement of evidence cited with approval by the court:

> In the past we had been unable to protect him from abuse both from others and himself. How could we subject our precious son to what was ahead. He had been through so much, and with a courage and determination most could only hope to achieve. He was such a brave soul. At this time in his life he deserved a reward, not what lay ahead of him. So with all the love we had for Matti, we borrowed from his strength and courage and released him from any more pain and suffering, *he had had enough.* We owed him nothing less. [emphasis added][38]

Although New South Wales has enacted laws specifically to deter crimes against persons with disability, and by persons in positions of trust and authority, the Dawes and Sutton cases suggest that the courts are incapable or unwilling to give effect to those laws. Another remarkable feature of both cases is the acceptance by the prosecution of the offenders' pleas to the lesser offence of manslaughter, instead of murder, and the courts' failure to reject pleas to the lesser offence. In both cases the manslaughter plea was founded on the statutory equivalent of the doctrine of diminished responsibility and formally relied on the diagnosis of mood disorder in the offenders. However, there also appears to be a subtle and complex interaction between the victims' impairment and disability and the doctrine of diminished responsibility. At one level, both cases appear to be activated by the latent belief that the 'burden' and 'suffering' caused by a child with disability *ipso facto* diminishes the culpability of parents for that child's murder.

Article 6 of the ICCPR does not contain any express provision in relation to euthanasia; nor does any other human rights instrument, including the CRPD. Nevertheless, the right to life has traditionally been interpreted as requiring states to refrain from non-voluntary euthanasia programmes such as those conducted by the German National Socialists in the lead-up to and during the Second World War, and as imposing an obligation on states to prevent private acts of non-voluntary euthanasia.[39] However, these obligations appear to have little application to euthanasia in its contemporary presentation.[40]

Many commentators have pointed to the risks to the lives of persons with disability presented by the contemporary advocacy for euthanasia.[41] Australia has produced some of the most strident advocates of euthanasia of persons with disability.[42] In 1995, Australia became the first country in the world to enact legislation permitting voluntary active euthanasia when the Parliament of the Northern Territory passed the Rights of the Terminally Ill Act, 1995 (NT). This Act was extremely controversial and very short-lived. In response to its enactment, the Commonwealth Government legislated to override the powers of the Australian territories to make such laws, and consequently, the Act was overturned.[43] While suicide has been decriminalized in all jurisdictions in Australia, it remains an offence to assist a person to commit suicide. Along with the general laws of homicide, this means that under Australian law euthanasia is a criminal offence. Nevertheless, euthanasia is, in reality, very widely practised[44] and approved of[45] in Australian health care settings, especially in the area of so-called end-of-life decision-making.

Paradoxically, the Northern Territory law, and the commonwealth legislation that negatived it, only ever concerned active voluntary euthanasia – the taking of active steps to terminate the life of a person who has specifically requested this. In fact, the most common forms of euthanasia practised in Australian health care settings are active and passive non-voluntary euthanasia. This involves withholding or withdrawal of life-sustaining treatments from, or the taking of active steps to hasten the death of persons who, at law, and for all practical purposes, do not have the capacity to consent to these acts or omissions. The commonwealth legislation specifically excepts this conduct from the prohibition on active voluntary euthanasia. Such decision-making is to some extent regulated by Australian guardianship and administration tribunals, which may appoint a close associate of a person or a public authority to make these decisions on the person's behalf,[46] and by state and territory supreme courts in their *parens patriae* jurisdictions,[47] which may also consent to such decisions, or appoint an associate of the person to do so. However, most decisions of this nature are not scrutinized by the law, and are instead determined in private between the treating physician and the person's family.

Although these cases are most likely to involve persons at the end stage of terminal illnesses, or at the end of their natural lives, persons with disability who are neither terminally ill nor at the end of their lives are also vulnerable to such treatment in Australian health care settings. In such cases, the person with disability is typically constructed as having 'no quality of life', and as 'being better off dead', and health care professionals, other service providers, and family may conspire to bring about the person's death during a period of health vulnerability. However, this practice is rarely formally acknowledged, and it is difficult to obtain objective evidence of it. One exception to this is the 2005 report by the New South Wales Ombudsman on his annual review of the deaths of persons with disability 'in care'.[48] In this report, the ombudsman notes a number of instances where 'not for cardiopulmonary resuscitation' (no CPR) orders and other treatment limitation decisions were placed on a person with disability's file without discussion with the person, the person's family, and without any documented reason. The report suggests that poor 'quality of life', as perceived by medical professionals, was a key factor driving the decision to limit treatment.[49] In a number of the cases reported, the person's impairment and disability are simply equated with poor quality of life, and treatable unrelated health conditions are conflated with impairment. In Australia, at common law, a health care provider has no obligation to offer or provide life-sustaining measures that they consider futile. However, in the case of persons with disability, the assessment of what treatment is futile is sometimes heavily influenced by factors extraneous to the specific condition being treated. In the cases reported by the ombudsman, treatment sometimes appears to have been considered futile only because it would not ameliorate or cure the individual's impairment, or overcome the social consequences of this, such as being forced to live in a nursing home or boarding house.

Australian law purports to provide stringent safeguards against abuse of power by substitute decision-makers formally entrusted with making end-of-life decisions on behalf of persons unable to make such decisions themselves. In this respect, key safeguards are the general requirement that such decisions must be made in the best interests of the person or to promote their health and well-being, and the supervision of such decision-makers by specialist tribunals.[50] In reality, the operation of these safeguards is not unproblematic. The functioning of specialist tribunals heavily privileges the medical model. Assessments of a person's quality of life are typically only viewed through a narrow medical lens. In tribunal hearings medical evidence and opinion typically trump all other evidence and opinion. This is also true for courts hearing similar matters in *parens patriae* jurisdictions. Additionally, in many cases, tribunal panels will be constituted so as to include medical experts. Statutory terms such as 'medical' and 'palliative' care are interpreted in light of contemporary medical practice, and in this respect are essentially elastic and entirely deferential to the medical model.[51] There are few, if any, independent legal norms to operate as constraints on medical power.

Under Australian law, the provision of nutrition and hydration by technological means, and potentially even by means of personal assistance,[52] is considered medical treatment.[53] Its characterization as medical treatment means that the person affected, or in the case of a person unable to make health care decisions, a court or someone appointed by a court or guardianship and administration tribunal to make such decisions on their behalf, may refuse this treatment or request its withdrawal. Failure to comply with such a request amounts to an assault of the person, and may attract civil and criminal penalties.[54] In substance, decisions to withdraw nutrition and hydration, and other forms of life-sustaining treatment, are passive euthanasia.

Article 25 (Health), sub-paragraph (f) of the CRPD provides that states parties have a particular obligation to 'prevent discriminatory denial of health care or health services or food or fluids on the basis of disability'. This provision was added to the draft CRPD text in the final stages of negotiations, although the issues it encompasses had been the subject of debate both in relation to the draft health and right to life articles at earlier points in the Ad Hoc Committee's deliberations.[55]

There can be little doubt that advocacy for this provision was directed in particular at the withdrawal of 'life-sustaining treatments' from persons with severe disability, including the withdrawal of hydration and nutrition provided from a nasogastric tube or percutaneous endoscopic gastrostomy (PEG) inserted into the stomach (often referred to as 'artificial' hydration and nutrition). In this respect, a key contextual factor that gave colour and content to the Ad Hoc Committee debates on this issue was the contemporary legal, political and social struggles in the United States of America concerning Michael Schiavo's decision to withdraw PEG-administered hydration and nutrition from his wife, Theresa Schiavo, against the objection of her parents. Ultimately, Michael Schiavo's decision prevailed in the courts, despite the intervention of the American Congress, and his wife died of dehydration and starvation. The drafting of the CRPD became a focal point for further activism by a number of interest groups who sought a supervening international law that would prevent such an outcome in the future. There have now been a number of cases similar to *Schiavo* litigated in Australian courts, with effectively the same outcome.[56] Article 25(f) therefore has interesting, and so far unrecognized, implications for Australian law in the area of so-called end-of-life decision-making, particularly as it affects persons with disability.

A potentially perverse outcome of the attempt to proscribe the discriminatory denial of food and fluids on the ground of disability in the health article of CRPD is the implied characterization of food and fluid (at least in specific circumstances) as medical treatment. As already noted, it is precisely this characterization that has led the Australian courts to conclude the person concerned or a person appointed to make decisions on their behalf can withhold or withdraw consent to such measures. The CRPD may thus inadvertently reinforce precisely the problem it seeks to resolve. This may have serious broader implications for the rights to life and survival of persons with disability. Following the Supreme Court of Victoria's decision in *re Gardner*,[57] one of the leading Australian cases in which the administration of 'artificial' nutrition and hydration is characterized as medical treatment, some specialist disability services in that state are reported to have refused to continue to administer PEG nutrition and hydration to clients of their respite and supported accommodation services on the basis that their staff were neither qualified, nor entitled under the relevant industrial awards, to administer 'medical treatment' to clients. The consequences of this are that those clients affected must be reaccommodated in a medical facility, or at least in a facility with medically qualified staff. If the person refuses to be reaccommodated, and if suitable alternative staffing arrangements are not put in place, the inevitable consequence is that the person will die of dehydration and starvation.[58]

The enabling of life

The scope of the right of survival in international law is subject to significant debate, principally because it lies at the intersection of civil and political rights with economic, social and cultural rights.[59] Some commentators seek to confine the right within the narrow framework of civil and political rights, arguing that it imposes an obligation on states merely to refrain, and prevent others, from arbitrary killing by means of the purposeful denial of the necessities of life.[60] According to this view, the right of survival must be distinguished from economic, social and cultural rights that seek to promote an adequate standard of living. Accordingly, it is argued that the right does not purport to provide any guarantee against death from famine, exposure, or disease, and that mere toleration of such conditions by the state would not breach the right. Alternatively, it is argued that the right of survival does purport to guarantee 'basic and minimum material goods and services essential to sustain life', and that a restrictive interpretation of the right is untenable as it would deprive millions of poor people around the world of any rights at all (the right of life and survival being primordial).[61]

As already noted, the Human Rights Committee has provided qualified support for the latter view by contending that right to life requires states to adopt positive measures, suggesting it would be '*desirable*' (emphasis added) for states parties to take all possible measures to reduce infant mortality and to increase life expectancy, especially in adopting measures to eliminate malnutrition and epidemics.[62] In our view, the CRPD codifies and extends this broader interpretation of the survival dimension of the right by requiring states to 'take all necessary measures' to ensure the effective enjoyment of the right to life of persons with disability on an equal basis with others. In our view, this terminology enlivens obligations in the economic, social and cultural spheres that are necessary for the realization of the rights of life and survival by persons with disability.

The CRPD also extends the scope of economic, social and cultural rights, not only in the sense that it incorporates many detailed requirements to enable all persons with disability to develop to their full potential, but also in that it incorporates an independent right to an adequate standard of living and social protection which is arguably much more expansive than any of its antecedents. It requires states to ensure access to: 'appropriate and affordable services, devices and other assistance for disability-related needs'; 'social protection programmes and poverty reduction programmes'; and, for persons with disabilities and their families living in situations of poverty, 'assistance from the state with disability-related expenses, including adequate training, counselling, financial assistance and respite care', as well as public housing and retirements benefits and programmes.[63] These measures, at least potentially, penetrate to the survival needs of persons with disability to a far greater extent than any pre-existing formulation of these rights.

Australian law contains few provisions codifying the right to survival, and those provisions that do exist are very limited in scope. In some states and territories the criminal law imposes a duty on persons with responsibility for the care and support of others to ensure the provision of the necessities of life.[64] These provisions potentially apply to those who have responsibility for the care and support of persons with disability. However, we are not aware of any reported case where this duty has been prosecuted or enforced in relation to a person with disability, even though, as the following discussion will reveal, there have been numerous instances where these provisions were apposite.

In Australia, coronial authorities have responsibility to investigate deaths of individuals who die of unnatural causes, or in suspicious or unusual circumstances. However, such authorities have been criticized for their perceived failure to apply sufficient attention or expertise to the deaths of persons with disability living 'in care'. In 1998, following a public outcry from disabled people's organizations, resulting from numerous reported incidents of persons with disability 'in care' dying as a result of abuse or neglect, including malnutrition,[65] the New South Wales Government established a Disability Death Review Team within the former Community Services Commission,[66] which had the role of systematically reviewing the circumstances of persons with disability who die in supported accommodation. In 2002 this function was incorporated into the NSW Ombudsman.[67] All deaths of persons with disability living in supported accommodation must be brought to the attention of the Ombudsman within 30 days. The Ombudsman is empowered to recommend, but not compel, policies and practices to be implemented by government and service providers for the prevention or reduction of deaths of persons with disability living 'in care'. The Ombudsman also has the power to undertake research and project work to assist in the formulation of strategies to reduce or remove risk factors associated with reviewable deaths that are preventable.

In their work to date the Community Services Commission and Ombudsman have identified and reported on a range of systemic issues adversely impacting on the survival of persons with disability in care. This has included poor identification and management of swallowing and nutritional risks; poor health care needs assessment, planning and review; failure to provide adequate first aid following critical incidents; poor risk management of epilepsy; medication errors; poor access to primary and secondary health care; premature hospital discharge and poor discharge planning; unexplained and unreasonable treatment limitation decisions; and, poor interagency coordination between health care and disability service providers.[68] However, government and service providers have been slow and ineffective in their response to the problems identified, and consequently, the survival rates of persons with disability living in supported accommodation have improved only marginally. In his last annual report, the Ombudsman noted that many of the problems identified in the previous 12

months 'are longstanding and have been the subject of previous recommendations'.[69] Additionally, in spite of its undoubted benefits, the
establishment of the disability death review function in an agency responsible for the administrative oversight of government and non-government
agencies, rather than in an agency responsible for criminal investigation or
the coroner,[70] has also resulted in a subtle detoxification of harms affecting
the survival of persons with disability.

The CRC requires states parties to 'ensure to the maximum extent possible the survival and development of the child',[71] and this requirement
applies to children with disability on an equal basis with others.[72] In spite of
this, there is widespread approval among Australian medical practitioners
for withholding altogether or limiting treatment to newborn children with
severe disability with the intention of 'allowing' these children to die.[73]
There is also considerable support for the taking of active steps, such as the
administration of analgesia sedation, to hasten or cause the death of these
children.[74] Although this would usually constitute a criminal offence,[75] we
are not aware of any case where such conduct has been prosecuted in
Australia. In fact, these 'treatment' decisions appear to have become so
commonplace as to be regarded as normative medical practice in spite of
the applicable law.[76] Decisions to withhold or limit treatment, or to hasten
or cause death by active measures, are typically justified on quality of life
grounds,[77] but also in terms of health economics, according to which it is
suggested that high-cost medical interventions and later social service
obligations for this group constitute an unjustifiable drain on finite
resources.[78] Such analyses are obviously deeply value-laden and ultimately
turn on the perceived social value of persons with disability.[79]

Australia is a relatively wealthy country with evolved income support,
health and social service systems.[80] This environment is undoubtedly
favourable by world standards, but persons with disability may nevertheless
struggle to secure the resources and support necessary for their survival.
Indeed, the treatment of persons with disability in Australia in a wide number of instances would appear to be in clear breach of the basic principle of
progressive realization that underpins economic, social and cultural rights:
their living conditions simply do not reflect the 'full and maximum use' of
the resources at the disposal of Australian governments to secure the economic, social and cultural rights of their citizens.[81]

Australia operates a universal income support system that purports to
provide a safety net against poverty. A number of payments are potentially
available to persons with disability and their associates including a
Disability Support Pension, Disability Support Pension for the Blind, Carer
Payment, Carer Allowance, and Mobility Allowance. Additionally, a number of price and tax concessions and subsidies are also potentially available
to persons with disability at both the commonwealth and state levels.[82]
Quite surprisingly, there is little published critical research about the
extent of disability-related poverty and the adequacy of income support

payments for persons with disability in Australia, and that which does exist is largely income-focused. Income-focused poverty measures tend to suggest that the Australian income support system provides a comprehensive, though modest, income safety net that protects most people from extreme income poverty.[83] However, this conclusion has been hotly contested by disabled people's organizations for its failure to take into account the extra costs of disability and the barriers to participation.[84]

Recent formative Australian research has attempted to identify the link between disability and poverty in terms of the incidence of financial hardship, the level of social participation, the incidence of severe financial stress, expressed need and the availability of support. This research suggests that having a household member with disability is associated with a substantial increase in the incidence of financial hardship, a higher probability of experiencing severe financial stress, and is more likely to result in seeking help from others. It also found that disability is associated with less social participation and a greater likelihood of no access to external financial support if it is needed. It has tentatively concluded that Australian households with a disabled member are not only more deprived than other households, but also at greater risk of deprivation in times of crisis.[85]

All Australian jurisdictions have in place early intervention and parenting programmes, which are directed towards the care and support of young children and their parents.[86] Some of these programmes are specifically focused on so-called 'especially vulnerable' families, which may include young children or parents with disability, and others are specifically focused on children with disability and their parents. These programmes offer both therapeutic and developmental interventions for children with disability, as well as parent education and support. They are, however, budget-capped and access to them is discretionary, rather than eligibility-based. Many children with disability have no access to these programmes, and access is also often delayed or insufficient resulting in significant loss of developmental opportunity.[87] Some of these programmes are also subject to very limited quality assurance and professional supervision requirements, and consequently lack potency and developmental focus.[88]

All Australian jurisdictions also provide programmes of specialist services for adults with disability, including supported accommodation, personal care and domestic assistance, supported employment, developmental day programmes, recreation services, therapy services, specialized transport, home modifications, aids and appliances, case work, clinical and advocacy services. However, these programmes are also budget-capped and under significant and long-standing stress. Many thousands of people with disability lack access to basic services and supports essential for their well-being, development and survival.[89] There have now been several cases of a person with disability committing suicide or refusing 'non-heroic' life-sustaining treatment in order to die, and of a parent killing their son or daughter with disability before committing suicide themselves, driven by despair at their inability to obtain necessary support services. The situation is especially acute within Australian mental health systems, which are chronically under-funded relative to demand.[90] There are now numerous documented cases of persons with mental illness committing suicide during periods of disorientation having been refused access to crisis mental health services.[91] This problem is especially critical in Australia's criminal justice facilities and immigration detention centres, which are notorious for their failure to provide adequate mental health services for prisoners and detainees.[92]

Persons with disability also experience widespread structural and personal discrimination in their access to general health services.[93] The Disability Discrimination Act, 1992 applies to health service provision, but has had limited impact to date. In the area of health prevention, disability discrimination may manifest in a failure to detect the onset of illness and disease (for example, screening for breast and cervical cancer is only rarely carried out for women with intellectual disability living in supported accommodation, and breast and cervical screening equipment is, in most cases, inaccessible for women with significant physical disability).[94] Population-based health promotion programmes are rarely tailored to the needs of persons with disability. For example, tobacco control programmes rarely focus on the provision of accessible and adapted education strategies, or on appropriate smoking cessation supports for smokers with disability, in spite of the fact that smoking prevalence is as high as 90 per cent among some population groups of disabled persons.[95] The prevalence of obesity among persons with intellectual disability is also up to three times that of the general population.[96]

There is a very high incidence of 'diagnostic overshadowing' in the treatment of persons with disability in Australian health care settings, in which health concerns are incorrectly assimilated with the person's impairment, resulting in the failure to diagnose and treat health risks. One Australian study found that 42 per cent of medical conditions went undiagnosed in people with intellectual disability, and half the diagnosed conditions were inadequately managed.[97] Australia's tertiary health care system is subject to critical cost pressures, and the allocation of resources is heavily influenced by rationalist utilitarian economic policies. These policies often result either overtly or covertly in the denial or limitation of medical services to persons with disability due to negative perceptions of their social value.[98] Australia also lacks a publicly subsidized national dental health scheme, which means that most persons with disability lack access to essential dental care.[99] Untreated dental problems can be a source not only of life-diminishing pain, but also of life-threatening infection.

The CRPD extends the right of survival to persons with disability in situations of risk and humanitarian emergencies. It imposes an obligation on states to take 'all necessary measures to ensure the protection and safety of persons with disabilities in situations of risk, including situations of armed conflict, humanitarian emergencies and the occurrence of natural disasters'.[100] Australian building standards provide little protection for persons who use mobility devices in the event of an emergency requiring evacuation of multi-storey buildings. Lifts are not required to be fire rated and emergency procedures typically advise persons using mobility devices to wait at the top of stairwells in the hope of rescue by emergency services. As they currently stand, Australian building standards also fail to require visual alarms that would serve to warn persons who are deaf of an event requiring evacuation. Most emergency response policies, procedures and products on the Australian market also fail to take into account the specific needs of persons with disability.

Australia is a bushfire and flood-prone country, and much of its extensive coastline, where most of the population is concentrated, is also subject to cyclonic storms. Although the continent is relatively stable compared with other regions of the world, earthquakes do occur, and severe earthquakes have occurred in urban areas. The risk of a tsunami hitting the coast following an earthquake offshore is also quite real. Apart from natural disasters, Australia also faces the constant threat of terrorist attack, particularly since its participation in the United States-led wars in Afghanistan and Iraq. In response to these threats, local, state and territory, and commonwealth governments have established designated emergency services responsible for planning, coordinating and implementing emergency responses to these risks. While some agencies have developed plans that may effectively protect the lives of persons with disability in some circumstances (for example, evacuation of people from supported accommodation services threatened by bushfire),[101] generally such planning has failed to take account of the specific needs of persons with disability, particularly in the event of a large-scale emergency. Consequently, there is every reason to suggest that, should a large-scale disaster occur, Australia would experience similar problems to those that became evident in the United States of America following cyclones Rita and Katrina.[102] This issue is the subject of attention by disability activists in Australia, but to date, there has been little response by government.

Conclusion

In the nearly 30 years since Australia signed and ratified the ICCPR, very few specific steps have been taken by Australian governments to ensure that persons with disability enjoy the right to life on an equal basis with others. Indeed, even those steps that have been taken, such as the legislating of specific measures to deter crimes against persons with disability and the establishment of the Disability Death Review Team – both in New South Wales – have been driven by specific domestic issues, rather than by any particular consciousness of Australia's international obligations. This complacency appears to be underpinned by a relatively high level of confidence that Australian law and social norms already sufficiently protect persons with disability against threats to their life and survival. However, this confidence is seriously misplaced. Despite living in a wealthy country, presided over by stable governmental and legal institutions that claim a commitment to human rights, Australians with disability face significant threats to their rights to life and survival, even from within those institutions specifically charged with the protection of these rights. The CRPD potentially establishes a new standard, and certainly brings a new focus, to international efforts to protect the rights of persons with disability to life and survival. In particular, it will place a stronger accent on the provision of the social resources persons with disability require in order to effectively realize these rights. This will be as important in developed countries, such as Australia, as it will be in developing and transitional states. However, at least at this stage, there is little consciousness of this in the Australian community. In particular, the Australian Government appears to be of the view that it already substantially complies with the requirements of the CRPD. The realization of the transformative potential of the CRPD in Australia will therefore require intelligent and persuasive advocacy by disability and human rights activists to illuminate the distance between rhetoric and reality, and the text of the law and its practice, in relation to the human rights of persons with disability. This will most especially be required in relation to the rights to life and survival.

Notes

1 Australia was a significant contributor to the crucial negotiations on the United Nations Charter to ensure that respect for human rights was placed alongside peace, security and development as the primary aims of the United Nations. Australia also participated in the eight-member committee charged with drafting the Universal Declaration of Human Rights, and its Minister for External Affairs also presided over the General Assembly when the Declaration was adopted by the United Nations in 1948.

2 Australia signed and ratified the International Covenant on Civil and Political Rights on 18 December 1972 and 13 August 1980 respectively.

3 Australia signed and ratified the Convention on the Rights of the Child on 22 August 1990 and 17 December 1990 respectively.

4 Australia signed the Convention on the Rights of Persons with Disabilities, but not its optional protocol, when they opened for signature on 30 March 2007.

5 Office of the High Commissioner for Human Rights, *General Comment No. 6: The Right to Life* (art. 6), 30 April 1982, *CCRP General Comment No. 6*, at paragraph 5.

6 For example, Article 9, 'Accessibility', which appears both as a stand-alone article and as a cross-cutting principle underpinning the Convention as a whole, and Article 20, 'Personal mobility'. Although these articles might be said to spring from the principle of non-discrimination and the right to liberty of the person respectively, their formulation clearly transcends any previously existing human right.

7 For example, Article 21, 'Freedom of expression and opinion, and access to information', which extends the formerly essentially 'negative' right of state

non-interference with personal opinion and expression into the 'positive' state obligation to provide public information in accessible formats and to recognize sign languages, Braille, and augmentative and alternative communication.

8 CRPD Article 10.

9 Arguably, the Convention on the Rights of the Child had already achieved this in Article 6(2) of that convention, but obviously only with respect to children.

10 M. Nowak, *UN Convention on Civil and Political Rights: ICCP Commentary*, Kehl, N.P. Engel, 1993, p.104; Y. Dinstein, 'The right to life, physical integrity and liberty' in L. Henkin (ed.), *The International Bill of Rights*, New York, Columbia University Press, 1981, p.114; B.G. Ramcharan, 'The concept and dimensions of the right to life' in B.G. Ramcharan (ed.), *The Right to Life in International Law*, Dordrecht, Boston, Martinus Nijhoff, 1985, p.6.

11 *Wake v. Northern Territory of Australia* (1996) 109 NTR 1.

12 Ibid. per Martin CJ at 37, Mildren J at 39, and Angel J at 19–35.

13 Courts may look to Australia's international obligations to assist in statutory interpretation, where ambiguity exists: *Minister for Immigration and Ethnic Affairs v. Teoh* (1995) 183 CLR 273.

14 Aspects of some obligations have been incorporated. The Sex Discrimination Act, 1984 (Cth) incorporates major aspects of the Convention on the Elimination of All Forms of Discrimination Against Women and the Race Discrimination Act, 1975 (Cth) incorporates major aspects of the International Convention on the Elimination of All Forms of Racial Discrimination. In the disability area both the Disability Discrimination Act, 1992 (Cth) and the Disability Services Act, 1986 (Cth) incorporate major aspects of the Declaration on the Rights of Mentally Retarded Persons (1971) and the Declaration on the Rights of the Disabled (1975).

15 The Hon. Michael Kirby, AC, CMG, Acting Chief Justice of Australia, 'The ALJ @ 80: Past, present and future', paper delivered to a conference to celebrate the 80th anniversary of the *Australian Law Journal*, 16 March 2007 (unpublished) p.29.

16 Section 4, Disability Discrimination Act, 1992; although cast as a definition of disability, it is essentially a definition of impairment.

17 This includes a mandate to develop mandatory Disability Standards in specific areas, incentives for the development of Voluntary Action Plans, and a time-limited exemption function that promotes staged compliance.

18 Both individual and representative complaints may be made under the Act. Such complaints may ultimately be adjudicated in the Federal Magistrates Court or Federal Court of Australia.

19 Crimes (Sentencing Procedure) Act, 1999 (NSW), s. 21A(2)(h).

20 Crimes (Sentencing Procedure) Act, 1999 (NSW), s. 21A(2)(l); see also Crimes (Sentencing) Act, 2005 (ACT), s. 33(1)(m).

21 Crimes (Sentencing Procedure) Act, 1999 (NSW), s. 21A(2)(k).

22 Crimes (Sentencing) Act 2005, (ACT), s. 33(1)(d); Criminal Law (Sentencing) Act, 1988 (SA), s. 10(d); Sentencing Act, 1995 (Vic) s. 5(2)(da).

23 This diagnosis resulted in the case proceeding under s. 23A of the Crimes Act, 1900 (NSW) on the ground of 'substantial impairment' of capacity by reason of an 'abnormality of mind arising from an underlying condition'. This provision codifies the principle of diminished responsibility, rather than insanity. *R v. Daniella Dawes* (unreported) District Court of New South Wales Criminal Jurisdiction Judge Ellis Parramatta Wednesday 2 June 2004 at p.1 of the transcript.

24 Ibid. at p.7 of the transcript.

25 *R v. Daniella Dawes* [2004] NSWCCA 363 (unreported) 5 November 2004 Dunford, J. at paras. 8 and 9; Hoeben J. agreeing; Barr J. at paras. 51–53.

26 This case invoked the aggravating factors of 'special vulnerability of the victim' Crimes Act, 1900 (NSW), s. 21A(2)(l), and 'the offender's abuse of a position of trust and authority in relation to the victim' Crimes Act, 1900 (NSW), s. 21A(2)(k).

27 *R v. Daniella Dawes* (unreported) District Court of New South Wales Criminal Jurisdiction Judge Ellis Parramatta Wednesday 2 June 2004 at p.9 of the transcript.

28 Ibid. at p.18 of the transcript.

29 Ibid.

30 *R v. Daniella Dawes* [2004] NSWCCA 363 (unreported) 5 November 2004 per Dunford and Hoeben JJ.; Barr J. held that there was no error on the part of the sentencing judge. This discretion arises from the principles governing Crown appeals on sentence in Australia.

31 The charge was reduced from murder to manslaughter on the basis that Mr and Mrs Sutton were also subject to a 'substantial abnormality of mind' – constituted by severe depression and anxiety – at the time of the offence: s. 23A of the Crimes Act, 1900 (NSW).

32 *R v. Raymond Douglas Sutton; R v. Margaret E Sutton* [2007] NSWSC 295.

33 Ibid. at paras. 12–13.

34 Ibid. at para. 26.

35 Philip Nitschke, interviewed for *ABC News* 7:00 p.m.; 4 April 2007.

36 Remarkably, this included the Chair of the NSW Government's official advisory body on disability, the Disability Council of New South Wales, who stated that Mr and Mrs Sutton were to be 'applauded' for their actions.

37 *Sutton supra.*

38 *Sutton supra.*

39 M. Nowak, 1993, op. cit., p.123; Y. Dinstein, 1981, op. cit., p.120.

40 Ibid.; see also G. Zdenkowski, 'The International Covenant on Civil and Political Rights and euthanasia', *UNSW Law Journal* 1997, 169.

41 In the Australian context, see for example: C. Newell, 'Medical killing and people with disability: A critique', in *Australian Disability Review*, 2: 28; J. Fitzgerald, 'Legalising euthanasia: Its implications for people with disability', in *Australian Disability Review* 2: 3; E. Liepoldt, *Good Life in the Balance: A Cross-National Study of Dutch and Australian Disability Perspectives on Euthanasia and Physician-Assisted Suicide*, a thesis submitted in fulfilment of the requirements of the award of Doctor of Philosophy (Human Services) at the Faculty of Community Studies, Education and Social Science, Edith Cowan University, May 2003.

42 For example, Peter Singer and Helga Kuhse, *Should the Baby Live? The Problem of Handicapped Infants*, Oxford, Oxford University Press, 1985.

43 The Northern Territory law was overturned by the Euthanasia Laws Act, 1997 (Cth).

44 A 1997 study reported that 1.8 per cent of deaths in Australia are by voluntary euthanasia or physician assisted suicide; 3.5 per cent of deaths involved termination of the patient's life without explicit request; in 24.7 per cent of deaths treatment was withheld or withdrawn with the intention to hasten death; and, in 6.5 per cent of deaths opioids were administered with at least the partial intent to hasten death: H. Kuhse, P. Singer, P. Baume, M. Clark and M. Rickard, 'End-of-life decisions in Australian medical practice', *Med J Aust*, 1997, 166: 191–196; A study conducted in 2001 reported that 36.2 per cent of general surgeons surveyed reported that they had given drugs in doses greater than was necessary to relieve symptoms with the intention of hastening death; 20.4 per cent reported that they had given drugs with the intention of hastening death, but without the explicit request of the patient; 1.9 per cent reported assisting with a suicide; and 4.2 per cent reported having acceded to

requests for voluntary euthanasia: C. Douglas, I. Kerridge, K. Rainbird, J. McPhee, L. Hancock and A. Spigelman, 'The intention to hasten death: A survey of attitudes and practices of surgeons in Australia, *Medical Journal of Australia*, 2001, 175.

45 In 1987, Kuhse and Singer reported that 62 per cent of doctors surveyed thought it was right for a doctor to take active steps to bring about the death of a patient who has requested the doctor to do this: H. Kuhse and P. Singer, 'Doctors' practices and attitudes regarding voluntary euthanasia' *Medical Journal of Australia*, 1988, 148: 632–627. A 1993 survey conducted by Baume and O'Malley reported that 59 per cent of doctors thought hastening death on request was sometimes right: P. Baume and E. O'Malley, 'Euthanasia: Attitudes and practices of medical practitioners', *Medical Journal of Australia*, 1994, 161:137–144; see also C.A. Stevens and R. Hassan, 'Management of death, dying and euthanasia: Attitudes and practices of medical practitioners in South Australia', *Journal of Medical Ethics*, 1994, 20: 41–46; I. Wilson, B. Kay and I. Steven, 'General practitioners and euthanasia', *Australian Family Physician*, 1997, 26: 399–401; M.A. Steinberg, J.M. Najman, C.M. Cartwright, S.M. MacDonals and G.M. Williams, 'End-of-life decision-making: Community and practitioner perspectives', *Medical Journal of Australia*, 1997, 166: 131–134; C.M. Cartwright, G.W. Robinson, M.A. Steinberg, G.M. Williams, J.M. Najman and W.B. Tyler, 'End-of-life decision making perspectives of Northern Territory doctors, nurses and community members', *Lancet*, 1997, 349, 9051: 477; H. Kuhse and P. Singer, 'Euthanasia: A survey of nurses' attitudes and practices', *Australian Nurses Journal*, 1992, 21, 8: 21–22; S. Aranda and M. O'Connor, 'Euthanasia, nurses and care of the dying: Rethinking Kuhse and Singer', *Australian Nursing Journal*, 1995, 3, 2: 18–21; B.A. Kitchener, 'Nurses' attitudes to active voluntary euthanasia: A survey in the ACT', *Aust. NZ Journal of Public Health*, 1998, 22, 2: 276–278; J. Iliffe 'Nurses' attitudes to voluntary euthanasia, *Journal of the NSW Nurses Association*, 1998, 55, 1: 37–39; C.M. Cartwright, G.M. Williams, M.A. Steinberg and J.M. Najman, *Community and Health/Allied Health Professionals Attitudes to Euthanasia: What are the driving forces?* Report to the National Health and Medical Research Council, University of Queensland School of Population Health 2002.

46 See for example: *Re MC* [2003] QGAAT 13; *BTO* [2004] WAGAB 2; *Re AG* [2007] NSWGT 1.

47 See for example: *Gardner; Re BWV* [2003] VSC 173; *Northbridge v. Central Sydney Area Health Service* [2000] NSWSC 1241; *Isaac Messiah (by his tutor Magdy Messiha) v. South East Health* [2004] NSWSC 1061.

48 Persons 'in care' are defined as those living in supported accommodation which is funded or licensed by the New South Wales Government.

49 NSW Ombudsman (2006) *Report of Reviewable Deaths in 2005: Volume 1: Deaths of People with Disabilities in Care*, NSW Ombudsman p.28.

50 Obiter in *Gardner; Re BWV* [2003] VSC 173.

51 A good example of this is: *Re AG* [2007] NSWGT 1 (5 February 2007); for background see C. Stewart, 'Problems with substitute decision-making', in NSW *Bioethical Inquiry*, 2006 3: 127–131 and *WK v. Public Guardian* (No 2) [2006] NSWADT 121.

52 For a discussion of this issue see B. White and L. Willmott, *Rethinking Life-Sustaining Measures: Questions for Queensland: An Issues Paper Reviewing the Legislation Governing Withholding and Withdrawing Life-sustaining Measures*, Queensland University of Technology, February 2005, pp.77–80.

53 Statutory provisions vary significantly across Australian jurisdictions. However, in most jurisdictions the term 'medical treatment' has been interpreted broadly to include such procedures, and this is also the case at common law: *Gardner; Re BWV* [2003] VSC 173; *Re MC* [2003] QGAAT 13; *BTO* [2004] WAGAB 2.

54 *Re Marion* (1992) 175 CLR 218 pp.309–310.
55 The paragraph was added to the draft text in the course of the Eighth Session of the Ad Hoc Committee, and the issues it agitates were discussed at the Committee's Third (2003), Fifth (2005) and Seventh (2006) sessions, and in the Ad Hoc Committee Working Group also held in 2003; for summaries of discussions see http://www.un.org/esa/socdev/enable/rights/adhoccom.htm
56 *Re MC* [2003] QGAAT 13; *BTO* [2004] WAGAB 2; *Gardner; Re BWV* [2003] VSC 173; *Northbridge v. Central Sydney Area Health Service* [2000] NSWSC 1241; *Isaac Messiah (by his tutor Magdy Messiha) v. South East Health* [2004] NSWSC 1061.
57 *Gardner; Re BWV* [2003] VSC 173.
58 At the time of writing this issue remains unresolved.
59 For an overview of this debate see F. Menghistu, 'The satisfaction of survival requirements', in B.G. Ramcharan (ed.) *The Right to Life in International Law*, Dordrecht 1985, pp.63–83.
60 See, for example, Y. Dinstein, 'The right to life, physical integrity, and liberty', in L. Henkin (ed.) *The International Bill of Rights: The Covenant on Civil and Political Rights*, New York, Columbia University Press, 1981, pp.114–137.
61 F. Menghistu, 1985, op. cit. p.64.
62 Ibid.
63 CRPD Article 28.
64 Criminal Code Act, 1924 (Tas), Chapter XVI; Criminal Code Compilation Act, 1913 (WA), Part V; Division XXVII; Crimes Act, 1900 (NSW), s. 44 (applies to wife, apprentice, servant and insane persons); Criminal Code Act (NT), Part VI, Division 1; Criminal Law Consolidation Act, 1935 (SA), s. 14; Criminal Code Act, 1899 (Qld) s. 285. Most states and territories have similar provisions in relation to those with responsibility for the care and support of children.
65 See for example, Community Services Commission, *Report on Nutritional and Mealtime Practices For People with Developmental Disabilities in Residential Care*, 1997; Community Services Commission, *Cram House: Inquiry into Care and Treatment of Residents*, 1998; Community Services Commission, *A Critical Event at the Grosvenor Centre: Review by the Disability Death Review Team of the Critical Event at the Grosvenor Centre*, 2000; Community Services Commission, *Disability, Death and the Responsibility of Care: A Review of the Characteristics of 211 People with Disabilities who Died in Care between 1991 and 1998 in NSW*, 2001; Community Services Commission, *Young Deaths – Children with Disabilities in Care: A Review of the Deaths of Eight Children and Young People at the Mannix Children's Centre*, 2002; Community Services Commission, *Food for Thought … a Report Card on Nutritional and Mealtime Practices in Accommodation Services for People with Disabilities – 1997 to 2002*, 2002.
66 The Community Services Commission was established in 1993 as an independent watchdog agency for community and disability services provided or funded by the New South Wales Government. It was abolished in 2002 and its functions absorbed by the NSW Ombudsman.
67 Community Services (Complaints, Reviews and Monitoring) Act, 1993, Part 6.
68 NSW Ombudsman *Report of Reviewable Deaths in 2005: Volume 1: Deaths of People with Disabilities in Care*, 2006; NSW Ombudsman *Report of Reviewable Deaths in 2004*; NSW Ombudsman, (2004) *Reviewable Deaths Annual Report 2003–2004*, 2005; see also reports cited at note 67.
69 NSW Ombudsman, 2006, op. cit. 'Ombudsman's Message'.
70 This disability death review function is additional to, rather than a replacement of, the role traditionally undertaken by the coroner. In fact, in parallel with the establishment of the disability death review function in the Ombudsman, specific jurisdiction was conferred on the NSW Coroner to review such deaths: Coroner's Act, 1980 (NSW) s. 13A; similar jurisdiction has now been conferred on the Queensland Coroner: Coroner's Act, 2003 (Qld), ss.9 and 11.

71 Article 6(2) Convention on the Rights of the Child.
72 By virtue of Article 2 Convention on the Rights of the Child.
73 K. Lui, B. Bajuk, K. Foster, A. Gaston, A. Kent, J. Sinn, K. Spence, W. Fischer, D. Henderson-Smart, 'Perinatal care at the borderlines of viability: A consensus statement based on a NSW and ACT consensus workshop'. *Medical Journal of Australia*, 2006, 185, 9: 495–500; P. Barr, 'Relation of neonatologists' end-of-life decisions to their personal fear of death', *Archives of Diseases in Childhood Foetal and Neonatal Edition*, 2007.doi:10.1136/adc.2006.094151.
74 P. Barr, 2007, op. cit.
75 Depending on the specific fact situation of the case and the jurisdiction in which it occurred such conduct may constitute unlawful homicide, failure to provide necessities of life, or child neglect.
76 Lui *et al.* 2006, op. cit.
77 Ibid; National Health and Medical Research Council, *Discussion Paper on the Ethics of Limiting Life Sustaining Treatment*, Canberra, 1988; C. Newell, 'A critical evaluation of the NH&MRC's *The Ethics of Limiting Life Sustaining Treatment* and related perspectives on the bioethics of disability', *Australian Disability Review*, 1991, 4: 46–57.
78 National Health and Medical Research Council, 1988, op. cit.
79 C. Newell, 1991, op. cit.
80 Australia has a gross domestic product equivalent to $US29,632.00 per capita and is ranked seventh in the world; Australia is ranked third (behind Norway and Iceland) in the United Nations Human Development Index (both 2003 figures): UNDP, *Human Development Report 2005: International Cooperation at a Crossroads: Aid, Trade and Security in an Unequal World*, 2005. For a profile of government services in Australia, including those available to persons with disability (Chapter 13), see Australian Government, Productivity Commission, *Report on Government Services*, 2007.
81 The Committee on Economic, Social and Cultural Rights outlines the requirements of the principle of progressive realisation in its *General Comment No. 3: The Nature of States Parties Obligations*, 1990, at paras. 9 and 10.
82 These include at the commonwealth level the Healthcare Card, Pension Concession Card, and Continence Aids Assistance Scheme, and at the state and territory levels transport concessions, the taxi subsidy scheme, and aids and appliance assistance schemes.
83 P. Saunders, 'Disability, poverty and living standards: reviewing Australian evidence and policies', Social Policy Research Centre Discussion Paper, 2005, pp.4–8.
84 See, for example, J. Frisch, 'Towards a Disability Allowance: Offsetting the costs of disability – an analysis', Physical Disability Council of Australia, Northgate, Queensland, 2005; C. O'Neill, 'The non-optional costs of blindness: Can we count the costs?' Blind Citizens Australia unpublished paper, 2002.
85 P. Saunders, 2005, op. cit. pp.8–9.
86 For example, the Commonwealth funds a range of early intervention and parent support services for vulnerable families under its Communities for Children Program. Similar services are funded at the state and territory level; for example, the New South Wales Government funds an extensive network of early intervention and family support services under its 'Families First' programme.
87 Australian Senate Standing Committee on Community Affairs, *Funding and Operation of the Commonwealth State/Territory Disability Agreement*, Commonwealth of Australia, 2007, at 91ff; Australian Institute of Health and Welfare, *Therapy and Equipment Needs of People with Cerebral Palsy and like Disabilities in Australia*, Disability Series, December 2006; L. Dowling,

'Children who live with equipment: Report to the Department of Ageing, Disability and Home Care', Issues Paper, February 2002 (unpublished).

88 Australian Senate Standing Committee on Community Affairs, 2007, op. cit. p.91.

89 Senate Standing Committee on Community Affairs. See Note 87, Chapter 4, 'Unmet Need'.

90 Australian Senate Select Committee on Mental Health, *A National Approach to Mental Health: From Crisis to Community*, First Report 2006, Commonwealth of Australia: see especially Chapter 4, 'Resourcing'; Mental Health Council of Australia and Human Rights and Equal Opportunity Commission, *Not for Service: Experiences of Injustice and Despair in Mental Health Services in Australia*, 2005, authors.

91 Mental Health Council of Australia and Human Rights and Equal Opportunity Commission, 2005, op. cit.

92 Australian Senate Select Committee on Mental Health, 2006, op. cit.: see especially Chapter 13, 'Mental health and the Criminal Justice System'; see also, NSW Coroner, *Inquest into the Death of Scott Ashley Simpson*, July 2006; *S v. Secretary*, Department of Immigration & Multicultural & Indigenous Affairs [2005] FCA 549.

93 However, two recent positive developments are the introduction of a National Auslan Interpreter Booking and Payment Service (NABS), which provides free Auslan interpreting for deaf persons attending private medical appointments, and changes to Medicare health insurance rebates which allow longer health checks for people with intellectual disability.

94 See generally, J. Bridge-Wright 'Waiting to be Included: Breast and cervical cancer screening, Where are the women with disabilities?', a paper presented by Jenny Bridge-Wright on behalf of Women With Disabilities Australia (WWDA) to the Inaugural Conference on Social Aspects of Disease, Disability and Disablement, Melbourne, 1 July 2004.

95 See generally A. Baker, R. Ivers, J. Bowman, T. Butler, F. Kay-Lambkin, P. Wye, R. Walsh, L. Pulver, R. Richmond, J. Belcher, K. Wilhelm and A. Wodak, 'Where there's smoke, there's fire: High prevalence of smoking among some sub-populations and recommendations for intervention', *Drug and Alcohol Review*, 2006, 25: 85–96.

96 L. Stewart, H. Beange and D. McKerras, 'A survey of dietary problems of adults with learning disabilities in the community', *Mental Handicap Research*, 1994, 7: 41–50.

97 H. Beange, A. McElduff and W. Baker, 'Medical disorders of adults with mental retardation: A population study', *AJMR*, 1995, 99: 595.

98 National Health and Medical Research Council, 1988, op. cit.; for a critical review of this discussion paper see C. Newell, 1991, op. cit.

99 G.D. Slade, A.J. Spencer and K.F. Roberts-Thomson (eds) *Australia's Dental Generations: The National Survey of Adult Oral Health 2004–06*. AIHW cat. no. DEN 165. Canberra: Australian Institute of Health and Welfare (Dental Statistics and Research Series No. 34), 2007; A. Scott, L. Marsh and M.I. Stokes, 'A survey of oral health in a population of adults with developmental disability: Comparison with a national oral health survey of the general population', *ADJ*, 1989, 43: 257–261.

100 CRPD, Article 11.

101 For example, Department of Human Services Victoria, *Fire Safety for Disability Accommodation Services*, 2002, second edition.

102 There is no published Australian research in this area; however, Australian emergency response plans tend to mirror the shortcomings evident in the United States in responses to Hurricanes Rita and Katrina: National Council

on Disability, *The Impact of Hurricanes Rita and Katrina on People with Disabilities: A Look Back and Remaining Challenges*, 2006. Available online at <http://www.ncd.gov/newsroom/publications/2006/hurricanes_impact.htm> (accessed 16 February 2007); National Council on Disability, T*he Needs of People with Psychiatric Disabilities During and After Hurricanes Katrina and Rita: Position Paper and Recommendations*, 2006. Available online at <http://www.ncd.gov/newsroom/publications/2006/peopleneeds.htm> (accessed 16 February 2007).

4 It's my life – it's my decision?

Assisted dying versus assisted living

Baroness (Jane) Campbell, DBE

I do not hold a moral, religious or ethical position on the right to live or die. Like many other disabled people who live close to death, my perspective is purely practical. In this chapter, I look at two sets of circumstances, one in which disabled people have sought to change the law and one in which we are fighting to maintain the status quo. The first concerns the existing right of doctors to cease to treat a patient if, in their clinical judgement, it has no benefit and would prolong intolerable suffering. The second involves the on-going campaign for the legalization of assisted dying and voluntary euthanasia.

Society today still discriminates against people with severe disabilities and illnesses. Our lives are seen by many as inferior to those of non-disabled people. Against this background, there is the inherent danger that actions to withdraw treatment and legalize assisted dying will place disabled people at greater risk. These issues were well explored in two recent attempts to change current UK legislation, one heard in the High Courts of Justice and the other in the House of Lords.

Withdrawal of treatment

The issue of withdrawal of treatment was central to the case of *R (Burke) v. The General Medical Council* (GMC)[1] heard in the High Court in 2004 which concerned Mr Oliver Leslie Burke, a 43-year-old man with cerebella ataxia. The GMC is the body charged by the UK Government with regulating the medical profession. Mr Burke challenged guidelines issued by the GMC concerning the withdrawal of life-prolonging treatment on the grounds that it was unlawful and incompatible with Articles 2, 3 and 8 of the European Convention on Human Rights (Articles 6 and 14 were also invoked). Specifically Burke claimed that 'a patient is entitled to have the question of whether or not care in the form of artificial nutrition and hydration is withdrawn resolved by a court or tribunal in accordance with Article 6(1)'.

And that

> where death is not imminent, the withholding or withdrawal of artificial nutrition and hydration, leading to death by starvation or thirst, not through natural causes, would necessarily be a breach of the claimant's rights under Articles 2, 3 and 8 and would be unlawful under domestic law.

To familiarize the reader with Leslie Burke's precise concerns, it is worth quoting brief extracts from the relevant Articles of the European Convention on Human Rights (1950) cited in his claim.

- Article 2 states: 'Everyone's right to life shall be protected by law'.
- Article 3 states: 'No one shall be subjected to ... inhuman or degrading treatment ...'
- Article 6 states: 'In the determination of his civil rights ... everyone is entitled to a fair and public hearing ... by an independent and impartial tribunal established by law'.
- Article 8 states: 'Everyone has the right to respect for his private and family life ...'
- Article 14 states: 'The enjoyment of the rights and freedoms set forth in this Convention shall be secured without discrimination ...'[2]

These rights are recognized by UK law – in both our common law and the Human Rights Act 1998. In the main the court found for Mr Burke, although the GMC overturned much of the judgement on appeal. Nevertheless, this case was of great significance to disabled people who felt as Leslie Burke did, that the withdrawal of life-prolonging ANH (artificial nutrition and hydration) should not be at the sole discretion of the doctor.

Leslie Burke's case challenged the current power relationship between doctor and patient. Burke believed *each* party had a breadth of knowledge and experience not available to the other. In addition, he argued that it should be ultimately his decision to continue receiving food and water and to 'die naturally'.[3] In the judgement, Mr Justice Munby considered the knowledge base of both patient and doctor to be of equal merit and determined that neither should take precedence over the other *as a matter of course.* He concluded that, if the patient so wishes, life-prolonging treatment should be provided unless, if by doing so, it prolonged a situation that 'from the patient's point of view [would] be intolerable'.[4]

Many of us saw the judgement as a significant achievement for disabled people's rights. First, for our future safety because many felt the quality of their lives would be questioned when they became highly incapacitated; and second, because the court understood, perhaps for the first time, that doctors should not be asked or expected to pass sole judgement on what is 'in the best interest' of the severely ill or disabled patient. Disabled people felt the judgement raised their status from passive recipient of care to 'expert patient'.[5] In addition many physicians across the UK were equally relieved, many agreeing that the patient or their chosen, trusted close relatives, friends and advocates are in the best position to make such life and death decisions.

In my opinion Mr Justice Munby sought to strike a balance between the patient's wishes and the doctor's professional judgement. He highlighted parts of the GMC's guidance that failed to give equal weight to patients' expertise in their own situations and their right to make decisions about the withdrawal of their end-of-life treatments.

For example, the doctor's only obligation under part of the guidance is to 'take account of' what are referred to as the competent patient's 'wishes', 'preferences' and 'views'. Having done so, he is not required to take heed of the same. It rests with the doctor in charge of the patient's care to 'make the decision' regarding whether or not to withdraw treatment.

In addition, the guidance places too much reliance on the doctor's assessment of the patient's 'quality of life' in determining 'best interests'. Recognizing that doctors can and do share many of society's fears and prejudices about disability, the court decided that a higher test of 'intolerability' was needed.[6]

This judgement, although short-lived, in my view, went some way to redress the balance of power as to who decides, and on what grounds, life-prolonging treatment is to be withheld or withdrawn. It challenged the historical relationship between doctor and patient and decided that greater equality was needed. For severely disabled people it made us feel safer too. It would have resulted in an environment of knowledge about the life, or expected life, of the patient, beyond their diagnosis.

Subsequently the Court of Appeal overturned much of the judgement. In the opinion of the Appeal Bench, common law provides sufficient safe-guards for the competent patient, i.e. a person who is able to communicate his or her wishes. In the case of incompetent patients, i.e. those no longer able to communicate their views, artificial nutrition and hydration should not be withdrawn until the doctor has considered the views of those caring for the patient and his or her relatives. In cases of doubt or conflict, the case must be referred to the courts to decide.

Mr Burke then appealed to the European Court of Human Rights (ECtHR). Regrettably, the Strasbourg Court approved the view of the Court of Appeal that it is not for the High Court to authorize medical actions but merely to declare whether a proposed action is lawful. Doctors are fully subject to the sanctions of the criminal and civil law and would only be recommended to obtain legal advice, in addition to proper sup-porting medical opinion, where a step is controversial in some way. Any more stringent legal duty would be 'prescriptively burdensome'.

In so far as having his views taken into account once he becomes incompetent the court considered that Mr Burke is able to make a living will or advance statement. Mr Burke's concern remains that once he loses competence to determine his own best interests, doctors may decide to withdraw ANH without being under an obligation to obtain the approval of the High Court first.

Mr Burke commented:

> I am to say the least extremely disappointed with the ruling from the ECtHR, I only hope that if I am lucky enough to be in hospital, the doctors treating me will not believe at some stage that it will be in my best interests for ANH to be withdrawn even when death is not imminent, effectively letting me die of starvation and thirst when I am no longer able to communicate my wishes.

> I will be making a living will, even though it will give me no comfort, for as it stands living wills are not legally binding and can be disregarded if the wishes contained conflict with the doctor's view.

Despite the reassertion that medical authority must prevail, Leslie Burke's case attracted significant media interest which sparked much debate both within groups of disabled people and wider society. Disabled people were shocked to realize that their lives could be ended prematurely against their wishes. In the mainstream media, the fact that a severely disabled person with a progressive condition did not crave death was seen as newsworthy, demonstrating yet again how disability is perceived as a fate worse than death. Mr Burke was well able to articulate his position and there was widespread sympathy for his desire for certainty that he would never experience the withdrawal of artificial nutrition and hydration, even when close to death. The Disability Rights Commission (DRC) intervened in his case and I was pleased to be one of those who gave expert witness testimony to the court in support of his application.

The Leslie Burke case sought equality in the relationship between patient and doctor. In essence his view (and mine) is that the doctor alone must not decide when to withdraw treatment. The intention of campaigners for the legalizing of assisted dying seeks to strengthen the patient's position further, so that he or she may request death. Would this step provide the ultimate choice and control over one's life that disabled people have fought for decades? In my opinion, such a move would not liberate us further, but would take us backwards, leading to less choice and control. It would be a 'negative right', endangering countless more disabled people than it seeks to help. In this next section I will set out my reasons for believing this to be the case.

Assisted dying

On 12 May 2006 the House of Lords debated Assisted Dying for the Terminally Ill, a Private Member's Bill presented by Lord Joffe. The Bill had the backing of the Voluntary Euthanasia Society (recently renamed Dignity in Dying) and, according to their polls, the support of the British public. Yet the Bill failed to get the endorsement of a single organization of disabled people, and the Disability Rights Commission came down firmly against its passage. Three major national disability charities condemned it and a fast growing number of individual disabled people mobilized under the banner Not Dead Yet UK[7] to make their concerns heard.

So why were so many people the Bill was intended to help, terminally ill and disabled people, so frightened by what it sought to achieve? The answer is that this is not a simple matter of increased choice for those disabled people who live their lives close to death. It raises deep concerns about how disabled people are viewed by society and by themselves. Many people who do not know anyone with motor neurone disease, multiple sclerosis or my own impairment, spinal muscular atrophy, believe we would be better off dead. Society's obsession with the body beautiful only reinforces the negative stereotype that disability is equal to a state worse than death. Even more assert, 'I couldn't live like that!'. Due to this predominant social negativity, life-and-death decisions about disabled people will always be influenced in a discriminatory way. Lord Joffe's Bill fed into this culture by endorsing these views and seeking to sanction the killing of terminally ill and severely disabled people (albeit at their request) as a solution to extreme situations of what they saw to be personal suffering.[8]

In order to understand the public's apparent call for voluntary euthanasia we need to explore further the social context underpinning this demand. Terms such as 'wheelchair bound' and 'handicapped' appear daily in the press without their pejorative meaning being questioned. Despite a growing international awareness of disability as a human rights issue, the notion of elimination of our specific diversity is supported.

In the words of Professor Mike Oliver:

> We know the Nazis killed 200,000 disabled people in Germany but we still practise death making in the here and now and still hidden from view. We avert our eyes just like the Germans did all those years ago. There are no gas chambers but there are things going on that we talk about in hushed tones using terms like 'euthanasia', 'mercy killing' and 'termination'.[9]

It is a sad fact that a large part of the public thinks disabled lives are flawed or simply not worth living. In a recent UK newspaper poll 32 per cent said they would want to abort the pregnancy if they found they were carrying a disabled child.

This societal backdrop influences the medical profession as it does everyone else. Doctors are subject to the same cultural messages and negative stereotyping of disability as everyone else. For example, as pointed out by Dr Ian Basnett, research on the attitudes of accident and emergency doctors found that only a fifth imagined they would be glad to be alive if they were quadriplegic, whereas over 90 per cent of people with quadriplegia reported they were glad to be alive.[10]

If therefore, assisted dying were to be made legal, we could not necessarily depend upon the medical profession to be the custodians of an assisted dying, 'second opinion' safeguard. Dr Ian Basnett illustrated this well in an article for the *Observer* newspaper,

> I became quadriplegic following a sporting accident 17 years ago. I was ventilator dependent for a while and at times said to people, 'I wish I was dead!' I am now extraordinarily glad no one acted on that and assisted suicide was not legal. I think the first difficulty I faced was the fact that, like many people, I had a terribly negative image of disability. When you suddenly become severely disabled you still have that viewpoint. Before I was disabled, I was working as a junior doctor. That brought me into contact with disabled people and I remember clerking in a man with quadriplegia. My reaction was, how could anyone live like that? I said to my then girlfriend, 'I'd rather be dead, if I couldn't play sport'.[11]

Proponents of the Bill claimed safety was not an issue, citing the 20-plus 'safeguards' contained in the Bill to 'ensure that only competent adults who have made a considered and persistent request would be entitled to use it'.[12] Supporters of the Bill claimed it was only intended to help that small minority who, in a similar situation to my own, do not think as I do but want to die. They say that the Bill was not about disabled people but those who are terminally ill, in the last few months of their lives. They cite people having conditions such as multiple sclerosis and motor neurone disease as the potential beneficiaries of this law. This angered the disabled people's movement in Britain, as people with these conditions *are* disabled people. The Dignity in Dying campaigners sought to separate out impairments like MS as 'terminal illnesses' and therefore feed into the medical model of disability.

One may feel it is a compassionate act to help someone end a life that is intolerable to them. The danger is the assumption that disability, in this case the physical conditions brought about by multiple sclerosis etc., is sufficient to explain the intolerable nature of a life.

The relentless dictate that certain medical conditions will affect our lives and those of the people around us is used unashamedly by Dignity in Dying and others who campaign for legalizing euthanasia. When the language used is of someone with MS being 'incurably ill', and descriptions of those who wish to assist them to die as performing 'supreme acts of compassion', we start to understand the strength of such a negative medical model.

Every day disabled people are made fully aware of how their quality of life is contingent on the goodwill of others. There is no right to Independent Living Support or palliative care. As the Joffe Bill said – the patient should be 'inform[ed] of the benefits of the various forms of palliative care', but there is no guarantee in law that such care will be available.

As might be reasonably expected, the views of individual disabled people are sometimes at odds with the collective consensus. Diane Pretty was a British disabled person who went as far as the European Court of Human Rights to fight for her legal right to be assisted by her husband to die. What alarmed me and confirmed my fears about assisted suicide was the public and press response to her situation. Every newspaper supported the 'mercy killing' of those who suffer from terminal impairments.

Diane Pretty was presented to the press as a tragic and pathetic individual. She received maximum coverage, none of which ever questioned, even fleetingly, her suicidal tendencies. Indeed when she said on camera, 'I'm already dead', her misery was in no doubt, no one bothered to look further than the illness for additional causes of hopelessness. The collective view was that ending her life was the only way to put her out of that misery. Against this backdrop the general public could be forgiven for believing that anyone with a substantial level of disability will inevitably be deeply depressed and preoccupied with thoughts of dying. However, when disabled people like me contemplate this reasoning we shudder. I never met Diane but I wish we could have spent some time together. Her life was very different from mine and I would have liked to know the reasons for that. Did she choose to live confined in a downstairs room rather than have adaptations to her home or be rehoused? Did she want her husband to be her full-time carer rather than accept more support from social services? Why was she not fully confident of how her medical team would take care of her as her illness progressed?

Whilst despair is a common reason for contemplating suicide, research evidence from palliative care specialists shows that most people who seek assisted suicide give 'not wanting to be a burden' as the principal reason for seeking death.

Epithets such as 'tragic', 'burdensome' and even 'desperate' are frequently used to describe disabled people's lives, and unless you are extraordinarily strong it's all too easy for disabled people to succumb to this negativity and internalize this oppression which could end in their suicide.

There is thus concern from disabled people's organizations about the language used to describe end-of-life situations for disabled and terminally ill people. Often words are used which convey the fears of the able-bodied rather than the realities of disabled people. That such conjecture might too easily be enshrined in law can be demonstrated by this extract taken from the report of the House of Lords Select Committee on the Assisted Dying Bill.

The need for qualifying conditions for assisted suicide or voluntary euthanasia to be set which reflect the realities of clinical practice as regards the prognosis of terminal illness and which define a patient's suffering in as objective a manner as possible – e.g. 'unbelievable' rather than 'unbearable' suffering.[13]

Unbearable suffering is not just a matter of physical pain. For example, someone may find life 'unbearable' when they have become physically unable to communicate and cannot afford the equipment that would enable them to have a vital connection with their family and others around them. In one US case a man fought vigorously for the right to die via the courts and media coverage highlighted his communication impairment. A software company provided specialist equipment and others raised funds to provide him with home-based support. With this support and equipment he regained the dignity and independence he thought was lost forever and decided that he no longer wished to die. Life was 'bearable' again.[14]

Returning to the Leslie Burke case, Mr Justice Munby emphasized a patient's right to refuse treatment when, 'from the patient's point of view', their situation has become intolerable. For outsiders to assume that the condition itself is the locus of unbearable suffering is to ignore the social, economic and personal context of disability. Society was content to consign Mrs Pretty to the graveyard, yet no one has proposed a similar end for Professor Stephen Hawking. Surely, if the Mrs Prettys of the world are so different that they would be better off dead then the same should be said of Stephen Hawking? Or do we want Hawking to live because of his intelligence? To grade the disabled population in this way one must rely on prejudice since no logic or reason is found there.

I have been fortunate to benefit from excellent medical care. I live in an adapted bungalow, my local authority (government) provides proper care support in the form of a direct payment package that enables me to select and employ personal assistants. I have a powered wheelchair and other assistive technology, some of which I used to write this chapter. Without this social and health care support, I am quite sure I would feel suicidal. Lord Joffe and others who supported his Bill place too little value on the importance of public service support with personal well-being.

Services inevitably involve costs and although in Britain we have a National Health Service and public social care provision, choices offered to disabled people are resource-based. Assisted dying could become an insidiously 'attractive' and inexpensive option in comparison to funding the treatment and support disabled people need. This is of particular concern given that a survey by the Nuffield Trust and the *Nursing Times* found that the NHS is already failing to care adequately for hundreds of thousands of patients who die each year, many without proper pain relief.[15] If assisted dying were to become law, the relationship between caregivers and receivers would be irrevocably damaged.

Apart from fears of burdening loved ones or indeed society, people also cite pain as a reason for wanting the option to call upon others to assist them to die. If you are asked, 'Would you prefer to be assisted to die rather than be in "unbearable" pain?', the answer seems straightforward. But is it? Alison's story is a powerful example of why pain as eligibility criteria for assisted dying is too tenuous.

> I am 47 and was born with severe spina bifida. I am completely depen-dent on my wheelchair for mobility. I am doubly incontinent and I have the lung condition emphysema which often makes breathing very diffi-cult. I also have osteoporosis (brittle bones) which has caused my spine to collapse, trapping nerves. This causes extreme pain which is not always controlled, even with morphine. When the pain is at its worst I cannot move or speak. This can go on for hours, and there is no prospect of relief. Some years ago a combination of the above led me to feel that I couldn't go on living. For ten years I wanted to die and I made several serious attempts to kill myself. I hoarded painkillers and swallowed huge overdoses, washing them down with whatever alcohol I could lay my hands on. I wanted death, and I knew exactly what I was doing.
>
> Fortunately for me, I have friends who were brave enough to intervene, who called 999 and had me rushed to hospital. I was treated against my will more than once.
>
> If euthanasia had been legal, I would certainly have requested it and I wouldn't be here now. In fact, under the rules that now apply in Holland, I would have qualified for euthanasia. Two things helped me realize that, in spite of my many disabilities, life can be sweet.
>
> The first was my friends who refused to accept my view that my life had no value. They helped me re-establish a sense of my own infinite human value, a value which isn't diminished by being severely disabled and having to depend on others.
>
> The second was that I went to India to visit two children I had been sponsoring through a project to help those with disabilities. They called me mother and I became part of their lives – they were to change my life completely.

Alison went on to form a charity providing assistance to disabled children in India. Alison is not unique. The Royal Association for Disability and Rehabilitation (RADAR) has published a booklet, 'Assisted dying – the facts', which includes a collection of personal stories similar to Alison's.[16]

Having looked at the evidence from Holland and listening to the emi-nent physician, Professor Lord McColl in the House of Lords last spring, I am also persuaded of the so-called 'slippery slope' argument against legal-izing assisted dying. He said,

When a Dutch doctor was asked what his first case of euthanasia was like he said, it was dreadful. 'We agonised all day. But the second case was much easier and the third case was a piece of cake.' Many elderly people in Holland are so fearful of euthanasia that they carry cards around with them saying that they do not want it.[17]

Lord Joffe's attempts to draft and redraft the Assisted Dying Bill further illustrate the problem of the slippery slope. Following each previous rejection, he has returned to Parliament with a more restrictive Bill. His most recent version of the Bill contained two further safeguards. First assistance would be given only to the 'terminally ill' – the 'disabled' were to be excluded, so we supposedly had nothing to fear. Second, the doctor would be permitted only to prescribe the lethal dose, requiring the patient to self-administer and thus protecting anyone requesting assistance to die but then having a change of heart.[18]

A moment's thought will quickly show that these are not safeguards but mere devices to silence objectors. The more restrictive the Bill, the easier it is to argue for its scope to be expanded once it has passed into law. None of us will be safe. Consider two patients lying side by side in hospital. Both ask their doctors to prescribe lethal medication. Although their symptoms and prognosis are similar, one has a terminal illness whereas the other is classed as disabled. One gets the drugs, the other does not. Or will the second patient be reclassified? Then consider the patient with a progressive condition. Better to swallow the lethal dose this week, than risk being too ill to do so next week. Were assisted dying to be legalized, such inequalities would create pressure for the safeguards to be relaxed. When would that process stop? When assisted dying becomes just another treatment option available to all?

Lord Joffe has said on more than one occasion that he does not believe legislation should be as restrictive as his proposed Assisted Dying Bill. To have any chance of success, he knows that he must play the long game as part of his strategy of eventually achieving legalized assisted dying for all groups who say they are suffering unbearably.

I would argue that society has a duty to relieve such suffering rather than use death as a way of sweeping it away. Without good palliative care, someone near death may find life 'unbearable'. Someone who is disabled long-term may find life 'unbearable', if there is inadequate home-based support, for example if they have to live in an institution or in undignified circumstances at home.

There is now increasing pressure from the Independent Living Movement to stop disabled people being institutionalized against their will. This has been taken up by Lord Ashley in a Private Member's Bill.[19] Some disabled people engaged in this campaign have spoken openly about how they would rather die than live in institutional care. Undoubtedly, this is campaign rhetoric; however there is more than elements of truth behind the fear.

There needs to be policy imperative from the British Government to introduce an agreed entitlement to essential community living support services and palliative care so that people do not feel a burden – this needs to extend to cover support for family members and carers. That way 'unbearable' suffering could be turned into a bearable life – and in turn a more bearable death.

Those who argue that sufficient safeguards can be included in any proposed legislation to weed out those who could be helped with palliative care or social service support need to reconsider. The last Joffe Bill claimed to apply to people with just weeks or months to live. The reality is that there can be no watertight safeguards to determine whether a person is indeed terminally ill and in the last months of life, neither whether they are 'suffering unbearably' nor whether the cause of that suffering is the actual illness or unmet physical, mental or social needs.

Who 'qualifies' for the right to be assisted to die under proposed legislation is therefore highly contestable. Not only would this present doctors with impossible dilemmas about when to treat and when to assist to die but, if physician-assisted suicide were once to be legally sanctioned, then *limiting* access to such assistance to die could be said to be discriminatory.

For this reason there would inevitably be calls to extend the legislation over time to include more and more people in the name of equality and human rights (as has proved to be the case in Holland). The slippery slope that so many reject as anecdote will reassert itself.

Legalizing premature death as a treatment option will place the seed of doubt about one's right to demand help – not to die – but to live with dignity. I believe it may place pressures on people who think they are close to the end of their lives to consider death as preferable to fighting for support to live with dignity.[20] It will be the cheapest, quickest and simplest option. In addition, consider older people who are anxious not to cause their families any distress.

Fear of dependency and being cared for is not without good grounds. A local newspaper reported in 2005 that an elderly mother was compelled to wash her disabled adult daughter with a bucket and flannel because support services were unable to fund the level-floor shower they had been assessed as needing.[21] This could be deemed 'unbearable suffering'. It may also be 'unbearable' to witness your partner become exhausted and to feel you are now nothing but a 'burden'. Studies in Oregon and Holland find that a substantial proportion of people seeking assisted deaths again give 'not wanting to be a burden' as their reason. Believing oneself to be a burden strikes at the heart of our feelings of self-worth.

Rachel Hurst, in her plea to the bioethics community at their fifth world congress said,

> It takes a particular sort of courage to rise above these negative impacts and have a faith in your own worth, or the worth of your disabled family

member. It takes courage and a clear understanding that disability arises from the social barriers of attitude and environment to your impairment, not the impairment itself. A similar sort of courage and understanding has been needed by women as they overcame the discriminatory images of subservience and earth mother or the courage and understanding that have been needed for black people to overcome slavery and apartheid. Just as we all recognise that society needs the difference of women and people of different races and backgrounds, so society needs people with impairments.[22]

I believe the background noise to this debate is reinforcing negative perceptions of disability. It feeds into desires for a body beautiful and a perfect life untroubled by illness. It promotes premature death as a choice option, especially for people with severe disability or terminal conditions. This choice agenda is false because it will insidiously lead to less choice. To make a real choice we need to live in a society that values us equally, where we can live with dignity and have access to proper pain relief. In the safety of that environment, perhaps then we can turn our attention to assisted dying. Disabled people who currently live under a cloud of uncertainty as to whether their lives are worth living will then be in a better position to debate about a real choice, to end their lives. Personally, when and if that time comes, I do not think people will want a right to assisted dying in such a supportive climate.

Thankfully, there is an antidote to Lord Joffe and his solution to personal distress. As mentioned earlier in this chapter, Lord Ashley's Right to Independent Living Bill seeks to guarantee the services that terminally ill and disabled people need to live with dignity. It is a Bill of hope whereas Lord Joffe's was the Bill of fear.

Sometimes academic debate does not get to the heart of the matter, so I will end this chapter with a poem. This poem was written by Micheline Mason, a disabled writer and poet whose leadership of the inclusion movement is known throughout the world.

Not Dead Yet

I have lived to see another spring
To breathe in the blossom's perfumed air
To feel again the sun warming my skin
To wonder at the life we share

I have another chance to notice
Shining eyes meeting my own
Some with love, some with questions
The hope, fear, pain we have all shown

I can touch again those I care for
With my hands, my mind, my heart

They touch me as if for the first time
New thoughts, our dreams just start

Physical pain I have known plenty
Impairment holds little fear for me
But to feel unwanted, a burden, a weight
Is the intolerable pain I flee

The answer cannot lie in murder made easy
In fuelling guilt, complicity and dread
It lies in the courage to create a kinder world
In which no one would choose to be dead

Happily, I am not dead yet
I have lived to see another spring
I will use every precious moment I have left
This welcome change to bring[23]

Notes

1 [2004] EWHC 1879 (Admin); [2005] 2 WLR 431.
2 Council of Europe, The European Convention on Human Rights (Rome, 4 November 1950) and its Five Protocols (Paris, 20 March 1952, Strasbourg, 1963–1966), considering the Universal Declaration of Human Rights proclaimed by the General Assembly of the United Nations on 10 December 1948.
3 Radio 4 news broadcast, 29 July 2005.
4 Judgement at para. 213(o).
5 The Expert Patients Programme (EPP) was instituted in April 2002 by the Department of Health, as a National Health Service programme that recognizes and supports patients' rights to take charge of their own conditions and treatment.
6 Judgement at para. 211.
7 Not Dead Yet UK, founded in 2006, is a network of over 100 UK-based disabled people opposed to assisted suicide and euthanasia. Their activities are organized through the website www.livingwithdignity.info. Not Dead Yet UK shares many of the principles and views with its US-based cousin, Not Dead Yet, founded in 1983: www.notdeadyet.org.
8 I refer the reader to my earlier point that the Disability Rights Commission has withheld its support of Lord Joffe's Bill, in part because people with terminal illnesses are likely to be classified as disabled people under the Disability Discrimination Act.
9 Oliver, M. (1999) 'Disabled people and the inclusive society', public lecture, Strathclyde Centre for Disability Research.
10 Paper presented by Dr Ian Basnett, Labour Party fringe 2004.
11 *Observer*, Sunday 31 March 2002.
12 Taken from 'Questions and answers on the Assisted Dying for the Terminally Ill Bill 2005–6', on the website: http://www.dignityindying.org.uk
13 Select Committee on the Assisted Dying for the Terminally Ill Bill Evidence 2004–05 [HL].
14 DRC Assisted Dying Policy Statement, October 2005.
15 'How do you deal with death?', *Nursing Times*, 1 February 2001.

16 Royal Association for Disability and Rehabilitation (RADAR) 'Assisted dying – The facts', 2006.
17 House of Lords Official Report (Hansard), 12 May 2006, column 1285.
18 The Assisted Dying for the Terminally Ill Bill [HL] states:

> 'terminally ill' means an illness which in the opinion of both the attending and consulting physician (a) is inevitably progressive, (b) cannot be reversed by treatment (although treatment may be successful in relieving symptoms temporarily), and (c) will be likely to result in the patient's death within six months.

Clause 1 of the Bill states:

> Subject to the provisions of this Act, it shall be lawful for (a) a physician to assist a patient who is a qualifying patient to die (i) by prescribing such medication, and (ii) in the case of a patient for whom it is impossible or inappropriate orally to ingest that medication, by prescribing and providing such means of self-administration of that medication.

19 Disabled Persons (Independent Living) Bill [HL], second reading in the House of Lords on 8 June 2006.
20 Among those denied euthanasia or PAS by the GPs, 'not wanting to be a burden', 'tired of living', and 'depression' were reasons most often given by patients to justify their death requests (p.1699). van der Weide, J. 'Granted, undecided, withdrawn, and refused requests for euthanasia and physician-assisted suicide', *Arch Intern Med*, 165, 8/22 2005.
21 *East Anglian Daily Times*, 16 July 2005.
22 Hurst, R. 'Ethics and disability, celebrating diversity', paper given to 5th World Congress on Bioethics, 2000, Sydney, Australia.
23 Micheline Mason, 2006.

5 Disability rights and resuscitation

Do not attempt reconciliation?

Tom Shakespeare and Bryan Vernon

Many disabled people and disability rights organizations have expressed concerns about barriers and discrimination in health care settings and medical treatment. These have covered specific issues including genetics (Disability Rights Commission (DRC) 2005) and sexual health (Shakespeare *et al.* 1996), access to treatment (DRC 2005) and normalizing treatments or corrective surgery (Parens 2006). More generally, there may be an inevitable tension between the disability rights perspective and the dominant ethos of biomedicine. The twin goals of medicine are to save life and to alleviate suffering. But where disability rights perspectives see life with impairment as a valid form of existence which may be different but not worse than the average, biomedical perspectives often see a life with disability as a harmed life, involving suffering. If the mission of medicine is to cure or prevent disability, the existence of disabled people implies medicine's failure. In particular, the use of quality-adjusted life years (QALYs) to assess the cost-effectiveness of health care tends to disadvantage and disturb disabled people and has been criticized by disabled commentators as discriminatory. Calculations used to determine QALYs measure a year of healthy life expectancy as one, while a year of unhealthy life expectancy will be less than one. Because disabled people's lives always start out scoring less than one, they are disadvantaged when different interventions are evaluated (Wasserman *et al.* 2005).

End-of-life issues raise particular concern. Past experience partly explains the sensitivity of the relationship between the disability community and the medical profession around end of life. The history of doctor-administered euthanasia under the Nazi regime has been well documented (Burleigh 1995). In modern times, the much publicized activities of murderers such as Dr Harold Shipman, or assisted-suicide entrepreneurs Dr Jack Kevorkian or Dr Philip Nitschke create a climate of suspicion and hostility among some disability activists. Recent UK attempts to legalize assisted suicide have generated impassioned opposition from many in the disability community (Campbell 2003; Davis 2004; Hurst n.d.): there are concerns that the UK may follow those countries that have liberalized end-of-life legislation; for example, in Oregon physician-assisted suicide is available for residents, in Switzerland it is available to anyone, while both Belgium and the Netherlands have legalized voluntary euthanasia.

There have been well publicized cases of disabled, sick or elderly people discovering that their medical notes had been marked with 'Do Not Attempt Resuscitation' (DNAR) without their knowledge or agreement. For example, in the UK the voluntary organization Age Concern launched a campaign after Jill Baker, a 67-year-old person with stomach cancer, found that her medical notes recorded a judgement that cardiopulmonary resuscitation (CPR) would be inappropriate in her case (BBC 2000). Some disabled people who have gone into hospital with infections or needing particular treatment have found that their notes have been marked with DNAR orders without their knowledge or consent. Leslie Burke suffered from a congenital degenerative brain condition and would need artificial hydration and nutrition to sustain his life at some point in the future. He went to court because he was concerned that doctors might withdraw this at some point in the future when he was no longer able to make decisions for himself. They could rely on GMC guidance if they did this, but he wanted the judge to say that this guidance contravened his common law rights, as well as the Human Rights Act. Although he was successful in the original case, it was overturned on appeal (*R (Burke) v. General Medical Council* [2006] QB 273).

In the UK, there has been considerable media focus on stories about older people being left to die, about withdrawal of care, about cases of assisted suicide or 'mercy killing', and about high-profile right-to-die cases such as that of Ms B. or Diane Pretty. Ms B. was a patient who was paralysed from the neck down who wished to have her ventilator withdrawn. There were doubts expressed about her competence, but the High Court decided that she was both competent and able to demand that the ventilator be withdrawn (*B v. An NHS Trust* [2002] EWHC 429). Diane Pretty, in contrast, wanted the Director of Public Prosecutions not to prosecute her husband if he killed her at her request. The court refused to make such an order, and an appeal to the European Court of Human Rights was unsuccessful (*Pretty v. UK* [2002] 35 EHRR 1). A recent survey by the UK Disability Rights Commission found that 63 per cent of respondents thought that there should be new laws to make euthanasia or assisted suicide possible (BBC 2003). In the Netherlands, the liberal regime around voluntary euthanasia has allegedly led to pressure on individuals with disabilities to end their lives. In response to what many activists feel is a growing movement to get rid of disabled and elderly people, disability rights campaigners have challenged infringements of human rights and called for legal scrutiny of medical treatment of end-of-life issues.

The context for this controversy is the perceived cultural assumption that it is better to be dead than disabled. The public, and medical professionals, and indeed those who have recently become impaired through accident and disease, usually underestimate disabled people's quality of life (Albrecht and Devlieger 1999). In a Western world which is fixated on youth, beauty, fitness and independence, disability and dependency are seen as the worst possible way of life. Jane Campbell, a Disability Rights Commissioner who lives with spinal muscular atrophy, argued in an article originally published in the *Independent* newspaper: 'We live with the negative stereotype that disability equals a state worse than death, an idea reinforced by our collective obsession with the body beautiful'.

She suggests that the social, economic and personal context of disability explains why particular individuals with impairments may find their lives not worth living, and that media reports reinforce the idea that ending a disabled life is rational and desirable (Campbell 2003). Judgements of quality of life are inherently subjective. They are amenable to change. Often, simple improvements – better pain management, provision of support, increase in social inclusion – may lead to people feeling better about their situation. When first impaired, it is common for individuals to feel extremely negative and pessimistic. With time, there is a natural tendency to become reconciled to a situation and to make the best of it, and many disabled people have gone through this very process themselves.

The end-of-life debate is emotionally powerful for disabled people for perhaps three major reasons. First, their own survival is at stake. Second, others claim to be able to evaluate their quality of life, thereby robbing them of the possibility of evaluating their own experience. Third, disabled people, particularly those with degenerative conditions, may have understandable anxieties about their own mortality and vulnerability which are heightened by the constant equation of disability with death. Disabled people may welcome the opportunity to think about these questions, but it must be in a safe context and at a time of their choosing.

Debates about disability and end of life are often undermined by the conflation of a range of different issues in disability rights response. For example, distinctions need to be made between voluntary euthanasia and assisted suicide on the one hand, and advance directives (living wills) and withdrawal of treatment on the other. While there are common themes and principles, each of the specific issues at end of life raise slightly different concerns. This paper will focus on CPR, combining clinical, ethical and sociological arguments in order to analyse the fears expressed by disabled commentators and campaigners.

Perceptions of CPR

We claim that lack of information and communication means that the debate on CPR and DNAR is sometimes misleading and impoverished. For example, some disability rights comments and claims may lack insight into the realities of resuscitation. Conversely, none of the professional documents and academic discussions we have surveyed for this paper mentions disability rights perspectives or the fears of the disability community. There is a need for improved dialogue between medical professionals and the disability community.

We believe that some of the fears of DNAR and withdrawal of treatment exaggerate the dangers to disabled people. Resuscitation Council UK guidelines (2001) suggest that Do Not Attempt Resuscitation (DNAR) orders may be appropriate in three situations:

- when attempting CPR will not restart the patient's heart and breathing
- when there is no benefit to restarting the patient's heart and breathing, for example when death would follow very shortly after, or when the patient would never regain awareness or the ability to interact, and would therefore not experience the benefit
- when the expected benefit is outweighed by the burdens.

The first two criteria are not problematic. The third is dubious: it is a rather bland and general phrase concealing considerable debate and complexity of judgement.

There are two prevalent and important misapprehensions about resuscitation: that DNAR orders are widespread, and that CPR is usually successful. However, contrary to perception, only a minority of patients are given DNAR orders. For example, a DNAR audit at a hospital in our region covered 150 patients on geriatric wards over a six- to eight-week period. There were only eight cases of DNAR orders being made (Mannix 1995).

Second, there is an important distinction between the terms Do Not Resuscitate (DNR) and Do Not Attempt Rescuscitation (DNAR). 'DNR' suggests that clinicians are deliberately not helping patients who could be saved from death. 'DNAR', a more recent term, more accurately suggests that CPR is a difficult procedure which is frequently unsuccessful.

Moreover, DNAR does not mean withdrawal of treatment or nutrition, as is sometimes wrongly assumed by both the public and by clinical teams (Hilberman *et al.* 1997:362). It should mark a limit to efforts to keep someone alive, not abandoning less invasive efforts and therapies. All other relevant treatment and care should be considered and offered.

There is ample evidence that the general public has an exaggerated view of the efficacy of attempts at resuscitation. Even professionals regularly overestimate the possibilities of CPR being successful (Wagg *et al.* 1995). This misapprehension arises partly because of general ignorance of medical procedures and overexpectations of doctors. It is fuelled by inaccurate representations in the media. Research shows that television medical soaps such as *ER* are a major source of information for patients. One study of television representation showed short-term survival (one hour) after resuscitation in 75 per cent of cases (Diem *et al.* 1996). By contrast, 40 per cent short-term success is accepted to be the upper limit, and most sources give a figure of 25 per cent of patients being successfully resuscitated in the short term (Mohr and Kettler 1997).

The same TV study found 67 per cent of CPR cases survived until discharge from hospital. By contrast, a range of studies of long-term survival have produced figures of 2 per cent to 30 per cent for those experiencing cardiac arrest outside a hospital, and 6.5 per cent to 15 per cent for those experiencing arrest while in hospital. For elderly patients, it is suggested that a figure of 5 per cent long-term survival after CPR would be more realistic (Morgan *et al.* 1994). Unrealistic media portrayal, therefore, reinforces the perception that CPR is a miraculous intervention with a high chance of success. Criticism of television representations of resuscitation has apparently led to a more realistic portrayal in recent years (Gordon *et al.* 1998).

A rational choice for DNAR

Many surveys suggest that most people would want to be consulted on CPR, and would want resuscitation (Cherniack 2002). Those who overestimate the success of CPR have no reason to decline the procedure. If no one in their right mind would choose to forgo a life-saving treatment, it seems doubly wrong that clinicians would deny particular individuals that possibility.

However, choosing to decline CPR may be a rational choice, given the realities:

> If CPR were a benign, risk-free procedure that offered a good hope of long-term survival in the face of otherwise certain death, few people would ever choose to have medical personnel withhold resuscitation. But controversy surrounds the use of CPR precisely because the procedure can lead to prolonged suffering, severe neurological damage, or an undignified death.
>
> (Diem *et al.* 1996:1581)

CPR is often a traumatic experience for patients, relatives and staff. It involves: checking that airways are clear, and sometimes inserting a tube into the mouth and airway; air or oxygen being pumped into the lungs; vigorous repeated pressure on the chest to pump blood to brain and other vital organs until normal heartbeat is restored; it may include the use of an electric shock (defibrillation) to restart the heart.

There are some disabled or elderly people for whom CPR would always be hugely traumatic or sometimes even lethal. For example, a person with osteoporosis or osteogenesis imperfecta has frail bones, which could be broken if clinicians attempted to restart their heart, resulting in a fractured sternum or ribcage and possibly lacerated lungs. In most circumstances, the outcome is likely to be either a much more painful death at the time, or temporary survival in a state of extreme discomfort.

Of the minority who survive CPR, research shows that 20 per cent to 50 per cent suffer neurological impairment, ranging from slight brain damage to persistent vegetative state (Mohr and Kettler 1997). While we agree with disability rights commentators who challenge the negative valuation of people with brain damage, it also needs to be recognized that many people would want to avoid this outcome, and the increased suffering both for the patient and for their relatives which might result.

Often, people who may be offered DNAR orders are elderly, or have degenerative or terminal illness. Evidence shows that people who are asked to consider CPR in the context of terminal illness or persistent impairment are less likely to desire it (Cherniack 2002:303). Death has become a taboo subject, and people find it difficult to contemplate their own mortality. But many traditional religions and ethical systems challenge this approach, maintaining that death is a natural part of life. For every person, there will come a time to die. Heroic efforts to keep someone alive for another few days or weeks may not always be helpful. If asked about death, most people desire a peaceful and painless death. Aggressive CPR can undermine that possibility, and undermine the important bioethical principle of non-maleficence ('do no harm').

Surveys show that when the realities of CPR processes and survival rates are explained to patients, they are less likely to request the procedure. For example, in one study, 41 per cent of acute patients initially opted for CPR. When informed of the evidence about efficacy and outcome, 22 per cent opted for CPR. In a group of people with chronic illness whose life expectancy was less than a year, only 11 per cent initially opted for CPR. After being informed of the evidence, only 5 per cent opted for CPR (Murphy *et al.* 1994). This data could be interpreted in two ways: either that effective communication leads to more rational decision-making, or that doctors are persuading their patients to comply with their regime of death-making for disabled and elderly people. Certainly there is evidence that the way in which CPR is explained influences people's choice of DNAR orders (Cherniack 2002:304).

The European Convention on Human Rights, now incorporated in UK law in the Human Rights Act (1998), has 'the right to life' as the second article, and this is often cited by the disability rights movement. But the third article, 'the right to be free from degrading treatment', is another important principle. The concept of dignity is central to human rights thinking. Aggressive CPR is not a dignified procedure.

Disability rights and autonomy

In practice, it seems probable that patients are more likely to be resuscitated against their will than left to die when they have expressed a preference for resuscitation. A minority of patients who have cardiac arrest have discussed their preferences with their physician. There is a default assumption of resuscitation, except where patients are of advanced age or suffering from terminal illness. This approach is reinforced by the February 2001 joint statement from the BMA, Resuscitation Council and Royal College of Nursing, of which the first guideline is that the goal of medicine is extension of life, and the second guideline is a presumption in favour of attempting resuscitation (Resuscitation Council 2001).

Autonomy is an important principle in bioethics, and dictates that individuals should have the right to refuse treatment, a right recognized in law. Competent adults have the right to refuse medical treatment, even if that refusal results in their death. When a patient requests or agrees to a DNAR notice, they are extending their autonomy into a crisis situation where they would be unable to decide for themselves.

Research has shown that 89 per cent of alert elderly patients wanted decisions about CPR to be discussed with them (Morgan *et al.* 1994). In the past, doctors did not have to discuss DNAR notices with their patients, and often did not do so. When patients discovered that they had been labelled 'not for resuscitation', they were understandably aggrieved, and adverse press coverage followed. The response was the introduction of the new guidelines in 2001, which make consultation a requirement, and recognize the legal and human rights of patients (Resuscitation Council 2001). Patients need written information on what DNAR is, to dispel myths and clarify the potential costs and benefits of the procedure.

Autonomy is also an important principle in the disability rights movement, which has campaigned for disabled people to be able to make choices about where to live, how to live, and what treatment they receive. It is paradoxical that when it comes to the end of life the dominant position of the disability rights movement is to deny individuals with impairment the choice of voluntary euthanasia or assisted suicide, and to question the morality of DNAR.

The explanation for the contradiction is the fear that individual choices will be influenced by a cultural context in which disability is devalued. Many people who express a wish to end their lives or refuse treatment have either recently become impaired, or have been denied access to independent living services and barrier-free environments. An end to discrimination and social exclusion for disabled people is vital, if people are to make decisions which are not merely responses to the oppression they face.

However, we believe that the principle of autonomy should extend to the right to refuse resuscitation attempts. Many disabled people, older people and medical patients are very keen to express their right to refuse treatments. Part of the fear of death is a fear of being kept alive in a state of total dependency or permanent lack of awareness, and knowing that there is a way out can be a source of comfort and security.

There remains an abiding problem around DNAR negotiations: forcing patients to make choices in a situation where they would prefer not to choose may be paternalism, not autonomy (Sayers *et al.* 1997). Discussing impending death is difficult for most people in a culture which makes it difficult for people to discuss and plan for their own deaths. DNAR conversations can be difficult and distressing for patients, relatives and clinicians themselves.

One option is for consultations to look at a wider range of treatment preferences, rather than focusing on just death and CPR. Such discussions could be preceded by an explanatory leaflet. Clearly, the patient still has the right to decline this discussion. Clinicians need training in communication skills, and where medical schools have initiated good programmes, this will begin to bear fruit in the next generation of doctors.

Cognitive impairment raises particular problems. This is why the concept of a living will or advance directive has been developed, in order to allow a person to exercise their autonomy while cognitively intact and decide how they want to be treated if a particular situation arises. Advance directives have been seen as an improvement on DNAR notices, as they reflect more discussion, and cannot be imposed by a clinician. However, some disability rights activists have also reacted against this expression of disabled people's autonomy: for example, a *Disability Tribune* editorial commented, of the Hammersmith Hospital Trust's decision to introduce advance directives, that 'this decision takes disabled people further down the slippery slope of having to justify our very existence' (*Disability Tribune* 2003). By contrast, the voluntary organization Help the Aged, while opposed to euthanasia and physician-assisted suicide, believes that advance directives can be a useful tool. Help the Aged also supports the right of older people to make decisions for themselves about treatment and refusal of treatment (Help the Aged 2002). In a society where nearly three-quarters of people who die do so without having made a will, let alone living wills, failure to anticipate or consider end-of-life issues is a common problem.

Conclusion: reconciliation around DNAR

There undoubtedly have been abuses of DNAR procedure, and the practice needs to be monitored by scrutiny organizations – in the UK, clinical ethics committees which currently operate in 52 NHS Trusts, and the Healthcare Commission which acts as a national health watchdog – as well as by organizations of patients and disabled people. Abuse sometimes has occurred where doctors have made paternalistic judgements about the quality of life they might expect a disabled or elderly person to experience, reflecting their own prejudices about disability. There is an important distinction between not resuscitating because it is believed that attempts would be unsuccessful or cause harm, and not resuscitating because of projected quality of life or discriminatory assumptions about disability or age. Blanket policies to deny attempts at resuscitation – based on age, or impairment, or social context – are discriminatory, unethical and probably illegal under the Human Rights Act.

Each NHS Trust needs to have a proper policy on DNAR, with improved communication of the realities of resuscitation to patients. DNAR orders and negotiation are a sensitive task that should not be left to junior doctors. Better training of staff at all levels is needed, to include disability equality and disability rights perspectives. This might enable professionals to understand and respect the concerns of members of the disability community. Where members of the disability community are actively involved in medical training – for example at the Bristol, Leicester and Newcastle Medical Schools – medical students gain an understanding of the fears and perceptions of disability activists, who themselves benefit from a better insight into medical practice and values.

There is also an onus on the disability rights movement itself to be responsible and careful. Disability rights advocates need to exercise care in their political rhetoric, distinguishing legitimate from illegitimate fears, rather than fuelling anxiety and undermining doctor–patient relationships. Careful analysis and evidence is needed. While it is vital to challenge the social perception of disability and ageing, we believe that it is wrong to deny the rights of individuals to make their own decisions to refuse treatment. The disability movement should reflect on its inconsistent use of the concept of autonomy.

The DNAR issue has wider implications for discrimination and communication in the medical encounter. The Resuscitation Council guidelines call for demystification of clinical procedures and better information and communication with patients. A combination of distorted claims by activists and poor medical procedures has the potential to breed a climate of fear and mistrust among disabled people. Trust is vital in the health care encounter, especially at the end of life. Ultimately, it is the clinician who decides when to resuscitate, and who is responsible for doing what is in the interests of the patient. A climate of better communication and mutual respect would be in the best interests of everybody.

While these measures may achieve some reconciliation in the DNAR debate, there is a wider contradiction which still needs resolution or at least recognition. The guidelines suggest: 'Doctors cannot be required to give treatment contrary to their clinical judgement, but should, whenever possible, respect patients' wishes to receive treatment which carries only a very small chance of success or benefit' (Resuscitation Council 2001:5.2). It would be a point of principle in the disability rights approach that no patient should be given a DNAR notice against their will. Yet treatment is always a matter of clinical judgement. In practice, doctors can withhold or withdraw futile treatments. Whether a patient has consented to a DNAR notice or not, no one has a right to a particular treatment, only the right to decline treatments, as debate around the Burke case has established. In other words, the language of rights has its limits, and not just at the end of life.

Acknowledgements

Thanks to Kathryn Mannix and Simon Woods and the editors for their helpful comments on this paper.

Bibliography

Albrecht, G.L. and Devlieger, P.J. (1999) 'The disability paradox: High quality of life against all odds', *Social Science and Medicine*, 48, 977–988.

BBC (2000) 'Age discrimination "rife" in NHS', 16 April 2000. Online at http://news.bbc.co.uk/1/hi/health/715071.stm. Accessed 27 April 2007.

BBC (2003) 'Euthanasia fears for disabled', 20 January 2003. Online at http://news.bbc.co.uk/1/hi/health/2668253.stm. Accessed 24 January 2003.

Burleigh, R. (1995) *Death and Deliverance*. Cambridge: Cambridge University Press.

Campbell, J. (2003) 'Don't be fooled, we don't all want to kill ourselves'. Online at www.bcodp.org.uk/about/campbell.shtml. Accessed March 2004.

Cherniack, E.P. (2002) 'Increasing use of DNR orders in the elderly worldwide: Whose choice is it?', *Journal of Medical Ethics*, 28, 303–307.

Davis, A. (2004) 'A disabled person's perspective on euthanasia'. Paper presented at UK Forum on Healthcare Law and Ethics, University of Newcastle.

Diem, S.J., Lantos, J.D. and Tulsky, J.A. (1996) 'Cardiopulmonary resuscitation on television: Miracles and misinformation', *New England Journal of Medicine*, 334, 24, 1578–1582.

Disability Rights Commission (2005) *Closing the Gap: Interim Report of a Formal Investigation into Health Inequalities*. London: Disability Rights Commission.

Disability Tribune (2000) 'Solihull declaration', *Disability Tribune* (Disability Awareness in Action), March. Online at <http://www.daa.org.uk/e_tribune%5 Ce_2000_03.htm>. Accessed April 2007.

Disability Tribune (2003) 'Editorial: UK hospital's new policy puts pressure on people to refuse treatment', *Disability Tribune* (Disability Awareness in Action), March, p.1.

Gordon, P.N., Williamson, S. and Lawler, P.G. (1998) 'As seen on TV: Observational study of cardiopulmonary resuscitation in British television medical dramas', *British Medical Journal*, 317, 7161, 780–783.

Help the Aged (2002) *End of Life*. Help the Aged policy statement.

Hilberman, M., Kutner, J., Parsons, D. and Murphy, D.J. (1997) 'Marginally effective medical care: Ethical analysis of issues in cardiopulmonary resuscitation', *Journal of Medical Ethics* 23, 361–367.

Hurst, R. (n.d.) 'Assisted suicide and disabled people: A briefing paper'. Online at www.daa.org.uk/assisted_suicide.htm. Accessed April 2004.

Mannix, K. (1995) Verbal communication.

Mohr, M. and Kettler, D. (1997) 'Ethical aspects of resuscitation', *British Journal of Anaesthesia*, 79, 253–259.

Morgan, R., King, D., Prajapati, C. and Rowe, J. (1994) 'Views of elderly patients and their relatives on cardiopulmonary resuscitation', *British Medical Journal*, 308, 1677–1678.

Murphy, D.J., Burrows, D., Santilli, S., Kemp, A.W., Tenner, S., Kelling, B. and Teno, S. (1994) 'The influence of the probability of survival on patients' preferences regarding CPR', *New England Journal of Medicine*, 330, 545–549.

Parens, E. (ed.) (2006) *Surgically Shaping Children*. Washington DC: Georgetown University Press.

Resuscitation Council (2001) 'Decisions relating to cardiopulmonary resuscitation: A joint statement from the British Medical Association, the Resuscitation Council (UK) and the Royal College of Nursing'. Online at www.resus.org/pages/dnar.htm. Accessed 5 February 2003. Also published in *Journal of Medical Ethics*, 27, 310–316.

Sayers, G., Schofield, I. and Aziz, M. (1997) 'An analysis of CPR decision-making in elderly patients', *Journal of Medical Ethics*, 23, 207–212.

Shakespeare, T., Gillespie-Sells, K. and Davies, D. (1996) *The Sexual Politics of Disability: Untold Desires*. London: Cassell.

Stewart, K., Spice, C. and Rai, G.S. (2003) 'Where now with Do Not Attempt Resuscitation decisions', *Age and Ageing*, 32, 143–148.

Wagg, A., Kinrions, M. and Stewart, K. (1995) 'Cardiopulmonary resuscitation: Doctors and nurses expect too much', *Journal of the Royal College of Physicians of London*, 29, 20–24.

Wasserman, D., Bickenbach, J. and Wachbroit, R. (eds) (2005) *Quality of Life and Human Difference: Genetic Testing, Healthcare and Disability*. Cambridge: Cambridge University Press.

6 Disability, human rights and redistributive justice

Some reflections from the North West Frontier Province of Pakistan on popular perceptions of disabled people

Shaheen Sardar Ali

At the outset I would like to make a disclaimer: I do not profess to have any significant knowledge or indeed understanding of issues of disability and rights of disabled people. That of course does not preclude sensitivity to their situation, needs and rights as equal members of society. Neither does it denote any lack of interest in the subject. My training and research interests place me at the intersection of Islamic law, human rights and gender issues. The position and perspective I adopt in the present chapter are informed by my understanding of human rights as inherent and inalienable entitlements of every human being throughout the life cycle. It reflects upon my interaction with people with disability during my time as Provincial Minister for Health, Population Welfare and Women Development in the Government of the North West Frontier Province (NWFP) of Pakistan and is presented in narrative form rather than what may be termed as a strictly 'academic' format.[1]

I have never quite fathomed how I got propelled into my ministerial position in the North West Frontier Province of Pakistan in 1999 where I served until 2001 before returning to the UK to resume my academic position at the University of Warwick.[2] Agonizing for me were the defining moments when it was decision time (both at entry and exit from government). Saying 'yes' to becoming a cabinet minister came at a heavy price. Having remained a member of the human rights and women's rights movement in Pakistan and espousing the position that the military had no business in politics, my decision will remain the proverbial albatross round my neck. My decision to hand in my resignation too was not easy to explain to a society where very few in ministerial positions exit of their own volition.

My reasons for agreeing to become part of a military regime ranged from the personal to the political. I have to admit that the decisive factor was the fact that for the first time in the history of Pakistan a Pukhtoon woman would become a cabinet minister. In a country where the NWFP was singled out (along with Baluchistan) for its stereotypical images of women, this opportunity overrode the many negatives of joining government.[3] Last, but

not least, I will admit my frustration at finger-pointing drawing-room ideal-
ists who sat on the fence, criticizing governments for everything and
anything. I felt that the offer created space to 'get my hands dirty' and try to
make some positive inputs in government. Ideally and ideologically not
quite the perfect scenario, but by far the most difficult experience was to
open oneself to continuous public scrutiny where everyone can criticize and
find fault with whatever one does. However controversial my induction into
a military government might have been, I must say that I came into the position as a believer in human rights, a sociolegal researcher and academic as
well as an activist. I strongly believed in the responsibility of government to
provide basic entitlements including health, education and access to justice
and accountability of persons in positions of authority. My perceptions of
issues, including those related to the rights of disabled people, were thus
informed by this 'baggage' I brought to the job.

By virtue of the sheer size of the department and range of responsibilities, the department of health consumed most of my time. But the range of
portfolios assigned to me, combined with my interest in human rights, provided me with insights to make connections with issues such as women's
problems in the workplace, rights and entitlements of disabled adults and
children, to name a few.[4] Speaking from a purely 'bureaucratic' division of
tasks, matters relating to disabled persons and disability fell within the
purview of the Ministry of Social Welfare and Special Education (unless
people with disability accessed facilities and or sought health care and services). Despite this bifurcation of ministerial domains, I tried to engage
with vulnerable groups including people with disability, an approach sometimes perceived as digression from the 'straight and narrow' path of
portfolios assigned to me.

Before we proceed further, Pakistan's governmental structure requires
some clarification here. It is a large (South Asian) country both in terms of
geography and population. Pakistan is a federation comprising four
provinces, Baluchistan, North West Frontier Province (NWFP), Punjab,
Sindh and (in a different legal framework), the Northern Areas (NA) and
Azad Jammu and Kashmir (AJ&K).[5] Two sets of governments, federal and
provincial, operate simultaneously and have each a legislature, executive
and judiciary. The constitution outlines areas of operation of each government with major overlaps in jurisdiction especially in the social sector
(health, education, social welfare, etc.) The federal government, however,
is more policy-oriented in the performance of its role because 'action' is in
the provinces as that is where the population is!

Let me now present you with the (in)visible hierarchy in ministries. The
Finance and Interior Ministries are, for obvious reasons, positioned at the
top of the governmental pyramid with Health and Education close sec-
onds. Social Welfare and Special Education, Women's Development,
Sports, Tourism, Archaeology, Youth Affairs, Religious Affairs and so on,
are spread at the lower end of this pyramid. Whereas the Finance Ministry

draws 'strength' because it holds the purse strings of government and the Interior Ministry commands and controls law-enforcing agencies including the police force, Education and Health Ministries are mainstream and have influence due to the number of employees as well as their direct dealing with the public. On the other hand, the Ministry of Social Welfare and Special Education has as its brief the welfare of vulnerable sections of society, women, children and persons with disability including the education of 'special children' and exists both at federal and provincial levels. Looking at its budgetary allocation, reach and importance within the governmental structure, it is evident that it has a low priority.

Now coming to the North West Frontier Province (NWFP),[6] this is one of the smaller provinces of Pakistan, not so much in terms of territory but by population, which is 14 million out of 150 million for the whole of Pakistan.[7] The infrastructure is very patchy and unevenly developed, not least due to the difficult terrain and economic development and opportunities.[8] Indigenous resources of the province are limited and potential wealth underexploited, hence funding for social sector development from provincial resources is not very high.[9] This inadequacy has implications for infrastructure (building and roads, health facilities, education, employment opportunities and so on). More importantly, poor infrastructure inhibits access to whatever resources and services are available to people in the NWFP. In view of meagre funding, the uneven terrain becomes a huge impediment to accessing existing institutions. NWFP has a few fertile valleys and urban centres where schools, colleges, universities and health facilities are relatively easy to approach.[10]

Professionals tend to concentrate on working and living here as their children can go to good schools, enjoy a better quality of life and so on. But major parts of the province are either mountainous or barren. Basic amenities of life are virtually non-existent in these areas and as a result, governmental presence in terms of health facilities, roads and educational institutions is thinner on the ground. Health professionals and other government personnel are reluctant to serve in these 'under-privileged' or 'difficult' stations and try to get posted out as soon as they possibly can. If the mainstream sectors of health and education are so inadequately serviced in these areas, what chance of service delivery does the social welfare department stand, catering for vulnerable groups of people with disability?[11]

This brings us to the chequered constitutional history and legal framework of Pakistan. The country was carved out of the Indian subcontinent to provide a separate homeland for the Muslims of India in August 1947 (on the departure of the British colonizers). The Government of India Act 1935 and the Indian Independence Act 1947 became the legal vehicles for running the newly found country whilst a constituent assembly was formed to deliberate on drafting a constitution. This proved to be a more daunting task than had been anticipated and a number of issues, central to nationhood, citizenship, rights and obligations and so on, led to protracted confrontation, controversy and thus a hindrance to consensus.[12] Laws and institutions in Pakistan are plural and often operating at parallel levels, resulting in a complex framework. If one were to present a graphic description of the legal pluralities informing people's lives in Pakistan, they would appear as concentric circles in the following order: the constitution of Pakistan and the statute law as outer rings of this circle with religious laws and customary practices as the resilient inner core closest to people's lives.

As I have indicated elsewhere,[13] a common element in postcolonial statehood is a written constitution inspired by either the 'Westminster' or the 'Capitol Hill' model. The constituent assembly of Pakistan too debated this issue, opting for a parliamentary regime of government. Later constitutions changed and rechanged tracks.[14] Coupled with incorporating parliamentary and/or presidential forms of government is the fact that the Universal Declaration of Human Rights (UDHR) has found a place in the fundamental rights chapters of more than two dozen Asian, African and Middle Eastern constitutions, including Pakistan.[15]

Whatever differences presented themselves in the form of governments espoused by various constitutions, all (constitutional) documents of Pakistan included a fundamental rights chapter, most of its provisions lifted almost verbatim from the UDHR. It is very interesting to note that at least 33 countries (mostly former colonies) have fundamental rights chapters inspired by and almost copied from the UDHR. I find it amusing that, on the one hand, there exists such close synergy between concepts of domestic, regional and international human rights regimes, and on the other, some societies are adopting the position that human rights is a construct alien to non-Western societies. How does one analyse this seeming contradiction in terms, especially when the UDHR has been 'internalized' into constitutions and laws?

To date Pakistan has had four constitutions,[16] coinciding with the fall of civilian regimes and installation of military governments. The present constitution of Pakistan is as modern and contemporary a document as you may find in any part of the world. Its fundamental rights chapter is justiciable and enforceable in a court of law,[17] and another chapter (2) entitled 'Principles of policy' contains a further catalogue of entitlements.[18] For the purposes of our discussion on people with disability, it is the latter that makes reference to protection of special groups and special needs. Despite their being cast in a welfarist framework and subject to available governmental resources, Articles 37 and 38 in particular are noteworthy in terms of the potential for advancing social justice. There is no dedicated constitutional provision addressing rights of disabled persons but Article 38 makes some oblique references to their protection:

> [38] Promotion of social and economic well-being of the people. – The State shall ... (d) provide basic necessities of life, such as food, clothing, housing, education and medical relief, for all such citizens, irrespective

of sex, caste, creed or race, as are *permanently or temporarily unable to earn their livelihood on account of infirmity, sickness or unemployment* [emphasis added].

But the problem here is that the working and the character of the Principles of Policy are different from fundamental rights. The latter are enforceable in a court of law, whereas the principles of policy document is prefaced by the proviso: 'subject to available resources of the government'. Recalling the internalizing and domestication of human rights, bifurcation of rights as 'fundamental' and 'principles of policy' follows a pattern similar to international human rights instruments (the International Covenant of Civil and Political Rights and the International Covenant on Economic, Social and Cultural Rights). Human rights literature continues to debate whether economic, social and cultural rights are as 'real' as their counterparts, civil and political rights.

From the perspective of disabled people, this dichotomy of rights has adverse implications because it is through principles of policy that their needs can be more usefully addressed. Whilst equal rights provisions exist, both in the constitution and statute laws of Pakistan, rarely are these actually invoked for rights of disabled people. It is almost as if by creating some affirmative action opportunities, they are somehow detached from mainstream legal mechanisms. As it is, these are people living on the margins and by creating a few special laws, society believes it has done its bit for disabled people!

Interpreting laws and applying them is always contested territory. Just as the (in)famous 'he includes she' approach in legislative enactments did not really envisage this 'she' as using the law, we have a similar approach towards people with disability. Since they are not considered 'mainstream' people there is a perception in some quarters that they require special laws and regulatory frameworks. These measures include affirmative action, quotas in schools, jobs and so on. But this approach is a double-edged sword. On the one hand there is the view that state and society ought to facilitate persons with disability to be perceived as mainstream citizens by using the equality provisions of the law. This approach opens up the question of whether such a policy leaves them vulnerable and disadvantaged in competing for resources with the non-disabled population. This fear becomes the rationale for special measures, laws and policies. Pakistan too has developed a regime of policies and laws for addressing the needs of persons with disability, a brief overview of which is presented below.

Governmental policies for disabled people: work in progress?

We spoke briefly of the fundamental rights and principles of policy outlined in the constitution of Pakistan. In order to supplement these general principles, special ministries in federal and provincial governments have been set up focusing on 'social welfare' including disabled persons. In response to the UN Year of Disabled Persons, the Government of Pakistan generated an awareness campaign on rights of disabled people. An important outcome was The Disabled Persons (Employment & Rehabilitation) Ordinance promulgated in December 1981. Under Section (3) of the ordinance, the National Council for the Rehabilitation of Disabled Persons (NCRDP) was established in the four provinces.[19] One important provision of the ordinance is the introduction of a quota system in relation to employment and the introduction of the entitlement to terms and conditions that are no less favourable than to other employees. In 2000, the quota for disabled persons in employment was raised to 2 per cent.[20] A similar quota is provided for places in technical and professional institutes. The new measures, among others, declare that disabled people are now entitled to free education, free health care, and fare concessions on airlines, railways and other public transport systems.

These policies of the government have their detractors who argue that government is perpetuating and institutionalizing a culture of hand-outs rather than creating opportunities for disabled people to become part of the national mainstream.[21] Government officials, on the other hand, respond by saying that they have made an earnest beginning and since this was a neglected area in the past, it will take some time to catch up. According to the 1998 census of the Pakistan government, the overall percentage of disabled persons is 2.49 per cent, which has been queried by a number of agencies and organizations and the actual statistics are believed to be much higher. For instance the website of the Asia-Pacific Development Center on Disability claims it is generally estimated that around one-tenth of the population of Pakistan, 150 million people, live with disability. It makes the point that the government is also trying to tackle the causes of disability which are seen to be mainly due to poor prenatal and post-natal health care facilities in most of the country.[22]

The Institutional Framework for addressing issues related to disabled persons in Pakistan means that responsibility is spread across a range of departments and ministries but as I have already mentioned, government policies and facilities for disabled people are limited. Most institutions in the private sector that do address these issues have developed as a result of the personal initiatives of parents or close family of disabled children who have tried to fill the gaps in the state system. I am personally aware of at least three such institutions in the NWFP that started as small play groups and gradually developed into fully fledged institutions.

In the context of Pakistan, there are two other sets of laws broadly defined which provide an overarching framework, stronger and more potent, than the constitution and the black letter law. The first of them is religion and the other, customary practices. So what does religion say in terms of how family, state or society ought to treat or meet the needs of people with disability, and second, what are customary norms regarding people with disability?

Conceptualizing disability in Islam: a brief overview

Pakistan is a predominantly Muslim country with 97–98 per cent of the population professing the Islamic religion. The Qur'an is believed by Muslims to be the very word of God revealed to the Prophet Muhammad over a period of 23 years. It acts as a constitution of social justice and, supplemented by Hadith or the words and deeds of the prophet Muhammad, constitutes the primary sources of Islamic law. The Qur'an and Hadith outline the rights of people with disabilities and special needs, conceptualizing them from a human rights perspective. But as noted by Bazna and Hatab in their study entitled 'Disability in the Qur'an: The Islamic alternative to defining, viewing and relating to disability', and I quote at length:

> we find that the concept of disability, in the conventional sense, is not found in the Qur'an. As a matter of a fact, our search for the word *disabled* and its derivates did not return any results. Rather, we find that the Qur'an concentrates on the notion of *disadvantage* that is created by society and imposed on those individuals who might not possess the social, economic, or physical attributes that people happen to value at a certain time and place. Since this disadvantage is created by society, it isn't surprising that the Qur'an places the responsibility of rectifying this inequity on the shoulder of society by its constant exhortation to Muslims to recognize the plight of the disadvantaged and to improve their condition and status.[23]

Some of the Qur'anic verses regarding treatment of persons with disability and Hadith include the following:

> [N]o blame attaches to the blind, nor does blame attach to the lame, nor does blame attach to the sick, and neither to yourselves for eating [whatever is offered to you by others, whether it be food obtained] from your [children's] houses, or your fathers' houses, or your mothers' houses, or your brothers' houses, or your sisters' houses, or your paternal uncles' houses, or your paternal aunts' houses, or your maternal uncles' houses, or your maternal aunts' houses, or [houses] the keys whereof are in your charge, or [the house] of any of your friends; nor will you incur any sin by eating in company or separately. But whenever you enter [any of these] houses, greet one another with a blessed, goodly greeting, as enjoined by God. In this way God makes clear unto you His message, so that you might [learn to] use your reason.
>
> (24:61)

This verse attempts to remove from people's minds superstitious notions attached to interacting with disabled persons, including the lame, alongside the blind and the sick.

Another Qur'anic verse states:

> Do you know the one who denies the (Day of) Judgement? It is he who pushes the orphan away, and urges not to feed the needy. Woe, then unto those praying ones, who are heedless of their prayers, who want to be seen and praised, and refuse (to give) even little things in charity.[24]

In some translations, the term 'indigent' has been used instead of 'needy' and includes those who are unable to fulfil their own needs.

> He frowned and turned away because the blind man approached him! Yet for all thou didst know, [O, Muhammad,] he might perhaps have grown in purity, or have been reminded [of the truth], and helped by this reminder. Now as for him who believes himself to be self-sufficient – to him didst thou give thy whole attention, although thou art not accountable for his failure to attain to purity; but as for him who came unto thee full of eagerness and in awe [of God] – him didst thou disregard![25]

The above verses indicate the sort of treatment that people with disabilities ought to be given, i.e. with full regard and respect as granted to the non-disabled.

Sabiq narrates a Hadith that epitomizes societal obligations towards disabled persons. When asked by one of his companions:

> '[F]rom what do we give sadaqah if we do not possess property?'[26] Muhammad replied, 'The doors of sadaqah are ... guiding the blind; listening to the deaf and mute until you understand them; guiding a person to his object of need if you know where it is; hurrying with the strength of your legs to one in sorrow who is appealing for help; and supporting the weak with the strength of your arms'.[27]

The Islamic ethos of equality of all human beings and mainstreaming disabled persons is evident in the following saying of the Prophet Muhammad:

> Verily, God does not look at your bodies or your appearances, but looks into your hearts.[28]

> Turn not your cheek away from people in scorn and pride, and walk not on earth haughtily; for God does not love anyone who acts proudly and boastfully. Be modest in your bearing and lower your voice; for the ugliest sound is the donkey's braying.[29]

From the Qur'anic verses and sayings of the Prophet Muhammad, it is evident that the overarching tone of these pronouncements is corrective, protective and non-discriminatory. Simultaneously, the Qur'an places clear obligations on family, state and society to share and care for people with disabilities. The contradiction is the stark contrast between the rhetoric of the Qur'anic text, Hadith, constitutional provisions, statutory laws and policies relating to people with disability and society's perception of them. This is where serious reflection and thinking are required. I am often concerned at how things written on paper in one form are applied in a very different spirit. What causes this contradiction, when the law acknowledges that we are not all the same, but being different does not necessarily mean one is any less a human being? Religion, too, is saying exactly that. So why are the perceptions of society on disability so confused, sterile and apathetic to the rights and needs of this section of society?

State and society's responses to disability: rhetoric and reality

Having placed persons with disability in the context of the legal framework, religion and customary norms, I would now like to share some of my specific experiences of contact with disabled people when I was a minister. The narrative below is also a synthesis of my understanding regarding non-disabled people's perceptions of those who are disabled in Pakistan. Any discussion of the rights of disabled people, including the right to life, has to take account of the ways that they are perceived and valued by others.

A major role of the ministerial office is to meet people and this of course included people with disability. The stream of visitors is heaviest in the early days, not least from a sense of curiosity regarding the new occupant of a ministerial office. I sensed a certain reluctance, bordering on sullen resistance and suspicion, on the part of employees in the various ministries when engaging with disabled persons. This reluctance extended to impeding access to me, especially when the request to meet was repetitive. Under-the-breath muttering of 'Oh my God, here they are again!' and 'Now what?', as well as snippets of conversation, suggested the impatience and a sense of what society was thinking of disabled persons. Once I was told to my face to reflect on the idea that 'There is something very sinister about how they came to be the way they are ... Have you ever thought that if God made them different, then there must be something to all this?' My response was quite simple, 'It is not for me to start acting like God and interpreting why some people are disabled and others not'. Then there would be the subsequent questions: 'Do you know that these people's disability has made them very aggressive and very devious? They know they are not able to access facilities and entitlements in the normal way, so they have to engage in a sort of play-acting'. In other words, there are some deviant thought processes amongst the disabled whereby they will 'come at you' and try to manipulate you. It was probably for the first time in my life that in my conversations with Janet Read, I mustered up the courage to speak out aloud and repeat these uncharitable comments and the degree of prejudice that I had encountered. I felt very uncomfortable expressing what others had said; I had to mull this over and ask people again and again at various junctures just to make sure that this really was what they were saying, and I wasn't extrapolating. In a nutshell, the formula was 'not normal, read deviant and not necessarily deserving of your support' because they are quite capable of looking after their own interests.

In some ways, the preconceptions, wariness, inhibitions and anxiety I witnessed are similar to those experienced when dealing with any 'difference' in the wider sense, be it ethnic, linguistic or religious minorities. What I find disturbing is how on earth society has come to the conclusion that disabled persons are inherently of lower value and competence than people seen as 'mainstream'. These issues and questions continue to trouble me. So for instance, what is the basis for interpreting people with disability as 'not normal' or defining them as 'deviant'? Is there any evidence that life histories, behavioural patterns and aspirations of people with disability are different from 'mainstream' people and if so, does this matter? Why does a flawed and unsubstantiated perception inform our world view of a section of society that is different from the one we occupy?

Here I am reminded of my encounter with the president of an association for the blind from one of the rural districts of the NWFP. He was very persistent in his request to call on me, and so a date was set for the meeting. I was impressed with how this man, who was himself blind, had set up an organization after undertaking a survey of all the visually impaired people in that district. He compiled a membership list of more than 200 visually impaired persons and registered an association. Everything from a register of members to a charter of demands including free health care, education and employment was included. He then set about lobbying relevant departments and institutions to actualize these demands using provisions of the constitution, as well as laws and policies of affirmative action to articulate their demands for jobs, places in educational institutions and so on. In his meeting with me, he raised the request for a hospital card that would give access to health facilities and free medicines and services. He also came up with a specific request: he wanted me to use my discretionary funds to supply 175 of his members with white canes. He had even worked out the unit cost of each cane and which shop we could order them from! My immediate response to all this information and lobbying was one of admiration and amazement. Here was a blind man from the backwaters of the province who had organized an entire community, searched for laws, rules and regulations to use to his advantage. If it had been any other group of people, words including 'proactive', 'politically savvy' and so on would have been employed in a positive way to describe this association and its members. The president would certainly have been described as a 'go-getter' with remarkable leadership qualities. Because this was a person with a disability, however, the response was: 'What a cheeky fellow; he is really devious, isn't he? Look how he is going round trying to dig up all these laws, to his advantage, and he is harassing you, the minister, in trying to extract more and more favours ...' It was telling that my decision to fund white canes from resources already set aside for such needs was interpreted by others as a 'favour'. I subsequently had a great deal of public and private contact with this man and the association he had formed and I was impressed with his political astuteness. He used any opportunity he could to raise the profile of the association and to lobby for changes that would benefit the membership of visually impaired people. His efforts and the success he achieved continued to give rise to negative comments by people in the ministry: 'You have given him a very bad habit Madam Minister'. I found this disconcerting and wondered whether we would have seen similar reactions had the recipient of ministerial attention been for instance a nurses' association, a paramedics' association or a doctors' association. Is it because the political process isn't seen to be for the likes of disabled people?

Following on from the episode of the president of the association for visually impaired people, I now want to share my interaction with persons at the 'mental hospital' (as it was called) in Peshawar which left me in grave distress. This group of disabled persons are undoubtedly subjected to some of the worst forms of neglect and treatment. Strangely enough, my most vivid introduction to the way that people with mental health problems are perceived by society came from the novel *Jane Eyre* which I read years ago as a teenager in a boarding school hundreds of miles away from home and the NWFP. Images of Mrs Rochester created so effectively in *Jane Eyre* more than a century ago came back to me on my visit to the mental hospital in Peshawar, thousands of miles away from Victorian England. It dawned on me that the culture of feeling 'ashamed' of a relative with disability, shunning them and restricting their liberty might well be a universal trend. So much for protagonists of cultural relativism!

As soon as I set foot in the courtyard of the mental hospital, I felt a chill run down my spine. It was not the physical temperature as it was a hot summer's day, but the air was emotionally cold, lacking warmth. I still remember the red brick floor, squeaky clean (in anticipation of a ministerial visit?), but the place was cold, its surroundings barren, grey and forlorn on a bright summer's day. The doctors were evidently a committed group who were doing their best but obviously were no replacement for loved ones. The institution was such that the lives of those living there were completely bereft of those things which are important to all human beings. I spent some time trying to make conversation with the patients but with little success. Some were totally disengaged, making personal contact and interaction almost impossible. There were women of all ages and from different parts of the province. Each one had a history that spoke volumes about the way that family, community and society can withdraw care, love and support from its disabled members because they are unable to or do not want to deal with 'difference'. The stories of two women provide examples of this.

I remember meeting an elderly woman, a long-term patient whose records went back about 20 years. No one knew her name and there were no details of her family. Some aspects of her history had been pieced together on those occasions years before, when she had lucid moments. It seemed likely that she came from Dir, a remote area 150 miles away from Peshawar. It was also likely that she had been brought to the hospital by the police 20 years earlier after she had been found wandering in the wilderness somewhere near to her home area. She had remained in the hospital since that time without contact with her family or community and without hope of being restored to a more ordinary life. There was also a young woman, barely 20 years old, who came from a well-off family in Kohat, a small town an hour's drive from the capital city of Peshawar. The doctor told me that she had explained to the family how the young woman's mental health problem had been a transitory phase and was cured and past – what the girl needed now was her own family and familiar environment. The relatives, however, said quite categorically that the hospital would have to look after the girl from now on because they did not wish to bring shame on their family by having a 'mad' person in their midst.

I felt sad and angry about the fact that the easy way for societies to deal with people with mental health difficulties is to keep them hidden from view. In other words, in the absence of not being able to wish them away, families and society at least keep them invisible. I see this as a main issue in addressing disability in Pakistan because societal perception of imperfection is akin to a shameful act. So, if a mother gives birth to a disabled child it is somehow believed to be an adverse reflection on the parents or family in general. This attitude is taken to a point where they try to hide the child from the world around them, pretending that this disabled person does not exist. I feel that this is a major right to life issue, because apart from issues of restriction of liberty, significant in themselves, there can be no doubt that in these circumstances the deaths of these disabled people are sometimes hastened by sheer neglect.

Following my reflections on the mental hospital visit, I discovered another link that also caused me deep distress: the geographical proximity of the mental hospital and prison in Peshawar. Although not the case any longer, for decades these two institutions existed side by side. They shared a common road, one main entrance and two gates side by side. There was one secure compound from which you entered either the prison or (through an adjacent gate), the mental hospital. I am not sure whether this description is able to portray the strong image and message this proximity brings to mind, but I was very concerned and distressed by the way that it was seen as appropriate for people who were mentally ill and those at variance with the law to be placed adjacent to each other and in similar circumstances. The atmospheres of the mental hospital and the prison were almost identical; attitudes towards the prisoners and those who were mentally ill were similar as were the perceptions of society towards their predicaments. The message coming across loud and clear in unspoken words was: dissociate yourselves from prisoners and the disabled because they fall outside the realm of normalcy and normality.

As I indicated earlier, these visits had a very intense impact on my thinking and priorities. I wondered what I could do to make life a bit more humane for the women in the mental hospital and the organization of a patients' support group brought some small benefits. In collaboration with this group, we were able to improve the material surroundings of the institution, by decorating the walls and getting carpets, furniture and a television. Tea and refreshments were introduced for the women to have mid-morning. The funds were raised to build a new gate so that the separation from the prison was emphasized. As with some of the other work in relation to disabled people, these developments bemused some of my colleagues in the civil service and I had to explain that for the women in the hospital and for me this was a human rights issue: the right to live with dignity and respect. But facilitating a small section of the population when resources for everyone are scarce does not really hold water for some, particularly when disability comes right down at the bottom of the priority lists of government, society and families.

Commodifying disability

Human nature throws up all sorts of contradictions and dealing with disability is one such instance where gaps between theory and practice, perceptions and actions simply do not add up. As indicated earlier, many if not most communities and families in Pakistan are not supportive of their disabled members. Many disabled people therefore end up on the streets, begging for food and money, and are thus vulnerable to abuse. Some of them are placed at shrines of saints where many people come to visit. A disabled beggar is a commoner sight than a non-disabled person begging and is seen to evoke a stronger sense of compassion and tendency to give. It is known that because of this, gangs kidnap children, maim them and send them out to beg. It is interesting to reflect on why people may be more prone to 'kindness' in coming across a disabled child begging in the street, when in all probability they would neglect or abandon that same child were it to be a member of their community or family? Perhaps it is that having transitory contact and giving alms to a disabled child who remains an outsider is very different from acknowledging that child as being part of the same human community as yourself.

Unfortunately, in some communities disability is also considered to be related to evil spirits and the disabled person as being 'possessed' of those spirits and acting at their behest. It is not uncommon to see a family taking their 'possessed' child (or adult) to shrines and faith healers in an effort to drive the evil spirit out of the person. I have heard dreadful stories of how faith healers have attempted to 'thrash' the evil spirit out of the disabled person. Now this problem requires active public campaigning and advocacy especially by members of the medical profession who have authority and a voice. Human rights advocates and NGOs too have an important role to play as have religious scholars.

At this point I would like to share another observation regarding strategies for reform and acceptance of policies seemingly extraneous to cultural and religious norms. The conceptual framework for reform has to take account of the plural legalities of a society and Pakistani society is no exception. Religion forms an important part of people's identity and their reluctance to accept certain governmental policies is sometimes based upon real or perceived contradictions with Islam. Population planning and contraception is one such area where popular perception was that this is un-Islamic and hence unacceptable. In relation to this, there was no point in using any other language but that of religion and so I based my arguments about population planning and contraception on the Qur'an and Hadith, recalling verses of the Qur'an as well as sayings of the Prophet Muhammad regarding human rights of women and children.

In understanding issues relating to disability too, I referred to the Islamic tradition and would gently remind colleagues of the verses of the Qur'an and Hadith (cited above) that refuted dominant oppressive attitudes towards disabled people. It was hugely uncomfortable for some to be reminded of God and duties to all humankind.

In this context, the institution of *zakat* and related concepts of *sadaqah* and *ushr* form the basis of the social justice framework of Islam and this is highly relevant to the position of disabled people. It stems from the belief that God has endowed different people with different capacities and each has the obligation to contribute to society according to this capability. Those who have more will share with those who are unable to meet their own needs. This giving is not a personal gift or charity but a redistribution of resources, a form of redistributive justice. *Zakat* is an *entitlement* for the vulnerable sections of society and because of the obligation that is entailed, an argument can be made that it was not owned in the first place by the person who makes the contribution. In this way, it is distinguished from charity. As a religious concept, *zakat* forms the third pillar of Islam and is calculated in accordance with well developed principles (usually as an annual payment of 2.5 per cent of all capital assets, savings and current income above a certain threshold known as *nisab*).

I believe that when addressing issues of social justice, rights and obligations in relation to disabled people or any other group, it is important for members of society to be able to internalize a concept or approach. Legitimacy, validation and action that stem from it are more achievable from within the sociocultural and religious normative framework in a particular context. It is easier to build an argument on it, and one is not accused of being culturally insensitive or imperialistic, and it is less likely to be seen as an imposition from above or outside.

Notes

1 The present chapter is the result of a number of extended conversations on the subject with Janet Read and credit for its inclusion in this collection is entirely hers! Thank you Janet for your perseverance and faith in my offerings.
2 I was also Chair of the National Commission on the Status of Women from September 2000–2001.
3 Very few academics have been offered cabinet positions and as a legal academic, I felt this was a positive initiative, despite the ideological controversies generated.
4 See my chapter entitled 'Where is the toilet? Getting down to basics in accessing women's rights', in Anne Hellum, Julie Stewart, Shaheen Sardar Ali and Amy Tsanga (eds) (2007) *Human Rights, Plural Legalities and Gendered Realities: Paths are Made by Walking.* Harare: Weaver Books, Chapter 12.
5 For a detailed discussion on this nomenclature of the Government of Pakistan and its federating units, see S.S. Ali and J. Rehman, (2001) *Indigenous Peoples and Ethnic Minorities of Pakistan Constitutional and Legal Perspectives.* London: Nordic Institute of Asian Studies Press/Curzon Press, p. 184.
6 The NWFP government website, www.nwfp.gov.pk describes the province in the following words:

> North West Frontier Province is a province of the Islamic Republic of Pakistan, located on both banks of the river Indus and stretches from the Himalayas in the north to the deserts in the south where it is bordered by the Baluchistan and Punjab provinces. On its western flank is the rugged terrain of neighbouring country Afghanistan, which is accessed via the historic Khyber Pass through the mountains of the Suleiman Range. Its borders touch or are close to those of China, the Tajikistan and the disputed territory of the state of Jammu and Kashmir in the north. The capital of the province is the city of Peshawar.

7 The figure of 14 million is taken from the NWFP government's official website. When I was in cabinet, the figures quoted were much higher and included approximately three million Afghan refugees, a majority of whom came into the country at the time of the Soviet invasion of Afghanistan.
8 NWFP covers an area of 74,521 sq. km. According to the 1998 census, the total population of NWFP was approximately 14 million of whom 52 per cent are male and 48 per cent female. Geographically the province may be divided into two zones: the northern zone extending from the ranges of the Hindukush to the borders of Peshawar basin; and the southern one extending from Peshawar to the Derajat basin. The northern zone is cold and snowy in winters with heavy rainfall and pleasant summers with the exception of the Peshawar basin, which is hot in summer and cold in winter. It has moderate rainfall. The southern zone has hot summers and relatively cold winters and scant rainfall. Its climate varies from very cold (Chitral in the north) to very hot in places like D.I. Khan (source: official website of the Government of the NWFP).
9 The major wealth of the province is hydroelectric power, but there is a lot of controversy there because it is considered a national resource, and we are only handed out a small fraction of that to feed back into developmental projects in the province.

10 These include Peshawar (the capital of the NWFP), Abbottabad, Mingora/Saidu Sharif, Dera Ismail Khan, Kohat and Bannu.

11 It is important to make the point that 70 per cent of the population of Pakistan live in rural areas where infrastructure is at a bare minimum.

12 It is not within the remit of the present chapter to engage in a discussion on these issues. Suffice it to say that implications of becoming an Islamic state were given conflicting meaning; rights of minorities, religious, linguistic and ethnic, caused dissent among a hitherto seemingly united polity.

13 S.S. Ali, (2000) *Gender and Human Rights in Islam and International Law: Equal Before Allah, Unequal Before Man?* The Hague: Kluwer Law International, p.94.

14 The 1956 constitution envisaged a parliamentary form of government whereas the 1962 constitution took a U-turn to a presidential form. The present constitution of 1973 presents a parliamentary form.

15 See A.H. Robertson and J.G. Merrills, (1989) *Human Rights in the World*. 3rd edn, Manchester: Manchester University Press, p.27.

16 Adopted in 1956, 1962, 1972 and the existing one 1973.

17 Articles 8–28 of Chapter 1 of the constitution of Pakistan. These rights include: security of person (Article 9), safeguards as to arrest and detention (Article 10), slavery, forced labour, etc. prohibited (Article 11), protection against retrospective punishment (Article 12), protection from double punishment and self-incrimination (Article 13), inviolability of dignity of man, etc. (Article 14), freedom of movement, etc. (Article 15), freedom of assembly (Article 16), freedom of trade, business or profession (Article 18), freedom of speech, etc. (Article 19), freedom to profess religion and manage religious institutions (Article 20), safeguard against taxation for purposes of any particular religion (Article 21), safeguard as to educational institutions in respect of religion, etc. (Article 22), provision as to property (Article 23), protection of property rights (Article 24), equality of citizens (Article 25), non-discrimination in respect of access to public places (Article 26), safeguard against discrimination in services (Article 27), preservation of language, script and culture (28).

18 Principles of policy include requiring government to enable an Islamic way of life (Article 31), promoting local government institutions (Article 32), discouraging parochial and other similar prejudices (Article 33), taking steps to ensure full participation of women in national life (Article 34), protecting marriage, the family, the mother and child (Article 35), safeguarding rights of minorities (Article 36), promotion of social justice and eradication of social evils (Article 37) and promotion of social and economic well-being of the people (Article 38).

19 Matters pertaining to disabled people belonging to ICT, FANA and FATA are directly processed by NCRDP.

20 A news item of *Daily Times* dated 3 December 2006 stated the following:

> NWFP Ministry for Social Welfare has asked the provincial government not to advertise jobs without mentioning two percent quota for disabled persons. The minister said that apart from the Provincial Council for the Disabled, a Council for Social Welfare was also helping special people, adding that 4 per cent of the total grants provided by the Department of *Zakat* to the districts was spent on the disabled.

21 This statement was cited in an article entitled 'Pakistan's disabled unimpressed by new welfare scheme' by Muddassir Rizvi, accessed from *Asia Times Online* in May 2000.

22 Ibid.

23 M.S. Bazna and T.A. Hatab (2005) 'Disability in the Qur'an: The Islamic alternative to defining, viewing and relating to disability', *Journal of Religion, Disability and Health*, 9, 5–27, at p.26.

24 The Qur'an 107: 1–7.
25 The Qur'an 80: 1–10. These verses relate to Amr bin Um Muktum, a blind companion of the Prophet Muhammad who came to him to seek a clarification on verses of the Qur'an. The Prophet is said to have been agitated with him as he intruded upon a very important meeting.
26 *Sadaqah* is a collective term that typically signifies giving of material possessions. It is something to be performed by each Muslim every day for her or his own good and reward in this life and the life hereafter.
27 Sabiq 3.98.
28 Muslim 2564.
29 The Qur'an 31: 18–19.

7 Human rights aspects of deaths of institutionalized people with disabilities in Europe

Jan Fiala and Oliver Lewis

Introduction

This chapter draws on the authors' work at the Mental Disability Advocacy Center (MDAC), an international non-governmental organization based in Budapest, Hungary. MDAC advances the human rights of adults and children with actual or perceived mental health problems or intellectual disabilities. It works in several European countries, predominantly former socialist countries of central and eastern Europe. With its partner organizations, the MDAC represents clients in domestic and international courts, conducts policy-oriented research and advocates for the advancement of human rights at the intergovernmental level.

In this chapter we outline the structure of services in central and eastern Europe and examine state obligations under the European Convention on Human Rights (ECHR) to protect the right to life and to investigate deaths.[1] We then analyse the extent to which countries in central Europe comply with convention obligations, and the chapter concludes with an examination of some obstacles which make it difficult or impossible for people with disabilities to access justice.

We argue that effective investigations of deaths and alleged ill-treatment are an important component in every country's legal system, because they can prevent unnecessary mistreatment and deaths in institutions by revealing circumstances of deaths, punish those responsible and can be used as the basis for remedying deficiencies.

Social care and psychiatric services in central and eastern Europe

The unifying feature of social care in former socialist countries of central and eastern Europe is institutionalization. The European Coalition for Community Living, a new pan-Europe umbrella group, sets out a definition of an institution:

> An institution is any place in which people who have been labelled as having a disability are isolated, segregated and/or compelled to live

together. An institution is any place in which people do not have, or are not allowed to exercise control over their lives and their day-to-day decisions. An institution is not defined merely by its size.[2]

Despite governments across the region promising to de-institutionalize large institutions and establish more humane community services, the legacy of large institutions ('social care homes' and psychiatric hospitals) remains, with little evidence of action. It is these institutions where many people with perceived or actual disabilities spend their entire lives, where violence is rife, where there are few trained staff, where there is overcrowding and boredom, and where there is little scrutiny of staff. In this environment abuse and neglect sometimes result in deaths. This chapter explores this phenomenon, and argues that preventable and un-investigated deaths are human rights concerns which governments, professional bodies and civil society stakeholders need to address in each country.

The Czech Republic is a good example of a central European country which relies on institutions. With a population of around ten million people, the Czech Republic belongs to the most developed post-Communist states. It joined the European Union in 2004 and has a gross domestic product similar to that of Portugal.[3] In 2004 there were more than 1,000 institutions with a capacity ranging from fewer than ten to more than 427, providing social care to approximately 80,000 people.[4] Two-hundred-and-eighty-three of these institutions had a capacity of 100 persons or more, 64 of them 200 persons or more. The majority were homes for the elderly or for people with disabilities.

In 2004 there were 275 'social care institutions' in the Czech Republic for people with disabilities, the institutions having a total capacity of 20,333 people. There were separate institutions for adults and children with 'mental' disabilities,[5] physical disabilities, sensory disabilities, combined disabilities, 'psychotics and psychopaths' and people with substance abuse problems. The figures are much the same for Hungary, a country with a similar population size as the Czech Republic. In Poland around 50,000 people lived in more than 400 institutions for people with psychosocial and intellectual disabilities.[6] Similar figures existed for other countries in the region.

In these institutions people with disabilities are isolated from society. Institutions typically provide long-term accommodation for people who have lost contact with their relatives or do not have any relatives. Residents rarely leave the institutions, seldom receive visitors and typically stay there until they die. In most countries there are no state-funded inspectorate mechanisms monitoring human rights compliance within institutions, and few non-governmental organizations carry out such visits. As a result, the lives and deaths of hundreds of thousands of European citizens remain hidden.

Accessing human rights data in institutions is difficult. Most governments do not keep statistics on the number and causes of deaths in institutions and therefore it is impossible to make comparisons between institutional and community mortality rates. However, the available figures raise questions.

For example, according to MDAC research, in the Czech Republic in 2004, 10,036 children under the age of 18 were living in 141 institutions for youth with 'mental disabilities'. During the same year there were 5,260 people living in 64 institutions for adults with mental disabilities. The fate of these children on reaching adulthood is unexplained, yet it is rare for a child with disabilities to be re-integrated into society, because (save for a few run by NGOs) there are no community support services available. On reaching the age of 18, most children are transferred to adult institutions, but adult institutions have capacity for only half of the children living in child institutions. One explanation for what happens to children reaching 18 is that some are kept in children's homes. Another explanation could be that a significant proportion of children in institutions die before they reach the age of 18. There is simply no data to support or refute this supposition.

Causes of death in institutions

Institutions are dangerous places. MDAC research suggests that there are many practices that endanger the lives of residents living in state care in central Europe. Governments make little effort to reveal the living conditions of people with disabilities, to investigate the reasons leading to deaths or to improve the situation in institutions. Our research and practice has unfortunately provided us with only limited access to institutions and their residents, and so we are only able to provide a few examples of life-threatening practices taken from different countries in the region.

Physical and chemical restraints

Restraints commonly used in social care and psychiatric institutions in the region include physical restraint by staff, leather straps, towels tied to chairs, cage (and 'net') beds, seclusion rooms and large doses of tranquilizers and other psychiatric medications.[7] To the best of our knowledge no government has statistics available on the frequency and circumstances of the use of these restraints. The authors' interviews with users of mental health services have revealed that restraints and seclusion are often used as a punishment or threat of punishment. For example, when one patient in a Slovakian psychiatric hospital became aggressive, others told him: 'Please be quiet. ... Don't do this because they might put you in a cage bed.'[8] It is accepted medical and human rights practice that restraints should never be used as punishment.[9]

In some countries cage beds continue to be used.[10] A cage bed is a regular hospital bed on which there is a metal frame which supports metal bars or netting, resembling a small cage. Despite the strong opposition to cage beds among users and international organizations,[11] they are still widely used in social care institutions in the Czech Republic and in psychiatric hospitals in Slovakia, the Czech Republic and Croatia. Until recently they were also used in Hungary and Slovenia.

Cage beds are used solely for reasons of staff convenience and institutional economy and particularly for 'difficult' patients who are often placed in such beds for weeks at a time,[12] causing obvious trauma and suffering. Such beds pose an enormous safety risk and evidence of such predictable tragedies is not difficult to find. For example in 2000 a man died in a Hungarian social care home when a fire broke out. The untrained nurses did not unlock the padlock which was keeping him locked inside the cage bed. He died of smoke inhalation and burns.[13] In 2003 in the Czech Republic a 14-year-old girl died when one of the iron bars of the cage bed fell on her.[14] In 2006 a woman died in Prague's Bohnice psychiatric hospital. She was locked in a cage bed, and suffocated from eating her own faeces. The circumstances suggest that she had been deprived of food for a very long time before her death, and had been unsupervised for hours prior to her death.[15]

Following the ban on cage beds in Slovakian social care homes in 2004, there is now evidence that in 2006 residents were tied to their beds with leather straps all night, whether agitated or not.[16] Slovakia's neighbour the Czech Republic still uses cage beds in long-stay social care homes.

As far as the MDAC is aware, no death in a mental health or social care institution in central Europe has ever been acknowledged as having been caused by chemical or physical restraint. In cases where there is prima facie causation between restraint and death, the cause of death appears to be recorded as 'cardiac insufficiency'. In cases that the MDAC is litigating in Estonia and Bulgaria, the evidence shows that the state prosecutors terminated their investigations into the deaths on the ground that the deaths resulted from 'heart failure' and it was not necessary therefore to investigate further. In some of these cases the victims died while physically restrained to a hospital bed and immediately after receiving high doses of psychiatric medication.

Violence

MDAC investigations and experience (detailed below) strongly suggest that overcrowding, lack of trained staff, the use of restraints and boredom all contribute to an anti-therapeutic environment and increased levels of violence in institutions. Vulnerable residents in particular are in a permanent state of danger from such attacks, with abuse by staff and residents most prevalent during the night, when few nurses are likely to be on duty. The MDAC has received allegations from residents of social care homes in Bulgaria, Estonia, Lithuania and Slovakia about constant physical threats and violence coming from other residents. Such complaints are frequently not investigated by staff.

The European Committee for the Prevention of Torture (CPT)[17] has documented violence in such institutions in Slovakia[18] and Estonia.[19] However, since the CPT visits just a tiny proportion of institutions, it falls on civil society organizations to carry out systemic monitoring. In Bulgaria one such organization has revealed that in some hospitals the nurses lock themselves in their offices because they are afraid to visit the residents' rooms even if a resident calls for help.[20] The MDAC has heard direct testimony from residents in Bulgarian institutions of severe beatings by other residents.

Violence by staff has also been documented. In a Slovakian social care home in early 2006 a nurse ordered three residents to beat another resident. The man died from his injuries. The nurse had decided to punish the victim for a previous suicide attempt. In this case criminal proceedings have been instigated against the nurse, and at the time of writing the case is pending. Beyond the narrow boundaries of criminal acts or omissions, however, it appears that wider circumstances of institutional violence are not investigated. For example, in the beatings case, there was some evidence that beating by sticks was a widespread method of punishment in that social care home,[21] yet no investigation is looking into this allegation.

Lack of health care

Experience suggests that residents of institutions generally have worse access to health care than the rest of the population.[22] Although social care homes are typically regularly visited by a doctor, this is, however, generally insufficient to take care of health care needs of the residents. Access to specialized care, including dentistry, is even more problematic.

The MDAC has direct evidence concerning Slovakian hospitals refusing to provide emergency care to residents of institutions. Hospitals have refused to send an ambulance to the institutions, reportedly claiming that the institutions should take care of their residents themselves or that 'it would be better if the client died'.[23] In one case an emergency doctor was called to an institution to resuscitate a child who was having an epileptic attack. For 15 minutes the doctor watched the institution's nurse trying to save the child's life, without assisting her. When the nurse asked the doctor to help, the doctor reportedly replied: 'Maybe it would be better to leave the child to die.'[24]

Lack of food and heating

Although lack of food and heating is no longer a typical feature of institutions in central Europe, some institutions in Bulgaria and Romania and in countries to the east are grossly under-funded (or funding is mismanaged) such that these basic needs go unmet. This sometimes results in malnutrition and large numbers of deaths during the winter. Examples include the Dragash Voyvoda social care home in Bulgaria, where 22 men (out of the total capacity of 140) died in 2001,[25] and Poiana Mare psychiatric hospital in Romania, where 17 people died in January and February 2004 due to malnutrition and hypothermia.[26]

Revealing causes of death

A common feature of the situations discussed above is that no countries in the region have mechanisms to effectively investigate deaths in institutions. Without investigations into deaths, the lives of people in institutions are unlikely to improve. Even if immediate perpetrators of violence are convicted by a criminal court, residents may still be subject to overcrowding, disproportionate punishment systems and seriously bad living conditions, all contributing to elevated levels of aggression, dealt with by punishments, isolation, restraint and over-medication. Investigations have the potential to break the circle of neglect and abuse.

International human rights law mandates states to protect the lives of people in their jurisdiction. States must thoroughly and effectively investigate deaths, including those that take place in mental health and social care institutions. In the following parts of this chapter we explore these international legal obligations and in the section that follows it, we examine the extent to which countries of central Europe comply with their international legal obligations.

Death and Article 2 of the ECHR

Apart from Belarus and Montenegro,[27] all countries in wider Europe have ratified the European Convention on Human Rights (ECHR). To date, no cases concerning the loss of life in central European institutions have reached the European Court, but many aspects of the right to life applicable to people with disabilities have been developed by the court in other areas. In this section we review the case law under Article 2 of the convention to establish the current standards.

Article 2 of the ECHR reads:

(1) Everyone's right to life shall be protected by law. No one shall be deprived of his life intentionally save in the execution of a sentence of a court following his conviction of a crime for which this penalty is provided by law.
(2) Deprivation of life shall not be regarded as inflicted in contravention of this Article when it results from the use of force which is no more than absolutely necessary:
  (a) in defence of any person from unlawful violence
  (b) in order to effect a lawful arrest or to prevent the escape of a person lawfully detained
  (c) in action lawfully taken for the purposes of quelling a riot or insurrection.

Article 2 obliges states to protect the right to life of 'everyone' in their jurisdictions. This involves not only the negative obligation to refrain from unlawful killing by state agents, but also extends to the positive obligation to protect life against actions of third parties.[28]

It goes without saying that governments cannot provide effective protection to everyone who feels threatened. Nor can it ensure zero loss of life. Combating crime has its important resource implications and the obligation to protect life against third persons is not absolute. The European Court set the standard in the case of *Osman v. the United Kingdom*,[29] holding that a state violates the convention if an applicant can 'show that the authorities did not do all that could be reasonably expected of them to avoid a real and immediate risk to life of which they have or ought to have knowledge'.[30]

The obligation to protect life is stronger if the victim dies in detention.[31] This standard was developed initially under Article 3 of the convention (prohibition of torture, inhuman and degrading treatment or punishment) to protect prisoners, who often have evidential difficulties in proving ill-treatment in custody.[32] The European Court has stated that 'where an individual is taken into police custody in good health but is found to be injured at the time of release, it is incumbent on the State to provide a plausible explanation of how those injuries were caused'.[33]

The shift of the burden of proof to the government is also the standard in cases where detainees have died. As the court expressed in *Salman v. Turkey,*

> [w]here the events in issue lie wholly, or in large part, within the exclusive knowledge of the authorities, as in the case of persons within their control in custody, strong presumptions of fact will arise in respect of injuries and death occurring during such detention. Indeed, the burden of proof may be regarded as resting on the authorities to provide a satisfactory and convincing explanation.[34]

This standard applies to all people deprived of their liberty, and therefore logically extends to such institutions as prisons, hospitals or social care homes.

In the case of *Paul and Audrey Edwards v. the United Kingdom,* the applicants' son was killed in a prison cell by his cellmate.[35] The court found that the UK failed to protect Christopher Edwards' life, and found a violation of Article 2 of the convention.[36] The court extended its *Osman* standard, noting that '[i]n the context of prisoners, the court has had previous occasion to emphasise that persons in custody are in a vulnerable position and that the authorities are under a duty to protect them'.[37] This 'duty to protect' provides more protection to people in institutions than those living in the community, although the precise limits are yet to be defined.

Intentional killing of residents in social care institutions or hospitals in central Europe is, we think, rare. As discussed in the earlier part of this chapter, the lives of people living in institutions are threatened by casual violence, neglect, and a denial of their basic needs such as health care, food and warmth. The court has however dealt with these questions in the context of prisons, reviewing them under Article 2 (right to life) and Article 3 (prohibition of torture, inhuman and degrading treatment or punishment). The judgements oblige state authorities to provide health care to persons in custody. Thus in *Ilhan v. Turkey* the court found a violation of Article 3 where the applicant, who had been severely beaten by gendarmes, was denied medical treatment while in a detention centre.[38] The court did not find a violation of Article 2, because notwithstanding the applicant's life-threatening injuries, the force applied by the gendarmes and the denial of treatment was not 'of such a nature or degree as to breach Article 2 of the convention'.[39]

Death and Article 3 of the ECHR

Lack of suitable medical treatment leading to loss of life has also been examined by the court under Article 3 in the case of *McGlinchey and others v. the United Kingdom.*[40] Judith McGlinchey was a heroin addict who experienced severe withdrawal symptoms while in prison, including vomiting and weight loss. The prison authorities tried to alleviate her suffering and transferred her to a hospital, but she died. The court found a violation of Article 3 on the grounds that the prison authorities failed to meet an appropriate standard of care '[h]aving regard to the responsibility owed by prison authorities to provide the requisite medical care for detained persons'.[41] Since the objective failures in the case were (on one level) of a minor nature (the prison officers could not accurately establish the victim's weight loss due to a discrepancy of the scales and she was not under constant medical supervision during the weekend), the court imposed an obligation on states to provide detainees with medical care of a high standard in order to avoid a violation of the convention in similar situations.

Judge Costa wrote a concurring opinion in which he noted that the decision,

> must be placed in a wider context, that of the special treatment to be given to prisoners whose state of health gives cause for concern. In cases like that of the victim, such concern might even entail a decision that their state of health is incompatible with committal to prison, or in any case with continued detention.[42]

Although the case concerned a heroin addict whose condition was known by the authorities, it seems likely that the court would adopt a similar approach to other serious medical conditions. States are required to make all necessary steps in terms of medical treatment to protect the lives of people detained in institutions, and even minor and avoidable failures can result in an Article 3 violation. It should be noted that the court did not examine the case under Article 2, because that article (curiously) was not raised by the applicants.

In the case of *Keenan v. the United Kingdom* the court examined whether the psychiatric treatment provided to a prisoner with mental illness met the standards of the convention. Mark Keenan killed himself in prison. The court criticized the lack of effective monitoring of his condition and the lack of informed psychiatric input into his assessment and treatment, especially because of his diagnosis of mental illness and his known risk of suicide. The court noted that the prison punished him with seven days' segregation in the punishment block and imposed an additional 28 days to his sentence two weeks after the event and only nine days before his expected date of release. The court found that this treatment 'may well have threatened his physical and moral resistance,' and found that it constituted inhuman and degrading treatment and punishment within the meaning of Article 3 of the convention. However, the European Court did not establish the required causality between what happened to him prior to his death and the suicide itself, and therefore found no violation of Article 2.

In a chapter about death and human rights, we need to examine whether Article 2 is the only convention provision that can be relied on in cases where a death occurs. The *McGlinchey* and *Keenan* cases demonstrate the court's autonomous approach to the relationship between Articles 2 and 3. Although in both cases the victims eventually died, the court found violations of Article 3 of the convention, but not of Article 2. The court found that the treatment before the death violated the convention, not the failure to prevent the death itself. In the *Keenan* judgement the court described the link between the treatment and the suicide as 'speculative'.[43] The same holds true with the *McGlinchey* case. Her symptoms of vomiting and weight loss were typical withdrawal symptoms of a heroin addict. There was little to suggest that she was subjected to treatment contrary to the convention, except her death.

In a case where an applicant survives, it may be difficult to persuade the court that the suffering reached the threshold of severity required by Article 3. Where ill-treatment leads to death, the death itself may add an objective element to the 'minimum level of severity' test, tipping the balance in favour of finding an Article 3 violation. People living in institutions being subjected to treatment that has caused the deaths of others could use those deaths as evidence for an Article 3 claim. An effective remedy for them would require improvement of the treatment or conditions which violated their Article 3 rights, and which resulted in the deaths of others. This could be, quite literally, a life-saving litigation strategy.

Living victims using death arguments

It is established jurisprudence that death is not a prerequisite to invoke Article 2. The Article can be used by living applicants to argue that their life is in danger, as at least four ECHR cases demonstrate. In the cases of *Osman v. UK* and *Yaşa v. Turkey*[44] the court examined state failures to protect the applicants against attacks of third parties despite the fact that in both cases the applicant survived. In *Ilhan v. Turkey* the question was whether the beatings by gendarmes and the subsequent denial of medical treatment endangered the victim's life to an extent to violate Article 2 of the convention. In that case the court stated that 'it is only in exceptional circumstances that physical ill-treatment by State officials which does not result in death may disclose a breach of Article 2 of the convention'.[45] The court found that Article 2 was not violated, but did find a violation of Article 3 on the account of the ill-treatment suffered.[46]

In *LCB v. the United Kingdom* the applicant was the daughter of a soldier who had been exposed to nuclear radiation while stationed on Christmas Island during British nuclear tests. She claimed that the testing caused her leukaemia. The court examined under Article 2 whether the state 'did all that could have been required of it to prevent the applicant's life from being avoidably put at risk'.[47] The court found that the British government did not fail in this regard given the information about the possible risks available to it at the relevant time.

It will be interesting to scrutinize the court's approach in future cases, especially in those where the state *is* aware of the risks. For example, in psychiatric institutions with high mortality due to lack of nutrition and heating, the state could not claim ignorance about the risk to life to other residents of the institutions, because it operates the institutions themselves. Along the lines of the *LCB* judgement, the state would be required to prevent lives 'being avoidably put at risk'.[48]

The obligation to investigate deaths

People applying to the European Court of Human Rights seeking remedies for the loss of the lives of their close relatives are often in a difficult situation. They have to prove the causal relationship between the death and action or negligence of the authorities in a situation in which they themselves were not present. The exact circumstances of the death may be unclear; often the only people with direct experience about the events are either dead or are themselves culpable to a greater or lesser degree. If most of the information is in the exclusive knowledge of the authorities, any legal action could be effectively blocked by the authorities refusing to supply information, or by not taking steps to gather, analyse or disclose the information.

The European Court of Human Rights has been faced with cases in which it was difficult to decide on the substance of a complaint because of the lack of information about the circumstances of the death. The court responded to these difficulties innovatively in the case of *McCann and others v. United Kingdom*, stating that, a general legal prohibition of arbitrary killing by the agents of the State would be ineffective, in practice, if there existed no procedure for reviewing the lawfulness of the use of lethal force by State authorities. The obligation to protect the right to life ... requires by implication that there should be some form of effective official investigation when individuals have been killed as a result of the use of force by, inter alios, agents of the State.[49]

The court created a 'procedural' obligation on governments to investigate deaths. While the 'substantive' limb of Article 2 obliges governments not to kill people, and protect the lives of people from actions of third parties, the procedural obligation requires that once death occurs the government take all necessary steps to find out the circumstances of the death and the persons responsible.

The procedural obligation should be an effective tool to combat unlawful taking of life, as it no longer permits the government to rely on the lack of information. If the information is not available, and the investigating authorities failed to take the necessary steps to discover the information, the court may find that this in itself constitutes an Article 2 violation.

Three years after *McCann*, the court created a similar procedural obligation under Article 3 of the convention. In *Assenov v. Bulgaria* the court stated that 'where an individual raises an arguable claim that he has been seriously ill-treated by the police or other such agents of the state unlawfully and in breach of Article 3, that provision ... requires by implication that there should be an effective official investigation'.[50]

The court has elaborated the state obligation to hold investigations under Articles 2 and 3. In the 2002 case of *Paul and Audrey Edwards v. the United Kingdom*, it stated that the purpose of the investigation is to 'secure the effective implementation of the domestic laws which protect the right to life and, in those cases involving state agents or bodies, to ensure their accountability for deaths occurring under their responsibility'.[51]

To comply with the European Convention on Human Rights, an investigation must meet the following requirements:

i) The persons responsible for carrying out the investigation must be *independent* from those implicated in the events.[52] This includes the lack of hierarchical or institutional connection and also practical independence.[53]

ii) The authorities must act on their *own motion*.[54] They cannot leave it to the initiative of the victim's relatives or other interested parties to lodge a formal complaint or to conduct the investigation.[55]

iii) The investigation must be *effective* in the sense that it is capable of leading to a determination of whether the force used was or was not justified in the circumstances[56] and to the identification and punishment of those responsible.[57] The court stressed many times that 'this is not an obligation of results, but of means':[58] the investigation may not be successful in every case. However, the

> investigating authorities must take the reasonable steps available to them to secure the evidence concerning the incident, including, *inter alia*, eyewitness testimony, forensic evidence and, where appropriate, an autopsy providing a complete and accurate record of injury and an objective analysis of clinical findings, including the cause of death. Any deficiency in the investigation which undermines its ability to establish the cause of death or the person or persons responsible will risk falling foul of this standard[59]

> Thus, for instance, in *Salman v. Turkey* the European Court dismissed the findings of a low quality autopsy report prepared by state officials, and came to a different conclusion as regards the cause of death from that of the domestic authorities.[60]

iv) The investigation must be *prompt*.[61] The logic is that witnesses' memories will become stale with time,[62] and that a speedy response by the authorities is needed to maintain public confidence in the rule of law.[63] There seems to be no uniform standard to the length of the investigation. However, a violation may be found where there has been an unreasonable or unexplainable delay.

v) There must be sufficient public scrutiny of the investigation.[64] The degree of publicity may vary with the circumstances. However, it is now clear that the next-of-kin must always be involved in the procedure to safeguard their legitimate interests.[65]

Investigation of deaths in central Europe

Having laid out state requirements to investigate such deaths, in this section we describe investigations after death in central Europe, and analyse whether the existing practices meet convention standards. The European Court has made it clear that states are free to choose the form of investigation as long as it satisfies basic convention requirements. Countries are thus not obliged to set up investigative committees or inquest bodies to investigate deaths. These are indeed rare in central Europe.

In central Europe the 'duty to investigate' typically rests with the prosecution service, whose general purpose is to investigate and prosecute crimes. Unlawful deaths, torture, beating and other forms of severe ill-treatment are actions prohibited by criminal law in all countries. Nothing therefore prevents prosecutors from investigating criminal allegations, and indeed they are usually legally obliged to do so. However, such criminal prosecutions fail to meet the standards of Articles 2 and 3 of the convention. We will analyse these prosecutorial investigations against the criteria established in the previous section where we outlined convention requirements.

Independence

Prosecution services in all central European countries are formally independent institutions, outside the control of the executive branch. Prosecutors are institutionally separated from providers of mental health and social services. However, the prosecution often carries out the investigation with the help of the police, bringing into question the independence of the whole investigation if police officers are implicated in the events. This is of course not specific to central Europe: it is always difficult to ensure objectivity in cases where crimes are committed by police officers or other justice officials.[66]

Own initiative

The prosecution must initiate an investigation if alerted to a possible crime. However, the effectiveness of the investigation can be endangered if the deceased's representative does not pursue the investigation. This is not an uncommon scenario in cases of institutional deaths, especially where a victim lacks close relatives.

Effectiveness

The investigation must be capable of leading to a determination of whether actions were justified in the circumstances and to the identification and punishment of those responsible. A prosecutorial investigation aims to determine whether a crime was committed by perpetrators. However this is not enough. The European Court has emphasized that the crucial issue under Article 2 is 'State responsibility under international law and not ... guilt under criminal law'.[67]

The case of *Ribitsch v. Austria* illustrates this important point. Here, the applicant sustained numerous injuries while detained in a police station.[68] The suspected police officer was prosecuted in domestic courts, and convicted in the first instance, but an appeal court overturned the decision and acquitted him because of lack of evidence. In proceedings before the European Court of Human Rights the Austrian Government argued that the appeal court had established that Article 3 of the convention was not violated. The European Court, however, disagreed:

> It is not disputed that Mr Ribitsch's injuries were sustained during his detention in police custody, which was in any case unlawful, while he was entirely under the control of police officers. Police Officer Markl's acquittal in the criminal proceedings by a court bound by the principle of presumption of innocence does not absolve Austria from its responsibility under the convention. The Government were accordingly under an obligation to provide a plausible explanation of how the

applicant's injuries were caused. But the Government did no more than refer to the outcome of the domestic criminal proceedings, where the high standard of proof necessary to secure a criminal conviction was not found to have been satisfied.[69]

The prosecutor's hands are tied if no crime was committed, even where he or she thinks there was a possible breach of Article 2 or 3 of the convention. To give an example in the mental disability context, nurses acting in accordance with local laws and policies physically restrain a person to a hospital bed with leather straps. The person dies during this process. A prosecutor opens an investigation. If what happened did not constitute a crime, the investigation is closed at the preliminary stage. This leaves the victim with no redress, no one is prosecuted and there is no public court hearing related to the incident.[70]

In other cases it may be clearer that a crime was committed (for example, a person dies in a social care home under suspicious circumstances), but there is not enough evidence to prove who specifically is responsible for the death. Alternatively, and throwing stigma and discrimination into the mix, the prosecutor may think that the residents of the social care home would not be credible witnesses. The prosecutor may close the investigation on the grounds that it is not possible to establish the identity of the perpetrator.

Another problem is that prosecutors cannot investigate deaths that result from systemic failures of institutional care. For example, if a nurse in an institution maliciously starves a resident to death, this would very likely constitute a crime which the prosecutor could investigate. However, if starvation is due not to individual negligence but to a lack of resources (e.g. the Romanian example, above), it is difficult to see the basis on which a prosecution would be brought, or who would be prosecuted. Likewise, a staff member who beats a resident to death could be convicted of homicide, but what if residents of the same institution are beaten to death by each other as a consequence of a fight over scarce food and serious overcrowding? The prosecutor would probably be powerless to investigate such deaths if the perpetrators lacked the necessary mental capacity to establish criminal responsibility.

Similarly, prosecutors cannot investigate allegations of acts or omissions which are not classed as a 'crime' in law. For example, certain psychiatric 'treatments' are not only permitted, but even explicitly provided for by law, for example, the use of cage beds in the Czech Republic. Whilst these might violate Article 3 of the convention, a prosecutor would not be able to investigate their case because these beds are legal in Czech law, irrespective of what the European Court of Human Rights might eventually find. Other examples in this category would include other 'treatments' used in central Europe such as hot and cold showers, overuse of medication, constant sedation, and mundane work performed as 'therapy'.[71] The European

Court of Human Rights may class these as inhuman or degrading treatment or punishment, but in the absence of domestic prohibition their use does not constitute a crime and accordingly they go un-investigated by prosecutors.

Investigation files concerning such deaths often include a pro forma medical report stating the immediate cause of death. On the basis of this, the prosecutor closes the investigation, concluding that no crime has been committed – particularly if the victim has no 'interested' relatives. In the MDAC's right to life cases in Bulgaria, Estonia and Hungary, relatives took an active role in finding out how their loved one died, yet prosecutors closed their investigations at an early stage on formal grounds. In some cases prosecutors sought to obtain signed statements from relatives waiving their right to have an autopsy performed. These statements were collected in a way in which persons signing them later stated that they did not know what they had signed and were not aware that by their signatures they had authorized the prosecutors to abandon the investigation.

Even where there is a criminal conviction, families have difficulties in obtaining a remedy from domestic authorities. The convention requires that 'in the case of a breach of Articles 2 and 3 ... compensation for the non-pecuniary damage flowing from the breach should, in principle, be available as part of the range of redress'.[72] However, in most central European countries only pecuniary damages can be recovered through the criminal process. This generally includes little other than funeral expenses and possibly time off work. The deceased's relatives can theoretically apply to civil courts for compensation, but it is questionable whether any civil court would, on the basis of criminal responsibility, award non-pecuniary damages which are unavailable in criminal proceedings. The authors of this chapter have been involved in right-to-life litigation in six central European jurisdictions, and are not aware of any court decision in which an award for non-pecuniary damages has been made in such death cases.

The convention requires a more holistic approach than that adopted in central Europe. It requires the state to investigate the circumstances which lead up to the death. It requires witnesses to be asked why the services failed to protect the victim's life. It requires the availability of non-pecuniary compensation. Lack of convention compliance is particularly poignant if one considers the access to justice problems people with mental disability face.

Publicity

The European Court requires a sufficient element of public scrutiny of the investigation or its results. Investigations in central Europe typically concentrate on the perpetrator, not on the victim or relatives. In most countries the deceased's relatives have access to the investigation file, but in practice this does not extend to all documents in the file. The prosecutor has discretion to withhold disclosure of documents which would violate the presumption of innocence or the interest of other parties.[73] Relatives may therefore be denied an effective challenge to the prosecutor's decision.

Relatives can also be prohibited from being present when testimonies or other evidence is taken,[74] contrary to findings in the *Edwards* case that family members have the right to be present and ask questions of witnesses. Relatives are not 'automatically' invited to take part in the investigation. Once they are informed about the decision not to investigate, they have a right to appeal and an opportunity to suggest that new evidence be gathered.[75] However, at this stage it is often too late to take effective investigative steps. Non-involvement of relatives directly links in with the effectiveness of an investigation.

It is not uncommon that people who have died in a psychiatric or social care institution have no contactable or interested relatives. In such a case there is a need for someone to represent the interests of the deceased in a subsequent investigation. However, in many countries there is no mechanism to appoint an *ad litem* representative for deceased persons, nor can friends, non-governmental organizations or other groups with an interest in the case act in the interests of the deceased. This is a serious deficiency, especially considering that relatives are often instrumental in demanding justice, and considering the many thousands of people in institutions who have no interested relatives.

The requirement of transparency with regard to the general public is also problematic. Since the alleged perpetrator is protected by the criminal law presumption of innocence, the public has no access to the prosecutor's investigation until the criminal trial. As discussed above, actual prosecutions are rare. Even if there is an investigation which is then closed pre-trial, the public is left in the dark because prosecutors do not publicly announce their decision to discontinue investigation.

Having revealed substantial weaknesses in the effectiveness of investigations, we turn to the fifth and final convention requirement, namely the speed with which investigations are carried out.

Speed

Since evidence must be secured on the scene to establish the circumstances of a death, an unreasonable delay of days or even hours might thwart the investigation. These failures are even more serious in light of the fact that it is not possible to remedy them. The requirement of speediness goes hand in hand with the effectiveness and publicity of the investigation. If the victims' relatives are involved automatically in the investigation from its beginning, they could spur on the investigation by arguing that evidence be collected quickly. Commonly in central Europe relatives are not involved in investigations into deaths in institutions, and such proceedings regularly last for two or more years.

Other forms of investigation in central Europe

Although central European prosecutors have statutory responsibilities for investigating crimes, they are not the only officers with power to investigate deaths. Ombudspersons have often an unrestricted mandate to investigate alleged breaches of the law or of human rights standards by public authorities. These investigations are sometimes commendably thorough and reveal information about closed institutions, yet they cannot be regarded as satisfying the requirements of Articles 2 and 3 of the convention because ombudspersons do not have the legal authority to punish perpetrators, provide compensation to victims, compel witnesses to appear or demand that evidence be produced. Their investigations cannot therefore be regarded as 'effective' in convention terms. Internal investigations are also sometimes performed by a ministry or other executive organ. These are limited to the actions of state bodies responsible to the body conducting the investigation. Such investigations typically constitute a financial audit.[76]

Conclusion

People with disabilities living in central European social care and health care institutions often live in conditions which put their lives in danger. They are subject to violence from staff members and other residents, outmoded and unregulated physical restraints, seclusion rooms and over-medication. People are detained in overcrowded facilities which provide little respect for privacy and autonomy. In some countries material conditions are still so bad that many residents suffer from malnutrition, hypothermia during the winter and are denied access to medical care. Since the institutions are isolated from society and mortality rates are not published, it is difficult to assess how many residents die yearly and the reasons for these deaths, but cases of violent deaths closely connected with the problems described above do occasionally reach the public domain.

All European states have international obligations to protect the rights of people with disabilities in their jurisdictions. The provision guaranteeing the right to life (Article 2) of the European Convention on Human Rights not only requires the state to refrain from unlawful killing, it also demands that it protects people from violence and death caused by lack of health care. There is an increased obligation to protect people living in institutions. The state has a further duty to investigate deaths that take place within their territories, with the aim of establishing the circumstances of the deaths, punishing any perpetrators and providing compensation to victims who are nearly always relatives of the deceased. Similar obligations exist under Article 3 of the convention, which prohibits torture, inhuman and degrading treatment or punishment. Some practices can be examined under both Articles 2 and 3, since they can constitute inhuman treatment and endanger the life of the victim at the same time.

In this chapter we have argued that central European countries do not have adequate mechanisms in place that satisfy convention requirements. Violent deaths are investigated by prosecutors with the aim of establishing whether a crime was committed. Systemic failures of institutional care fall outside the scope of such an investigation. The investigation is terminated if a crime committed by a specific individual cannot be proven, even if other circumstances of the death are not yet revealed. Victims and their relatives do not receive compensation for clear violations of the convention but which do not breach domestic criminal law. Even if a crime was possibly committed, the effectiveness of the investigation depends very much on the activity of the victim or his or her representatives. Relatives are not automatically involved in the investigation. Criminal investigations also fall short of the convention requirement of promptness. Criminal investigations thus do not satisfy states' obligations under the convention. The same is true about other forms of investigation in central Europe which are investigations by ombudspersons and ministries.

Establishing convention-compliant and functioning investigative machinery would force public scrutiny of other issues which rarely surface. These include policies of physical and chemical restraints, prescribing guidelines for psychiatric medication, legal criteria for admission to psychiatric hospitals, court reviews of psychiatric detention, and the abuses created by de facto detention in social care institutions via guardianship. Maintaining the status quo where deaths go uninvestigated means that those responsible are not punished, the causes of systemic elevated mortality go unexplored, grieving relatives do not know why their loved ones died, and needless deaths will not be prevented.

Notes

1 For a further discussion, see P. Bartlett, O. Lewis and O. Thorold, *Mental Disability and the European Convention on Human Rights*. The Netherlands: Brill Publishing, Martinus Nijhof, 2006.
2 Taken from <http://www.community-living.info>, (accessed 1 May 2007).
3 In purchasing power standard; see *EC Economic Data Pocketbook*, Luxembourg: Office for Official Publications of the European Communities, 2006, available online at <http://epp.eurostat.ec.europa.eu/cache/ITY_OFFPUB/KS-CZ-06–001/EN/KS-CZ-06–001-EN.PDF>, p.16 (accessed 1 May 2007).
4 These data were gathered from August to December 2005 from different sources, such as the Czech Statistical Office, the Ministry of Labour and Social Affairs, regional and local governments and the institutions themselves. Data from year 2005 were still not available at the time of drafting this chapter.
5 This includes people with psychosocial (mental health) and intellectual disabilities.
6 *Included in Society: Results and Recommendations of the European Research Initiative on Community-Based Residential Alternatives for Disabled People*. Brussels: Inclusion Europe, Autism Europe, Mental Health Europe and the Open Society Mental Health Initiative, 2005.
7 Bartlett *et al.*, 2006, op. cit., Chapter 3.

8 'Cage beds: Inhuman and degrading treatment in four EU Accession countries', Budapest: Mental Disability Advocacy Center (MDAC), 2003, available online at <http://www.mdac.info> p.33 (accessed 1 May 2007).

9 Standards of the European Committee for the Prevention of Torture and Inhuman or Degrading Treatment or Punishment (CPT), ref CPT/Inf/E (2002) 1 – Rev. 2006.

10 See 'Means of restraint in psychiatric establishments for adults' in CPT Standards, ibid.

11 See the 'Concluding Observations' of the United Nations Human Rights Committee: Slovakia, 22 August 2003, CCPR/CO/78/SVK, para. 13. See also the 'Report to the Czech Government on the visit to the Czech Republic carried out by the European Committee for the Prevention of Torture and Inhuman or Degrading Treatment or Punishment (CPT) from 21 to 30 April 2002', published on 12 March 2004; response of Günter Verheugen, (then) European Union Commissioner for Enlargement, to John Bowis MEP at the European Parliament, 17 December 2003.

12 See documentary on Slovakian psychiatric hospitals on the *Reporters* programme, BBC World, 24 October 2004, available through the MDAC's website: <www.mdac.info> (accessed 1 May 2007); also 'Ústavy stále zavírají lidi do klecí' (Institutions still lock people into cages), Eliška Bártová, Ludvik Hradílek, *Aktuálně* (Czech newspaper), 7 April 2006, available online at <http://aktualne.centrum.cz/domaci/kauzy/clanek.phtml?id=116581> (accessed 1 May 2007).

13 'Halálesetek egy elmeotthonban' (Deaths in a mental institution), Doros Judit, *Népszabadság*, (Hungarian newspaper), 14 December 2000.

14 'My z ústavu' (Us from an institution), Eliška Bártová, *Respekt* (Czech newspaper), 10 February 2003.

15 'Smrt v Bohnicích: Rath žádá vysvětlení' (Death in Bohnice: Rath asks for explanation), Eliška Bártová, *Aktuálně* (Czech newspaper), 26 April 2006, available online at <http://aktualne.centrum.cz/domaci/kauzy/clanek.phtml?id=135761> (accessed 1 May 2007).

16 Viera Šimkovičová ová, 'Dodržiavanie udských práv v zariadeniach sociálnych služieb na Slovensku' (Satisfying human rights in social service institutions in Slovakia), *Report for the International Helsinki Federation*. Banská Bystrica, Slovakia: ANNWIN, October 2005, p.2.

17 See <www.cpt.coe.int> (accessed 1 May 2007).

18 See 'Report to the Slovak Government on the visit to the Czech Republic carried out by the European Committee for the Prevention of Torture and Inhuman or Degrading Treatment or Punishment (CPT) from 22 February to 3 March 2005', published on 2 February 2006, ref CPT/Inf (2006) 5, para. 86.

19 See 'Report to the Estonian Government on the visit to Estonia carried out by the European Committee for the Prevention of Torture and Inhuman or Degrading Treatment or Punishment (CPT) from 23 to 30 September 2003', published on 27 April 2005, ref CPT/Inf (2005) 6, para. 89.

20 'Inpatient Psychiatric Care and Human Rights in Bulgaria in 2005', Bulgarian Helsinki Committee, December 2005, Sofia, p.35.

21 'Ošetrovatel'a vinia, že privodil smrt' klienta' (Male nurse accused of causing the death of client), Mikuláš Jesenský, *SME,* (Slovak newspaper), 11 January 2006, available online at: <http://www.sme.sk/clanok.asp?cl=2540583>

22 ANNWIN report, op. cit., p.3.

23 Ibid.

24 Ibid.

25 'Bulgaria: Residents of Dragash Voyvoda are dying as a result of gross neglect', *Amnesty International*, 15 April 2002, available online at: <http://www. bghelsinki.org/press/2002/en/04–02.htm> (accessed 1 May 2007).

26 'Romania: State duty to effectively investigate deaths in psychiatric institutions', Amnesty International, 30 November 2005, AI Index: EUR 39/008/2005, available at <http://web.amnesty.org/library/Index/ ENGEUR390082005?open&of=ENG-2U2> (accessed 1 May 2007); see also 'Report submitted by the Special Rapporteur on the right of everyone to the highest attainable standard of physical and mental health, Paul Hunt, Mission Report to Romania, 21 February 2005', UN Ref: E/CN.4/2005/51/Add.4.

27 With the dissolution in 2006 of the Union of the States of Serbia and Montenegro, Serbia has remained a Council of Europe member and Montenegro is in the process of rejoining as a contracting state in its own right.

28 *Osman v. the United Kingdom*, Application No. 22414/93, judgement 15 November 1996.

29 Ibid.

30 Ibid., para. 116.

31 See *Salman v. Turkey*, Application No. 21986/93, judgement 27 July 2000, para. 99.

32 *Tomasi v. France*, Application No. 12850/87, judgement 27 August 1992, paras. 108–111.

33 *Selmouni v. France*, Application No. 25803/94, judgement 28 July 1999, para. 87.

34 *Salman v. Turkey*, op. cit., para. 100.

35 *Paul and Audrey Edwards v. the United Kingdom*, Application No. 46477/99, judgement 14 March 2002.

36 For an analysis of this case, see O. Lewis, 'Right to life: European Convention on Human Rights, Case Commentary on *Paul and Audrey Edwards v. the United Kingdom*' (2003) *Journal of Mental Health Law*, 75–84.

37 *Paul and Audrey Edwards v. the United Kingdom*, op. cit., para. 56.

38 *Ilhan v. Turkey*, Application No. 22277/93, judgement 27 July 2000.

39 Ibid.

40 *McGlinchey and others v. the United Kingdom*, Application No. 50390/99, judgement 29 April 2003.

41 Ibid., para. 57.

42 *McGlinchey*, op. cit., concurring opinion of Judge Costa, para. 4.

43 *Keenan v. the United Kingdom*, Application No. 27229/95, judgement 3 April 2001.

44 *Yaşa v. Turkey*, Application No. 22495/93, judgement 2 September 1998.

45 *Ilhan v. Turkey*, op. cit., para. 76.

46 *Ilhan*, op. cit.

47 *LCB v. UK*, Application No. 23413/94, judgement 9 June 1998, para. 36.

48 Ibid.

49 *McCann and others v. the United Kingdom*, Application No. 18984/91, judgement 27 September 1995, para. 161.

50 *Assenov v. Bulgaria*, Application No. 24760/94, judgement 28 October 1998, para. 102.

51 *Paul and Audrey Edwards v. the United Kingdom*, op. cit., para. 69.

52 *Gülec v. Turkey*, Application No. 21593/93, judgement 27 August 1998, para. 81.

53 *Hugh Jordan v. the United Kingdom*, Application No. 24746/94, judgement 4 May 2001, para. 120.

54 *Ilhan v. Turkey*, op. cit., para. 63.

55 *Slimani v. France*, Application No. 57671/00, judgement 27 July 2004, para 47.

56 *Kaya v. Turkey,* Application No. 22729/93, judgement 19 February 1998, para. 87.
57 *Ogur v. Turkey,* Application No. 21594/93, judgement 20 May 1999, para. 88.
58 *Paul and Audrey Edwards v. the United Kingdom,* op. cit., para. 71.
59 Ibid.
60 *Salman v. Turkey,* op. cit.
61 *Mahmut Kaya v. Turkey,* Application No. 22535/93, judgement 28 March 2000, para. 106–107.
62 *Slimani v. France,* op. cit., para. 32.
63 *Paul and Audrey Edwards v. the United Kingdom,* op. cit., para. 72.
64 Ibid.
65 *McKerr v. the United Kingdom,* Application No. 28883/95, judgement 4 May 2001, para. 148.
66 See *Slimani v. France,* op. cit., partly dissenting opinion of Jugde Loucaides, para. 3.
67 See *Nachova v. Bulgaria,* Application No. 43577/98, judgement 26 February 2004, para. 166.
68 *Ribitsch v. Austria,* Application No. 18896/91, judgement 4 December 1995.
69 Ibid., para. 34.
70 The MDAC is currently litigating a case in Estonia with exactly these facts.
71 All of these examples come from the MDAC's cases in Bulgaria, Czech Republic and Estonia.
72 *Paul and Audrey Edwards v. the United* Kingdom, op. cit., para. 97.
73 Slovak Code of Criminal Procedure, Law no. 141/1961 Col as amended, para. 65(2), which allows the prosecutor to withhold information for 'important reasons'.
74 Czech Code of Criminal Procedure, Law no. 141/1961 Col as amended, para. 43.
75 Slovak Code of Criminal Procedure, op. cit., para. 166.
76 MDAC, 2003, op. cit., p.53.

8   Demonstrably awful

The right to life and the selective non-treatment of disabled babies and young children

Janet Read and Luke Clements

Introduction

Over the past 25 years, there have been deeply troubling cases which centred on the highly contested issue of whether there are circumstances that permit parents, doctors or the courts to take a decision that a young disabled child, often a baby, should not survive. In the United Kingdom and elsewhere, such cases have provoked substantial debate in medical literature and the wider public domain. The issue has emerged and re-emerged across this period: recent examples include *re A (Children) (Conjoined Twins: Surgical Separation)* (2000)[1] *Glass v. UK* (2004)[2] and *Portsmouth NHS Trust v. Wyatt and others* (2004).[3]

This paper considers the sociolegal context of a small number of landmark judgements concerning selective non-treatment of disabled infants or young children: the trial of Leonard Arthur in 1981; *re B (A Minor) (Wardship: Medical Treatment)* (1981),[4] sometimes known as 'Baby Alexandra'; the Canadian case of *In re (Superintendent of Family and Child Service) and Dawson* (1983)[5] and *In re J (A Minor) (Wardship: Medical Treatment)* (1990).[6] In a paper mainly concerned with the United Kingdom jurisdiction, the Canadian case is included because of the way it developed the principles in *re B* (1981) and in turn provided the foundations for the key precedent case of *re J* (1990).

Much of the analysis of medical treatment cases such as these has traditionally been the province of medical ethics[7] or medical law. This paper seeks to review the cases in a different way, viewing them primarily as a litmus test of the then contemporary attitudes towards disabled people. An analysis of relevant features of that contemporary context provides indicators as to why the cases were brought. In turn, the cases themselves together with the associated press coverage and public debate may be regarded as an arena where both dominant attitudes towards disabled people and emerging challenges to such attitudes are played out. They expose tensions around the most fundamental of disabled people's rights, the right to life, and they indicate the changing benchmarks used to establish which lives were seen to warrant protection and which were not.

These cases remind us that only 25 years ago it was common practice to bring about the deaths of some children with learning disabilities or physical impairments, particularly if their parents' social or personal situation was 'unfavourable'. What an analysis of the sociolegal contexts of these cases also reveals is that in the United Kingdom the primary impetus for change did not come from the civil liberties lobby (such as the National Council for Civil Liberties) and drew no inspiration from the European Convention on Human Rights or other international human rights treaty. This radical change resulted from concerted action by members of the Roman Catholic church, small numbers of progressive health and welfare professionals and a few pressure groups with a membership mainly of families with disabled children.

The cases of Leonard Arthur and *re B* in 1981 were unprecedented in that they brought the law to bear on issues that had hitherto been left in the domain of professional discretion. It follows that an analysis of these cases from the perspective of their sociopolitical genesis provides significant insights into the different, overlapping and competing worlds of law and medicine: two powerful value systems that in this study came into conflict.

Tempting as it is to view these cases as examples of 'true social change' being wrought through the medium of the law',[8] their legacy remains indeterminate and in any event beyond the scope of this emergent study. Undoubtedly they illustrate a process by which external sociopolitical change moved through the legal system to effect a profound change outside that system. These external forces used the law to challenge the largely closed domain of medical conduct/practice, resulting in significant change that has materially affected the lives of many thousands of families. These cases cannot, however, be explained solely in terms of their social contexts, and in many respects are illustrative (echoing Cotterrell's observation) not so much of 'how law is produced by society but with the way "society" is produced by the law'.[9] The result of these cases can be measured, not merely by the number of children living who would have died – but of the wider consequences of this fact: of the families who then lived with disability, rather than being severed from the experience; of communities and municipalities having to cater for and accommodate disability and, in turn, of the need to reconfigure our intellectual understanding of disability such that it has now become articulated in social rather than medical terms.

The trial of Leonard Arthur (1981)

In November 1981, Leonard Arthur, a consultant paediatrician at Derby City hospital, was acquitted of attempted murder. He had been charged with the murder, later reduced to attempted murder, after having prescribed the drug dihydrocodeine and nursing care only for a baby with Down's syndrome whose parents did not wish him to survive. It was well known that this procedure would preclude feeding and bring about a child's death. The baby, John Pearson, died 69 hours later. While it was revealed at the trial that the autopsy had shown that John Pearson was suffering from some heart, lung and brain damage, there was no evidence that Leonard Arthur was aware of this when he made his clinical decision. His notes suggest that the decision to prescribe sedation and nursing care only was made solely on the dual grounds that the child had Down's syndrome and that his parents were rejecting him. It was the findings of the autopsy, however, that led Farquarson J., the trial judge, to direct that the original charge of murder should be reduced to one of attempted murder.

The prosecution was instigated by the organization Life, after the events had been disclosed to it by someone working in the hospital. Life, a pressure group with a largely Roman Catholic membership, had been founded to campaign for the repeal of the 1967 Abortion Act. The policy it adopted in relation to disabled infants can be seen as a logical extension of the stance that all life post-conception should be safeguarded.

Leonard Arthur's acquittal, the tactics of the defence in failing to disclose their evidence until the cross-examination stage,[10] the fact that Leonard Arthur did not give evidence, and the summing up of the trial judge,[11] Farquarson J., have been the subject of critical commentary. The defence lawyer, George Carmen, is said to have considered this his finest case.[12] For the purposes of this paper, however, the trial is of importance because it provides a contemporary, high-profile snapshot of popular, judicial and professional sentiments concerning the legal rights to be afforded to disabled babies and the circumstances that were seen to make it permissible to bring about their deaths. It is also of importance because of the fierce public debate that it triggered.

Most significantly, in his summing up, the judge determined that the law merely required agreement between the physician and the parents concerning 'non-treatment'.[13] Kennedy summarizes:

> In his instructions to the jury, Farquarson J. indicated that it was lawful to treat a baby with a sedating drug and offer no further care by way of food or drugs or surgery if certain criteria were met. These criteria appear to be, first, that the child is 'irreversibly disabled' and, second, that it is 'rejected by its parents'. By way of clarification for the jury, the judge drew a distinction between sedating a baby and passively letting it die, 'allowing nature to take its course', and doing a positive act to kill the baby, for example, giving it a death-dealing dose of drugs. The latter, he said, would be unlawful, the former lawful.[14]

Booth,[15] referring to news coverage of the trial,[16] also draws attention to the fact that the judge regarded it as of the greatest importance to establish at the outset that none of the jury had had any dealings with disabled children or belonged to any organization which concerned itself with their affairs. It was made clear, therefore, that only those with no knowledge or experience of childhood disability could be regarded as having the required capacity both to be objective and not to hold strong feelings. As Booth observes, such a condition was not applied to others involved in the case: the medical experts and the parents.

Booth,[17] referring to Kennedy,[18] highlights the fact that those medical experts who gave evidence at the trial unanimously endorsed the practice carried out by Leonard Arthur. Thus, despite evidence available at the time that there were differences of view on the issue, the only position presented as authoritative medical practice was that which normalized the actions of Leonard Arthur. Inevitably underpinning such an approach was a particularly bleak perception of disability and of its impact both on the disabled individuals concerned and those around them. By such means was it sought to justify the ending of a child's life.

re B (1981)

The case of *re B* or 'Baby Alexandra', in August 1981, also concerned a newborn baby who had Down's syndrome. In addition, however, 'Alexandra' had a duodenal atresia which required surgery to save her life (a routine operation for a not uncommon condition). When her parents refused to give consent, the hospital alerted Hammersmith and Fulham local authority. After a number of meetings between the parents and social workers, the parents' decision remained the same. The Director of Social Services, David Plank, therefore, made a successful application for 'Alexandra' to be made a ward of court and gave consent for her to have surgery. 'Alexandra' was transferred to Great Ormond Street Children's hospital but medical staff there refused to operate without the consent of her parents. The Director then sought High Court authority for the surgery. Ewbank J. deferred full judgement until a further hearing two days later and having heard the parents' views, rescinded the wardship order. The same afternoon, the local authority successfully appealed the decision and 'Alexandra' again became a ward of court. As a result, a surgeon was then found who was willing to operate and David Plank gave consent once more. It was reported in the press that the surgery was successful and that the baby was making good progress.[19]

The brevity of Templeman L.J.'s *ex tempore* judgement (only three pages) is striking. It cites one precedent case – and that being of marginal relevance[20] – and makes no reference to any human rights treaty or other legal authority. Yet it is a judgement that fundamentally recast the legal landscape. Ewbank J. had considered the law and the competing interests at two separate hearings and his conclusions were not obviously contrary to precedent law. Templeman accepted the local authority's argument that arrangements could be made for 'Alexandra' to have a 'happy life' and determined that it was not for the parents to decide the fate of their children. Rather, he determined, the court must decide whether the life of this child is demonstrably going to be so awful that in effect the child must be condemned to die, or whether the life of this child is still so imponderable that it would be wrong for her to be condemned to die ... The evidence in this case only goes to show that if the operation takes place and is successful then the child may live the normal span of a mongoloid child with the handicaps and defects and life of a mongol child, and it is not for this court to say that life of that description ought to be extinguished.

As Morgan[21] observed, the judgement in *re B* was 'clearly going to need elaboration', but the elaboration required related to the underpinning of the legal reasoning rather than any modification of principle. Templeman in his extraordinary judgement simply came down in favour of life at a time when many respected physicians and large swathes of the public (not to mention Ewbank J. and Farquarson J.) were not prepared to accord parentally rejected disabled babies this right. The fact that a child would live with disability was not sufficient grounds to justify ending a life. Elaboration came in 1983 with the Supreme Court of British Columbia judgement *In re (Superintendent of Family and Child Service) and Dawson*.

The Dawson case (1983)

In re (Superintendent of Family and Child Service) and Dawson (1983) (hereafter the 'Dawson case') concerned a young child, 'S.', who shortly after birth suffered profound brain damage through meningitis. The child remained in hospital care and a shunt was inserted to drain excess cerebro-spinal fluid. He was blind, partially deaf, incontinent, unable to feed himself, stand, walk, talk or hold objects. Immediately prior to the court proceedings, when the child was seven years of age, his shunt became blocked. The parents refused their consent to remedial surgery on the ground that they believed that he was in constant pain and should be allowed 'to die with dignity rather than continue to endure a life of suffering'.

The application was brought by the Superintendent of Family and Child Service and the case came before the Provincial Court of British Columbia. The evidence put to the provincial court judge (and subsequently to McKenzie J.) did not contradict the profound nature of S.'s impairments. However, his physicians stated that he responded to others and smiled or laughed when stimulated and was a 'happy little fellow despite his handicaps'. A paediatric specialist at the hospital reported that she thought that he was capable of further development and that she saw 'great changes in such children with schooling and therapy'. His occupational therapist gave evidence as to the great pleasure he drew from music therapy, how he 'smiled a great deal in vocalizing sounds' and that this suggested that 'he was previously grossly understimulated and has more potential than he previously exhibited'.

After a five-day hearing, the judge ruled that shunt revision surgery would amount to an 'extraordinary' intervention which was not 'necessary medical attention', and that the wishes of the parents should prevail. The case was appealed to the supreme court where McKenzie J. handed down a truly remarkable decision. Although in his judgement, he makes reference to various reported decisions, in reality only one 'authority' is cited, namely *re B*, and indeed, virtually the whole of Templeman's judgement is quoted verbatim. While relying heavily on *re B*, McKenzie's judgement articulated the case 'for life' in such affirmative and fundamentalist language that it has become the jurisprudential inspiration, if not the benchmark, for all subsequent legal contestations in this domain.

McKenzie commenced from the 'best interests' principles identified in *re B*. Careful consideration of the views of the parents was required but their opinions did not override the court's view of the child's best interests. The court in turn, was not overriding the views of the physicians. Apart from the fact that this was not its role, there were in this case doctors willing to undertake the disputed remedial surgery. In addressing the central principle, 'best interests', the judge held that

> the laws of our society are structured to preserve, protect and maintain human life and that in the exercise of its inherent jurisdiction this court could not sanction the termination of a life except for the most coercive reasons. The presumption must be in favour of life.

He then delivered one of the most insightful judicial statements made in relation to the rights of disabled children:

> I do not think that it lies within the prerogative of any parent or of this court to look down upon a disadvantaged person and judge the quality of that person's life to be so low as not to be deserving of continuance.

In so doing he adopted comments made by Asch J. of the Supreme Court, New York County:[22]

> It is not appropriate for an external decision maker to apply his standards of what constitutes a liveable life and exercise the right to impose death if that standard is not met in his estimation. The decision can only be made in the context of the disabled person viewing the worthwhileness or otherwise of his life in its own context as a disabled person – and in that context he would not compare his life with that of a person enjoying normal advantages. He would know nothing of a normal person's life having never experienced it.

McKenzie concluded his analysis of the best interests' assessment by approving the surgery recommended by the physicians and rejecting the parents' view that 'S.' would be better off dead, stating:

If it is to be decided that 'it is in the best interests of S.D. that his existence cease', then it must be decided that, for him, non-existence is the better alternative. This would mean regarding the life of a handicapped child as not only less valuable than the life of a normal child, but so much less valuable that it is not worth preserving. I tremble at contemplating the consequences if the lives of disabled persons are dependent upon such judgements.

It is not, as we have made clear at the outset, our intention to review the current state of the law as it applies to contested treatment/non-treatment decisions affecting disabled children. However it is the case that since *Dawson* there have been surprisingly few reported cases of this nature heard by the courts.[23] These have, as Morgan correctly predicted, elaborated upon the principles expounded in *re B* (1980) without in any way detracting from their basic soundness. In 1990 the Court of Appeal reviewed the law in *re J (A Minor) (Wardship: Medical Treatment)* (1990)[24] in the context of a decision concerning the future treatment of a six-month-old child. Lord Donaldson's analysis of both *re B* and *Dawson* results in there now being five fundamental legal principles in play in such cases, namely: that the paramount consideration is the child's best interests; that this must be informed by the views of the parents but their views are not determinative of the question; that respect for the sanctity of human life creates a strong presumption in favour of life-preserving treatment; that in exceptional circumstances, the courts can sanction non-intervention which may not prolong life (but not treatment designed to foreshorten life); that it cannot require physicians to provide treatment which is contrary to their professional judgement.

The medical context of Leonard Arthur and *re B*

In order to appreciate the significance and impact of *re B* and the trial of Leonard Arthur, it is necessary to be aware of established and accepted medical policy and practice in relation to disabled infants prior to these cases.

Between the late 1960s and early 1980s, rapid advances in the medical and surgical care of infants meant that medical staff experienced new dilemmas. Over time, the increased survival rates for very-low-birth-weight babies together with new procedures to save life meant that doctors were more likely to find themselves making ethically based, clinical decisions about the degree and type of neonatal intervention or care that should be given to babies who were very ill or who had considerable impairments.[25] There is also ample evidence that clinicians in the United Kingdom and elsewhere were making equally crucial decisions about other infants with a range of impairments not exclusively associated with very low birth weight.[26]

It was the medical advances between the late 1950s and early 1970s in relation to infants born with myelomeningocele (spina bifida), however, that triggered one of the first open debates about 'selective non-treatment' of disabled babies. In Weir's view, it was the explicit nature of the medical papers in the 1970s on babies born with spina bifida that had the effect, over the next few years, of bringing a wider range of related issues 'out of the closet' in both the United Kingdom and the United States.[27] At this time, however, 'out of the closet' mainly meant greater specificity and openness within the confines of medical journals and conferences. Broader public and legal debate was to come later.

By the 1960s, the work of Zachary, Lorber and Sharrard at the Sheffield Children's Hospital had ensured that it was seen as a world centre for the treatment of infants with spina bifida. Surgical techniques had been developed to close spinal lesions in babies soon after birth, and hydrocephalus could be treated by the insertion of a shunt system first developed in America in the 1950s. Leaving the spinal lesion and the associated condition, hydrocephalus, untreated substantially increased the likelihood of death. By the late 1960s, surgery for these babies had become a routine practice.[28]

Zachary and Lorber, however, developed very different and equally strongly held opinions about the appropriateness of 'selective non-treatment'. The Zachary–Lorber conflict offers an insight into the ways in which a wide range of disabled children and adults were perceived by those who had considerable, sometimes ultimate power over their lives. Because in many respects, their exchanges presage debates to be reworked in one form or another for the next three decades, they are worth considering in detail. Many others who published in medical journals in the wake of the Zachary–Lorber exchanges placed themselves somewhere along a continuum between the positions adopted by the two men from the Sheffield centre.[29]

Zachary was a paediatric surgeon with an international reputation. A Roman Catholic, he was described in an obituary by a colleague, as someone who 'had more faith in moral than statistical truths' and who reputedly identified with children with spina bifida because of his own impairment of the spine.[30] In 1968 in an article in the *Lancet*, he makes a strong ethical case for taking active steps to give all such children the best chance of survival.[31] Having ruled out the direct and intentional killing of the children, he confronts head on the practice of 'allowing to die' by withholding food or not treating for complications such as infections: 'To leave a child without food is to kill it as deliberately and directly as if one was cutting its throat. Even the prescribing of antibiotics for infection, must now be considered as ordinary care of patients.'

His emphasis on antibiotics as an 'ordinary' intervention was in keeping with the Roman Catholic doctrine requiring individuals to use ordinary but not extraordinary means to safeguard life. Arguing in a way that was unusual for its time, Zachary suggests that instead of ending children's lives, the community as a whole should take responsibility for ensuring that they have the educational and other provision which would enable them to develop their full potential. He offers a positive view of the options which could be available for disabled children and adults and their families, given commitment and resources.

By contrast, his colleague Lorber describes the fruits of 'indiscriminate use of advanced techniques' as being to keep alive 'those who would have died but who now live with distressing physical or mental handicaps or both, often for years, without hope of ever having an independent existence compatible with human dignity'.[32] After conducting a series of follow-up studies of children and young adults who had had surgical intervention, he began publishing on the possibility of withholding treatment from some infants.[33] A policy of 'selective non-treatment' began in Sheffield in 1971 with the stated objective of avoiding treating those who would survive with 'severe handicaps'.[34] Consequently, it was argued that only children likely to have 'moderate handicaps' should be given treatment. It is apparent from his writing that the category of children with 'moderate handicaps' was not intended to encompass those who would be 'retarded'.[35] 'Considerable paraplegia, often with gross deformities of legs and feet' also appears to have been regarded as a severe 'defect'[36] as does 'paraplegia requiring callipers, crutches or wheelchair for locomotion'.[37]

Lorber developed a set of medical criteria designed to predict which children would develop 'severe handicaps' and therefore, be unsuitable for treatment.[38] In addition, however, he argued that the infant's social situation was also to be taken into account with the result that if the child's circumstances were seen as unfavourable, the threshold for treatment could be raised still further. In a paper published in 1975, Lorber reasons that 'the fate of an abandoned or unwanted child is very grave, even if his physical condition is a little better than those with major adverse criteria'.[39] He concedes that by employing his criteria, some children who would have survived 'with normal intelligence' would die as a result of being excluded from treatment. He seeks to legitimate this, however, on the grounds that intelligent individuals, being more aware of their situation, would have suffered even more than those who were 'retarded'. According to the protocol described in the 1975 paper, decisions about selection were to be made by a consultant and expert in this field of medicine. Parents should be consulted but were not to decide because they were seen as 'hardly ever sufficiently informed' and also under emotional strain. In all of this, there was no discussion of the law or consideration of the legality of the procedures being instituted.

Lorber's approach was explicitly underpinned by a number of assumptions: that specific impairments or levels of impairment could by and large, be taken as the main predictors for a future quality of life without reference to the potential impact of other factors;[40] that the doctor's right to make

the judgement was justified with reference to scientific or technical expertise; that judgements about a projected quality of life formed a legitimate
basis for decisions about whether a child should survive; that the children
themselves who were selected for non-intervention would have had lives
characterized as not worth living; that the survival of such children would
have had 'disastrous effects' on the family as a whole and on individuals
within it; that their care was costly. Finally, he adds: 'Perhaps worst of all,
because severely affected infants were "saved", many more potentially normal lives never started because their parents did not dare to have other
children.'[41] Thus, the right to life of non-disabled children who may or may
not be conceived was argued to take precedence over the right to life of a
living disabled child.

It is crucial to note that the practice that Lorber developed was influential, widely respected, and enduring. By the mid-1970s, he reported that the
approach had already been adopted by a number of other centres in the
United Kingdom.[42] In some places, his criteria for determining which children should be given treatment to help them survive and which children
should be left untreated were still being applied well into the 1980s.[43] As has
already been noted, the Zachary–Lorber conflict was also instrumental in
generating a significant debate within medical and medical-related literature and one which encompassed decision-making in relation to disabled
infants with impairments and conditions other than spina bifida.[44]

Partly because of the internalized private nature of the decision-making
process at the time of the Leonard Arthur and *re B* cases, it is difficult to be
certain how common was the practice of withholding treatment or taking
other steps to ensure that babies who were considered to be severely disabled did not survive.[45] The relevant international medical and related
professional literature of the period leaves no doubt, however, that the
practice of ending life was by no means unusual.[46] In 1981, Lorber was
reported to have estimated that 300 children with spina bifida were
allowed to die each year.[47] The practice of ending life appeared in a number of guises. Frequently, terms with passive connotations such as
'allowing to die' or 'letting nature take its course' were used to obscure
practices designed to bring about death. Sometimes, euphemisms such as
'selective non-treatment' or even 'tertiary prevention'[48] masked the nature
of the activity, on paper at least. Sometimes, bringing about death was presented as a positive and caring form of intervention.[49] Debates about what
constituted an act of commission as opposed to an act of omission were
also common, the assumption being that the former usually required
greater justification than the latter. As has already been discussed, distinguishing between 'ordinary' and 'extraordinary' means of preserving life
was often regarded as important. Practitioners held a range of opinions on
the degree to which parents' wishes should be taken into account.[50]

Before the Leonard Arthur and *re B* cases, few outside medicine became
involved in the debate. A working party of doctors, church leaders and lay

people which was set up under the auspices of the Newcastle Regional Hospital Board to investigate selective non-treatment and spina bifida reported in 1975. In many respects, it endorsed the stance adopted by Lorber, concluding that while doctors were required to use 'ordinary means' to sustain the lives of disabled children, they were not obliged to use 'extraordinary means'. The application of the principle of 'ordinary' or 'extraordinary' means was, however, judged to be legitimately affected by matters such as the degree of the 'abnormality', the child's future quality of life, and the 'burdens' that would be placed on the family and society.[51]

In short, there were four main arguments used to legitimate the ending of life. Shearer in her seminal monograph, *Everybody's Ethics*, dubs them simply: 'it's better for the family', 'it's better for the child', 'it's better for society' and 'they're not really human anyway'.[52]

The social and political context of *re B* and Leonard Arthur

At the end of the 1970s and beginning of the 1980s, the medicalization of these issues, combined with the largely unchallenged position and authority of doctors, is undoubtedly significant. An exploration of the wider contemporary social context, however, also gives some indication why the ending of disabled children's lives did not become an immediate issue for public debate and legal intervention. It also offers clues about the factors which began to trigger some challenges to the status quo.

In the 1970s in the United Kingdom, disability was still not generally accepted as an issue that warranted a place on the mainstream public policy agenda.[53] Disabled adults and children were largely segregated and, as a consequence, the greater part of the non-disabled population had little contact with them and was ignorant of their lives.[54] The notion that disabled children and adults should be seen as having the rights and considerations routinely accorded to the non-disabled population was simply not part of dominant discourses. It was not unusual for some at least to be regarded as not having the attributes of human beings.[55]

While small numbers of disabled people in the UK in the 1970s and early 1980s were beginning to develop and articulate their own alternative perspectives on the experience of disability,[56] they had virtually no audible public voice nor visible public presence. Disability when discussed at all was mostly presented from the perspective of the non-disabled professional. A review of the professional literature of the period indicates that their orientation was dominated by overwhelmingly negative views of disability.[57] Thomas argues that in their search for the pathological, contemporary writers from the professions routinely ignored the conventional aspects of disabled people's lives on the assumption that it was impossible for disability to co-exist with things ordinary.[58]

In addition to these damaging perceptions, disabled children and adults were offered very little that was positive and much that was negative by way of service provision. The very poor quality of the limited services available to disabled children and adults and their families may be taken both as an indicator of the value accorded to them and as a factor which contributed to the view that they would be better off dead. The dominant spectre of the large, long-stay hospital had considerable impact on thinking about whether disabled children and adults could have lives worth living. As Kennedy observes, it undoubtedly fed people's fears that the fate of those who survived was not far removed from 'living death'.[59] Outside of the education system, the large institution was often still the main public provision available to disabled children and adults. For example, in the mid-1970s in England, there were still 6,500 children with learning difficulties who spent their childhoods in the inhumane and depriving conditions of the long-stay hospitals.[60] Oswin describes the conditions revealed by the research she undertook at that time:

> Observers in the long-stay hospitals in the 1970s recorded a continuation of appalling deprivations; for example, children were growing up without ever seeing shops or food being cooked; they never mixed with children outside the hospitals; they were denied affection; they were out of bed at 4.30 am and were left half naked in cots for many hours; some spent hours sitting on potties on concrete floors with cockroaches crawling round their bare feet; some were tied to chairs all day.[61]

As adults, many others (more than 50,000 in England in 1976) could also look forward to long-stay hospitals being their place of residence for long periods.[62] In the mid-1970s, 39 per cent of these hospitals in England and Wales had 1,000 beds or more.[63] Services and financial support for children and adults who lived at home were also poor or non-existent and individuals and families who resisted hospital placement were largely reliant on their own personal and material resources.[64] The majority of disabled children living with their families received their education segregated from their non-disabled peers. The fact that they were in schools termed 'special' could in no way be taken as a reliable indicator of the quality of the provision.[65] It was not until 1970 that children with learning disabilities were accorded the right to education.

It is also important to note that while the late 1970s and early 1980s saw mounting public, professional and political concern about the problem of child abuse, particularly in the context of the family,[66] reference was rarely made to disabled children. It was not until the 1990s that they were accorded even a shadowy presence on the mainstream child protection agenda.[67] Such was their degree of marginalization, that they had, in effect, to be *argued into* the category of 'children' who were deemed to have the need for and right to protection. In this climate it would have been highly unusual for any connection to be made between widespread professional concerns over infant deaths generally, and those medical practices which brought about the deaths of disabled babies. They were quite simply regarded as entirely separate matters.

It was not only within the mainstream political and policy agenda that disability was marginalized. Contemporary political groups and movements which spoke the language of liberation for those who were oppressed did not usually recognize disabled children and adults as being within that category. For example, the politics of the visible and active political Left of the time rarely embraced the interests of disabled people.[68] Similarly, feminism's neglect of disabled women during the 1970s and early 1980s has also been a source of comment.[69] Among other things, the defining of motherhood and caring as activities oppressive to women led some to disregard the rights and needs of those children and adults who needed care and assistance. There was, however, one specific factor which guaranteed that some feminists would have had difficulty in challenging publicly the practice of ensuring that disabled babies did not survive. As we have seen, it was the organization Life that took action against Leonard Arthur. In the 1970s, when a rallying point for many feminists was the 'woman's right to choose' position on abortion law reform,[70] some undoubtedly felt that they could not afford to muddy the waters by giving consideration to any of Life's policies.[71]

Taken together, the overwhelmingly negative and burdensome images of living with disability, the barriers which prevented disabled people living ordinary lives, the segregated and frequently dehumanizing service provision, the tendency to characterize disabled children and adults as falling outside majority definitions of personhood, and the exclusion of disabled people and disability issues from political and policy agendas may be seen as significant factors in a context where practices to curtail disabled children's lives were legitimated.

This period, however, also saw the beginnings of change. In the 1970s, the needs of disabled children and their families began to attract some government recognition mostly as a result of media attention given to Thalidomide and vaccine damage, the landmark ruling of the European Court of Human Rights in the Thalidomide case (*Sunday Times v. UK*) occurring in 1979. In the mid-1970s, some financial benefits were introduced to offset the costs of living with disability, and the Family Fund was set up to give grants to families of disabled children. The Warnock Committee reporting in 1978 proposed a radical overhaul of special education provision for all disabled children and paved the way for the 1981 Education Act.[72] In coining the term 'parents as partners', Warnock also gave expression to a new perspective held by a relatively small number of professionals whose practice was regarded as progressive. This gave recognition to the fact that parents frequently had a great deal of expertise, had been largely ignored by dominant professional practice and deserved better.[73] In a situation where parents had been misunderstood and discounted for so long, attempts to appreciate their knowledge and perspectives can undoubtedly be regarded as positive. Many were clearly their child's most reliable advocates and were accomplishing a great deal in very taxing circumstances.[74] Unfortunately, a more appreciative approach to parents sometimes went hand in hand with a failure to recognize that their rights and their children's rights and wishes were not always coterminous, a dangerous assumption particularly when a life-and-death decision is being made in relation to any child.

The publicity given to the revelations of the degrading and inhumane conditions in Ely mental handicap hospital[75] triggered new government policy initiatives for adults with learning difficulties, in the form of *Better Services for the Mentally Handicapped*.[76] This aimed over time to reduce the numbers of people in long-stay hospitals and to shift resources to smaller, locally based community facilities. In 1975, concerns about the slow rate of progress prompted the Secretary of State for the Social Services to establish the National Development Group for the Mentally Handicapped to advise ministers. Between 1976 and 1986, the population of people in the mental handicap hospitals was reduced by 30 per cent. The population of resident children, however, fell by more than 80 per cent.[77]

The end of the 1970s and beginning of the 1980s also saw the work of a small number of academic centres beginning to question dominant orthodoxy about disability through their publications, research and teaching. Research began to focus more on poverty and on the material problems that went hand in hand with living with disability. It also began to place centre-stage the inadequacy of service provision and to introduce the notion of rights to services.[78] Work emerged which emphasized the importance of enhancing disabled children's opportunities to learn.[79] A challenge was beginning to be mounted in relation to segregation and its negative impact, particularly in relation to education,[80] and accounts began to appear of a small number of experimental independent living schemes, sometimes organized by disabled people themselves.[81] The notion that disability could be seen as a social and political issue began to emerge in both orthodox and grey literature,[82] and early attempts were being made in university courses to reframe the ways in which disability was understood. At this point, those wishing to argue that there was a different and better way of understanding and responding to disability frequently looked to Scandinavia and the United States for inspiration.[83] State social welfare provision in Scandinavian countries was generally regarded as more progressive and better-resourced than in the United Kingdom. By the mid-1970s in the United States, there existed an active disability rights movement composed mainly of disabled adults and parents of disabled children.[84] This movement had identified disabled children and adults as a minority group subject to discrimination[85] and had successfully campaigned for anti-discrimination legislation which was passed in 1973.

In the late 1970s and early 1980s in the United Kingdom, a new breed of local and national pressure group started to emerge. These were often

made up of parents who were prepared to be much more vocal in arguing
for a better deal for their disabled children. Demands for more responsive
services and inclusion in mainstream education often provided a common
focus for campaigning.[86] Sometimes parents were joined by professionals
and academics who wished to see more progressive services and changes in
attitudes. They, too, often looked beyond the British context for inspiration.
The Campaign for Mentally Handicapped People (CMH) provides an
example of one such organization which brought to the fore the notion of
rights for children and adults with learning disabilities and campaigned for
improved services.[87] CMH also provided arguably the most clearly articulated contemporary challenge to the practice of ending the lives of disabled
infants by publishing Shearer's position pamphlet, *Everybody's Ethics*.[88]

Finally, during this period, the beginnings of a climate change can be
seen in relation to children's rights.[89] While disabled children did not feature in the forefront of such work at this point, the notion that children
should be given a voice in their own right separate from adults who had
parental or professional responsibility for their welfare was gaining ground
among some social services workers and lawyers.

Important as these developments were to further the interests of disabled children and adults, it needs to be recognized that at the end of the
1970s and beginning of the 1980s, they were in the minority and were only
just beginning to make an impact on old typologies and established attitudes and practices.

Leonard Arthur and *re B*: precipitating factors

As we have seen, the prosecution of Leonard Arthur was initiated by the
pressure group Life which had gone on the offensive in its campaign to
safeguard the lives of disabled babies and to redefine as murder the medical practices which aimed to bring their lives to an end. In the same year as
the Arthur prosecution, the organization was also reported to have made
complaints against other doctors alleged to have brought about the deaths
of five babies with spina bifida and another with Down's syndrome. Press
coverage indicates that two of those cases were referred to the Director of
Public Prosecutions but no further action was taken.[90]

The reference points of those involved in taking wardship proceedings
in respect of 'Baby Alexandra' were different. While such intervention by a
local authority was unprecedented and was subsequently presented by
many as highly controversial, for David Plank, the director of Social
Services responsible, what needed to be done appeared 'reasonable and
rather obvious':

> We decided that clearly it was right that the baby should have the oper-
> ation because the baby was an independent person and had a right to
> life ... The most fundamental right is the right to live ... It was our legal

responsibility as a social services authority to intervene on behalf of the child and in support of the medics who wanted the operation to go ahead in order that she should live ... She was a *child* first and had Down's syndrome second. All the issues around quality of life seemed really immaterial, legally immaterial. They were not immaterial to the parents and I understood what they were going through ... but the arguments that were being made against having the operation, basically did not distinguish between the parents and the child and saw the child wholly as a possession of the parents. And in law, that's not right and morally that's not right ... The 1948 Act and the 1969 Act clearly applied to all children and there's no distinction between disabled and non-disabled children in the legislation. Therefore, not to have acted in the case of the disabled child would have required quite extraordinary justification and I can't see what justification could have been given.[91]

Public and professional reactions to the cases of Leonard Arthur and *re B*

The trial of Leonard Arthur and the case of 'Baby Alexandra' had considerable impact. It was not only that a respected paediatrician had been put on trial for murder; medical practice itself was publicly interrogated in a way that was highly unusual for the time. Kennedy points out how rarely the law had been involved in cases of medical ethics prior to this case, and suggests that the increased visibility of complex medical–ethical issues reduced the possibility of their continuing to be resolved by private arrangement.[92] In addition, in the case of 'Baby Alexandra', the duties and powers of a local authority were also brought to bear on decisions that had usually been taken within the confines of the doctor–patient relationship. Public reactions were strong and the local authority found itself in the midst of controversy. David Plank recalls that he received many hundreds of letters, the majority of which took issue with the fact that he was seen to have interfered and contravened parents' rights. Despite the fact that social services' intervention was triggered by the concern of doctors and action taken with their full support, some also accused him of having trespassed on medical territory. Others expressed concern about the cost of care for 'Alexandra', should she survive. Even though his stance was different in many respects from that of Life and other similar organizations, some of the public support for his action inevitably came from them.[93]

The cases generated a new wave of articles and papers in the medical literature in the United Kingdom and elsewhere.[94] Doctors were in no doubt about the significance of the trial of Leonard Arthur. Gillon, the editor of the *Journal of Medical Ethics*, identified 38 ethical issues raised by the Leonard Arthur case and used it as the basis for a series of papers on an introduction to medical ethics in the *British Medical Journal*.[95] Links were made between the concerns of British medical practitioners and their peers in the United States. On the heels of the cases in the United Kingdom, the case of 'Baby Doe' in America and the issuing of what became known as the 'Baby Doe Regulations' established that the issue of bringing about the deaths of disabled infants was now firmly in the public and legal domains.[96] The death of 'Baby Doe' as a result of selective non-treatment caused a political storm and was, in part at least, responsible for the Reagan administration issuing guidance to the effect that such practices contravened the 1973 Rehabilitation Act. The Act precluded programmes supported by federal funding from discriminating against disabled individuals.[97] The medical publications of the time reflect a range of positions on a similar continuum to that already established through the earlier Zachary–Lorber conflict. Both Zachary[98] and Lorber[99] entered the debate generated by the cases of Leonard Arthur and *re B*, reaffirming their established positions on the issue of bringing about the deaths of disabled babies.

The cases also resulted in substantial public debate and mass media coverage. For example, in 1981 and 1982, there were a number of television and radio debates[100] and MORI conducted opinion polls for the BBC and the Human Rights Society.[101] During the same period, *The Times* alone carried more than 50 items about the cases or issues directly related to them. Once more, a detailed review of these features, news items and letters is beyond the scope of this paper, but it is important to note that this coverage gives an indication of how widespread was the debate. The opinions were reported of church leaders, politicians, lawyers, doctors, philosophers, pressure groups, parents of disabled children and other individual members of the public. Parliamentary bills were drafted both to protect the lives of disabled babies and to give doctors the legal authority to bring life to an end. A range of bodies made proposals for drawing up practice guidance. New organizations were formed by those with opposing and equally strongly held opinions on the issues.

There were some who, as we have seen, abhorred the practice of bringing the lives of disabled babies to an end. Religious faith and other ethics and values led some to believe that *all* children had the right to live.[102] There were parents of disabled children and their organizations who felt that in a climate of ignorance about disability, the positive aspects of their own and their children's lives went unrecognized.[103] In addition, in a context where the concept of *disability rights* was not yet part of the dominant discourse, there were a small number of commentators and groups such as the CMH intent on recasting the debate as one which concerned *the* most fundamental of rights of disabled children and of disabled people more generally.[104]

1981 was the International Year of the Disabled Person but precious little space was given in the press and professional literature to the views of disabled people themselves. The impact on them of the frequently harsh public debate on disabled children cannot be stressed too strongly.

Micheline Mason, the disabled writer and activist and one of the few disabled people afforded the opportunity to express a view, wrote:

> I do not want to discuss the issue. You are speaking about my life. You wish me to discuss whether or not, as a woman born with a 'severe' disability, I think I should have been murdered. It does not sound reactionary to me to hear of people who want to put an end to the killing of babies because they have disabilities. It sounds wonderful ... The Leonard Arthur case was very distressing to me and many of my friends with disabilities. We became afraid to turn on the TV or radio in case we were landed with another dose of 'Should we let them live?' When you suspect that the world would rather you weren't there, this sort of baggage can be most depressing. We felt the overall result was to legitimise and make respectable the most appalling aspects of our oppression.[105]

For many, however, bringing about the deaths of at least some disabled babies was considered desirable, though there was a variety of opinion about who came within the category of those who should live, and who fell outside it. Shearer draws attention to the widespread public support for the actions taken by Leonard Arthur.[106] It was revealed in a Mori poll shortly after his acquittal that 86 per cent of those polled said that if a doctor, with parents' consent, saw to it that a severely handicapped newborn baby died, she or he should not be found guilty of murder.[107] A later Mori poll found that 37 per cent of those who participated thought that it should be arranged for such babies to die.[108]

The 1980s to the present: a changing social and political climate

By the time *re J* was heard in 1990, some of the social changes which were emerging at the beginning of the decade had gained a stronger foothold. The need to close the large institution had won widespread acceptance[109] and government plans for community care reform were under way.[110] Concern over child protection and the need to introduce more effective ways of safeguarding children's welfare resulted in the Children Act 1989 which brought together most public and private law relating to children. The impact of the beginnings in attitude change towards disabled children can be seen in that the Act determined that disabled children should be included as 'children first' under legislation designed to safeguard the interests of all children.[111] In other words, the new legislation made explicit those very sentiments and ethics which had shaped David Plank's decision in relation to 'Baby Alexandra' nearly a decade earlier.

The 1980s and 1990s also witnessed the start of major efforts in the United Kingdom to redefine disability as a social and political issue. While the impetus for this came from a number of the sources identified earlier in this paper, there emerged across the 1980s an additional and most significant force for change. During this decade and the one that followed, the disabled people's movement gained in strength and influence and began to revolutionize thinking on disability.[112] Disability was beginning to be politicized in an effort to change its definition from one of a private misfortune to one of a matter of public responsibility. Across a period of two decades, this movement and its sympathizers were instrumental in gradually bringing about a major reframing of the way disability was construed in public consciousness.

The process of politicizing disability was accelerated by the growing number of disabled academics establishing the field of 'disability studies'.[113] The beginnings of an alternative discourse was established which validated disabled people's subjective experiences and enabled them to redefine themselves, their lives and aspirations in ways that frequently ran counter to the dominant orthodoxy to which many professionals subscribed. Central to the work of disability studies and the disabled people's movement was the notion that some of the most restrictive and damaging aspects of their lives were not inevitable consequences of having impairments. Major problems were seen to derive from social and political factors which were external to the person and which could be changed by social and political means. Utilizing what became known as the 'social model of disability', disabled activists and academics increasingly argued that they experienced discrimination because of the way that society was designed to exclude and oppress them. They identified and exposed the multilayered nature of the discrimination that disabled children and adults experienced in their daily lives.[114] Within this work, the established language of restrictive impairments and lives-not-worth-living was challenged head on and gradually countered by discourses of oppression, discrimination, human and civil rights and citizenship.[115] This has not been a matter confined to academic debate. Disabled activists and academics have been successful in winning widespread acceptance, at least in principle, of the need to validate the perspectives of disabled people and to forward an anti-discrimination and rights agenda. While the achievements of the movement are impressive, particularly when consideration is given to the range of arenas where change has been achieved, it has to be recognized that, for many disabled children and adults, the barriers that prevent them aspiring to the things that their non-disabled peers take for granted may still seem dispiritingly prevalent and insurmountable.

Discussion

The cases which have been the focus of this paper provide a lens through which we can view the changing sociolegal climate in relation to disability. In addressing the most fundamental of disabled children's human rights, the right to life, they allow us access to contemporary discourses in relation to disabled people in a particularly concentrated form. The cases and related debates show clearly the changing benchmarks that have been used in law and professional practice to make decisions about the circumstances that are seen to permit the deaths of disabled babies and young children. These cases also connect us to the wider social context and allow us to follow major changes in understandings and responses to disability more generally. In many respects, they reflect the tensions in that context.

In 1981 it was being established for the first time that the law could and should be brought to bear on the issue of protecting the lives or bringing about the deaths of disabled babies. Hitherto, it had been left solely to the professional discretion of doctors in consultation with parents. Consequently, whether a baby's life was protected or brought to an end could to a large degree be determined by the personal and professional ethics of the doctor responsible for treatment. It is clear what a major challenge the two cases presented to contemporary thinking.

In an age where medicine was seen to be all-conquering, the law was used as a tool (and as an intellectual force) to challenge this primacy, and open up to public scrutiny what had hitherto been a closed private domain. While the law did not challenge the professional autonomy of doctors, it identified the dilemmas in relation to these disabled children as fundamentally non-medical. It established that, as a general rule, no one – not judges, not the general public, not parents, not even doctors – were able to decide whether the life of a disabled child was or was not worth living. The presumption has to be in favour of life. Through the cases discussed in this paper, it was established that only when a life was so demonstrably awful in terms of being intolerable, racked by extreme pain and lack of consciousness, could it be contemplated that ordinary treatment be withheld.

When we analyse the cases of Leonard Arthur and *re B* in context, it is apparent how very fragile was the position of disabled babies at that time: the protection that the law afforded to other children could in no way be taken for granted in their case. As we have seen, arguments that would never have been countenanced in relation to non-disabled children were frequently advanced to support the ending of disabled babies' lives. As far as many were concerned, disabled babies and children were implicitly placed in a separate category from their non-disabled peers with the consequence that they need not be afforded the same rights or protections. It is telling that for many, there was no apparent contradiction between the heightened public, professional and legal concern about child protection generally running in parallel with widespread acceptance of the ending of the lives of disabled babies and young children.

Some, like Lorber,[116] were explicit not only in construing the lives of some disabled children as not worth living but also in subordinating their rights and needs to those of non-disabled people. It is chilling to recall the range of children whom Lorber and those who adopted his criteria regarded as too disabled to survive. It is equally chilling to reflect on the fact that those criteria were still being applied to some, as babies, who are now young disabled adults only in their twenties. It is also important to recognize that while Lorber may have figured large and been prepared to be more explicit than most, he represented a position that was by no means unusual. In many ways, it can be argued that Lorber and those in the medical profession who shared variants of his views, merely reflected, from a position of authority and power, a spectrum of commonplace attitudes towards disability in wider society, attitudes which were built into the bricks and mortar of the large institutions and, in turn, reinforced by their existence. The same might be said of the judge's summing up in the Leonard Arthur trial. Disabled people have been acutely aware of the dangers when this degree of power rests in the hands of those non-disabled professionals who place little value on their lives. In the mid-1990s, Nasa Begum, the disabled activist and writer reflected:

> Life and death decisions about disabled babies are vested in the hands of people who have very little understanding of the reality of disabled people's lives. The issue of selective treatment is full of complications because of the way that practical, ethical, legal, moral and financial issues are intertwined. However, it is absolutely critical that this is recognised as a fundamental part of the fight for civil and human rights ... Whilst some people might think that the notion of selective treatment being analogous to the Nazi Euthanasia programme is extreme, there is every reason to believe that much of the criteria and quality of life indicators that have been put forward, endorse the concept of 'lebensunwerten' (or lives unworthy of life).[117]

Challenging such institutionalized and enduring attitudes and practices was extremely difficult but an analysis of the four cases shows change over time. In the Leonard Arthur case, the existence of disability in itself was held to be the key justification for ending life. Parents, it seemed, were allowed to contribute to a decision about life and death in a way that would have been inconceivable in relation to a non-disabled child. In the slightly earlier and more far-reaching case of *re B*, however, the judge made his decision purely in relation to the best interests of the child. In addition, he introduced the concept that a disabled child's life should be seen in its own terms and that it was not for the court to decide that lives like this should be ended. In the *Dawson* case, this notion is further strengthened. McKenzie argues that a disabled person's life must not be judged and found wanting using benchmarks that apply to those who are non-disabled. Thus, he makes the case for something that disability rights movements across the world have fought for, a recognition of 'the authenticity of impaired modes of being'.[118] In addition, at a time when disabled people were so undervalued, there is a particularly clear and strong statement by McKenzie that disabled children's lives must in no way be seen to be less valuable than those of others. Donaldson in *re J* confirms the best interests' principle and a strong presumption in favour of life.

The challenges to the practice of ensuring that disabled babies should die came from a number of sources. As we have seen, one of the most visible and sustained of these was from Roman Catholic doctors and lay organizations. While some individual Roman Catholics may of course have had particular connections with disabled people and disability issues, their stance was mainly related to a more general theological stance on the fundamental right to life of all, a position made clear in 1981 by the Roman Catholic Bishops' Conference of England and Wales.[119] Some of different faiths later made known a similar view underpinned by a similar rationale.[120]

This was a rather different position from those who challenged such practices from a disability rights perspective. In the early 1980s some health and social welfare progressives, academics, vocal families of disabled children, and initially small numbers of disabled adults began to define disabled people as a group whose rights were routinely infringed. As is clear from David Plank's recollections, some also emphasized that disabled children were 'children first' and should be afforded the same rights and protections as their non-disabled peers. At the beginning of the 1980s, those who took this view were still a minority. As is clear from the outcome in relation to 'Baby Alexandra', however, the health or social welfare progressive with a personal awareness of disability and a professional commitment to the emerging 'non-institutionalized' opportunities for disabled people could prove to be an effective and persistent minority. Templeman's summing up shows that he was persuaded that for 'Alexandra' and others like her, positive alternatives to parental care were feasible and that there was the possibility that she could have a happy life. The influence of health and welfare staff with more positive perceptions of disabled children's lives can also be seen in the Dawson case.

In the longer term, the politicization of disability has arguably been the factor that has had the greatest impact in terms of measures to safeguard and promote disabled people's rights. Particularly through the wide-ranging activities and influence of the disabled people's movement, the last two decades of the twentieth century witnessed the notions of rights for disabled people gradually taking root in social institutions and processes and becoming more firmly embedded in public consciousness.

Despite this progress, the issue of the right to life and the value accorded to the lives of disabled people continues to emerge in different forms and to be a source of grave concern to disabled people and their organizations. The Disability Rights Commission (DRC) is to make submissions in *Ms B v. An NHS Hospital Trust*[121] (currently pending). The case, which in its opinion is by no means an isolated one, concerns a disagreement between the mother of a disabled child and the clinicians as to whether or not the child should be resuscitated, if a relapse occurs. The issue is thus the opposite of that in *re B* and the *Dawson* cases – since here it is the parent arguing in favour of life. A spokesperson for the DRC summarized the importance of the case:

> I hope this case will draw attention to the issue of the assumptions that can be made about the lives of disabled children and adults who have significant impairments, and I hope it will make clear what the Human Rights Act really does require.
>
> Disabled people want to be consulted and involved but they also want to be treated as equal citizens. Disabled people don't want their lives to be judged in different terms or to have a different value, that's all.[122]

Acknowledgements

This chapter first appeared as J. Read and L. Clements (2004) 'Demonstrably awful: The right to life and the selective non-treatment of disabled babies and young children', in the *Journal of Law and Society*, 31, 4, 482–509. The authors thank the editors of the *Journal of Law and Society* and Blackwell Publishing, PO Box 805, 9600 Garsington Road, Oxford, for their kind permission to reproduce the paper in this publication. We also thank Professor Nick Spencer, Professor Phil Fennell and Professor Tony Booth for helpful advice, David Plank for giving a valuable interview, and Katrin Bailly for assistance with library searches.

Notes

1 [2001] 2 WLR 480; [2000] 4 All ER 961.
2 9 March 2004; No. 61827/00.
3 7 October 2004; [2004] EWHC 2247 (Fam.).
4 [1981] 1 WLR 1421; [1990] 3 All ER 927.
5 [1983] DLR (3d) 610; [1983] 3 WWR 618; 42 BCLR 173.
6 [1990] 2WLR 140; [1990] 3 All ER 930.
7 Gillon, R. (1985) 'An introduction to philosophical medical ethics: The Arthur case', *British Medical Journal*, 290, 1117–1119, 13 April.
8 Friedman, L.M. (1973) 'General theory of law and social change', in J.S. Ziegel (ed.) *Law and Social Change.* Agincourt, Ontario: Osgood Hall Law School, pp.17–33, at p.21.
9 Cotterell, R. (1998) 'Why must legal ideas be interpreted sociologically?', *Journal of Law and Society*, 25, 2, pp.171–192, at p.175.
10 The failure of the defence to disclose evidence that John Pearson may have had other impairments until the cross-examination of the prosecution pathologist resulted in a procedural change to the law requiring technical evidence to be treated like an alibi defence and disclosed to the court beforehand – British Medical Journal (1998) 'Obituary Alan Usher' *BMJ*, 317, 1457, 21 November.
11 See Kennedy, I. (1988) *Treat Me Right: Essays in Medical Ethics.* Oxford: Clarendon Press; Morgan, D. (1989) 'Severely handicapped babies and the

courts', *NLJ*, 139, 6409, 723 (26 May 1989); and Wright, G. (1999) 'The culture of death', *Catholic Medical Quarterly*, November, 19–22.

12 *BBC News Online*, 29 August 2000. 17:29 UK.

13 Kennedy, I. (1988) op. cit.; Wright, G. (1999) op. cit.

14 Kennedy I. (1988) op. cit., p155.

15 Booth, T. (1982) *Eradicating Handicap*. Course E241. Milton Keynes: The Open University.

16 *Guardian*, 5 November 1981, p.3.

17 Booth, T. (1982) op. cit.

18 Kennedy, I. (1982) 'Reflections of the Arthur trial', *New Society*, 13–16, 7 January.

19 *The Sunday Times*, 16 August 1981.

20 *J v. C* [1969] 1 All ER 788; [1970] AC 668 – a custody case not involving a disabled child.

21 Morgan, D. (1989) op. cit.

22 *In re Weberlist* (1974) 360 N.Y.S.2d 783; N.Y.Sup. 1974: a case concerning profound cosmetic and dental surgery for a disabled adult.

23 See for instance *In re C (A Minor) (Wardship: Medical Treatment)* [1990] Fam 26; *In re R (A Minor) (Wardship: Consent to Treatment)* [1992] Fam. 11; *In re J (A Minor) (Child In Care: Medical Treatment)* [1992] 3 WLR 507; [1992] 4 All ER 614; *R v. Portsmouth Hospitals NHS Trust, ex parte Glass* [1999] 2 FLR 905, 50 BM LR 269 and *A NHS Trust v. D and others* (2000) 55 BMLR 19; *Glass v. UK* (2004) 9 March 2004; No. 61827/00.

24 [1990] 2WLR 140; [1990] 3 All ER 930.

25 Kennedy, I. (1988) op. cit.

26 Booth, T. (1982) op. cit.; Weir, R. (1984) *The Selective Nontreatment of Handicapped Newborns*. New York: Oxford University Press; Zachary, R. (1968) 'Ethical and social aspects of treatment of spina bifida', *Lancet*, 2, 274; Lorber, J. (1971) 'Results of treatment of myelomeningocele: An analysis of 524 unselected cases, with special reference to possible selection for treatment', *Developmental Medicine and Child Neurology*, 13, 279–303.

27 Weir, R. (1985) 'Selective nontreatment – one year later: Reflections and a response', *Social Science and Medicine*, 20, 11, 1109–1117.

28 Lorber, J. (1975) 'Ethical problems in the management of myelomeningocele and hydrocephalus', *Journal of the Royal College of Physicians*, 10, 47–60.

29 Weir, R. (1984) op. cit., gives a detailed account of the range of positions adopted by doctors in the United Kingdom and the United States in the 1970s.

30 'Obituary: Emeritus Professor Associate RB Zachary', Sheffield University Staff Newsletter 23, 7, p.5, February 1999.

31 Zachary, R. (1968) op. cit. p.274.

32 Lorber, J. (1975) op. cit. p.47.

33 See for example, Lorber, J. (1971) op. cit. Lorber , J. (1972) 'Spina bifida cystica: Results of treatment of 270 consecutive cases with criteria for selection for the future', *Archives of Diseases in Childhood*, 47, 856; Lorber, J. (1975) op. cit.

34 Lorber, J. (1975) op. cit.

35 Lorber, J. (1975) op. cit.

36 Lorber, J. (1975) op. cit.

37 Lorber, J, (1972) op. cit.

38 Lorber, J. (1975) op. cit.

39 Lorber, J. (1975) op. cit. p.53.

40 It has been noted that while Lorber places great emphasis on the predictive validity of his criteria in relation to future medical and developmental outcomes, their definition lacks essential clarity and specificity. Neither is it always absolutely clear which outcomes he regards as falling within the category of

'severe handicaps' which he believes legitimate the policy and practice on selective non-intervention. Spencer, N. (2003) Personal correspondence. University of Warwick.

41 Lorber, J. (1975) op. cit. p.52.

42 Lorber, J. (1975) op. cit.

43 The debate within medicine specifically about selective non-treatment of children with spina bifida, however, was seen to be largely redundant as the number of live births of such children declined. This came about as a result of widespread prenatal screening and research on nutritional supplements during pregnancy.

44 Weir, R. (1985) op. cit.

45 Kennedy, I. (1988) op. cit.; Frader, J. (1985) 'Selecting neonatal ethics', *Social Science and Medicine*, 20, 11, 1085–1090.

46 *Lancet* (1975) 'Ethics of selective treatment of spina bifida'. Report by a working party, 11 January, 1, 85–88; Hauerwas, S. (1975) 'The demands and limits of carer-ethical reflections on the moral dilemmas of neonatal intensive care', *American Journal of the Medical Sciences*, 269, 2, 222–236; Duff, R. and Campbell, A. (1976) 'On deciding the care of severely handicapped or dying persons: With special reference to infants'. *Paediatrics*, 57, 4, 487–493; Wolfensberger, W. (1980) 'A call to wake up to the beginning of a new wave of "euthanasia" of severely impaired people', *Education, Training and Mental Retardation*, 15, 3, 171–172; *Lancet* (1981) 'The doctors' dilemma: A thought from the Medical Services Study Group of the Royal College of Physicians', 18 April, 1, 8225, 887–888; Johnson, P. (1981) 'Selective non-treatment and spina bifida: A case study in ethical theory and application', *Bioethics Quarterly*, 3, 2, 91–111; Deitch, R. (1981) 'The treatment of severely handicapped infants', *Lancet*, 12 September, 2, 8246, 592–593; Garrow, D. (1981) 'A loving thing to do', *Nursing Mirror*, 30 April, 27–28; Weir, R. (1984) op. cit.; *Lancet* (1975) 'Ethics of selective treatment of spina bifida'. Report by a working party, 11 January; Devlin, D. and Magrab, P. (1981) 'Bioethical considerations in the care of handicapped newborns', *Journal of Paediatric Psychology*, 6, 2, 111–119; Editorial: 'The cost of salvage!' (1982) *Public Health: The Journal of the Society of Public Medicine*, 96, 1, 2, January; Frader, J. (1985) 'Selecting neonatal ethics', *Social Science and Medicine*, 20, 11, 1085–1090; Harris, J. (1982) 'Reply to Lorber, Cusine and Anscombe', *Journal of Medical Ethics*, 8, 1, 40–41.

47 *The Times*, 13 August, 1981, p.1.

48 Booth, T. (1982) op. cit.

49 Garrow, D. (1981) op. cit.

50 For example, in contrast to the Lorber position noted above, the British Paediatric Association and the British Medical Association were reported to place the onus on parents being finally responsible for the decision as to whether a disabled baby received treatment. *The Times*, 19 August, 1981, p.2.

51 *Lancet* (1975) op. cit.

52 Shearer, A. (1984) *Everybody's Ethics*. London: CME.

53 See Clements, L. and Read, J. (2003) *Disabled People and European Human Rights*. Bristol: Policy Press.

54 Morris, J. (1991) *Pride Against Prejudice*. London: The Women's Press.

55 Shearer, A. (1984) op. cit.; Read, J. (1987) 'The structural position of mentally handicapped adults, children and their carers: Some implications for practice', in CCETSW *Policy, Politics and Practice: Training for Work with Mentally Handicapped People*. Rugby: Central Council for Education and Training in Social Work; Begum, N. (1995) 'Rock-a-bye baby, or the treatment might stop:

A discussion on selective treatment of disabled babies', *Critical Public Health*, 6, 2, 30–37.

56 For accounts of early political organization by disabled people, see Sutherland, A. (1981) *Disabled We Stand*. London: Souvenir Press, and Campbell, J. and Oliver, M. (1996) *Disability Politics*. London: Routledge.

57 For a review of the literature of this period on disabled children and their families, see, for example, Philp, M. and Duckworth, D. (1982) *Children with Disabilities and their Families: A Review of Research*. Windsor: NFER/Nelson; Read, J. (2000) *Disability, the Family and Society: Listening to Mothers*. Buckingham: Open University Press.

58 Thomas, D. (1982) *The Experience of Handicap*. London: Methuen.

59 Kennedy, I. (1988) op. cit.

60 Oswin, M. (1998) 'An historical perspective', in C. Robinson and K. Stalker (eds) *Growing Up with Disability*. London: Jessica Kingsley Publishers.

61 Ibid.

62 DHSS (1976) *Mental Health Enquiry for England*. London: HMSO.

63 DHSS (1975) *Facilities and Services of Mental Illness and Mental Handicap Hospitals*. London: HMSO.

64 Read, J. (1987) op. cit.

65 Booth, T. and Potts, P. (eds) (1982) *Integrating Special Education*. Oxford: Blackwell.

66 See, for example, Carter, J. (ed.) (1974) *The Maltreated Child*. London: Priory Press; Parton, N. 'The natural history of child abuse: A study in social problem definition', *British Journal of Social Work*, 9, 431–451.

67 Westcott, H. (1993) *Abuse of Children and Adults with Disabilities*. London: NSPCC.

68 See, for example, in Sutherland, A. (1981) op. cit.

69 Begum, N. (1992) 'Disabled women and the feminist agenda', *Feminist Review*, 40, 3–6; Morris, J. (1993) '"Us" and "Them"? Feminist research and community care', in J. Bornat, C. Pereira and F. William (eds) *Community Care: A Reader*. Basingstoke: Macmillan in association with the Open University.

70 Greenwood, V. and Young, J. (1976) *Abortion in Demand*. London: Pluto Press.

71 Shapiro, R. (1982) 'Life: A doctor's right to choose', *Spare Rib*, 114, 26.

72 DES (1978) *The Report of the Committee of Enquiry into the Education of Handicapped Children and Young People* (Warnock Report). Cmnd 7212. London: HMSO.

73 Mittler, P. and McConnachie, H. (1983) *Parents, Professionals and Mentally Handicapped People: Approaches to Partnership*. London: Croom Helm.

74 For discussion of the ways in which parents of disabled children were characterized during this period, see, for example, Read, J. (2000) op. cit.

75 DHSS (1969) *Report of the Committee of Enquiry into the Allegations of Ill-treatment and Other Irregularities at Ely Hospital, Cardiff* (Howe Report). Cmnd 3785. London: HMSO.

76 DHSS (1971) *Better Services for the Mentally Handicapped*. Cmnd 4683. London: HMSO.

77 Booth, T., Simons, K. and Booth, W. (1990) *Outward Bound: Relocation and Community Care for People with Learning Difficulties*. Buckingham: Open University Press.

78 Walker, A. and Townsend, P. (1981) (eds) *Disability in Britain: A Manifesto of Rights*. Oxford: Martin Robertson.

79 See for example, the work of the Hester Adrian Research Centre at Manchester University and its related publications, including Cunningham, C. and Sloper, P. (1978) *Helping Your Handicapped Baby*. London: Souvenir Press.

80 The work of the Open University Special Needs in Education team was notable: see, for example, Booth, T. and Potts, P. (1983) *Integrating Special Education*. London: Basil Blackwell Publisher Ltd.

81 Shearer, A. (1981) *Living Independently*. London: CEH and Kings Fund.

82 UPIAS (1976) *Fundamental Principles of Disability*. London: The Union of the Physically Impaired Against Segregation; Ryan, J. and Thomas, F. (1980) *The Politics of Mental Handicap*. London: Penguin Books; Sutherland, A. (1981) op.cit; Brechin, A., Liddiard, P. and Swain, J. (1981) *Handicap in a Social World*. Sevenoaks: Hodder & Stoughton in association with the Open University Press.

83 For example, Shearer, A. (1981) op. cit.

84 Asch, A. (2001) 'Disability, bioethics and human rights', in G. Albrecht, K. Seelman and M. Bury (eds) *Handbook of Disability Studies*. California and London: Sage Publications.

85 Gliedman, J. and Roth, W. (1980) *The Unexpected Minority: Handicapped Children in America*. New York: Harcourt Brace.

86 For example, Booth, T. and Statham, J. (1982) *Parent's Choice: Establishing a Unit for Children with Down's Syndrome in an Ordinary School*. London: CME; Family Focus (1983) 'Parents underrated but undeterred', *Special Education: Forward Trends*, 10, 4 27–28; Family Focus (1984) *Swimming Against the Tide: Working for Integration in Education*. Coventry: Coventry Resource and Information Service.

87 Tyne, A. and Wertheimer, A. (1980) *Even Better Services*. London: Campaign for Mentally Handicapped People.

88 Shearer, A. (1984) op. cit.

89 At the end of the 1970s and beginning of the 1980s, the establishment of the Who Cares movement, The Voice for the Child in Care and the Children's Legal Centre may be seen as practical manifestations of this climate change. Page, R. and Clark, G. (1977) *Who Cares? Young People in Care Speak Out*. London: National Children's Bureau, provides an early example of publications which focused on children's perspectives.

90 *The Times*, 14 August, 1981, p.22; *The Times*, 6 October, 1981, p.1.

91 Plank, D. (2003) Personal interview, 12 September.

92 Kennedy, I. (1988) op. cit.

93 Plank, D. (2003) op. cit.

94 Weir, R. (1985) op. cit.

95 Gillon, R. (1985) op. cit.

96 President's Commission for the Study of Ethical Problems in Medicine and Biomedical and Behavioural Research (1983) *Deciding to Forego Life-Sustaining Treatment: A Report on the Ethical, Medical and Legal Issues in Treatment Decisions*. Washington DC: Government Printing Office.

97 For a discussion of the American cases and their context, see Asch, A. (2001) op. cit.

98 Zachary, R. (1981) '"To let live" or "cause to die"', *Nursing Mirror*, 30 April, 4–5.

99 *The Times*, 13 August, 1981, p.1.

100 For example, *Live and Let Die*, ATV, March 1981; *Panorama*, BBC1, November 1981; *You the Jury*, BBC, Radio 4, November 1981.

101 *The Times*, 10 November, 1981, p.3; *The Times*, 26 March, 1982, p.5.

102 *The Times*, 6 November, 1981, p.1

103 *The Times*, 7 November, 1981, p3.

104 Shearer, A. (1984) op. cit.

105 Mason, M. (1982) *Spare Rib*, 115, p.26.

106 Shearer, A. (1984) op. cit.

107 *The Times*, 10 November, 1981, p.3.

108 *The Times*, 26 March, 1982, p.5.

109 Booth, T., Simons, K. and Booth, W. (1990) *Outward Bound: Relocation and Community Care for People with Learning Difficulties.* Buckingham: Open University Press.
110 McCarthy, M. (1989) (ed.) *The New Politics of Welfare: An Agenda for the 1990s.* Basingstoke: Macmillan.
111 *The Children Act 1989, Guidance and Regulations Volume 6. Children with Disabilities.* London: HMSO.
112 Campbell, J. and Oliver, M. (1995) op. cit.
113 For example, Abberley, P. (1987) 'The concept of oppression and the development of a social theory of disability', *Disability, Handicap and Society,* 7, 2, 139–155.
114 For example, Barnes, C. (1991) *Disabled People in Britain and Discrimination.* London: Hurst and Co in association with the British Council of Organisations of Disabled People.
115 See for example, Morris, J. (1991) op. cit.; Oliver, M. (1996) *Understanding Disability.* London: Macmillan.
116 Lorber, J. (1975) op. cit.
117 Begum, N. (1995) op. cit.
118 For example, Abberley, P. (1997) 'The limits of classical theory in analysis and transformation of disablement –(Can this really be the end: to be stuck inside Mobile with the Memphis blues again?)', in L. Barton and M. Oliver (eds) *Disability Studies: Past, Present and Future.* Leeds: Disability Press, p.26.
119 *The Times,* 7 November, 1981, p.3.
120 *The Times,* 12 November, 1981, p.2.
121 CO/163/2003 – leave granted by Newman J. on 11 July 2003 – and see Hinsliff, G. (2004) 'Mother seeks right to life for disabled', *Observer,* 4 January.
122 Sayer, L., DRC Director of Policy, quoted in *Observer,* 4 January, 2004, p.12.

9 End-of-life decisions in neonatology and the right to life of the disabled newborn child

Impressions from the Netherlands

Jozef H.H.M. Dorscheidt

Introduction

As a result of the increased possibilities offered by medical technology, many newborn children who in earlier days would have died due to their severe abnormalities nowadays stay alive and are often successfully treated. Yet for some children even the technological advances in medicine are no consolation. Sometimes this leads to dilemmas as to whether or not a physician must start, continue or withdraw lifesaving medical treatment. In exceptional cases the condition of a newborn child raises the question of whether deliberate medical termination of the child's life could be justified.

Recently, this issue has gained much attention in the international media, not least as a result of developments in the Netherlands. An existing protocol[1] concerning this question, produced by paediatricians of the University Medical Center Groningen, caught the eye of the public and has led to several misleading newspaper and television reports claiming that disabled newborn children would be killed in Dutch hospitals for more or less eugenic reasons. I have elsewhere commented on this inaccurate view on the actual Dutch medical practice in this regard and stressed that in the last decades Dutch efforts to find adequate ways of dealing with this end-of-life issue have always been based on the utmost respect for human life, human dignity and individual autonomy: there have been no recent changes in the Dutch interpretation of these values that would clearly infringe on disabled newborn children's best interests.[2] Nevertheless, the legal admissibility of end-of-life decisions regarding these children remains one of the most difficult issues in Dutch health law.[3]

A starting point for a review of the legal admissibility of these decisions against the background of the disabled newborn child's inherent right to life is the response of the UN Children's Rights Committee in January 2004 to the First Periodic Report of the Kingdom of the Netherlands. In its response the committee paid specific attention to this issue and urged the Netherlands to take measures in order to ensure the newborn child's legal protection in view of the UN Children's Rights Convention (CRC). Part of the committee's recommendations was that it be furnished with additional information on this matter in the Second Dutch Periodic Report, due in March 2007. This chapter aims to provide a preview of this forthcoming report on this question.

It commences by clarifying the substance of the UN committee's Concluding Observations. It then outlines the legal context of the Dutch discussion on the deliberate termination of severely disabled newborn life, developments in jurisprudence and the current Dutch medical practice. Finally the chapter addresses the compatibility of end-of-life decisions regarding a severely disabled newborn child with this child's inherent right to life. In this context, I argue that developments in the United States in the 1980s and the remarkable Baby K. case in the early 1990s are of special significance in interpreting the scope of Article 2 of the CRC (non-discrimination).

Concluding Observations of the UN Children's Rights Committee

In its 35th Session in January 2004 the UN Children's Rights Committee delivered its Concluding Observations on the First Periodic Report of the Netherlands on the implementation of the UN Children's Rights Convention into the Dutch legal system.[4] In the context of information regarding the child's inherent right to life as in Article 6 of the CRC, the committee addressed the recent Dutch regulations on euthanasia and physician-assisted suicide and focused in particular on the position of minors within these regulations. The committee also considered the issue of deliberate termination of the lives of newborn infants who are expected to die shortly after birth, as they are born with – and suffer 'unbearably' from – severe disabilities.

Like the Human Rights Committee (HRC), in the summer of 2001[5] the UN Children's Rights Committee expressed its concerns about two Dutch cases in which the lives of severely disabled newborn children were deliberately terminated by physicians. In both cases, however, the physicians in charge were acquitted of murder as they had acted in accordance with – for the first time accepted – requirements of careful practice. In consequence of this information the committee, referring to the earlier HRC's recommendations, recommended that the Netherlands should

> frequently evaluate – and if necessary revise – the regulations and procedures with respect to euthanasia in order to ensure that children, including newborn infants with severe abnormalities, enjoy special protection and that the regulations and procedures are in conformity with Article 6 of the Convention.

In a second recommendation, the committee addressed the need to take all necessary measures to strengthen control of the practice of euthanasia, to prevent non-reporting and to ensure that the mental and psychological status of the child and parents or guardians requesting termination of life are taken into consideration when determining whether to grant the request. In a third recommendation the committee sought additional information from the Dutch Government – to be provided in its next Periodic Report.

Through these recommendations the committee actually recognized the issue of end-of-life decisions in neonatology as a freestanding children's rights issue. It follows that the committee is likely, in future years, to address this topic in reports in other countries: for example in the next Belgian report, as research suggests a not dissimilar medical practice exists in Flanders regarding end-of-life decisions concerning disabled neonates.[6]

The Dutch legal context

According to Dutch law a physician who deliberately terminates the life of a severely disabled newborn child commits a crime under the Penal Code. This act is regarded as homicide or murder, being considered to be an act where human life is deliberately terminated without the explicit request of the person involved. According to Dutch literature and jurisprudence this thanatic act can only remain without legal consequences if the physician can successfully appeal to a ground for impunity. The applicable ground in this matter refers to an emergency situation known under Dutch criminal law as a conflict of interests, as in Article 40 of the Dutch Penal Code.

The Dutch Euthanasia Act, which came into force on 1 April 2002, does not apply to cases of deliberate termination of the life of an incompetent person. This Act only applies to cases of deliberate termination of life on the explicit request of the person involved. The parents or any other legal representative of a newborn child cannot request the termination of the child's life on the child's behalf, as this would be in conflict with the concept of the child's inherent right to life. Moreover, such a request cannot count as a request within the meaning of the Euthanasia Act.

The only regulation within Dutch law, apart from criminal law, applying to the deliberate termination of newborn life is the reporting procedure, based on Article 10 of the Act on the Burial of the Dead, valid as of June 1994. According to this procedure, a physician who has deliberately terminated the life of a newborn child is not allowed to issue a form declaring the child's natural death. Instead, the physician must inform the local coroner about his course of action. The local coroner on his part informs the Public Prosecutor and declares that the physician has reported that the child died as the result of an act of deliberate termination of life without the patient's request. The local coroner then holds a post-mortem on the body of the child and contacts the Officer of Registry of Births, Deaths and Marriages. Furthermore, the local coroner declares by a special form that the physician has provided a report and a well founded and completed list of points of special interest.

Although physicians are legally obliged by the reporting procedure to report their cases of deliberate termination of newborn life, only a few such cases have been reported since the procedure came into force. This reluctance to report is almost certainly due to an earlier Ministry of Justice policy – namely to commence a criminal prosecution in any case so reported to it. This policy led to the two cases the UN Children's Rights Committee referred to in its Concluding Observations. These cases are known as the Prins and Kadijk cases.

The Prins and Kadijk cases

In the mid 1990s the Prins case and the Kadijk case were the first proceedings that addressed the issue of medical neonaticide in a Dutch court of law. In both cases a physician was charged with murder of a severely disabled newborn child. Unlike the Dutch Supreme Court in the earlier Baby Ross decision,[7] the courts in the cases against Prins and Kadijk undertook an in-depth review of the facts. Unfortunately, neither case reached the Dutch Supreme Court.

In both cases a child was born with unexpected and severe abnormalities. In the Prins case the child had a severe spina bifida; in the Kadijk case the child suffered from trisomy 13. Both children also had additional malformations. In both situations no medical treatment was initiated because the responsible physician decided – after consulting different medical experts – that medical intervention was medically futile because of the seriousness of each child's condition. This resulted in a situation where the children's death was considered to be inevitable. Both children's life expectancies were believed to be severely limited and each child appeared to be suffering severe pain which could not be relieved adequately by medication. Prins as well as Kadijk considered that there were no other options to help their baby patients and decided therefore – in consultation with the children's parents – to administer lethal medication, as a result of which both infants died.

Both physicians reported their actions to the juridical authorities, which reviewed their medical conduct against the requirements of careful practice resulting from Dutch criminal law and jurisprudence. As a result, the Board of Procurators General decided not to press criminal charges against the physicians. However, the Dutch Minister of Justice thought otherwise and concluded that both cases offered an opportunity for judicial review. Accordingly the minister ordered the prosecution of Prins and Kadijk, believing that court rulings would contribute to a better legal understanding of the matters at stake. Both physicians were however acquitted by the Court of Appeal in their separate cases. The basis for these acquittals was the 'emergency situation' that existed and the conflict of interest as in Article 40 of the Dutch Penal Code.

The route that led to the acquittal of Prins[8] and Kadijk[9] consists of two elements. The first element involves the justification of the decision not to treat the serious abnormalities of the children. In both cases the diagnosed disabilities were considered to be of such severity that many surgical interventions would have been necessary to open a reasonable life perspective for the children. Undergoing such major surgery would have caused the children very severe suffering. Besides, the positive outcome of these operations was far from certain. This led to the conclusion that operating on the children was medically futile, an estimation that was also shared by other physicians involved in the decision-making process. In both cases the courts consulted independent experts in order to determine whether or not the medical opinions held by Prins and Kadijk were accurate. In court these experts confirmed that the medical and ethical conclusions of the accused physicians were in accordance with current medical understanding and reasonable ethical norms. The evidence of these experts was accepted by the courts.

The second element relates to the line of policy initiated from the moment it was clear that the children would not receive medical treatment. In symbolic terms the decisions not to intervene were considered synonymous with deciding to let the children die, as both children suffered from immense pain for which no cure or adequate measures of relief could be offered. Both physicians consequently came to the conclusion that it was their moral and professional duty to prevent the children suffering such unbearable pain. In this regard Prins as well as Kadijk consulted anaesthetic experts as to the potential for adequate pain relief – which they were advised was very limited. The physicians were therefore confronted by a serious dilemma: what was the most appropriate course of action: keeping the child alive and waiting for nature to take its course or ending this inhumane situation and granting the child a peaceful, yet hastened death? By choosing to deliberately terminate the lives of the children and following requirements of due care in doing so (that is to say, to act according to current medical understanding and accepted medical–ethical values, being careful in the decision-making process as well as in the execution of the decision and taking good notice of the wishes of the parents), the courts concluded that both physicians had acted in an emergency situation under which their actions had been lawful.

The principles established in the Prins and Kadijk proceedings are now used as a standard by the Public Prosecutor in deciding whether or not to prosecute a physician who has deliberately terminated the life of a disabled newborn child.

Characteristics of reported cases

The significance of the cases against Prins and Kadijk – especially the Prins case – is confirmed by a study of paediatricians in Groningen.[10] This study shows that 22 cases of deliberate termination of disabled newborn infants were reported to the Dutch juridical authorities in the period 1997–2004.

All cases involved children with severe spina bifida and hydrocephalus. In all cases at least two independent physicians were consulted regarding the decision as to whether or not the child should be treated; in 17 of the 22 cases, a multidisciplinary spina bifida team was involved in the decision-making process. In all cases the parents agreed to the earlier decision not to treat the child. In all cases the physician in charge finally considered the active termination of the life of the child to be justified as the child suffered unbearable pain, which could not be relieved adequately. In all cases the parents agreed to this decision; in four cases the parents actually requested that their child's suffering be brought to an end.

In all cases the Public Prosecutor decided not to prosecute the physician in charge, as he was believed to have acted in an emergency situation in which the termination of the child's life was considered to be the last remaining humane option. All decisions not to prosecute were reached with the consent of the Dutch Minister of Justice.

This analysis of the reported cases clarifies a few matters. First, the Prins and Kadijk cases appear to have set a standard for the circumstances under which the deliberate termination of severely disabled newborn life can be admissible according to Dutch criminal court law. Second, the study gives a first reliable account of the quantity as well as the characteristics of the cases reported to the juridical authorities. This is important information, as up until January 2005 the Dutch public knew hardly anything about the existing medical practice regarding the deliberate termination of severely disabled newborn life. The only information available up to that moment were the results of the studies by Van der Maas and Van der Wal, published in 1996[11] and 2003.[12] These studies have shown – among other things – that the proportion of end-of-life decisions in neonatology is only 1 per cent of all neonatal deaths in the Netherlands. Furthermore, these studies offer some insight into the considerations of physicians who admit to having terminated disabled neonatal life in the past and show that an average of three cases per year is reported to the juridical authorities although, according to estimates within the Dutch medical community, some 60–90 of such cases occur every year. Third and finally, the results of the analysis by Verhagen caused further debate among Dutch paediatricians as to what extent neonates with spina bifida are capable of experiencing unbearable suffering. Some commentators have argued that, according to their experience in the field of paediatric neurology, these children hardly ever suffer from such an intensity of pain that terminating their life is unavoidable. The lack of an adequate standard for 'unbearable suffering in neonates with severe spina bifida' demands that the assumption of such suffering needs to be crystallized. This also goes for the specific content of the medical decision not to start lifesaving treatment, as well as for the distinction between palliative care and the deliberate termination of life.[13]

This development, I believe, demonstrates that criticisms expressed by foreign commentators, suggesting that the Netherlands definitively went down the slippery slope, are unjustified. On the contrary, the debate still continues in the Netherlands and – in my opinion – in a necessarily open, but critical, cautious and incremental fashion.

In the autumn of 2005 the Dutch Government informed the Dutch Parliament of its decision to establish a multidisciplinary committee that would function as an advisory board to the Public Prosecution. This committee, which consists of medical, ethical and legal experts, will review cases where a physician has deliberately terminated the life of a severely disabled newborn child in view of specific requirements of due care.[14] The Public Prosecution may use the committee's conclusions as an aid in deciding whether or not to start criminal pre-investigations or to press charges against the physician.

The committee is not part of the judiciary and has, formally speaking, no influence on the prosecution policy of the Public Prosecutor. The committee commenced its work on 1 November 2006.[15]

Article 6 of the CRC: the child's inherent right to life

The CRC was adopted by the General Assembly of the United Nations on 20 November 1989 and aims to protect children because of their vulnerability and dependence on others. The CRC covers civil and political rights as well as economic, social and cultural rights of the child, accepting the interdependence of individual and social rights, which is also a basic assumption of both UN covenants of 1966. As of December 2006 the CRC had been ratified by 193 states making it the most ratified human rights convention.[16]

The idea of adopting a right to life into the CRC was first expressed by Professor Lopatka, the Polish chairperson of the working group that prepared the text of the Convention. In the chairperson's opinion, the right to life of the child is the most important of all children's rights and requires a positive approach. Furthermore, he stated that a child's exercise of its right to life could not be dissociated from economic, social or cultural factors.[17]

In view of the recommendation of the UN Children's Rights Committee mentioned above, it is necessary to clarify the meaning of Article 6 of the CRC. Section 1 of this provision requires that States Parties to the Convention recognize that every child has the inherent right to life. Section 2 requires that States Parties ensure to the maximum extent possible the survival and development of the child.

The provision holds three existential claims of the child and refers, although implicitly, to related obligations for States Parties. In this respect the wording of Article 6 (1) of the CRC differs from provisions such as Article 3 of the Universal Declaration on Human Rights, Article 6 of the International Covenant on Civil and Political Rights or Article 2 of the European Convention on Human Rights. What States Parties must do in order to fulfil their obligations under Article 6 of the CRC is not quite clear. It is assumed that they enjoy a certain liberty of interpretation as to their duties and responsibilities in this respect – given that an obligation 'to recognize' a right is generally deemed to be of a lower order than rights that States Parties need 'to respect', 'to ensure' or 'to guarantee'.[18]

The obligation to ensure the survival and development of every child engages other aspects of the right to life, such as the child's claim to an adequate state of health, to adequate food, water and shelter.[19] The wording 'to the maximum extent possible' articulates the awareness that the fulfilment of the corresponding obligations by States Parties depends on economic, social or cultural factors.[20]

Article 6 of the CRC does not clarify when the inherent right to life of the child begins. Following from a discussion on a draft version of Article 1 of the CRC[21] it was deemed to be a purpose of the CRC to offer legal protection to the child's life only from the moment of birth.[22] In this respect the CRC appears to be in line with a generally accepted view on the position of the unborn child under international human rights law.[23]

The essence of the right to life is that it contains the basic legal prohibition of deprivation of life; a prohibition to be ensured by law. It is reasonable to assume that this prohibition includes arbitrary as well as intentional deprivation of life, being requirements following from Article 6 of the ICCPR and Article 2 of the ECHR. The reach of this prohibition has significance for the legal admissibility of medical end-of-life decisions regarding severely disabled neonates. In order to understand how these end-of-life decisions relate to Article 6 of the CRC one must understand the main characteristics of the child's right to life.

The inherent character of the child's right to life as articulated in Article 6 of the CRC connotes an inalienable right intrinsic to the human person; one that cannot be taken away, suspended or transferred to others. It is a right regarded as self-evident and for which contracting states have positive obligations under human rights law.[24]

An understanding of the characteristics ascribed to the right to life and the current methods of treaty interpretation[25] are decisive factors in determining the true reading of this right. The search for an authoritative interpretation of the right, however, is complicated by the fact that no ultimate method of verifying the rightness of any given interpretation of these characteristics is available. Yet the need for an authoritative interpretation is beyond dispute as this is essential to establishing whether or not specific conduct, i.e. medical termination of neonatal life, is compatible with this fundamental right of the child. An additional problem is that the right to life's wording in several human rights provisions is not univocal. Provisions such as Article 6 of the ICCPR and Article 6 of the CRC mention the inherence of the right to life. Other provisions, such as Article 2 of the ECHR, Article 4 of the ACHR, Article 4 of the African Charter or Article 2 of the Cairo Declaration do not state this character. Another difference between treaty provisions that mention the right to life is whether the particular provisions identify States Parties' obligations in order to recognize or to ensure the right to life. This recalls an important distinction of approach to the right to life. This distinction, made by Ramcharan, stresses the difference between the right to life as a general principle and concept being part of international customary law on the one hand and the right to life as a human right made explicit in human rights conventions and the meaning of which must be determined through applicable rules of treaty interpretation on the other.[26]

The compatibility of end-of-life decisions regarding severely disabled newborns with the inherent right to life of the child has not been broadly discussed in children's rights literature.[27] As a result lines of thought on the meaning of this fundamental right in this very context remain largely unexplored.[28] In the Netherlands Rood-De Boer anticipated (in the mid-1980s) aspects of this debate when she related these decisions to the concept of 'the best interest of the child', nowadays one of the central concepts of the CRC. She argued that although every child has the right to life, in certain situations it could be in the child's best interest not to have it prolonged: that its life be terminated. In her opinion however, the decision-making process had to comply with an ultimate standard of carefulness.[29]

Brands-Bottema voiced doubts about the use of 'medical futility' as a criterion for medical decisions concerning the termination or withdrawal of life-prolonging medical treatment of severely disabled newborn infants, as these decisions had potential to conflict with the idea of the legal equality of human beings. In particular, criteria that link a treatment decision to certain (missing) capacities of the child or to the (limited) acceptance of the child by others were in her view problematic, as these engaged questions in relation to Article 2 of the CRC, the provision – at that moment still in preparation – concerning the prohibition of discrimination. In this context Brands-Bottema also referred to States Parties' special obligations under Article 23 (2) of the CRC and the care for the disabled child.[30]

Kilkelly considers the particular meaning of Article 6 of the CRC in relation to disabled children, as (1) the mortality among these children is significantly higher than among non-disabled children and (2) third persons not infrequently consider that their quality of life is devalued because of their disability. Kilkelly also focuses on the importance of Article 6 of the CRC for disabled newborn infants. In her view physicians throughout the world tend to withhold medical treatment to disabled neonates – treatment that would ordinarily be provided to non-disabled children. It also occurs that a disabled neonate is denied adequate food and care. In consequence this child's inherent right to life is less protected than that of a child without disabilities. In such cases a disabled child's right to die often appears to be regarded as more important than its right to life. Kilkelly considers this to be a flagrant violation of fundamental human rights law.[31]

However plausible and important these views may be, they do not clarify whether or not certain motives for end-of-life decisions in neonatology are compatible with the disabled newborn child's right to life and how the characteristics of this right combine to answer this question. To illustrate the meaning of, and at the same time, the difficulties that arise out of these characteristics I will bring into focus the Dutch Government's view on the inalienable character of the right to life, expressed during the preparation of the Dutch Euthanasia Act which came into force in 2002.

According to the Dutch Government, the content of the Euthanasia Act is not contrary to the right to life, set forth in Article 2 of the ECHR. As early as 1985 the Dutch State's Commission on Euthanasia concluded that a regulation on the deliberate termination of life on a patient's request is not necessarily incompatible with this provision. In consequence it has become common Dutch legal understanding that one cannot be obliged to accept the protection of one's right to life against one's own free will. The *Pretty v. UK* (2002) judgement of the European Court of Human Rights[32] did not alter this view.

Legalization on the deliberate termination of the life of an incompetent patient has, also in the Netherlands, always been considered to be in conflict with the right to life embodied in Article 2 of the ECHR. Yet, up to this day, this view has hardly ever been analysed. The Dutch Government's interpretation of the inalienable character of the right to life, as well as the recommendation of the UN Children's Rights Committee mentioned above, clearly provide an opportunity to do so.

According to the Dutch Government, the right to life is inalienable when a person has no reasonable interest in the possibility of waiving the right. This view seems to add two important characteristics to the inalienability of the right – characteristics, I believe, that also have important implications for the interpretation of the newborn child's right to life. The first characteristic is the idea of a reasonable interest in the possibility of waiving the right. The second refers to the capacity of the bearer of the right to express an interest in such waiver.

Following the government's line of thought, a neonate's right to life must be taken as inalienable as the child is not capable of expressing any reasonable interest in waiving the protection of this right. Does this mean a neonate can never have any reasonable interest in abandoning the right? Isn't it at least arguable that a child could have a reasonable interest in waiver if the exercise of the right is accompanied by unbearable and incurable pain and suffering? Accepting such an alternative reasonable interest of the child raises the question of whether a third party should decide whether or not the legal protection of the neonate's right to life should be lifted. An affirmative answer to this question, however, would mean a substantive concession to the idea that the exercise of the right to life is non-transferable to others. It would also introduce the risk of creating a thanatic practice in which other interests than those of the child become a motive for giving up the legal protection of the child's right to life.

The view that one cannot be obliged to accept the protection of one's right to life against one's own free will links the non-inalienable character of the right to life to the capability of the bearer of this right to express his or her will. The capacity to waive the protection of the right as the cornerstone of the non-inalienability of the right to life leads to the conclusion that those who lack this capacity cannot ascribe a non-inalienable character to their right to life. It therefore seems reasonable to assume that it is not the inalienable character of the right to life that stands in the way of regulating the deliberate termination of the disabled newborn child's life, but the fact that this child is incapable of divesting its right to life of its inalienable nature.

The logical consequence of this line of argument is one of legal inequality between the unbearably suffering competent person and the equally unbearably suffering incompetent newborn child. For, which concept of legal equality demands that a competent person should be able to prevent the exercise of his right to life conflicting with his personal interest in avoiding a life of unbearable pain, and at the same time denies the unbearable suffering newborn child the very same benefit?

I believe it is therefore unwise to hold on unconditionally to the concept of the inalienable right to life of a newborn child. To do so would be to make a newborn child suffering from unbearable pain and whose life expectancy is severely limited a prisoner of its inalienable right to life. This, I believe, would distort the fundamental aim of this elementary right. Accepting such a proposition logically requires a process by which such cases can be identified. However, the categorization of such cases inevitably creates an intermediate category, namely 'cases of doubt', which contains cases in which a neonate's abnormalities are not necessarily life-threatening although the child's future life with severe disabilities is a certainty, the prognosis remains unsure and a situation of untreatable suffering is at hand.

Article 2 (1) of the CRC: non-discrimination on the basis of disability

Among legal scholars it is quite common to approach the question of the legal admissibility of deliberate termination of disabled newborn life from the perspective of the right to life. In my view, however, this is not the only relevant way of addressing this question.

A largely unexplored approach is offered by Article 2 (1) of the CRC. This provision states that States Parties shall ensure that all the rights of the child set forth in the Convention shall be enjoyed without discrimination of any kind. Significant to our topic is that Article 2 (1) of the CRC is the first legally binding human rights provision in which 'disability' is expressly recognized as a forbidden ground for discrimination. This fact offers the possibility of investigating from a children's rights perspective whether or not end-of-life decisions regarding disabled newborn children are compatible with such a prohibition of discrimination on the basis of disability.

The idea of forbidding discrimination on the basis of disability within the context of end-of-life decisions in neonatology was widely discussed in the mid-1980s in the United States in the aftermath of the Baby Doe case. This case concerned a newborn child, born in April 1982 in Bloomington, Indiana. The child was born with a tracheaoesophageal fistule, a condition that made it impossible to take nourishment in a normal way. This condition, clearly life-threatening, was capable of being corrected by an operation that, if performed in time, had a very high chance of success. If no surgery were to be performed, the child would die. The child, however, differed from other children born with such a condition, in that she had Down's syndrome and a successful operation to remove the fistule would not change this fact. Based on considerations expressed by the obstetrician the parents of the child agreed not to authorize surgery and to refuse nutrition and hydration for the child. After protests by the nursing staff the hospital sought the court's assistance. Ultimately the Indiana Supreme Court upheld the ruling of the lower courts which recognized the parents' right to make the decision. While the attorneys in this case filed a petition to have this case reviewed by the US Supreme Court, the child died of pneumonia, six days after birth.[33]

Later, the Baby Doe case as well as the Baby Jane Doe case[34] caused the Reagan administration to issue the so-called Baby Doe Regulations, which prohibited discrimination against disabled individuals in the availability and delivery of medical services if based solely on the fact of their disability (contrary to Section 504 of the Rehabilitation Act of 1973). Although the Baby Doe Regulations were invalidated by the US Supreme Court in *Bowen vs. American Hospital Association* (1986),[35] the importance of the issue raised by the Baby Doe Regulations is unquestionable.[36]

The continuing debate on this issue in the USA resulted in 1989 in an authoritative report by the US Commission on Civil Rights, *Medical Discrimination against Children with Disabilities*.[37] In this report the US Commission noticed an increasing number of cases in which medical treatment for disabled newborn infants was denied solely because they were (or were perceived to be) disabled. The commission stated that in some cases the discriminatory denial of medical treatment was based on ignorance and false stereotypes about the 'quality of life' of persons with disabilities and, in others, on misconceptions about the nature of the particular disability the child would have if it were permitted to survive. The commission recommended that the US Government review its national enforcement mechanisms that guarantee the right of persons with disabilities to accessible health care, to design legislation to prevent discrimination against persons with disabilities and to initiate further fact-finding activities.[38]

The commission's report was published in September 1989, two months before the CRC was adopted by the General Assembly of the United Nations in New York. The coming into force of the CRC has, I believe, created the legal opportunity for States Parties to enter the debate on 'medical discrimination against children with disabilities' or even to reshape it within the context of their own legal systems in view of Article 2 (1) of the CRC. In consequence, research on the compatibility of end-of-life decisions regarding the disabled newborn child with the legal prohibition of discrimination on the basis of disability does not have to be limited to the USA any more. Such research can take place within any domestic legal system.

The importance of the question as to whether end-of-life decisions regarding disabled newborn children are compatible with the legal prohibition of discrimination on the basis of disability was broadened by the challenging Baby K. case in the USA in 1993. In this case a child was born with extreme congenital defects, known as anencephaly, in which large parts of the infant's skull and brain were missing. Notwithstanding this major impairment the child showed breathing reflexes and responded to touch and sound. Furthermore, the child had a normal blood pressure, a regular heartbeat, good functions of liver and kidneys and a regular metabolism. As the child had breathing difficulties the medical team of Fairfax Hospital (Virginia) decided to start mechanical respiration, although the team expected the child to die very soon. As a result of this intervention the child started autonomous breathing. On occasions, however, she developed respiratory distress, to which the medical team responded by initiating mechanical respiration. In due course the child left hospital and was transferred to a nursing home where, at times, the child developed further breathing difficulties which resulted in her emergency readmission to Fairfax Hospital. At this stage, however, the medical team refused to treat the child, on the basis that further mechanical respiration was medically futile. The child's mother disagreed such that the hospital sought a court order allowing the medical team to withhold artificial respiration.

The US Supreme Court held[39] – in short – that the denial of an emergency medical treatment to a child suffering from acute respiratory distress, solely because of the child's anencephalic condition amounted to discrimination on the basis of disability, which was prohibited under federal law.[40] The medical team's motive for this denial, namely that the treatment was considered to be medically futile, was held to be incompatible with the prohibition.

The case highlights the thin line that exists between acceptable professional reasons for decisions to withhold medical treatment and those which constitute disability discrimination. The difficulty, however, is that reasons for a medical decision may sometimes legitimately have regard to a patient's disability. When therefore is a distinction made by a physician on

the basis of disability acceptable as a justification for a non-treatment decision and when does such a distinction amount to unlawful disability
discrimination? In all respects, this is an intriguing problem. The fact that
the Court of Appeal's ruling in the Baby K. case was a split decision illustrates the difficult nature of this issue.[41] Nevertheless, although the
application of the principle of non-discrimination on the basis of disability
in our context still holds many obscurities, I believe that applying this fundamental norm when end-of-life decisions regarding severely disabled
neonates occur is essential and that disabled infants have an equal right to
protection against discrimination to non-disabled infants.

Non-discrimination and end-of-life decisions in neonatology

In recent years, the importance of this issue has been acknowledged by UN
human rights scholars. By way of example, during the preparation of the new
UN Convention to Promote and Protect the Rights and Dignity of Persons
with Disabilities the delegates discussed several proposals of a provision on a
disabled person's inherent right to life. Here, deliberations took place as to
whether or not such a provision should make reference to the fact that disability is unacceptable as a reason for infringing a disabled person's inherent
right to life.[42] The draft version of Article 10 of this convention currently
reads: 'States Parties reaffirm that every human being has the inherent right
to life and shall take all necessary measures to ensure its effective enjoyment
by persons with disabilities on an equal basis with others.'[43] This provision
reflects the idea that it is a violation of the Convention to permit legally the
termination of a disabled newborn child's life because of the child's disability. In consequence, the withdrawal of lifesaving medical treatment from a
disabled newborn child (such as mechanical respiration from an anencephalic child) which causes the child to die, when the same treatment
would have been given to a non-disabled child, would prima facie be unlawful discrimination on the basis of disability.

There is however a normative possibility that could provide an escape
for a sound physician in despair: a possibility that was not addressed in the
Baby K. case. A discriminatory reason for a medical (non-treatment) decision may be legally acceptable if it can be 'objectively justified'. This
concept, widely accepted in national and international jurisprudence,[44]
aims to make more explicit the reasons for a particular distinction and to
review whether or not realistic alternative options for conduct are available.
The essence of the concept of 'objective justification' is to determine
whether a discriminatory measure is made for a legitimate aim and
whether the means are suitable and necessary to achieve that aim.

There are several aspects that need consideration in order to establish
whether or not a non-treatment decision based on the newborn child's disability is objectively justified. Such aspects, I believe, are:

- the fact that the measure must meet a child's real need (topical demand)
- that the aim should not be articulated in abstract, vague or overly general terms (specific demand)
- that all interests involved have been identified and that their relative weight has been assessed on explicit grounds
- that the discriminatory measure must be necessary, bearing in mind the extent according to which the measure is regularly used by professionals in order to achieve the selected aim, and
- that it is clear and beyond doubt that there is no suitable alternative course of action.

It is clear, however, that the application of this 'objective justification' test in this end-of-life decision-making context needs further exploration in order to clarify what can be gained by it in terms of a better legal quality of the decision-making process.[45] In my opinion the application of this test provides the opportunity to prevent medical end-of-life decisions based solely on a child's disability (or disabilities) and therefore amounting to an inadmissible exclusion of a child's enjoyment of its inherent right to life.

Whether or not the Baby K. case can be regarded as a legal authority for the interpretation of Article 2 (1) of the CRC is a question that, of course, needs further investigation. What the Baby K. case does demonstrate, however, is that there is an area where medical deontology can come into conflict with fundamental human rights norms. This should therefore be interpreted as a signal to the medical profession to reflect further upon the real motives that underlie its professional goals in order that a satisfactory resolution can be achieved with the seemingly inevitable legal restrictions that may be placed on these goals.

Conclusion

In this chapter I have argued in favour of the plausibility of studying and analysing the admissibility of end-of-life decisions regarding disabled newborn infants in view of specific requirements for a child's legal protection under the CRC. I have tried to show that it is reasonable to ask how these end-of-life decisions, which obviously infringe on the newborn child's inherent right to life, relate to the CRC's prohibition of discrimination on the basis of disability as in Article 2 (1), especially when these decisions are based on an estimation of the child's future life's perspective and this perspective is considered to be limited because of an intrinsic bad health condition of the child.

I believe that end-of-life decisions in neonatology need (further) recognition as a children's rights issue and that further research on the significance of the CRC to the legal admissibility of these end-of-life decisions is necessary in order to safeguard the equal protection of the fundamental rights of the disabled newborn child.

Notes

1 This document became known as the 'Groningen Protocol'. The content of this protocol is discussed in A.A.E. Verhagen and P.J.J. Sauer, 'The Groningen Protocol: Euthanasia in severely ill newborns', *New England Journal of Medicine*, 352, 2005, 959–962.

2 J.H.H.M. Dorscheidt, 'Assessment procedures regarding end of life-decisions in neonatology in the Netherlands', *Medicine and Law*, 24, 2005, 4, 803–829.

3 For a legal analysis of this issue according to Dutch law and international human rights law according to current Dutch legal understanding, see J.H.H.M. Dorscheidt, *Levensbeëindiging bij Gehandicapte Pasgeborenen: Strijdig met het Non-Discriminatiebeginsel?* (Medical Termination of Disabled Neonatal Life: Compatible with the Principle of Non-Discrimination?). Sdu: Den Haag, 2006.

4 CRC/C/117/ Add.1.

5 Concluding Observations of the Human Rights Committee: Netherlands. Seventy-second Session, 20/07/01, CCPR/CO/72/NET.

6 V. Provoost, F. Cools, F. Mortier, J. Bilsen, J. Ramet, Y. Vandenplas and L. Deliens, 'Medical end-of-life decisions in neonates and infants in Flanders', *Lancet* 65, 2005, nr. 9467, 1315–1320.

7 In this case the parents of a baby, born with Down's syndrome and suffering from duodenal atresia, did not consent to surgery on the child necessary to lift the intestinal block. In consequence, the child would die. The Public Prosecutor's office intervened and parental authority was temporarily suspended from the parents. The appointed child care and protection board, however, agreed with the parents that surgery on the child would not be in the child's best interest and refused to consent to the operation as well. As a result the surgeon in charge did not operate on the child. A few days later the child died. The surgeon and the director of the child care and protection board were prosecuted for omitting to take responsibility for the child and to prevent the child's death. Yet the criminal proceedings against both men were discontinued. See Hoge Raad (Dutch Supreme Court), 28 April 1989, NJ (Dutch Jurisprudence) 1990, 46. The case was introduced to the public in J.C. Molenaar, K. Gill and H.M. Dupuis, 'Geneeskunde, dienares der barmhartigheid', *Nederlands Tijdschrift voor Geneeskunde* (Dutch Journal of Medicine) 132, 1988, nr. 42, 1913–1917. An analysis of this case is offered in J.H.H.M. Dorscheidt (2006), op. cit., 216–241.

8 District Court Alkmaar 26 April 1995, *Tijdschrift voor Gezondheidsrecht* (Journal of Health Law) 1995/41; Court of Appeal Amsterdam 7 November 1995, *Tijdschrift voor Gezondheidsrecht* (Journal of Health Law) 1996/1.

9 District Court Groningen 13 November 1995, *Tijdschrift voor Gezondheidsrecht* (Journal of Health Law) 1996/2; Court of Appeal Leeuwarden 4 April 1996, *Tijdschrift voor Gezondheidsrecht* (Journal of Health Law) 1996/35.

10 A.A.E. Verhagen, J.J. Sol, O.F. Brouwer and P.J.J. Sauer, 'Actieve levensbeëindiging bij pasgeborenen in Nederland: Analyse van alle 22 meldingen uit 1997/2004', *Nederlands Tijdschrift voor Geneeskunde* (Dutch Journal of Medicine), 149, 2005, nr. 4, 183–188.

11 P.J. van der Maas and G. van der Wal, *Euthanasie en andere Medische Beslissingen rond het Levenseinde: De Praktijk en de Meldingsprocedure* (Euthanasia and other Medical Decisions Regarding the End of Life: The Practice of the Reporting Procedure). Sdu: Den Haag, 1996. The results of this study relating to disabled neonates are discussed in A. van de Heide, P.J. van der Maas and G. van der Wal, 'Medical end-of-life decisions made for neonates and infants in the Netherlands', *Lancet*, 350, 1997, 251–255.

12 G. van der Wal, A. van der Heide, B.D. Ontwuteaka-Philipsen and P.J. van der Maas, *Medische Besluitvorming aan het Einde van het Leven: De Praktijk en de Toetsingsprocedure Euthanasie* (Medical Decision-Making at the End of Life: Dutch Practice and the Euthanasia Assessment Procedure). De Tijdstroom: Utrecht, 2003. As for the perspective of disabled neonates, A.M. Vrakking, A. van der Heide, W.F.M. Arts, R. Pieters, E. van der Voort, J.A.C. Rietjens, B.D. Onwuteaka-Philipsen, P.J. van der Maas and G. van der Wal, 'Medical end-of-life decisions for children in the Netherlands', *Archives of Pediatric & Adolescent Medicine*, 159, 2005, 802–809; A.M. Vrakking, A. van der Heide, B.D. Onwuteaka-Philipsen, I.M. Keij-Deerenberg, P.J. van der Maas and G. van der Wal, 'Medical end-of-life decisions made for neonates and infants in the Netherlands, 1995–2001, *Lancet* 365, 2005, 1329–1331.

13 E.J.O. Kompanje, T.H.R. de Jong, W.F.M. Arts and J.J. Rotteveel, 'Problematische basis voor "uitzichtloos en ondraaglijk lijden" als criterium voor actieve levens-beëindiging bij pasgeborenen met spina bifida', *Nederlands Tijdschrift voor Geneeskunde* (Dutch Journal of Medicine), 149, 2005, nr. 37, 2067–2069. See also T.H.R. de Jong, E.J.O. Kompanje, W.F.M. Arts and J.J. Rotteveel, 'Laten sterven of doen sterven', *Medisch Contact* (Medical Contact) 61, 2006, nr. 16, 669–671. It should be noted that Kompanje *et al.* do not exclude the possibility that a neonate with severe spina bifida can suffer unbearably. Apparently their main argument is that deliberate termination of such a child's life is simply not the right professional way to deal with this situation.

14 Furthermore, the committee will review cases of late termination of pregnancy.

15 'Regeling centrale deskundigencommissie late zwangerschapsafbreking in een categorie 2-geval en levensbeëindiging bij pasgeborenen', *Staatscourant* (Government Gazette), 2007, nr. 51, 8.

16 Status of ratification as of 13 July 2007. See <http://www.ohchr.org/english/countries/ratification/11.htm>

17 E/CN.4/1988/28, para. 21.

18 Regarding the right to health care, see B.C.A. Toebes, *The Right to Health as a Human Right in International Law,* Antwerpen/Groningen: Intersentia-Hart, 1999, pp.293–294.

19 Van Bueren refers to an 'umbrella approach' and argues the need to recognise the inner relationship between these special aspects and the child's right to life. See G. van Bueren: *The International Law on the Rights of the Child,* Dordrecht: Martinus Nijhoff, 1995, pp.293–294.

20 L.J. LeBlanc, *The Convention on the Rights of the Child: United Nations Lawmaking on Human Rights,* Lincoln and London: University of Nebraska Press, 1995, p.76.

21 In this regard P. Alston, 'The unborn child and abortion under the Draft Convention on the Rights of the Child', *Human Rights Quarterly,* 1990, 12, 165–172.

22 P. Alston (1990), ibid., p.170. The observer of the Vatican holds a different viewpoint. See E/CN.4/ 1988/28 para. 25.

23 J.H.H.M. Dorscheidt, 'The unborn child and the UN Convention on Children's Rights: The Dutch perspective as a guideline', *The International Journal of Children's Rights,* 7, 1999, nr. 4, 303–347.

24 J.H.H.M. Dorscheidt (2006), op. cit., p.293–297.

25 See Articles 31–33 of the Vienna Convention on the Law of Treaties (1969). This treaty came into force on 27 January 1980.

26 B.G. Ramcharan, 'The right to life', *Netherlands International Law Review,* 30, 1983, 297–329, in particular p.299, as well as B.G. Ramcharan, 'The concept and dimensions of the right to life', in B.G. Ramcharan (ed.), *The Right to Life in International Law,* Dordrecht: Martinus Nijhoff, 1985, pp.1–32, in particular p.3.

27 Hodgson is an exception to the rule. See D. Hodgson, 'The child's right to life, survival and development', *The International Journal of Children's Rights*, 2, 1994, 369–394. Hogdson considers the fact that the CRC does not address the euthanasia issue to be a lost opportunity to prescribe minimum guidelines and to express that mercy killing of severely disabled children and foetuses is not a matter exclusively within domestic jurisdiction. Hodgson states:

> An attempt might have been made for the benefit of those States Parties which sanction or tolerate the practice of child euthanasia to articulate appropriate safeguards concerning such matters as the duty to consult, what constitutes sufficient consultation, what constitutes an informed and authentic consent, the form of the consent, the problem of 'consent by proxy', the desirability of a 'cooling off' period, and so on.

The issue is also addressed in J. Dorscheidt, 'Levensbeëindiging bij gehandicapte baby's', *Tijdschrift voor de Rechten van het Kind* (Journal on the Rights of the Child), 16, 2006, nr. 3, pp.K2–K4.

28 Leenen (not H.J.J. Leenen) discusses the medical termination of a minor's life from a children's rights perspective and focuses on the issue as to whether the Dutch Euthanasia Act is compatible with Articles 5 and 12 of the CRC. See C. Leenen, 'Children's rights and the Dutch Termination of Life on Request and Assisted Suicide (Review Procedures) Act', in J.C.M. Willems (ed.), *Developmental and Autonomy Rights of Children: Empowering Children, Caregivers and Communities*. Antwerpen–Oxford–New York: Intersentia, 2002, pp.141–164.

29 M. Rood-De Boer: *Evolutie van een Rechtsbegrip 'Het Belang van het Kind'* (Evolution of a Legal Concept 'The Interest of the Child'). Arnhem: Gouda Quint, 1984, p.15.

30 G.W. Brands-Bottema, 'Het recht van zwaar-defecte pasgeborenen op gezondheidszorg: Een kwestie van leven of dood', in M. de Langen and J.H. de Graaf (eds), *Kinderen en Recht: Opstellen over de Positie van Minderjarigen in het Recht* (Children and the Law: Essays on the Legal Position of Minors). Deventer/Arnhem: Kluwer/Gouda Quint, 1989, pp.39–50, in particular pp.42–43.

31 U. Kilkelly, 'Disability and children: The Convention on the Rights of the Child (CRC)', in G. Quinn and T. Degener, *Human Rights and Disability: The Current Use and Future Potential of United Nations Human Rights Instruments in the Context of Disability*. New York/Geneva, United Nations, 2002, pp.119–140, especially p.121.

32 *Pretty v. United Kingdom* (Appl.nr. 2346/02) 29 April 2002, (2002) 35 *EHRR* 1.

33 *In re Infant Doe*, No. GU8204–00, Indiana Circuit Court, Monroe County, 12 April 1982.

34 The Baby Jane Doe case occurred in Port Jefferson, New York, and concerned a baby girl, born on 11 October 1983 with spina bifida, microcephaly and hydrocephaly. After consultation with neurologists, nurses, a priest and a social worker the parents did not consent to surgery on the child. They only agreed to 'warm care' and nourishment. A lawyer from Vermont, who was not involved in the case, protested in court against the parents' decision as this would surely lead to the child's death. The Court of Appeal, however, dismissed the lawyer's views. The parents were considered competent to decide on the basis of current medical understanding and not to seriously endanger the child's life by their choice. See *Weber v. Stony Brook Hospital*, 456 N.E. 2nd, 1186 (1983), idem 467 N.Y.S 2nd, 685. (1983), as well as 469 N.Y.S. 2nd 65 (1983).

35 *Bowen v. American Hospital Association*, 106 U.S. 2101 (1986).

36 A further discussion of the Baby Doe Regulations is offered in J.H.H.M. Dorscheidt (2006), op. cit., pp.475–480.

37 United States Commission on Civil Rights, *Medical Discrimination against Children with Disabilities,* Washington DC, 1989.

38 For an analysis of the Report of the US Commission, see J.H.H.M. Dorscheidt (2006), op. cit., pp.480–485.

39 US Supreme Court, 513 US 825 resp. 115 S. Ct. 91; 63 USLW 3258, 3 October 1994 upholding decisions by the US Court of Appeals for the Fourth Circuit (*In re Baby K,* aff'd 16 F.3d 590 (4th Cir. 1994) and the Eastern District Court of Virginia (*In re Baby K,* 832 F. Supp. 1022, ED Va).

40 In particular under the Emergency Medical Treatment and Active Labor Act (1986), the Rehabilitation Act of 1973 and the Americans with Disabilities Act (1990).

41 A reflection on this ruling and the dissenting opinion by Justice Sprouse is offered in J.H.H.M. Dorscheidt (2006), op. cit., pp.493–499.

42 See in this regard some earlier proposals of the USA and of international disability organizations at: <http://www.un.org/esa/socdev/enable/rights/ahcstata10fiscomments.htm>. For a discussion of these proposals, see J.H.H.M. Dorscheidt (2006), op. cit., pp.395–399.

43 This text was adopted by the Working Group, which prepares the text of the Convention, during its Eighth Session (10–24 August 2006). See <http://www.un.org/esa/socdev/enable/rights/ahc8docs/ahc8draftconv.doc>.

44 An analysis of this concept is offered in I.P. Asscher-Vonk, 'Towards one concept of objective justification', in T. Loenen and P.R. Rodrigues (eds), *Non-discrimination Law: Comparative Perspectives.* The Hague–London–Boston: Martinus Nijhoff – Kluwer Law International, 1999, pp.39–51.

45 An impulse to this has been given by J.H.H.M. Dorscheidt (2006), op. cit., pp.511–515.

10 The right to life and the right to health of children with disabilities before courts

Some Latin American examples

Christian Courtis

Introduction

The emergence of human rights in South America over the last 25 years is a distinct narrative. From their nadir in the 1980s, their rehabilitation has been slow but inexorable. If, as appears to be the case, the shape and speed of such developments are moderated by social and economic forces, then it is little wonder that South American developments have been so idiosyncratic – given that the region has had more than its fair share of social and economic upheavals during this period.

The revival of democracy and respect for the rule of law in many South American states has during this period resulted in many constitutional re-enactments and amendments.[1] Most of the new constitutional texts have included social rights of various kinds and some have also entrenched rights relating to vulnerable groups or minorities, including children and disabled people.[2] Contemporaneous with these developments has been the widespread ratification of international human rights treaties – both regional and universal – including, *inter alia*, those recognizing social rights, such as the International Covenant on Economic, Social and Cultural Rights; the Convention on the Rights of the Child; the Convention on the Elimination of All Forms of Discrimination against Women; and the regional Protocol of San Salvador. Some countries have gone further along this path, granting international instruments a privileged legal status – higher than national laws, and sometimes equivalent to the constitution.[3] In most cases, in any event, since the prevalent constitutional position in the region has been monist (meaning that international treaties, once ratified, are considered to be part of domestic law) this has had the effect of further entrenching human rights principles in domestic laws.

In some cases, the constitutional provisions dealing with social rights are drafted, not in the language of rights, but rather in the language of goals, principles or directives purporting to guide social policies. By way of example (in the context of this paper) the Dominican Constitution provides that: 'The state will stimulate the progressive development of a social security system, so that every person can enjoy adequate protection against unemployment, illness, disability and old age.'[4] In similar fashion the Colombian Constitution includes, under its chapter 'On Economic, Social and Cultural Rights', a provision that refers to the goals of public policies in respect of disabled people.[5]

In contrast, however, many new constitutional norms (and of course those contained in international human rights instruments) are expressed as 'rights' – such as the right to health care, the right to education and the right to adequate housing.[6] Nevertheless even when drafted in the language of rights, the question of how best to conceive of social rights remains controversial. Putting aside workers' rights and social security rights – whose status as judicially enforceable rights was hardly ever contested – social rights have traditionally been treated in constitutional doctrine as 'programmatic' rights, that is, as mere statements of goals to be pursued by the political branches, not as judicially enforceable individual or collective entitlements. The renewed recognition and expansion of social rights in Latin American constitutions, and to a certain extent the influence of the jurisprudence of international treaty-monitoring bodies such as the UN Committee on Economic, Social and Cultural Rights, have led to a less monolithic view, and to a growing discussion about the possibilities and limits of the judicial enforcement of these rights. In the same vein, concrete judicial experiences in different countries have challenged the idea that social rights are not judicially enforceable, and in some contexts, there is a growing case law showing exactly the opposite trend. Generally speaking, one can identify some countries where the traditional doctrine still prevails among courts and academia – Chile, Mexico and the Central American states[7] – and countries where there is a growing acceptance of the possibility of invoking social rights before courts – Argentina, Brazil and Colombia being good examples of this trend.

Constitutional, legislative and judicial evolution in this field has been dramatic in some Latin American countries, such as Argentina, Brazil, Colombia and Costa Rica. In Argentina, the judicial development of a new constitutional action provided by the 1994 constitutional amendments, collective *amparo*, even without statutory regulation, is surprising.[8] In Brazil, the use of a novel procedural mechanism called 'public civil action' (*ação civil pública*) to trigger judicial protection in environmental, consumer and occupational safety and health cases has been generalized since its regulation in 1985.[9] In Colombia, a number of new procedural mechanisms – namely, *acción de tutela* before the constitutional court, *acción popular* before ordinary courts, and *acción de cumplimiento* – have radically changed the possibilities of challenging state activities or omissions before the judiciary. In Costa Rica, a centralized and rather simplified *amparo* jurisdiction before the constitutional section of the supreme court has led to noteworthy results – for example, oral suits brought by children challenging educational decisions by school directors. Even acknowledging all the difficulties that every innovation presupposes, the doctrinal and institutional evaluation of these new procedural mechanisms has been positive, and countries where they still have not been adopted are pushing for change.[10] Many of the signals detectable in this field today are rather promising.[11]

It is not possible to review the entire recent South American jurisprudence concerning disabled people and the right to life and accordingly in this chapter I consider the experiences of two countries where innovative developments recognizing these rights have occurred, namely Argentina and Columbia. These countries have, in contradistinction to the European and US experiences, approached these questions from a predominantly socio-economic rights perspective.

The distinction between civil and political rights, on the one hand, and economic, social and cultural rights, on the other hand, has been pervasive for decades in Latin American courts. Despite their equal constitutional enshrinement in many countries of the region, the dominant doctrine stressed the difference between the two sets of rights – stating that while civil and political rights are 'operative', and thus enforceable before courts, economic, social and cultural rights are 'programmatic', and thus only directed to inspire the political branches but not suited to judicial adjudication.[12] Interestingly, this trend is gradually changing, and the domestic courts of some countries of the region have become more assertive about the justiciability of economic, social and cultural rights.[13]

Indeed the field of children's rights and that of children with disability have been groundbreaking areas regarding these developments. The acknowledgment of the positive duties stemming from civil rights has been an important entry point for the growing recognition of enforceable rights to access social services, such as health care or education.[14] This article will briefly present some of the cases where the judiciary, drawing on the positive duties stemming from the right to life, ordered different forms of access to medical treatment and medication to the administration or to other health care providers, when the situation of children with disabilities was at stake. I will illustrate this trend with some cases from Colombia and Argentina, but there are more examples available from other countries of the region, such as Brazil and Costa Rica.

Colombian case development

Colombia went through an important constitutional amendment process in 1991, adopting a new constitution with an extensive list of fundamental rights, and the establishment of a constitutional court, which was granted broad powers of constitutional review.[15] While the constitutional court originally stuck to the traditional theory of the differential treatment of civil and political rights, on the one hand, and economic, social and cultural rights, on the other hand, in terms of constitutional review, the difference soon started to blur through an original modification made by the court to the traditional doctrine. According to this modification, while economic and social rights were in principle not suitable for constitutional adjudication, they could be, however, subject to adjudication when the alleged infringement connected them with a fundamental civil and political right. Thus this doctrine, known as the 'interconnection doctrine', encouraged plaintiffs to find links between violations of economic, social and cultural rights which could 'overlap' with violations of civil and political rights enshrined in the constitution. One of the main paths through which this strategy was undertaken consisted of exploring the links between the right to life and the right to health assistance, especially in cases where the lives of children – and particularly, of children with disabilities – were involved. Indeed, the Colombian Constitution provides for special protection of persons with disabilities (sections 13 and 47), and for children and teenagers (sections 44 and 45). It follows that in cases that engage questions concerning the protection of the lives of children with disabilities the courts have subjected arguments by the state to particularly detailed analysis to ensure that these fundamental rights have been properly addressed.

Most of these cases have been channelled through constitutional injunctions (*acción de tutela*), since the constitutional court has the power to order that health care be provided or that treatment or medication regimes be maintained.

This trend can be seen as originating in 1992 with a decision (T-067/94)[16] concerning a child with neurological impairments caused by a parencephalic injury, which required constant medical care. While treatment was provided by the social security agency, the child's health improved; however, when this was interrupted, the child deteriorated. The plaintiff – the child's father – alleged that the denial of treatment put the child's life at risk, and amounted to a violation of the child's constitutional rights to life and to health. The government argued that the constitutional guarantee only obliged the provision of treatment during the first year of life, and that the social security agency had discretion to interrupt treatment when the disease was deemed to be incurable.

The court held the right to life to be 'the first and most important right enshrined in the constitution', and that it imposed

> on public authorities the permanent obligation of protecting its intangibility, not only through activity directed towards preventing conducts that put life in risk, but also through an active function directed to preserve it by all institutional and legal means within their realm.

It further held that

> the concept of life enshrined by the constitution is not simply limited to the biological aspect, which would only mean maintaining the vital signs, but also implies a necessary qualification: the kind of life that the state should protect requires conditions of dignity. Mere survival will be

of little or no use if it does not offer the minimum which defines a human being as such.

Relying on its previous case law, the court held that the right to health 'becomes a fundamental right when its threat or violation necessarily amounts to a risk or damage (to life), so that health should be protected immediately to prevent a threat against the right to life'. In its opinion, the interruption of the treatment had put the life of the child at risk whereas the treatment had had the effect of progressively ameliorating the child's health. The court accordingly held that the interruption of treatment was illegal, and directed the social security agency to restore the care regime.

A key issue that was not resolved by T-067/94 concerned the extent of the constitutional right – particularly whether it was engaged in cases where there was no imminent risk to life. This question was addressed directly in T-068/94,[17] decided in February 1994, where the court ruled that although the fundamental constitutional guarantee in relation to the right to health was – in general – only engaged where a real risk to life arose, this was not the case in respect of children, for whom the right was always a fundamental one (by virtue of article 44 of the Colombian Constitution). T-068/94 concerned a decision by the social security agency to suspend ongoing treatment for a disabled child. Although this decision did not put the child's life at risk, it did have a material affect on her development. In finding the actions of the social security agency to be unlawful, the court stressed that the notion of life protected by the constitution required the state to take positive steps to prevent a permanent deterioration of the quality of life. In this sense, the court did not restrict the notion of 'life' to a mere biological conception (i.e. being dead or alive), but expanded its content to the possibility of making meaningful choices – thus, redefining 'life' as 'dignified life' or 'free development of personality'. The court additionally rejected the social security agency's argument that the lack of certainty concerning the curative potential of the treatment justified the suspension of funding. In the court's opinion the constitutional guarantee in relation to the protection of life and health did not merely cover treatments that could cure but also extended to treatments that were likely to result in appreciable amelioration of the harmful symptoms.

The principles established in T-068/94 were reaffirmed in Case No. T-204/94[18] which also concerned an interruption by the social security agency to the treatment of a disabled child (in this case with hyperkinesia). The court reiterated its view that the lack of prospect of a cure could not justify a decision by the social security agency to suspend funding for treatment, if the treatment held out the prospect of an appreciable improvement in the child's health and life prospects. The court ruled that treatment would be obligatory if it had the effect of mitigating or neutralizing serious symptoms of the disease, such as aggressive behaviour, future lack of control of his sexual conduct or his potential to reproduce. In Case

No. T-571/94[19] (in a case concerning a child with hydrocephaly) this principle was further extended to require funding for non-curative treatment that had the potential merely to aid the child's integration in the social environment.

The constitutional court's procedures provide for representative and group complaints – and these have been important in clarifying the scope of the constitution's right to life and health guarantees. As a consequence of a 1995 complaint filed by the ombudsman (T-020/95)[20] on behalf of 229 children with a broad spectrum of disabilities (Down's syndrome, cerebral palsy, hydrocephaly, amongst others) the court required the social security agency to recommence the treatment and the provision of medication for children on the basis that this would improve their 'quality of life'.

The collective complaints process provides extensive opportunities and in Case No. T-049/95[21] the minor's rights defender submitted such a complaint on behalf of 69 children with developmental disabilities suffering institutionalization in inhuman conditions in public juvenile institutions. The complaint was formulated on the basis of sections 44 and 45 of the Colombian Constitution (concerning the right to life and health and the duty of special protection that the state has with respect to children and teenagers) and additionally on Article 23 of the Convention on the Rights of the Child. The court found that the children had suffered intolerably: that they were malnourished, naked or in straitjackets, and locked in at night. In its view the institution lacked even basic conditions of hygiene, staffing levels were inadequate and the quality of the therapeutic services provided was non-existent. The court held that the situation amounted to a violation of children's right to life, physical integrity, health, nutrition, care, education and recreation. It ordered that the responsible public authorities take remedial action and in the interim provide alternative accommodation for the children.

Since these landmark judgements of the constitutional court, further (albeit less dramatic) advances have occurred and the scope of the protection further clarified. Accordingly in T-179/00,[22] in a collective complaint concerning five children with different disabilities, the court held that its powers extended to outsourcing contracts for which the social security agency had responsibility and in T-1101/03[23] that the state obligation could be engaged indirectly. The case concerned the termination of the contract of an employee of a public hospital which had the collateral impact of excluding her disabled daughter from social security protection. Invoking the constitutional guarantees concerning the child's right to life, health and the state obligation to protect children and especially children with disabilities, the court ordered the provisional reinstatement of the mother.

The above cases all relate to the special protection afforded to disabled children by the Colombian Constitution. T-1034/01[24] concerned the interruption of treatment by a health care provider of a young man who had just turned 18. In this case it resorted to a 'due process' approach. It considered on the facts that the young man's right to health (as an element of his right to life) was engaged. Having emphasized the general and special protection due to all persons with disabilities it ordered that a fresh assessment be undertaken by the authorities of his health care needs and that pending this, the treatment be maintained.

The Argentinian experience

While labour and social security rights were already established fields of litigation in Argentina, judicial enforcement of socio-economic rights dramatically expanded to health rights in the 1990s. The social and economic crisis of the 1980s and 1990s led to a growing use of courts to ensure inclusion in medical plans, health coverage, access to medication, and to oppose forced termination of health coverage.

The Argentine health system is composed of three subsectors: a private market, which operates mostly through health insurance plans, a so-called 'social sector', which provides health coverage to permanent workers of the formal sector and is administered by trade-union-run entities, and a public sector aimed at covering the health needs of people with no other protection. Legal regulations have gradually imposed a mandatory minimum health coverage to all providers of the health system. As soon as litigation was perceived as a successful means to ensure health rights, the span and variety of cases broadened remarkably.[25] Constitutional litigation regarding health issues was also fostered by the concession of constitutional hierarchy to a number of international human rights treaties, including the International Covenant on Economic, Social and Cultural Rights, and the Convention on the Rights of the Child.[26] Special attention was paid by courts to the duties that all actors within the health system (both public and private) had to protect the health of children and of persons with disabilities.

An important supreme court precedent in 2000 involved a claim for individual coverage regarding children with disabilities.[27] In the case *Campodónico de Beviacqua, Ana Carina c. Ministerio de Salud y Banco de Drogas Neoplásicas*,[28] the court upheld an appellate court decision ordering the government to continue providing medication to a child with a disability. The government had previously delivered the medication, but interrupted the provision with notice that previous delivery was based on 'humanitarian reasons' and its interruption did not constitute a breach of a legal duty. The appellate court's rejection of this analysis was upheld by the supreme court.

In its opinion:

* the right to health was a constitutionally protected right: a right included in international human rights treaties and accordingly granted constitutional hierarchy

- the right to health imposed a positive and immediate obligation on public authorities to guarantee health care provision, regardless of other duties imposed on different actors.

The supreme court placed considerable reliance upon the ratification by Argentina of international human rights treaties specifically protecting children's rights to life and health. In particular it had regard to the recognition by the International Covenant on Economic, Social and Cultural Rights (ICESCR) of the right of 'everyone to the enjoyment of the highest attainable standard of physical and mental health' and of the concomitant state obligation to satisfy this right. Citing Article 12 of ICESCR, the court had especial regard to the state's duty to adopt a plan to reduce child mortality, to guarantee children a healthy development and to provide assistance and medical services in case of illness. It additionally cited Articles 23, 24 and 26 of the Convention on the Rights of the Child which guaranteed effective access to health and rehabilitation services for children with disabilities.

The supreme court summarized its doctrine in the following terms:

> the government has assumed explicit international duties to promote and facilitate health treatment required by children, and cannot validly refuse to comply with those duties with the excuse of the inactivity of other public or private entities, especially when all of them participate in the same health system and when the best interests of the child are at stake: this interest shall be protected beyond other considerations by all branches of government (citing Article 3 of the Convention on the Rights of the Child).

The court had occasion to review its decision the following year in *Monteserin, Marcelino c. Estado Nacional – Ministerio de Salud y Acción Social – Comisión Nacional Asesora para la Integración de Personas Discapacitadas – Servicio Nacional de Rehabilitación y Promoción de la Persona con Discapacidad* (2001), a case which concerned a claim for social insurance coverage made on behalf of an indigent child with a disability.[29] The facts in *Monteserin* were similar to those in *Campodónico de Beviacqua*: the father of the child filed a petition against the state in order to register him under the social insurance scheme and thus to entitle him to medical and rehabilitation support. The claim was successful, with the court requiring the child's social insurance registration to ensure that his medical and rehabilitation needs were protected. The supreme court agreed with the attorney general's summary of the relevant implications of the judgement in *Campodónico de Beviacqua* in the following terms:

> According to the international human rights treaties granted constitutional hierarchy, the court reaffirmed the right to the preservation of

health and stressed the compelling obligation of public authorities to guarantee this right with positive actions, regardless of the duties of local jurisdictions.[30]

In the court's view, the state, by ratifying the relevant conventions, had made an explicit commitment before the international community to promote and facilitate the health care needs of children, and could not

> validly disdain these duties under the excuse of the inactivity of other public or private entities, especially when they make part of the same health system, and when what is at stake is the best interest of the child, which should be protected over any other consideration by all governmental departments.[31]

In the court's opinion the general duty included more specific positive obligations

> to promote and facilitate the effective access to the medical and rehabilitation services needed by children, especially those with physical or mental impairments; to make its best effort for them not to be deprived of those services, and to undertake the full realization of the right to benefit from social security.[32]

There have since been many other supreme court cases which have found in favour of HIV-positive patients,[33] claims for medical coverage against private parties (such as for-profit health insurance companies, trade-union-run entities and state-run social entities),[34] and preliminary measures to ensure access to medication and treatment.[35] The lead given by the supreme court has now led to lower courts taking action and reaching similar decisions.[36]

Conclusion

As some of these cases can show, at least the courts of some countries of the region have taken the lead in enforcing positive obligations regarding access to treatment and medications, and the fact that children, and especially children with disabilities, are constitutionally declared to be subjects of special protection has been a key element in this trend. The trend has been replicated in other countries of the region, such as Brazil and Costa Rica, and there are also signs of its adherence by the regional human rights court, the Inter-American Court of Human Rights.[37] While previous judicial approaches were reluctant to review administrative decisions regarding medical coverage, the present trend has shown to be much more sensitive to children in need of treatment, rehabilitation or medication.

The cases I have reviewed reveal at least two kinds of intertwined developments in the field of human rights/fundamental constitutional rights. On the one hand, an expansive interpretation of the right to life, both in its extent – 'life' is not solely understood in a biological sense, but in the sense of 'dignified life' or 'free development of personality' – and in the legal obligation it creates for the state and for some qualified private actors – thus requiring not only negative, but also positive obligations, including the provision of health care, medication and rehabilitation. This expansive interpretation blurs the traditional divide between civil and political vis-à-vis economic, social and cultural rights, and has the practical effect of making justiciable, through the right to life, some components of the right to health. On the other hand, the protection of children (and especially of children with disabilities) has been an important factor for the operation of this expansive interpretation of the right to life. Constitutional and international human rights provisions requiring the state to adopt special measures of protection for children, and even interpretations of the exigencies of the constitutional 'social and democratic state' or 'welfare democratic state' formula when it comes to the situation of disadvantaged groups, including children and children with disabilities, have played an important role in these developments.

These changes appear not to be merely casual or contingent: they reveal a steady pattern in a number of countries of the region, which is consistent with the jurisprudence of the regional human rights court. Their consolidation and replication in other jurisdictions of the region would thus not be surprising.

Notes

1 See Roberto Gargarella (1997) 'Recientes reformas constitucionales en América Latina: Una primera aproximación', in *Desarrollo Económico: Revista de Ciencias Sociales*. IDES, Buenos Aires, 36, 144, January–March, pp.971–990.

2 See, for example, Argentina (amendments of 1994), Bolivia (amendments of 2002), Brazil (1988), Colombia (1991), Dominican Republic (2002), Ecuador (1998), Guatemala (1992), Mexico (several amendments), Paraguay (1992), Peru (1993), and Venezuela (1999).

3 This is the case, for example, in Argentina, Bolivia, Colombia, Costa Rica, Ecuador, El Salvador, Guatemala, Honduras, Paraguay, Peru and Venezuela.

4 See Dominican Constitution, art. 8.17.

5 See Colombian Constitution, art. 47: 'The State shall promote a social insurance, rehabilitation and social integration policy for persons with physical, sensorial and mental disabilities, to whom it shall provide special assistance.'

6 See, for example, Brazilian Constitution, art. 6: 'Education, health, work, housing, leisure, security, social insurance, protection of maternity and childhood, and assistance to indigents are social rights, according to this Constitution.'

7 For Mexico, see the comments of J.A. Cruz Parcero (2001), 'Los derechos sociales como técnica de protección jurídica' in M. Carbonell, J.A. Cruz Parcero and R. Vázquez (eds), *Derechos Sociales y Derechos de las Minorías* (2nd edn.) Mexico: UNAM-Porrúa, pp.89–112; J.R. Cossío (1998) 'Los derechos

sociales como normas programáticas y la comprensión política de la constitución', in E.O. Rabasa (ed.), *Ochenta Años de Vida Constitucional en México*. Mexico: Cámara de Diputados-UNAM, pp.295–328.

8 Directly applying section 43 of the Constitution (as amended in 1994), Argentinean courts have overcome the traditional narrow approach to *locus standi* in constitutionally based actions. Courts have granted, for example, *locus standi* to a subway user, for challenging an illegal increase in ticket prices; to a user of the telephone service, for demanding a public hearing before increasing prices; to a neighbour, for challenging the building of a toxic treatment plant without an environmental impact assessment; to an inhabitant of an area affected by an epidemic disease, for requiring the production of a vaccine; and to a disabled user of the suburban train service, for challenging the introduction of architectural modifications in train stations which made them inaccessible. None of these cases would have been admissible under the previous doctrine, which required proof of an individual grievance.

9 See, for example, R. de C. Mancuso (1999) *Açao Civil Pública*. (São Paulo: Ed. Revista dos Tribunais, pp.46–55; M.F.M. Leal (1998) *Açoes Coletivas: História, Teoria e Prática*. Porto Alegre: Sergio Fabris, pp.187–200.

10 For example, Mexico is witnessing an extensive debate about the need for a change in the *amparo* regulations. The experience of some other countries, such as Brazil, constitutes an important contribution to this debate. See J. Ovalle Favela and E. Ferrer MacGregor, *Juicio de Amparo e Interés Legítimo: La Tutela de los Derechos Difusos y Colectivos (Mexico: Porrúa, 2003)*; A. Gidi and E. Ferrer MacGregor (eds) (2003) *La Tutela de los Derechos Difusos, Colectivos e Individuales Homogéneos: Hacia un Código Modelo para Iberoamérica*. Mexico: Porrúa-Instituto Iberoamericano de Derecho Procesal; A. Gidi and E. Ferrer MacGregor (eds) (2003) *Procesos Colectivos: La Tutela de los Derechos Difusos, Colectivos e Individuales en una Perspectiva Comparada*. Mexico: Porrúa.

11 See L. Bujosa Vadell (1995) *La Protección Jurisdiccional de los Intereses de Grupo*. Barcelona: J.M. Bosch, Chap. 3.

12 For a critique of this doctrine, see Magadalena Sepúlveda (2003) *The Nature of the Obligations under the International Covenant on Economic, Social and Cultural Rights*. Antwerp: Intersentia; Víctor Abramovich and Christian Courtis, *Los Derechos Sociales como Derechos Exigibles* (2nd edn). Madrid: Trotta.

13 For a brief panorama, see Christian Courtis (2006) 'Judicial enforcement of social rights: Perspectives from Latin America', in Roberto Gargarella, Pilar Domingo and Theunis Roux (eds), *Courts and Social Transformation in New Democracies: An Institutional Voice for the Poor?* Aldershot: Ashgate, pp.169–184.

14 See, for example, *15 Interights Bulletin* (2006), wholly dedicated to this issue.

15 See Rodrigo Uprimny Yepes (2006) 'The enforcement of social rights by the Colombian Constitutional Court: Cases and debates', in Roberto Gargarella, Pilar Domingo and Theunis Roux (eds), *Courts and Social Transformation in New Democracies: An Institutional Voice for the Poor?* Aldershot: Ashgate, pp.127–151; Rodrigo Uprimny Yepes (2006) 'Should courts enforce social rights? The experience of the Colombian Constitutional Court', in Fons Coomans (ed.), *Justiciability of Economic and Social Rights: Experiences from Domestic Systems*. Antwerp: Intersentia-Maastricht Centre for Human Rights, pp.355–388. Constitutional Court cases (in Spanish) can be downloaded from www.constitucional.gov.co.

16 T-067/94 (February 1992) Constitutional Court Decision.

17 T-068/94 (February 1994) Constitutional Court Decision.

18 T-204/94 (April 1994) Constitutional Court Decision.

19 T-571/94 (December 1994) Constitutional Court Decision.

20 T-020/95 (February 1995) Constitutional Court Decision.

21 T-049/95 (February 1995) Constitutional Court Decision.
22 T-179/00 (February 2000) Constitutional Court Decision.
23 T-1101/03 (December 2003) Constitutional Court Decision.
24 T-1034/01 (May 2001) Constitutional Court Decision.
25 For a complete account, see Christian Courtis, (in press) 'La aplicación de tratados e instrumentos internacionales sobre derechos humanos y la protección jurisdiccional del derecho a la salud: Apuntes críticos', in Víctor Abramovich, Alberto Bovino and Christian Courtis (comps), *La Aplicación de los Tratados de Derechos: Humanos en el Ámbito Local: La Experiencia de una Década (1994–2005)*. Buenos Aires: Editores del Puerto. On social rights adjudication in general, see Christian Courtis (2006) 'Socio-economic rights before courts in Argentina', in Fons Coomans (ed.), *Justiciability of Economic and Social Rights: Experiences from Domestic Systems*. Antwerp: Intersentia-Maastricht Centre for Human Rights, pp.309–353.
26 See the articles contained in Martín Abregú and Christian Courtis (comps) (1997), *La Aplicación de los Tratados sobre Derechos Humanos por los Tribunales Locales*. Buenos Aires: Editores del Puerto-CELS.
27 Supreme Court cases (in Spanish) can be downloaded from www.cjsn.gov.ar.
28 Argentine Supreme Court, *Campodónico de Beviacqua, Ana Carina c. Ministerio de Salud y Banco de Drogas Neoplásicas*, 24 October 2000.
29 Argentine Supreme Court, *Monteserin, Marcelino c. Estado Nacional – Ministerio de Salud y Acción Social – Comisión Nacional Asesora para la Integración de Personas Discapacitadas – Servicio Nacional de Rehabilitación y Promoción de la Persona con Discapacidad*, 16 October 2001.
30 See *Monteserin*, Attorney General's brief of 30 March 2001, para. VII.
31 See *Monteserin*, Attorney General's brief, para. VII.
32 Citing Articles 23, 24 and 26 of the Convention on the Rights of the Child – see *Monteserin*, Court decision, para. 12.
33 Argentine Supreme Court, *A., C. B. C. Ministerio de Salud y Acción Social s/amparo ley 16.986*, Attorney General's brief of 19 March 1999; Court decision of 1 June 2000.
34 Argentine Supreme Court, *N., L. M. y otra c. Swiss Medical Group S. A.*, Attorney General's brief of 11 June 2003, Court decision of 21 August 2003; *Martín, Sergio Gustavo y otros c. Fuerza Aérea Argentina – Dirección General Bienestar Pers. Fuerza Aérea s/amparo*, Attorney General's brief of 31 October 2002, Court decision of 8 June 2004; *M., S. A. s/materia: previsional s/recurso de amparo*, 23 November 2004. In the same sense, Federal Administrative Court of Appeal, Chamber II, *R., R. S. c. Ministerio de Salud y Acción Social y otro s/amparo*, 21 October 1997; National Civil Court of Appeals, Chamber C, *T., J. M. c. Nubial S.A*, 14 October 1997.
35 See, for example, Argentine Supreme Court, *Alvarez, Oscar Juan c. Buenos Aires, Provincia de y otro s/acción de amparo*, 12 July 2001; *Orlando, Susana Beatriz c. Buenos Aires, Provincia de y otros s/amparo*, 4 April 2002; *Díaz, Brígida c. Buenos Aires, Provincia de y otro (Estado Nacional – Ministerio de Salud y Acción Social de la Nación) s/amparo*, 25 March 2003; *Benítez, Victoria Lidia y otro c. Buenos Aires, Provincia de y otros s/acción de amparo*, 24 April 2003; *Mendoza, Aníbal c. Estado Nacional s/amparo*, 8 September 2003; *Rogers, Silvia Elena c. Buenos Aires, Provincia de y otros (Estado Nacional) s/acción de amparo*, 8 September 2003; *Sánchez, Enzo Gabriel c. Buenos Aires, Provincia de y otro (Estado Nacional) s/acción de amparo*, 18 December 2003; *Laudicina, Angela Francisca c. Buenos Aires, Provincia de y otro s/acción de amparo*, 9 March 2004; *Sánchez, Norma Rosa c/Estado Nacional y otro s/acción de amparo*, 11 May 2004. The court declared itself incompetent but notwithstanding ordered preliminary injunctive relief in *Diéguez, Verónica Sandra y otro c. Buenos Aires, Provincia de s/acción de amparo*, 27

December 2002; *Kastrup Phillips, Marta Nélida c. Buenos Aires, Provincia de y otros s/acción de amparo*, 11 November 2003; *Podestá, Leila Grisel c. Buenos Aires, Provincia de y otro s/acción de amparo*, 18 December 2003. Cases were dealt under the original jurisdiction of the supreme court because plantiffs sued both the federal state and a province.

36 See, among many others, Bahía Blanca Civil and Commercial Court of Appeals, Chamber II, *C. y otros c. Ministerio de Salud y Acción Social de la Provincia de Buenos Aires*, 2 September 1997 (imposing treatment to public hospital); Tucumán Administrative Court of Appeals, Chamber II, *González, Amanda Esther c. Instituto de Previsión y Seguridad Social de Tucumán y otro s/amparo*, 15 July 2002 (imposing treatment to public 'social' entity); Buenos Aires Administrative Court of Appeals, Chamber II, *Sociedad Italiana de Beneficencia en Buenos Aires c. GCBA s/otras causas*, 7 October 2004; Buenos Aires Administrative Court of Appeals, Chamber I, *Centro de Educ. Médica e Invest. Clínicas Norberto Quirno c. GCBA s/otras causas*, 22 June 2004 (backing the legal imposition of coverage duties on private providers); Buenos Aires Administrative Court of Appeals, Chamber II, *Trigo, Manuel Alberto c. GCBA y otros s/Medida Cautelar*, 12 May 2002; Buenos Aires Administrative Court of Appeals, Chamber I, *Rodríguez Miguel Orlando c. GCBA s/otros procesos incidentales*, 22 December 2004, Buenos Aires Administrative Court of Appeals, Chamber I, *Defensoría del Pueblo de la Ciudad de Buenos Aires (Denuncia incumplimiento respecto a la afiliada Brenda Nicole Deghi) c. GCBA s/otros procesos incidentales*, 10 February 2005 (providing treatment through preliminary measures); Buenos Aires Administrative Court of Appeals, Chamber I, *Zárate, Raúl Eduardo c. GCBA s/daños y perjuicios*, 21 August 2002; Buenos Aires Administrative Court of Appeals, Chamber II, *Villalba de Gómez, Leticia Lilian c. GCBA (Hospital General de Agudos Franciso Santojani) y otros s/daños y perjuicios*, 8 April 2003; Buenos Aires Administrative Court of Appeals, Chamber II, *Echavarría, Adriana Graciela c. GCBA y otros s/daños y perjuicios*, 22 April 2003; Buenos Aires Administrative Court of Appeals, Chamber I, *B. L. E. y otros c. OSBA s/daños y perjuicios*, 27 August 2004 (awarding compensation for damages caused by denial or inadequate treatment); Buenos Aires Administrative Court of Appeals, Chamber I, *Roccatagliata de Bangueses, Mercedes Lucía c. OSBA s/otros procesos incidentales*, 10 June 2002; Buenos Aires Administrative Court of Appeals, Chamber I, *Urtasun, Teodoro Alberto c. Instituto Municipal de Obra Social s/Cobro de Pesos*, 22 April 2004 (imposing treatment to public 'social' entities).

37 The Inter-American Court of Human Rights has not delivered yet any decision dealing with children with disabilities, but it has vigorously affirmed in a number of cases that, specially in the case of children in a vulnerable condition, the right to life encompasses positive obligations for the State, including the provision of health care. See, for example, Inter-American Court of Human Rights, *case of the 'Street Children' (Villagrán-Morales et al.) v. Guatemala.* Judgement of 19 November 1999, Series C No. 63, paras. 194–196; *case of the 'Juvenile Reeducation Institute' v. Paraguay.* Judgement of 2 September 2004 (only in Spanish), Series C No. 112, paras. 148–149, 161 and 174; *case of the Indigenous Community Yakye Axa v. Paraguay.* Judgement of 17 June 2005, Series C No. 125, paras. 163, 165, 167 and 169; *case of Sawhoyamaxa Indigenous Community v. Paraguay.* Judgement of 29 March 2006, Series C No. 146, paras. 167–168, 170 and 177–178. The case law of the Inter-American Court of Human Rights can be found at its webpage, www.corteidh.or.cr.

11 Access to care and the right to life of disabled children in Bulgaria

Boika Rechel

Introduction

This chapter looks at barriers to protecting the rights of disabled children in Bulgaria, focusing particularly on those living in institutions. It draws on documented cases of violation of the right to life and discusses existing structural, institutional and cultural factors which are contributing to failures to ensure access to quality care and protection of children with disabilities. It focuses on the rights to life and access to care for disabled children in Bulgaria – how these basic human rights are understood by professionals, policy-makers and the wider community, and what mechanisms are in place to protect them. This text is derived from broader research on access to health care for children in Bulgaria, and presents specifically only those results that are relevant to children living with disabilities.

The research employed a case study strategy using multiple sources of evidence and data collection. It is based on 42 in-depth interviews with policy-makers, physicians providing care for children, users of health services, and representatives of NGOs concerned with children's rights and health, in addition to analysis of official government statistics, and reports of governmental institutions and NGOs. Qualitative interviews were selected as the method as they present a flexible research tool for accessing the participants' interpretations and the meanings they attach to the studied phenomena.[1] Data analysis was informed by the grounded theory approach, which implies that all explanations or theories are derived from the data themselves.[2]

Setting the scene

Political, social and economic transition

After the fall of the Communist regime in 1989, Bulgaria began a transition towards democratization and market economy. Frequent changes of government and political instability resulted in slow social, economic and legislative reforms.[3] The early years of transition were associated with severe economic decline, with the real GDP in 1997 plummeting to 63.2

per cent of its 1989 level,[4] followed by slow recovery. The living standards of the larger part of the population deteriorated significantly with widening socio-economic inequalities.[5] The economic decline resulted in a fall in real incomes, high unemployment and deterioration in the provision of social benefits such as health care, child care and education.[6] In 2001, poverty in Bulgaria was 31.9 per cent at a poverty line of $4.30 per day.[7] Poverty rates were four times higher in rural areas, and the Roma minority were ten times more likely to be poor than ethnic Bulgarians.[8] Children, in particular those in rural households with many offspring, were overrepresented among the poor.[9]

The UN Convention on the Rights of the Child (CRC) recognizes children's right to the highest attainable standard of health and access to health care services.[10] Member states that have signed the CRC are obliged to ensure that 'every mentally or physically disabled child enjoys a full and decent life, in conditions which ensure dignity, promote self-reliance and facilitate the child's active participation in the community'. Bulgaria ratified the CRC in 1991 and has been working towards meeting the standards set in the convention. The Bulgarian Parliament adopted the Child Protection Act in May 2000,[11] followed by the rules for its implementation in 2003.[12] The State Agency for Child Protection was created in October 2000, and began its activities in January 2001. The Child Protection Act stipulates special protection for children at risk. One of the groups of children at risk is defined as those who 'suffer from mental or physical disabilities, as well as difficult to treat conditions'. Considerable progress has been made in adopting legislation to protect the rights of people with disabilities. The Law on Integration of People with Disabilities which came into force in January 2005 aims to guarantee equal rights, non-discrimination, support and social integration of disabled people.[13] However, there is still more to be achieved in the practical implementation of the laws to ensure equal rights of disabled people in Bulgaria. In a survey among 1,350 adult citizens conducted in January 2002, 48 per cent of the participants state that in Bulgaria children with disabilities do not receive the special care that should guarantee for them dignified life, independence and active participation in society.[14] In the same study, the participants ranked the following problems faced by disabled children as the most severe: poor health (55 per cent), isolation from society (49 per cent), not having enough knowledge and skills for independent life (24 per cent), lack of security (23 per cent) and negative societal attitudes towards them (19 per cent).

Prevalence of disability among children

In the latest census in Bulgaria (March 2001), people with disabilities are defined as those who have been assessed formally by expert medical commissions and possess a document for disability status or a document for loss of capacity to work. According to this census, the total number of disabled people is 224,550 or 2.8 per cent of the population, including 18,189 disabled people under the age of 30 years.[15] According to the official census statistics, in 2004 there were 5,899 children in Bulgaria up to the age of 16 years with a recognized disability status, or five per 1,000 children in this age group.[16] However, this number seems to be an underestimate and to exclude a large number of children with disabilities who live in institutions. The most common causes of disability included neurological conditions and diseases of the sensory organs (31 per cent), diseases of the respiratory system (24.3 per cent), congenital malformations (14.1 per cent) and psychiatric disorders (12.4 per cent).[17] Interpretation of these statistics, however, is difficult because of the changing definition of disability, changing regulations for entitlement to disability benefits (which entails obtaining official disability status), lack of a national register of disabled people, and lack of reliable medical assessment of children placed in institutions.

In Bulgaria there are currently 332 institutions for children.[18] In 2001, the total number of children in institutions was 31,102, or nearly 2 per cent of the population of young people in Bulgaria (1,607,515 children). The children's institutions are under the authority of different governmental departments, and include:

- 244 institutions under the responsibility of the Ministry of Education and Science with 24,147 children. These include homes for children without parents, schools for children with impaired vision or hearing, schools for children with other chronic health conditions, and special schools for children with intellectual disabilities
- 32 homes for children under the age of three years under the Ministry of Health, caring for 3,563 children (formerly called 'mother-and-child homes'); these include healthy and disabled children; disabled children may remain in these institutions until the age of seven
- 56 institutions under the responsibility of the Ministry of Labour and Social Policy, which care for over 3,392 children with mental and physical disabilities between the ages of three and 18. About a quarter of the residents of these institutions are young people over 18 years of age.

The total absolute number of institutionalized children has been decreasing from 34,122 in 1999 to 31,102 in 2001. This decrease, however, is not due to deinstitutionalization, but to a declining birth rate and falling children's population in Bulgaria over recent years.[19] The proportion of the total child population in Bulgaria placed in institutions has been increasing.[20]

There is no accurate assessment of what proportion of children placed in institutions have any disability. According to one estimate, more than 5,400 of these children have a registered disability.[21] A UNICEF report indicates that 14,032 children with disabilities in Bulgaria were in public institutional care in 2001.[22] According to a study by the State Agency for Child Protection, the number of children with intellectual, psychological, physical or sensory disabilities placed in institutions is 18,695, of which 11,776 are in institutions of the Ministry of Education, 5,440 in institutions of the Ministry of Labour and Social Protection, and 1,479 in institutions of the Ministry of Health.[23] These discrepancies may arise from the inclusion in this figure of children who attend special schools for children with learning difficulties. According to the Ministry of Education, 8,957 children were studying in 74 special schools in the academic year 2003–2004.[24] About half of these schools are full-time boarding schools and share many common features with orphanages, as children have little contact with their parents.[25]

The placement of children into institutions is frequently based on unscientific diagnosis, not on the specific interventions and level of support they need.[26] There is a lack of standardized assessment procedures and a lack of a unified definition of disability.[27] Most children placed in institutions are assessed before three years of age, and usually are not reassessed until the age of 16 when they qualify for a state disability pension.[28] Interestingly, in all institutions the number of boys significantly exceeds the number of girls,[29] indicating that social factors, rather than solely medically ascertained need, play a role in the parental decision to leave their child in institutional care. Prevailing attitudes that girls are more vulnerable than boys and more in need of parental support may be one reason for the observed gender imbalance.

Why are so many disabled children placed in institutions?

The institutionalization of children can be seen as a result of interaction of multiple factors from the Communist tradition and contemporary phenomena. Poverty is one of the main reasons at the individual and family level which force mothers to surrender their children to social homes. This is especially true for Roma minority families with many children who are faced with the real threat of physical survival. Negative social attitudes towards disability and widespread stigma coupled with lack of services for disabled children in the community and lack of opportunities for their integration in society together form a major social deficit leading to institutionalization. Finally, the grossly underdeveloped child protection system leaves institutions as the only refuge from domestic violence, child neglect and abuse.

Many countries of central and eastern Europe inherited from their Communist past a large number of institutions for children cut off from their families and segregated from the community.[30] In Bulgaria, the institutionalization of children became a social phenomenon after its transition to a socialist country in 1945.[31] In 1939, for example, only one institution for social child care existed, in 1948 there were 31 such institutions, while by 1968 their number had risen to 133.[32] One participant in the study suggested that institutionalization 'is related to the socialist state that considered the family as something secondary. The communist state was something primary'. The first socialist constitution from 1947 stated that 'the family must follow the common public interest of the society'.[33] The state in the form of the institution becomes the only 'parent' of the child. As one Bulgarian NGO worker explained:

> Another reason for disabled children to be surrendered to institutions is that the state has since the 1950s pursued the policy of taking over all care for such children. Previously there was ideological reasoning that the state cares for these children, because the socialist society must be nice and beautiful, and such people hardly exist. They tucked them away in the black mountains, to live there like cattle. And they simply flickered and died.
>
>   (Participant from an NGO working with ethnic minorities)

Poverty

Pressures to put children in institutions often arise from the disadvantaged economic background of families. According to a survey conducted in 1993/1994 among 615 children from nine mother-and-child homes for children up to three years of age, only 11.8 per cent were placed in a home for medical reasons, including congenital malformations, malnutrition, prematurity, mental retardation or psychiatric illness of the parents.[34] Most children (67.1 per cent) were institutionalized for purely social indications, such as lone motherhood, poor living conditions, large number of children within the household, or imprisonment of the parent/s. Very few children (fewer than 5 per cent) were orphans. Most children were born out of marriage (56.3 per cent), many were born to young mothers aged between 13 and 20 (32.6 per cent) and 55.6 per cent were of Roma ethnic origin.

> I remember a case of a mother with three children. Her husband was in prison. I was doing research on the effectiveness of the programme for prevention of institutionalization. This mother wanted to place her baby, because she could not breastfeed after having two older children, and she was desperate. There was no Humana [infant formula] and she was going to bring the child to the institution. There is nothing to feed the baby, she doesn't know where to go. The only place she knows in the community is this institution. And she goes there.
>
>   (Psychologist, academic institution)

Studies among single mothers have shown that they leave their children in institutions because, first, they have insufficient financial means to care for them, and second, because they fear people's negative attitudes towards themselves and their children.[35] As one mother of a disabled child noted: 'In all cases of abandoned children one of the problems is the lack of money. Lack of possibility to support this child' (Mother of child with cerebral palsy).

Disability also leads to impoverishment because one of the parents has to look after the child at home and cannot work. The disability benefits are insufficient to cover the needs of the child: 'The disability pension of my son is 120 lev [approx. 60 Euro or 40 GBP per month]. It is 78 lev plus an addition for an assistant. Simply with this money if he has to survive on his own ... it is absolutely impossible' (Mother of child with cerebral palsy).

Many children are placed in special schools for social reasons, mainly by parents lacking the means for bringing up their child. These schools provide social assistance in the form of food, clothes, accommodation and textbooks which serves as an incentive for poor parents to enrol their children.[36] There is a recognition of a widely spread practice of special schools actively recruiting children from disadvantaged social backgrounds regardless of their intellectual ability, in order to keep these schools running. About 90 per cent of the children in special schools are labelled as having 'minor mental disabilities'.[37] The lasting effect of this on children was described by an NGO worker:

> They ruin these children totally. They can't even have a driving licence because they have a 'mental disability'. In other words, they remain employable only in a small segment of occupations, where you can work with a mental disability. It's written in their diploma 'graduated an auxiliary school'. The end. He can neither continue in a normal secondary school, nor go to the university, nothing.
>
> (Participant from an NGO working with ethnic minorities)

In Bulgaria, as in other countries of central and eastern Europe, Roma children are overrepresented in special schools for children with intellectual and physical disabilities. Different estimates indicate that 35 per cent to 50 per cent of those attending special schools for children with learning disabilities were Roma, while Roma children make up about 10 per cent of the general population.[38] Lack of standardized diagnostic procedures and overdiagnosis of mental disability among Roma children makes the reliability of the official statistics on disability questionable.[39]

The poverty trap is most difficult for Roma ethnic families with many children. Newly trained social workers feel helpless in assisting families to solve complex social problems and still opt for the institution as a means to provide basic physical care and nutrition for the children:

> Because most of the children are Roma, and the staff believe that it is better in an institution than in the Roma ghetto. I simply know social workers who when they enter in a gypsy house and see the misery there

– the baby eating a bread crust and boza [fermented wheat sugary drink] and so on ... In this sense the institution (depending on the institution) offers better conditions. Again, only the conditions, the material side of the conditions is seen, but not the emotional side.

(Psychologist, academic institution)

Such perceptions that for Roma children the institutions are better than their family home, that 'the gypsy mother is terrible', encourage their placement in children's homes. The institutions may provide for the basic physical needs of the children – nutrition, clothes and shelter. However the aspects of children's emotional needs and secure attachment with parents are very often neglected.

Lack of care options in the community

There is little community support for families caring for disabled children.[40] The risk of institutionalization of disabled children is associated with the lack of social and psychological support for their parents as early as at the maternity ward where the child is born. The most common social assistance service rendered to these children is residential care. At present, day centres for disabled children which were established very recently as a result of the World Bank funded Child Welfare Reform Project provide the only alternative to institutionalization:

There have been real social services in the community for one–two years now. And they are relatively few in the big cities. Most of them were created with the efforts of NGOs and foreign donors which started working on this years ago. In ten cities such centres for complex social services were created in the community. But this is a drop in the ocean, these are first steps, and the state has been subsidizing these centres only since July 2006.

(Participant from an NGO working with ethnic minorities)

Despite the existing law on the social integration of people with disabilities[41] many directors of mainstream kindergartens and nurseries refuse to admit children with disabilities, for example children with Down's syndrome.[42] Lack of day care and specialized community support services is a problem for many parents and their disabled children:

The problem with institutionalization of children is not a result of lack of health care, although some parents may claim so. It is more a social problem of the families in terms of lack of environment in the broadest sense, to support the families in the upbringing of the different child. Because he is different. [...] Starting from these social attitudes, to the lack of any support at all in the community like peer-to-peer counselling or any day care, to lack of rehabilitation services in the broadest sense, not only medical rehabilitation, although such is lacking as well, but not as dramatically as the social rehabilitation. Including lack of support for integration in school or kindergarten. These are the true reasons. In other words, this social mass of deficiencies, of social deficiencies, which do not help families to deal with the inherently difficult situation, to bring up a child with disability.

(Participant, disability rights NGO)

The destiny of children born with a disability is often decided by the health staff in the maternity unit, without provision of adequate counselling and support to the parents (Kubratova 2005).[43] According to a study among 60 mothers of children aged three to 18 with moderate and severe intellectual disability, the majority of parents (73.3 per cent) were dissatisfied with the way they were informed about the child's diagnosis.[44] It was communicated hurriedly (21.7 per cent), rudely (13.3 per cent), without sufficient information about the condition itself (80 per cent) and without further referral to appropriate specialists (48.3 per cent).

Doctors still reportedly encourage parents to surrender children with physical or mental disabilities to state-run institutions.[45] Particularly in small district hospitals, there is no expertise to assess the nature of the child's health condition and disability and to develop a comprehensive plan for treatment and rehabilitation. The only alternative suggested to the mother is to leave the child in an institution:

If she happens to give birth in a small town, she will be told: 'Yes. This child has a disability. We think that, firstly, these children live very short lives, because this is severe brain damage. And secondly, you will not be able to take care of a child with such a disability. And obviously, you have to leave it here and from here we will transfer it to a home for babies'.

(Lawyer, human rights NGO)

Many children born with a disability are referred to institutions for children from birth to three years of age and after that are transferred to another institution for older children. Lack of care in the community and lack of adequate social and professional support to parents of children with disabilities are some of the reasons why parents decide to leave their children in an institution:

The medical staff paint such a catastrophic picture of the future of the child – that in most cases he will die very soon, and that the parent will absolutely not be able to manage on their own. And it is true that bringing up a disabled child is very difficult. Especially if the parent is single, not two parents. In reality until recently there were no services to support them, apart from day centres for children with disabilities. If you have a disabled child you need to devote your life to them – to remain at home and to look after them all your life.

(Policy-maker, governmental department for social issues)

A real concern about the child's safety may be another reason for institutionalization. The system of child protection is still underdeveloped and it is likely that many instances of violence and abuse against children remain unreported. The issues of domestic violence have only recently become a subject of public debate.[46] As one of the participants explained, placement in institutions may be the only way to protect children from violence or neglect:

Social workers prefer to place children in institutions because it is less risky. They entrust the child totally to somebody who looks after them. Otherwise, as they weigh the risk, assess neglect and violence, because they cannot trust the family, because they don't know what to do, because there are no alternative services, the simplest way out is to institutionalize the child.

(Psychologist, academic institution)

Public attitudes towards disability and institutions

Traditional prejudiced attitudes towards people with mental and physical disabilities result in stigma for disabled children and their families. Stigma associated with disability and the social isolation of the family have been pointed out as obstacles to the integration of children with disabilities:[47] 'There is a stigma, which is obvious; the parent is ashamed to take the child out in the community for any service, regardless whether to bring him to the doctor or to enrol him in a kindergarten' (Lawyer, human rights NGO).

In small rural communities the problem of stigma, shame and guilt may be extreme with grave consequences for the child born with disability:

These are children with many disabilities, they look very severely ill, and before they were placed in the home, there has been a hard period when they were kept in basements or barns, or in attics, isolated from everyone else, they were kept hidden. Even the neighbour doesn't know that there is a child, she was announced dead or as if she was given away after she was born. But she is in reality kept in the house in such conditions. These are the children that are the most self-aggressive in the institutions, the ones that are being tied up there.

(Lawyer, human rights NGO)

The stigma extends to the family and relatives and may lead to disruption of family relations, which makes care for the disabled child by the single parent very difficult: 'When [the child] has chronic illness, men often leave the family. The woman remains alone to look after the disabled child, which is simply impossible when the disability is severe' (psychologist, academic institution).

> The stigma of the disability is transferred to the whole family when there is a disabled child. Especially if the impairment is from birth. There is a difference between inborn disability and acquired disability as a result of trauma or even a mistake in the vaccinations if you like. And the attitudes towards the family are different when the handicap is inborn. These are different things. In the first case, it is perceived as a sort of karma, punishment and all sorts of prejudices. In the other case, it is perceived as the tragedy, you see, which happened to that family. A healthy, well child and suddenly see what happened to her.
>
> (Participant, disability rights NGO)

In Bulgaria the medical model of disability still prevails. Disability is viewed as a medical condition requiring lifelong treatment, thus justifying placement in a health facility for long term care. There is less understanding of disability as a result of a 'disabling environment' and little appreciation of the need to ensure the best possible conditions for full social functioning of people with disabilities.

Bulgaria has one of the highest rates in Europe of institutionalization of children, and children with disabilities in particular. The relative proportion of institutionalized children has increased since the early 1990s. A recent report on children with disabilities in central and eastern Europe suggests that countries with a higher share of disabled children in institutions are countries where there is a social acceptance of institutionalization.[48] In a recent survey in Bulgaria, 78 per cent of the participants believed that the conditions in the children's institutions were poor, 70 per cent that children in institutions did not receive adequate care, 82 per cent said that they did not receive adequate nutrition, and 68 per cent that they were not being prepared to live independent lives.[49] Despite this recognition that the services provided by institutions were grossly inadequate, 31 per cent of the respondents still thought that placement in institutions was the most appropriate care for disabled children. Regarding options for reform in institutional care, 50 per cent of the public were categorically against the option of reducing the number of children's homes and reducing the number of children in homes.[50]

There is a lack of local studies from Bulgaria about the development of children under the age of three years who live in institutions,[51] and in general there is little understanding of the adverse consequences of institutionalization. A recent study found that a large proportion of mothers who surrender their children to institutions have themselves been in institutions as children, thus they were replicating this 'parenting' model.[52] As one social worker explained, often children who leave institutions at the age of 18 hold ambivalent attitudes towards the institution which was their (only) home:

> Nowadays young people who have grown up in institutions already start gathering and start forming some organizations. They say the upbringing there was very poor. There has been violence, hunger, there has been abuse, humiliation, and all those things. But if they don't have another parental figure, the institution becomes the only one. That's like the abusive parent. He is beating me, he is throwing me out and so on, but that is my parent. Thus, it is very complicated. Very complicated. I went to one gathering and there was lobbying there, graduates from different homes had gathered, and one group was so fiercely defending the benefits of the institutions that I got scared.
>
> (Psychologist, academic institution)

The stigma attached to disability and the public acceptance of institutions remain major challenges to recent attempts for deinstitutionalization. Other barriers to closing the institutions are administrative issues related to the funding of the children's homes and staff salaries, which depend on the number of children placed there. Institutions do not actively maintain links with the parents and do not undertake work designed to reintegrate children back into their families.[53] As one participant described:

> Institutionalization is a serious problem because it cuts off the person from participation in society. It absolutely isolates. The Bulgarian institution becomes the only 'parent' of the child. The child once placed in an institution ceases to be part of the family. Any regulation for visits of parents to the institution, any encouragement of the parents to take care of their child, any work with the stigma, work that the parents and life at home can contribute to the child's development and so on, all this the institution is not doing. On the contrary, it deepens the breakdown of the relationship between the child and the parent.
>
> (Psychologist, academic institution)

Cases have been reported where institutions have discouraged and prevented contacts with relatives with no justification.[54]

> Due to this greediness of institutions to swallow more and more and to establish themselves firmly as a presence and to say 'You can't do without us'. They prolong the stay [of the children] and definitely do not encourage minimal length of stay there.
>
> (Psychologist, academic institution)

One recent survey on attitudes towards foster care found that fewer than 13 per cent of families interviewed as potential foster parents were inclined to accept a child with a disability or with a medical condition.[55] This proportion was the highest for candidate foster families in the capital (13 per cent) and lowest for families from the villages (6.8 per cent). Among the reasons stated was the lack of appropriate services and the difficulty to provide in the family the special care such a child would need.

> The exit from the institution is difficult. There are no families who want to take their children back. Foster care is not developed. Adoption is extremely difficult. One must be very open-minded to adopt a disabled child, and especially with severe disabilities.
>
> (Social worker, NGO working with institutions)

According to official statistics of the State Agency for Child Protection, a total of 1,622 children from institutions were adopted in 2002, of whom 710 children were adopted in Bulgaria, and 912 abroad. From all children from institutions who were adopted in Bulgaria, 41 (5.7 per cent) had established disability or a long-term condition, while 241 (26.4 per cent) children with disabilities were adopted abroad. A reluctance of Bulgarian parents to adopt disabled children was reported by some service providers:

> Well, the Bulgarian families want [to adopt] healthy children. They don't take children if they have even the slightest problem, something which can be corrected like strabismus, let alone children with more serious problems. They are also very afraid of psychiatric illness, the biological parents shouldn't have such. There is a questionnaire, although an anonymous one, and they [the adoptive family] have the right to know. And in general, the children that remain, they have such deviations, and from there their unhappy fate is to go from institution to institution.
>
> (Paediatrician, regional hospital)

The rights to life and access to health care for disabled children

The right to life of disabled children depends on access to continuous, quality and timely health care. It is also interlinked with the wider political and socio-economic environment, and prevailing cultural attitudes and norms. Children with disabilities may experience premature death not simply because of their medical conditions, but because they do not receive optimal physical care and emotional stimulation, they are neglected or have accidents, are not brought in time to hospital when ill, or because nobody has the expertise to treat their conditions. The underlying cause of all these pathways is lack of political guarantees of their right to life and health care, and failure to implement child protection policies for children without parental support and children with disabilities. In a culture where children are highly valued, it is difficult to understand why there has been little societal engagement with the rights of disabled children. Possible clues may be sought on the one hand in the Communist tradition of presenting a society free of evil and disease, and on the other hand in the still-prevailing stigma attached to disability and the discriminatory low value accorded to a life with disability.

Conditions and care in institutions

State funding for social care homes is insufficient. Most care homes are situated in economically deprived areas, where possibilities for supplementing state funding from local municipalities and for fundraising in the communities are non-existent.[56] According to a recent assessment of 19 institutions for children with intellectual or physical disability by the State Agency for Child Protection, 15 homes are situated in small villages and only four in towns.[57] In recent years, funding for refurbishment of the homes and for improving general conditions has come mainly from external sources, while local investment has been limited.

The annual budget of the institutions and the salaries of staff depend on the number of children in their care. Thus, they are willing to prolong children's stay and actively promote their services by visiting vulnerable families and single mothers.[58]

A number of cases of death among disabled people living in institutions have been attributed to inadequate care and negligence by staff. The Bulgarian Helsinki Committee, a human rights NGO, reported that several people died in 2004 in Bulgarian institutions for adults with intellectual disabilities as a result of violence between residents and inaction and inadequate care by the personnel.[59] In late 2005, two children died in the Dobromirsti home in southern Bulgaria. One of them, a five-year-old blind girl, was scalded by boiling water in a bathroom where she had been left unsupervised.[60] Staff working in institutions usually lack the qualifications and training to be able to provide adequate care and rehabilitation for children placed there: 'Most of these people are extremely negligent. Firstly, they aren't given a job description or pre-defined standards of care to follow. And secondly, nobody is giving them any instructions and training, nor is controlling how they fulfil their obligations' (Lawyer, human rights NGO).

Most of the staff working in institutions are recruited from the villages where the institutions are located and do not have formal training. According to participants in this research, staff often have fatalistic attitudes towards deaths in children's homes. Staff believe that children are destined to die very soon because of their 'severe disabilities' and when a child dies nobody questions the circumstances of their death or whether it could have been prevented.

During the winter of 1996/1997, 13 children died from hypothermia and malnutrition in a home for children with mental disabilities in the village of Dzhurkovo near Plovdiv. Eight years later, in February 2005, the director of the institution and two members of the health care team were taken to court and charged with causing the death of the children through negligence of their professional duties.[61] The investigation found that some of the children were never examined by a physician. One of the children who died, a nine-year-old girl, weighed only seven kilograms, while another 18-year-old girl, weighed 11 kilograms.[62] In May 2005, the District Court of Plovdiv acquitted the three members of staff, but found that neglect on the part of the state had left the home without the means to pay for food and heating, resulting in living conditions that were cruel, inhuman and degrading.[63]

According to observations of the Bulgarian Helsinki Committee, in the late 1990s there was high mortality in other homes for disabled children: in the home for children and young people with mental disabilities in Vidrare, 18 children died in 1997 and 12 children died in 1998; in a similar home in Fakia, six to eight children were dying every year until 1999.[64] In the children's home in Mogilino there was a high mortality rate, with six deaths in 2001, out of about 90 children with developmental disabilities living in the home at that time.[65] One of the children, a nine-year-old boy with cerebral palsy, died of pneumonia. Children with cerebral palsy need to be fed in an upright position, to prevent food entering the windpipe and causing pneumonia. According to reports from visits to the home, these children were fed in a reclining position with bottles only.[66]

> It is obvious that most of these children do not die from their disabilities, contrary to the official explanation that persons with such disabilities are not expected to reach the age of 15 or 20 in any place of residence. On the contrary, these children die because nothing at all has been done for them from the moment of their birth, and nothing at all concerning therapy and treatment appropriate for their disability.
>
> (Lawyer, human rights NGO)

A survey conducted in 1993/1994 among 615 children in mother-and-child homes under the age of three years showed that 41.7 per cent weighed below the normal range, and 26.5 per cent were under the normal height range.[67] With efforts from NGOs and the government, conditions in the homes have been improving and since the early 2000s many institutions have been providing better nutrition and physical environment.

Many children living in institutions have parents who have not lost their parental rights, but do not visit their children for many years and do not have anything to do with them. In order to make a court case to investigate a child's death, normally it is the parents who should make a claim.

Children in institutions often do not have a guardian to defend their rights. This is one of the reasons why most of the premature deaths occurring in institutions remain without official investigation by the prosecution or the police.

> They don't want to visit the institution, neither to engage with anything related to the child. Even at that stage after the child has died, they don't want to get involved to make a court case in order to prove something.
>
> (Lawyer, human rights NGO)

There is a lack of official statistics on mortality rates as these data have not been reported by the institutions and have not been collated and analysed at national level. The case records in the children's homes are inaccessible for state organizations for control or quality assurance purposes.

> Because whatever way you look at it, these are closed institutions. In practice, no other state authority is interested in these institutions. They are closed to society. Neither a journalist enters them, nor a controlling authority manages to get in there, very often simply because they are situated in such remote and difficult to reach places, that they cannot get there, there is no transportation there, infrastructure is lacking.
>
> (Lawyer, human rights NGO)

Due to the lack of medical expertise, it is difficult to establish the real cause of death for children dying in institutions. Causes of death are registered on death certificates by general practitioners on the basis of the information provided by the medical staff on duty in the institution at the time. According to a report by Amnesty International the majority of death certificates stated that death resulted from 'the failure of the heart and respiratory function' but did not actually state what had caused it.[68] In cases when a post-mortem examination was performed, often there was a discrepancy between the clinical and pathological diagnosis. Post-mortem examination was introduced for children dying in institutions only in 1999. Until 2002, there was no means of reporting the number and circumstances of death of children dying in institutions, resulting in a lack of official statistics on mortality.

Another barrier to ensuring that laws are fully implemented is that institutions are closed to independent bodies for monitoring and control to ensure prompt and impartial investigation of deaths among residents or reported abuse.[69]

> The big problem is that no controlling authority ever enters the children's institutions. There is no person who is truly independent to review the documentation and to examine the child itself, in order to

be able to say what their concrete needs are, what is necessary to be done for them, in order to prevent a lethal outcome. We don't have anything like that. We don't have such expertise.

(Lawyer, human rights NGO)

Access to medical care

In Bulgaria, the Law on Health Insurance was enacted in 1998. The system of health insurance is compulsory for the entire population.[70] Children are exempted from health insurance and are entitled to free medical care. The problem of low quality care in institutions has been recognized by the Ministry of Health in a recent analysis of the health care reform.[71] Since the reform of primary health care provision in Bulgaria in 2000, general practitioners (GPs) have been the first point of contact for children in social care homes in need of medical services. As one of the participants pointed out, the provision of health care to children in institutions is regulated, and all homes have assigned medical staff. However, professional self-regulation is underdeveloped in the medical field in Bulgaria and it is likely that cases of negligence or malpractice remain unknown or not investigated. The key problem is the uncertain quality of care, which according to the respondent is difficult to regulate with a law, but is a question of personal responsibility of the physicians and nurses:

The problem is solved there. Depending on the institution, the problem is solved, there is a state-appointed doctor, who is paid for this work, or a nurse, or if the institution is small, several institutions are served by one doctor. Thus, the question is solved. Well, to what extent it is good quality, what is the quality of the service, this is another theme, this is not possible to regulate with a law only, it is necessary to have personal engagement of the staff. But there are requirements, there is a regulation, according to which these people receive health care.

(Policy-maker, governmental department)

In most institutions for disabled children there are no physicians.[72] Dental care is usually restricted to tooth extraction.[73] General practitioners are usually based far away from the children's institutions and they need to travel great distances to realize the chain of referral–child–GP–specialist–hospital – which for a child in a high-risk situation may be fatal.[74] In Mogilino, the GP is 17 km from the home, the paediatrician and psychiatrist 30 km away.[75]

In January 2000, two boys suffering from fever died in the social care home at Fakia, where 40 children with mental disabilities were placed.[76] The village of Fakia is situated in the mountains and transportation to the nearest health facility can be difficult especially in the winter. The children who died could not be taken promptly to a hospital because roads were impassable in the snow.

There are physicians working in the institutions under the Ministry of Health, which care for children up to the age of three years. The children still need to be registered with a GP. Although this is a reflection of the uniformity of access to primary health services through a GP-based system, on some occasions the registration with a GP is only a formality and adds bureaucratic complexity and delays in accessing specialized and hospital services. One of the participants in the study explained this situation:

> There is even another extreme, that the children who are placed in mother and child homes, where there are doctors working, they also have to be registered with a GP. And to be referred to the hospital, this is such an anomaly, to be referred to the hospital, you know the doctor on duty in the institution has seen the child, treated him, has written a referral medical summary, but he still has to call the GP to ask for a referral, for the child to be admitted to a hospital.
>
> (Paediatrician, regional hospital)

There are also financial implications arising from the system of per capita payment to GPs according to the number of patients registered with them. One participant perceived that as a diversion of resources from the children's homes:

> These doctors [GPs] don't treat them. The money should go instead to the institutions, they are so problematic. The children are registered with one GP, who I don't know when and how he sees them, but they are cared for and treated by the doctors in the institutions. And still the GP has to agree for the child's hospitalization. He has to provide the document.
>
> (Paediatrician, regional hospital)

Children in institutions receive practically no therapy or rehabilitation. Those with severe disabilities may be left all day confined in their beds, without any stimulation or organized activities.[77] Lack of adequate treatment and rehabilitation for children in institutions impairs their development and the possibility of leading a more meaningful life. According to an assessment by Amnesty International, many of the residents of adult social care institutions would have been able to lead independent lives if they had been adequately rehabilitated and trained in the institutions for children where they had previously resided.[78]

Although recent legislation requires that all new public buildings should be accessible for wheelchair users, the law has not yet been consistently implemented. For disabled children living in the community, physical access to health facilities may be problematic because most buildings have not been designed for people with impaired mobility:

The architectural access affects many people. It is important even for the elderly people who have difficulties walking. [...] We don't see them [disabled children] on the streets because they can't possibly get there. It is very difficult. He can't go anywhere without an accompanying person. In our case it is good that our flat is small and narrow and he moves along holding to the walls. However, outside alone, he can hardly get anywhere on his own. Someone must be with him all the time. The access is very important, regardless where. Even in the polyclinic [outpatients] which the ill need the most. Even if we drive him there by car, he will need to climb stairs. There is no normal access.

(Mother of a child with cerebral palsy)

One of the changes in the health system is that doctors have no incentives or obligations to visit patients at home. Combined with difficult physical access, this means that nowadays disabled children experience more barriers to receiving care when needed, compared with times before the health reform:

They don't make home visits. This is another problem which I cannot understand. You have to be dying, but even if you are dying they would not come to your home nowadays. You will have to pay for the ambulance, or you have to go and pick him [the doctor] up by car to bring him home. We have had bad conflicts over this issue. My husband was going to beat them up once. Because they simply drive you mad. The person has 39 degrees temperature but they say 'Bring him here'. But in order to bring him, we have to literally carry him.

(Mother of a child with cerebral palsy)

The problem of lack of knowledge and clinical expertise among medical staff was acknowledged by many participants. Physicians often lack training and experience to diagnose and manage complex conditions.

Because at present there is a widespread opinion that this [operation for hydrocephalus] is one impossible intervention, that this is of course a damage for life. Firstly, because many of the physicians really don't know that. Especially when a child is born in a small town or somewhere in a village a woman is pregnant and needs to be brought to the nearest town ... You know a physician there would not tell you that the hydrocephalus of your child is treatable.

(Lawyer, human rights NGO)

Health services are free for children, but parents may still experience financial barriers when accessing specialized services or buying drugs for treatment of chronic conditions. One problem that was raised was the changing lists for drugs which are reimbursed by the National Health

Insurance Fund. The drugs that are reimbursed are not always the ones needed by a particular child with a chronic condition. As another example, one respondent mentioned the valves for the shunt operation for hydro-cephalus, which are not provided by the state health care system and need to be purchased by the parents. Parents from poor socio-economic back-grounds face first the information barrier and second they cannot afford to purchase this piece of equipment necessary for the operation.

> The parent himself needs to obtain the valves. The parent can obtain the valve, if he is sufficiently informed, from an American foundation, for example, which is providing them ... The valve costs around two thousand lev. These parents usually don't have so much money. This is obvious. These children are born in families with low social status. They have to either start knocking from door to door to look for money, or to get the money from somewhere as a lump sum under cer-tain conditions, and to pay it back over a long period of time, or to receive it as charity.
>
> (Lawyer, human rights NGO)

As in many other low- and middle-income countries, in Bulgaria there are limited possibilities to perform some very complex surgical operations or to make the latest modern medical technologies available to all patients. One participant told a story of a young girl with a congenital heart malfor-mation from an institution who was adopted in the USA and there she had successful heart surgery. The adoption abroad for that child was a chance to live, because there were no surgery centres in Bulgaria where such an operation could be performed, and there was nobody to advocate provi-sion of lifesaving surgery for that particular child:

> There was a child we felt very much for, because the child had a life-threatening condition – a serious heart malformation, and an American woman [adopted her] in Houston, there was a cardiology centre. And after that, I went to the home, and I saw a whole photo album [...] Because they are subject to follow up [after adoption]. [Photos] from the hospital – how she was operated. After that from her birthday, later already older. And here you see a saved life. Here she would have died, and nobody even wants to hear.
>
> (Paediatrician, regional hospital)

Recent reforms

A trigger for more intensive reforms in child protection and welfare recently was the Child Welfare Reform Project in Bulgaria, funded mainly by a loan from the World Bank, but also with significant contributions from the Bulgarian Government, foreign governments and agencies.[79] It was implemented during the five years from May 2001 until June 2006, and aimed at institutional capacity building for child protection and family welfare, prevention of institutionalization, development of services for families in the community and services for street children. The planning of the different project components involved extensive research on public knowledge and attitudes to institutionalization. It provided the first comprehensive knowledge base on existing practices in child protection and barriers to deinstitutionalization. The attempt to involve all stakeholders in the process of reform has been an innovative approach for Bulgaria, where traditionally there has been little community participation in policy development and implementation.

The Council of Ministers adopted regulations for criteria and standards of social services for children in 2003, setting standards of care and protection of children and mechanisms for control of their implementation with regards to social support to families, placement of children with relatives and friends, foster care, and placement in institutions.[80] The National Strategy for Children 2004–2006 set the aim to create conditions for ensuring the rights of the child and improving child welfare.[81] Among the main objectives of the strategy were decreasing the number of children in institutions and improving the living conditions within them; provision of a guaranteed minimum of services for families in all municipalities; protection from violence and exploitation; equal access to education; establishment of a system of monitoring and control of the quality of services for children; and creating a national information system for child protection.

Conclusion

Bulgaria inherited from the Communist past a large number of institutions for children from disadvantaged backgrounds. Many children with disabilities spend all their childhood in institutions and most of them are then transferred to homes for adults with disabilities, if they are lucky enough to survive and reach the age of 18. The reasons for institutionalization are complex but are mainly related to negative public attitudes towards disability, underdeveloped services in the community and lack of opportunities for social integration of disabled children. A powerful driver for institutionalization is the widespread poverty which disproportionately affects the ethnic minorities, and leaves families unable to provide the necessary care for their child born with disability. The lack of clinical expertise and inadequate medical treatment and rehabilitation contribute to this phenomenon.

In the 1990s severe economic crisis led to dramatic deterioration of the conditions in children's homes and many children died of malnutrition and inadequate care. The conditions and physical care in the homes have been improving over recent years. Since 2000, work of NGOs, foreign investment and influence of international agencies resulted in growing appreciation of issues of human rights and children's rights as related to disability. Considerable changes were achieved in adoption of legislation on child protection and social services for families at risk and social integration of people with disabilities. Reforms were undertaken to improve standards of care in children's institutions, prevention of institutionalization, development of services in the community for disabled children and efforts to develop foster care and other alternatives to institutional care. The challenge ahead is to implement the legislation in practice and to promote public acceptance of the difference and full integration of children with disabilities in society.

Acknowledgements

I undertook this work as a part of my research towards a PhD degree at the University of Warwick in Coventry, United Kingdom. I would like to thank Professor Nick Spencer, Dr Clare Blackburn and Dr Janet Read from the School of Health and Social Studies at the University of Warwick for their advice and comments on earlier drafts of this paper. I am indebted to all participants in this research who openly shared their experiences, knowledge and views. Funding for this research was provided by the UK Economic and Social Research Council.

Notes

1 Murphy, E., Dingwall, R., Greatbatch, D., Parker, S. and Watson, P. (1998) 'Qualitative research methods in health technology assessment: A review of the literature', Health Technology Assessment, 2, 16.
2 Strauss, A. and Corbin, J. (1990) *Basics of Qualitative Research: Grounded Theory Procedures and Techniques*. London: Sage.
3 Raycheva, L., Hristova, K., Radomirova, D. and Ginev, R. (2004) 'Bulgaria: Childhood in Transition' in A.-M. Jensen, A. Ben-Arieh, C. Conti, D. Kutsar, M.N.G. Phádraig and H.W. Nielsen (eds) *Children's Welfare in Ageing Europe*. Trondheim, Norway: Norwegian Centre for Child Research. Volume II: 469–526.
4 UNICEF (2001) *A Decade of Transition, Regional Monitoring Report No. 8*. Florence: UNICEF Innocenti Research Centre.
5 World Bank (2002) *Bulgaria: A Changing Poverty Profile*. Poverty Assessment Report No. 24516. Washington and Sofia: The World Bank.
6 Raycheva, L., Hristova, K., Radomirova, D. and Ginev, R. (2004) op. cit.
7 World Bank (2002) op. cit.
8 Ibid.
9 Carter, R. (2000) *The Silent Crisis: The Impact of Poverty on Children in Eastern Europe and the Former Soviet Union*. London: EveryChild; Gantcheva, R. and A. Kolev (2001) *Children in Bulgaria: Growing Impoverishment and Unequal Opportunities*. Working paper No. 84. Florence: UNICEF Innocenti Research Centre.
10 United Nations General Assembly (1989) *Convention on the Rights of the Child*. New York, NY: United Nations.
11 Bulgarian Parliament (2000) 'Child Protection Act [in Bulgarian]' *State Gazette*, 48 (13 June 2000).

12 Bulgarian Council of Ministers (2003b) 'Rules for the implementation of the Child Protection Act [in Bulgarian]', *State Gazette*, 66 (25 July 2003).
13 Bulgarian Parliament (2004) 'Law on integration of people with disabilities [in Bulgarian]', *State Gazette*, 81 (17 September 2004).
14 MBMD (2002) *Analysis of the Public Views about the Reform of the Institutionalization of Children* [in Bulgarian]. Sofia: Institute for Marketing and Social Research MBMD.
15 National Statistical Institute (2005b) *Population and Demographic Processes.* Sofia, Bulgaria: National Statistical Institute, p.61.
16 National Statistical Institute (2005a) *Healthcare.* Sofia, Bulgaria: National Statistical Institute, National Centre for Health Information, Ministry of Health, p.15.
17 National Statistical Institute (2005a) ibid.
18 SACP (2002) *Children in Specialized Institutions in 2001* [in Bulgarian]. Sofia, Bulgaria: State Agency for Child Protection.
19 Ibid.
20 UNICEF Innocenti Research Centre (2005) *Children and Disability in Transition in CEE/CIS and Baltic States.* Florence: UNICEF Innocenti Research Centre.
21 UNDP, UNDESA and the World Bank (2000) *Social Assessment of Child Care in Bulgaria.* Sofia, Bulgaria: UNDP, UNDESA, The World Bank.
22 UNICEF Innocenti Research Centre (2005) op. cit.
23 SACP (2003) 'National Strategy for Protection and Social Integration of Children with Disabilities (2003–2005): Framework, objectives, principles, activities', *Bulletin of the State Agency for Child Protection. All Children are Different, but with Equal Rights*, 1, 12–19.
24 Open Society Institute (2005) *Rights of People with Intellectual Disabilities: Access to Education and Employment: Bulgaria.* Budapest and New York: Open Society Institute and EU Monitoring and Advocacy Program.
25 Bulgarian Helsinki Committee (2002) *General Overview of the Bulgarian System of Special Schools.* Sofia, Bulgaria: Bulgarian Helsinki Committee.
26 Amnesty International (2002b) 'Bulgaria: Far from the Eyes of Society: Systematic discrimination against people with mental disabilities', Amnesty International: AI Index: EUR 15/005/2002. Accessed 10 September 2007.
27 Open Society Institute (2005) op. cit.
28 Amnesty International (2002b) op. cit.
29 SACP (2002) op. cit.
30 UNICEF Innocenti Research Centre (2005) op. cit.
31 Markova, G. (2005) 'The relationship between parental mental representations, attachment style, and institutionalization of children in Bulgaria', PhD thesis. Smith College School for Social Work. Northampton, MA.
32 Ibid.
33 Stoykova, E. (2006) *Ideological Model of the Family and its Crisis in Socialist Bulgaria.* Amsterdam: International Institute of Social History. Available online at www.iisg.nl/~womhist/stoykova.doc. Accessed on 21 December 2006.
34 Doychinova, A., Todorova, G., Georgieva, L. and Salchev, P. (1996) 'Medical and social factors, compelling mothers to leave their children in mother and child homes [in Bulgarian]', *Sotsialna Meditsina*, 2, 16–17.
35 Antonova, Z., Gatev, V., Tatyozov, T., Tzvetkova, M. and Pravchev, V. (1996) 'Some medical and social characteristics of children brought up in mother and child homes [in Bulgarian]', *Sotsialna Meditsina*, 4, 33–34.
36 Bulgarian Helsinki Committee (2002) op. cit.
37 Ibid.
38 Ibid. UNDP (2003) *Avoiding the Dependency Trap: A Human Development Report on the Roma Minority in Central and Eastern Europe.* Bratislava: UNDP and ILO.

39 Open Society Institute (2005) op. cit.
40 Amnesty International (2002b) op. cit.
41 Bulgarian Parliament (2004) op. cit.
42 Kubratova, G. (2005) 'Project "Accept this child" of the Foundation Psychological Support: Counselling services for parents of children with Down's syndrome [in Bulgarian]', *Bulletin: National Information Centre on the Problems of the Street Children*, IX, 87.
43 Ibid.
44 Stancheva-Popkostadinova, V. (2002) 'Attitudes and needs of families with children with intellectual disabilities [in Bulgarian]', *Pediatria*, 3, 41–44.
45 Amnesty International (2006) *Amnesty International Report 2006: The State of the World's Human Rights.* Amnesty International. Available online at http://web.amnesty.org/report2006/bgr-summary-eng. Accessed on 10 August 2006.
46 Gospodinova, L. (2002) 'The violence which reproduces itself [in Bulgarian]', *Bulletin of the State Agency for Child Protection: The Institutions – Past and Present*, 1, 44–47.
47 Kubratova, G. (2005) op. cit.
48 UNICEF Innocenti Research Centre (2005) op. cit.
49 MBMD (2002) op. cit.
50 Ibid.
51 Antonova, Z. (1996) 'Influence of the conditions and the organisation of care in mother and child homes on the health status and psychological development of children [in Bulgarian]', *Pediatria*, 2, 9–11.
52 Markova, G. (2005) op. cit.
53 SACP (2004) *Report on the Conditions in the Specialised Institutions for Children with Disabilities.* Sofia, Bulgaria: State Agency for Child Protection. Council of Ministers. Republic of Bulgaria.
54 ASA (2004) *Report on the Provision of Social Services for Children and Families.* Sofia: Agency for Socio-Economic Analyses.
55 UNICEF and SACP (2006) *Report from the National Survey on Attitudes towards Foster Care in Bulgaria.* Sofia, Bulgaria: Institute for Social Work and Practice, Agency for Socio-Economic Analyses.
56 Amnesty International (2002b) op. cit.
57 SACP (2004) op. cit.
58 Markova, G. (2005) op. cit.
59 Bulgarian Helsinki Committee (2005) 'Human rights in Bulgaria in 2004: Annual report of the Bulgarian Helsinki Committee', *Obektiv*, (March).
60 Smith, N. (2006) 'Plight of Bulgaria's lost children: Tied up and neglected in care homes', *The Sunday Times*, 16 April 2006.
61 Bozhilova, V. (2005) 'Three days were not sufficient for the case 'Dzhurkovo', shocking facts came to light [in Bulgarian],' *BG Factor.* Available online at http://www.bgfactor.org/index_.php?ct=1&id=4517. Accessed on 26 July 2006.
62 Amnesty International (1997) 'Bulgaria: Government should prevent further deaths in children's homes', Amnesty International: AI Index: EUR 15/002/1997 – News Service 40/97. Accessed 10 September 2007.
63 Amnesty International (2006) op. cit.
64 Bulgarian Helsinki Committee (2003) *Institutions for Children with Disabilities.* Sofia, Bulgaria: Bulgarian Helsinki Committee.
65 Amnesty International (2002b) op. cit.
66 Ibid.
67 Antonova, Z., Pravchev, V., Gatev, V., Tayozov, T. and Petrova, M. (1998) 'Physical development of children looked after in mother and child homes [in Bulgarian]'. *Pediatria*, 3, 42–44.

68 Amnesty International (2002b) op. cit.
69 Amnesty International (2002b) op. cit.
70 Koulaksazov, S., Todorova, S., Tragakes, E. and Hirstova, S. (2003) *Health Care Systems in Transition: Bulgaria.* Copenhagen: European Observatory on Health Care Systems.
71 Ministry of Health (2004) *Report on the Health of the Nation in the Beginning of the 21st century: Analysis of the Reform.* Sofia, Bulgaria: Ministry of Health.
72 Bulgarian Helsinki Committee (2003) op. cit.
73 Ibid.
74 Parmakova, M. (2003) 'Homes for children with intellectual disability: Change is necessary [in Bulgarian]', *Bulletin of the State Agency for Child Protection: All Children are Different, but with Equal Rights,* 1/2003, 23–25.
75 Amnesty International (2002a) 'Bulgaria: Arbitrary detention and ill-treatment of people with mental disabilities', Amnesty International: AI Index: EUR 15/008/2002. Accessed 10 September 2007.
76 Amnesty International (2003) 'Public appeal. Bulgaria: Fakia social care home for children', Amnesty International: AI Index: EUR 15/011/2003. Accessed 10 September 2007.
77 Amnesty International (2002a) op. cit.
78 Amnesty International (2002b) op. cit.
79 World Bank (2000) *Bulgaria: Child Welfare Reform Project.* Report No. PID9362. Washington DC: The World Bank.
80 Bulgarian Council of Ministers (2003a) 'Regulation for the criteria and standards of the social services for children [in Bulgarian]', *State Gazette,* 102 (21 November 2003).
81 MLSP (2003) *National Strategy for the Children.* Sofia, Bulgaria: Ministry of Labour and Social Protection.

12 Unheard voices

Human rights issues of disabled youngsters from Romanian institutions

Mirela Saupe

Introduction

Romania is known to many as a country with a lot of abandoned children. Soon after the fall of the Communist regime in 1989, shocking images of Romanian institutionalized children were transmitted across the whole world. Living in extremely poor conditions, denied every human right, these children suffered from what we sometimes call 'hospitalism', a syndrome characterized by poor physical development, impaired intellectual development and affective disorders.

This chapter focuses mainly on the present situation of disabled youngsters from Romanian institutions and on the impact that these institutions have had upon them. An account is given of the history of provision for disabled children and young people in Romania, recent changes in the care system, an outline of the current legal framework and a short description of the development of the national protection policy for disabled youngsters. Central to the chapter is a report of an intervention project with a group of seven disabled youngsters who had spent their childhoods in Cighid, one of the classic institutions for disabled children and young people. The project created the opportunity for the young people involved to form friendships with people outside the residential institution and researched what these relationships meant to them. Finally, there is a discussion of the changes that need to occur in the care system in order to serve better the needs of its beneficiaries.

According to the statistics of the National Authority for Persons with Handicap (NAPH) at the end of 2005, the number of disabled people in Romania was 459,552, or around 2.11 per cent of the total population. Around 4 per cent of the population of disabled people were reported to be living in institutions and these included children, young people and adults.

The situation of youngsters in institutions is precarious and there are a range of factors which mean that a large number who are due to leave institutions will not have their needs adequately met. By law, those living in children's institutions should leave the system when they turn 18, or, if they are enrolled in some form of education, at the age of 26. Fifty per cent of the children still living in these institutions are over 14 years old and the majority are between 18 and 29 years old. This means that many of these youngsters will soon reach the age to leave. What happens next to these young people depends on their age and the degree and type of impairments that they are assessed as having. The great majority of children and young people in institutions are assessed as having 'mental disability'.[1] As they reach 18, those with severe disabilities are usually transferred to another institution, either a residential establishment for older people or a psychiatric hospital. Those with less severe and mild disabilities leave, or more accurately, are 'abandoned' by the protection system. Many of these will find themselves dependent on social security. Only a few who remain within the system become residents of specially designed houses and apartments. Without adequate financial resources and any real chance of getting a job, many disabled youngsters are reported to resort to prostitution and crime. The risk of abandonment of their future children is also extremely high. This is due mostly to financial difficulties, lack of support from the community and also problems with their parenting abilities. Many of these youngsters inevitably have a limited repertoire of solutions to their life problems, not only because they are disabled and live without support, but also as a result of their experience of being raised in institutions.

The care and protection system: changes and difficulties

The system of child protection and that of the protection of disabled children and adults has undergone many changes which reflect the transitions in Romanian society which took place after the changing of the political regime in 1989. After the fall of Ceausescu and the end of the Communist period, the evolution of the child protection services followed three main stages.[2] The early 1990s saw a stage characterized by 'quick fix' solutions. The period 1992–1996 saw a period of contradictory reforms and legislative attempts. From 1997, a more consistent and coherent reform of the system ensued.

The Communist era: pre 1989

The Communist period is characterized by a total disrespect for human rights issues, especially the rights of disabled persons and children from institutions. This period started in 1945 when Nicolae Ceausescu was elected president of the Socialist Republic of Romania, and lasted till the end of 1989, when a popular revolt put an end to what had become a cruel and inhumane regime.

During the Communist period, the state had a demographic policy designed to encourage an increase in the population. There were two means to accomplish this. First, the state introduced a decree[3] that stipulated that any woman under 45 had to have at least four children. Women who had a lot of children were even given the 'Heroic Mother' medal. Second, the state prohibited abortion. Women had the right to abortion only if they had at least four children or if there were special medical circumstances. Abortion was considered to be an 'evil enemy of the biological future of the people', an affront to the 'Parental State'.[4] Even gynaecological surgery was controlled by the state. Every hospital had a 'plan' regarding the number of babies born by caesarian section and there could be no deviation from it. In this way, the state invaded the private life of people through a regime of terror.

During this period, a measure that was very significant for disabled persons was a law that promoted the institutionalization of both disabled persons and abandoned children.[5] The rationale was that the state was characterized as the parent, was responsible for its citizens and therefore became the sole protector of these children.[6] Until 1989, the official data regarding persons with disability or institutionalized children were totally missing or could be accessed only by those working in the system. The existence of persons with disability was known only by close family members, neighbours and friends, or by the medical staff. This situation may be seen as a clear reflection of the state's attitude towards disabled persons. Since their ability to work was reduced and they were not seen as contributing to the welfare of a perfect state, the logical solution was their social isolation or institutionalization.

The consequence of the demographic policy was a huge increase in the number of abandoned and institutionalized children, many of whom were disabled. The abandoned children were put in different institutions according to their age and whether they had a disability. Of the non-disabled children, those below three years old were put in nurseries while the older ones went to orphanages. Those who were disabled were placed in special institutions. In some ways, these institutions had a 'medical' character and their organization reflected that of hospitals,[7] but this, of course, is quite ironic if we reflect on the inhumane conditions endured by those who lived there and the consequences for their health, well-being and development. The children's fundamental right to life was violated. They did not receive proper feeding and care. They had no activities during the day. They were just left to lie on dirty mattresses and wait for the next time someone came by and gave them something to eat. In many cases the children did not have any beds, tables or chairs. They sometimes ate from the ground and because they were not given enough to eat, food stealing became a habit, difficult to change even today. The mortality rate was very high, almost 50 per cent during one year in some institutions, as will become apparent in the discussion of the situation in Cighid later in this chapter. A lot of children died because of the abuse and neglect. No better than 'death camps', these large institutions were homes for almost 500 children. They were located in isolated, rural areas, and members of staff were people from the neighbourhood, only a few of whom had any professional qualifications. At this time, anyway, psychology and the social sciences were prohibited in universities because they were seen as subversive to the Communist regime and so this, too, contributed to a general shortage of trained professionals. Consequently, most of the staff working in the institutions were either not trained at all, or in the case of a few, were qualified as physicians. One staff member was responsible for the care of around 30 children. There were no rehabilitation plans and the only treatment provided was psychiatric medication.

The lack of proper feeding and hygiene and also the total affective disengagement of the staff produced profound delays in the development of the children.[8] The institution was itself debilitating. The children's personal records had the label 'irreparable mentally defective', an expression that could be seen as a hallmark of the system at that time. Even after leaving the institutions, many of these children and young people were unable to overcome the developmental delays caused by their upbringing.

It is hard to know exactly how many institutions there were like this in Romania at that time. Unofficial data indicate the number of institutions as being in the region of 150 and the number of disabled children resident in them as being around 100,000. However, the statistics of the National Authority for Protection of Children's Rights (NAPCR) indicate that at the beginning of 2005, there were 233 classic institutions still functioning. Whatever the accurate number, however, we are left with the shocking images showing the conditions in 1990, and the testimonies of those who 'lived to tell the tale'.

The period of reactive 'quick fix' solutions and interim measures

In the years 1990–1991, many Western organizations were outraged by the situation in Romania, and the government was forced to take action. All eyes seemed to be focused on the starving children from Romanian orphanages. Because of the seriousness of the situation, speedy solutions needed to be found. No long-term planning was undertaken and efforts were concentrated on doing something to remedy the poor living conditions in the institutions and the health and neglect of the children.

More funding was made available to these large institutions and they received food, medical supplies, vaccines and clothes for the children. As a consequence, the situation of the children was improving, mostly with help from abroad. Some NGOs were founded and began to offer services. Thinking that 'any place is better that an institution', one 'quick fix' solution was to promote national and international adoptions. Although adoption was seen initially as a positive measure aimed to bring about immediate improvements in the quality of life of the children, in the years that followed, it developed in an uncontrolled way that gave rise to great concern. Anybody could adopt a child who was declared abandoned if his biological parents had not visited him for six months. It was not until the period 1992–1996 that any restrictions were placed on international adoptions. Like all the 'quick fix' solutions of this period, adoption could never be a long-term solution and it did not change in any way the protection system which began to be reformed only from 1997.

A decade of more sustained policy development

From 1997, Romania's proposed entry to the European Community became a central feature of state policy. As a result, the situation of the institutionalized and disabled children, and also other issues of human rights, became important topics on the agenda of the reform. The main objective of the reform was the abolition of the large institutions and the promotion of human rights. Some smaller institutions began to emerge as alternatives to the larger ones. The Law 3/1970, which promoted institutionalization, was abrogated only in 1997. In 2003 the National Authority for Protection of Children's Rights was set up and in the same year the National Authority for Persons with Handicap was founded. As these two bodies began to elaborate strategies for the next decade, a programme of reform of the system was begun. In 2005, the NAPH developed care quality standards for institutions.

The human rights of mentally disabled people in Romania became a public issue only after 1997. During the Communist period, human rights were widely violated not only for disabled persons but also for the entire population. Disabled children and adults were often denied every right in the hostile conditions of the institutions. As we have seen, some died and others barely survived. The International Convention on the Rights of the Child was adopted by Romania in 1990.[9] In accordance with this covenant, the enforcement of children's rights is a priority and a necessity.[10] In 2001, the Romanian Government adopted a strategy regarding the protection of the child in need. In the same year, NAPH, along with 50 other NGOs, elaborated a policy according to the standard rules of the United Nations. NAPCR policy is built around three fundamental rights: the right to family life, the right to protection against abuse, and the right to be free from discrimination.[11]

The state is also now beginning to support NGOs that offer social services. Some NGOs can obtain the status of 'public utility' and have priority access to funding applications. In addition, some extra legal measures have been taken to protect and promote the rights of disabled people, mostly in relation to education, protection against discrimination and access.

While there are special schools for children with learning disabilities, they also, in theory at least, have access to mainstream schools where they are individually assisted by 'support teachers'. The children from urban areas have more access to education than those from rural and more isolated areas. Because of this, only a few of those who are institutionalized receive proper education.

In relation to protection from discrimination,[12] the disabled adult has the right to work, to be equally paid and to be protected against work discrimination. Every public institution is recommended, but not forced, to employ disabled persons (at least four per cent of the total workforce should be disabled), and the state offers financial benefits to the employers who hire disabled persons. Despite these measures, few disabled adults and youngsters are currently employed and the situation is worse among disabled youngsters from the institutions. There are no qualifications or training courses for this section of the population and the youngsters leave the institutions without developing the skills they would need as an employee. When employed, they tend to have jobs which are considered unworthy or shameful by other workers (washing dishes, taking out garbage, carrying heavy loads) and the attitude of the other employees is frequently a discriminatory one.

Recently, close attention has been paid to the right to be protected against abuse. Article 3 of the European Convention for Human Rights prohibits 'torture, ill-treatment and degrading punishments'. This includes child abuse and neglect.[13] Because of the high incidence of abuse in institutions, there are a few programmes which are beginning to raise awareness about abuse. Disabled children are more prone to be abused than other children, and 35.5 per cent of abused children are disabled.[14] Abuse may be inflicted by older children, adults or staff members. Emotional and physical abuse was a frequent practice in institutions during the Communist period. However, many of the people who were on the staff at that time are still employed and so it might be assumed that they continue to abuse children. The disabled children and adults often do not know how to recognize abuse or how to report it so official reports about abusive behaviour of staff are rare.

There have also been a few attempts at raising public awareness about disabled people in Romania. A lot of prejudice still exists about disabled youngsters from institutions, and public attitudes vary between pity, compassion and rejection. The term 'handicap' is still used when talking about disabled persons at both formal (laws, official institutions) and informal levels. While these negative attitudes are slowly beginning to change, there is much to be done.

The decade since 1997 has been a period of more sustained policy development as Romania started to comply with European legislation regarding disabled persons. Many of the large institutions were abolished or restructured. Much has been done in the area of protection against discrimination and respecting human rights but changes are still at the level of legislation, and efforts are being made to find ways of implementing them. For the first time, attention is now focused on the quality of care received by institutionalized youngsters and children. Conditions have been changed and now some rehabilitation programmes are starting to be put into practice in institutions. There have already been some attempts to develop appropriate interventions for young survivors of the institutions, projects designed to offset some of the damaging effects of their upbringing. One of these took place in western Romania and was planned and put into practice by the author. The following section of the chapter gives a brief account of its aims and what it achieved.

Working with survivors: a peer education programme for young disabled people experiencing attachment disorder

Case study: Cighid Rehabilitation Centre

Background

Situated in the western part of Romania, near a rural settlement, Cighid Recovery and Rehabilitation Centre for Persons with Handicap was one of the large institutions for disabled and abandoned children and young people. Images of the children living there and the inhumane conditions were typical of Romania's orphanages. As in all the large institutions, the mortality rate was very high, almost 50 per cent per annum. Figures provided by the first manager who was put in charge of Cighid after the revolution indicate that in 1989, 137 of the 237 children resident there died within one year. The youngsters living in Cighid Rehabilitation Centre have learning disabilities. For many, it is not known to what extent their intellectual impairment was an antecedent of their abandonment or a consequence of institutionalization. Even after 1989, the rate of adoption was extremely low because of the severity of the children's disabilities.

Reactive attachment disorder is a frequent diagnosis for these children and without intervention it may become what would be identified as a personality disorder in adult life. Attachment is ordinarily formed during early childhood and is related to the psychological and physical availability of a primary caregiver or attachment figure to a child.[15] Attachment behaviour is designed to get a child into a protective relationship with their attachment figure when they experience anxiety. The child learns from this relationship and thus forms an internal working model of representations of self, others and of relationships with others. This model will then be used to activate specific behaviour when experiencing new relationships.

The institutional environment of Romanian orphanages prevented young children from forming attachment relationships of this kind. If we think of the abuse, neglect and food deprivation practised in the institutions before 1989 and in the early 1990s, we have to acknowledge a strange and disturbing paradox. Because of the way that they perpetrated abuse, the primary caregivers for these children were simultaneously also a major source of anxiety and distress for them. Activation of attachment behaviour (getting close to a caregiver) in order to reduce anxiety was instead likely to enhance it. Inconsistency and rapid staff turnover in the institutions were additional factors that prevented attachment. As a result of these circumstances, the children formed a disorganized pattern of attachment, often called the non-attached type.[16] Cognitively, the children's internal working model construed the self as being of no value, and others as being bad, aggressive and ambivalent. Consequently, consistent relationships with others became of no interest or importance and contact was at best conceived of as instrumental and transitory. The children and young people were superficially involved in relationships. While they craved contact, they could not get involved emotionally. As they grow up, these children face a lot of problems in the area of interpersonal relationships, impulse control and regulation of aggression. Ainsworth *et al.*[17] also correlated attachment with exploration behaviour and argued that the attachment figure is a secure base from which children can explore their world. For children from institutions, exploration behaviour is reduced and this in turn affects their levels of intellectual and emotional development. The quality of care received in institutions disables a child and has a negative impact on his development as young person or adult. Many of the problems faced by former institutionalized youngsters (emotional problems, poor parental skills, restricted social circle and problems in the workplace) may, in part at least, be related to their attachment problems.

The conditions in Cighid changed after 1989 with a lot of help from abroad, especially Germany. At the time of the project in 2005, 114 children still lived at Cighid. There were rehabilitation programmes centred on music therapy, physiotherapy, speech therapy, occupational therapy and informal education that was compatible with the level of impairment.

Despite their mental disability and the harsh conditions in which they were raised, approximately 20 youngsters from Cighid received special education at the local village school. They were then transferred to Casa Franz Max (a small centre which was a satellite of Cighid) in Oradea, a large city in the western part of Romania. The basic idea was to prepare these youngsters for adult life. They began to take classes to train for occupations. Casa Franz Max was home for 14 youngsters and had a staff made up of a psychologist (the author), a speech therapist, a support teacher, a social worker and a cook. This team of colleagues provided all the care and assistance needed by the resident young people and we aimed to create a family atmosphere. No additional care staff were appointed.

The one-year intervention project and the research and evaluation that accompanied it took place at Casa Franz Max house and involved seven of the residents and an equal number of volunteers. All of the disabled young people who took part had previously been resident in Cighid. Similar to a 'buddying' or peer support programme, the project aimed to provide the opportunity for the establishment of an individual relationship between each of seven disabled participants and a designated volunteer. Focusing on the emotional problems of these youngsters and the impact on their adult relational life, the project aimed to explore the effects that a constant, warm, secure relationship with a volunteer across the course of a year might have upon the youngsters who participated.

Specifically, the research and evaluation element investigated the effects on the young people's self-esteem, self-image and social circle as well as their understanding and representation of friendship. The study investigated at a descriptive level the efficacy of using peer education as an intervention strategy to ameliorate attachment disorder and the indiscriminate friendliness of institutionalized youngsters.

Participants

DISABLED YOUNGSTERS

Seven disabled youngsters participated in the study. All of them had an intellectual disability which ranged from mild to severe. The youngsters had been institutionalized from birth and had suffered physical and emotional abuse. They had low self-esteem, poor self-image and a restricted social circle. Their age range was between 17 and 21 years. Six of the participants had received special education in a village school near Cighid. The effects of institutionalization (neglect and abuse) were still evident in the form of restricted physical development, self-harm, rocking, self-stimulation behaviours, stealing and aggression towards others. At the point of entering adulthood, the youngsters were emotionally withdrawn and had poor social skills. Almost all of them had difficulty in relating to others and had a relational life that was negatively affected by indiscriminate friendliness, a lack of confidence in others and passive–aggressive behaviour. All the participants had been diagnosed as having reactive attachment disorder.

VOLUNTEERS

Seven volunteers were involved in the project. They were all undergraduate psychology students and were selected though an interview with the psychologist who was employed at the centre. The psychologist was the only staff member involved in the project.

The project design

The project involved three phases. First, the volunteers were trained by the centre psychologist. The training involved presentations about the characteristics of the institutionalized children and youngsters, some background about reactive attachment disorder and also information about communication strategies and the development of relationships. After training, the second phase began. A party was organized and the volunteers were invited. Volunteer–child dyads were formed taking into consideration the way that the youngsters and the volunteers interacted at the party. The psychologist then gave each volunteer information about the youngster assigned to him or her, the intervention procedures so far and the rehabilitation plan. The volunteers were specially instructed to form a 'therapeutic' relationship. The aim was to encourage the expression of feelings, have discussions about the personal attributes of the youngster with whom they were working, develop trust and create a sense of security. Each volunteer met the youngster once a week for one year. The meeting took place outside the institution and included walking in the park, going to the cinema or shopping, talking and playing games. The third phase of the project involved a trip in which all the volunteers and the youngsters participated.

The project had a research element to evaluate the outcomes of the intervention. Data were collected and processed by qualitative procedures. In order to assess the representation of friendship, semi-structured interviews and focus groups were conducted during the development and at the end of the project. Analysis of written materials, including letters, was also undertaken, and clinical observations by members of staff were also used along with measures of self-esteem, self-image and the size of a young person's social circle. Self-esteem and self-image were assessed using qualitative interviews and drawings representing the self. The social circle was measured before and after the project by a socio-diagram made by the youngster. The type of attachment formed between youngster and volunteer was assessed by the psychologist. Data generated by semi-structured interviews were processed using thematic analysis.

Results

The evidence from staff, volunteers and young disabled people indicated many positive outcomes as a result of the project. At the end of the year, the participants had an improved self-image and had developed their self-presentation skills. Their level of self-esteem was raised. In addition to any impact that the friendship with the volunteer may have had on self-esteem, the fact that the youngsters were also considered privileged to participate in the programme may have had a positive effect. It needs to be recognized that we cannot be sure of the differential impact of these two factors. There was an obvious extension of the social circle of the participants. The relationship with the volunteer was perceived to be positive and the qualitative data analysis indicated two elements of this relationship that were important from the perspective of the young disabled person. First was the private character of the relationship, and second, the special attention that they received through it.

One young person said this:

'It is mine ... We talk ... She comes especially for me, we know each other.'

(Angela, 17 years old)

Another explained:

> 'What do I like about her? Well ... I saw that she liked me.'
>
> (Ioana, 21 years old)

It was clear that the young people had a need for the relationship to be reliable and predictable even though this was often accompanied by a sort of passivity towards interaction with the volunteer and affective involvement.

While there were positive benefits for all participants, the level of mental disability appeared to mediate the effect of the relationship. Those who were less affected by their impairment seemed to benefit most.

The young people's understanding and representation of the friendships also varied and the differences appeared, in part at least, to be associated with the degree of impairment. For those who were severely disabled, the main features of the friendship were presented as a combination of non-violence and acceptance on the part of the other person. Physical characteristics of the volunteer (such as good looks) were also important in developing a friendship and the need for reciprocity in the relationship appeared less. This group of young people also emphasized their own conforming, sometimes almost submissive behaviour as a key feature of the relationship. It may be that this is related to the fact that these young people are most likely to have been exposed to the highest levels of abuse in their former institution.

Angela, for example, described her friendship with Mary in the following way:

> 'What is a friend? Mary is a friend ... I get along with her, she is my friend. I'm good with her when we go out, I don't misbehave.'
>
> (Angela, 17 years old)

The phrase 'I don't misbehave' was used by this participant also to mean a lack of aggression, rocking and self-stimulating behaviour. Also, control of emotional outbursts was perceived by these youngsters to be appropriate behaviour with people close to them. Common activities and doing things together were central themes in the relationship of those who had severe impairments.

Those who were less mentally disabled identified other features that were important in the relationship and these included trust, intimacy and personal support. Friendship was a mixture of closeness and security for those who were less disabled.

The young people described it this way:

> 'A friend? ... I like her because she is open and she tells me stuff about her. We talk about us, about relationships. I told her so much about me I hope she keeps the secret.'
>
> (Sarmanca, 18 years old, mild mental disability)

'She is my friend. I already get used to her.'

(Ana-Maria, 20 years old)

This group also expressed a strong need for reciprocity of affect in the relationship:

'I saw that we are friends but we still need something. I think I feel more for her than she feels for me. It is not right.'

(Renata, 18 years old)

Despite the importance to them of reciprocity, these youngsters showed a lack of initiative in relation to their volunteers and felt unable to influence the course of the relationships.

Feelings of a lack of control over the relationships were characteristic of all the young people who participated in the project and this may be explained by the social deficits in their lives, long-standing attachment problems and difficulties in emotional development derived from their institutional upbringing. They all had difficulty in recognizing emotions, expressing feelings and differentiating between emotional states. Also, their affective involvement in relationships was usually quite low because they assumed that the person would leave, so there was no point to affective investment.

In relation to attachment issues, the psychologist used a classification developed by Bartholomew and Horowitz (1991)[18] and applied by Howe and Brandon (1999)[19] to assess the young people's internal working model of attachment, the way they perceived the relationships. According to the classification, just two of the participants can be said to have made attachments to the volunteers but they did so in a rather insecure way. Others expressed ambivalent behaviours in the presence of the volunteers and did not form attachments. Despite this, in all the cases, there was a significant amelioration of the indiscriminate friendliness that had been evident before and this meant that they were able to begin choosing between people and having preferences. This applied especially to those participants who were satisfied with the relationship with their volunteer. One young woman said:

'I don't need Mary, I've got Corina, she is my friend.'

(Ioana, 21 years old)

While the level of disability seems to have been important in shaping the nature of the friendship and attachment on the part of the institutionalized youngsters, it is also important to recognize the possible effect of the participants' awareness that the project would last for only one year. For this reason, some may not have been willing to invest emotionally in the friendship. The volunteers were instructed to tell the youngsters that the project was just for one year but that the relationship could continue after this period if they got along. It is worth considering whether the outcomes might have been different if the period of the project had remained unknown to the participants, if the project had lasted longer or if the volunteers had had more frequent meetings with the youngsters. It has to be recognized that despite some very positive outcomes in this project, attachment behaviour is very difficult to change in these disabled youngsters who have experienced such abuse.

Reflections on future practice implications

The results of this study might be used to help us to reconceptualize the quality of care provided by institutions for mentally disabled abandoned children. In spite of mental disability, peer education and support can have positive effects on the emotional and social development of institutionalized youngsters and can assist them to develop new social skills that are an asset for an independent adult life. Positive relationships built self-esteem, improved self-image and extended the social circle. Unfortunately, the opportunities of experiencing such relationships is limited for youngsters from institutions.

Currently, in large institutions and even in smaller ones, the attitudes of members of staff towards these children and youngsters vary from pity and compassion to detachment and indifference. Those less disabled are also those most likely to be more highly appreciated. In addition, the good-looking children and those who are not gypsies tend to receive the most appreciation, attention and care. The staff are frequently cold and keep a 'professional' distance. In many cases this distance seems to be used as an excuse for their non-involvement rather than indicating a valuable professionalism. Cold, detached and impersonal, the protection system does its duty of caring for the basic needs of the young service users, but it debilitates them on the social, human dimension. The strong and constant message that the staff from institutions still send out to the residents is that people are cold, dangerous and aggressive, and the still high rate of abuse is a strong indicator of this fact. To the child, the world becomes a dangerous place where one has no control over relationships with others. If you get lucky, someone will be good to you. Rapid changes in staff structure and the rotation of care workers – with as many as three shift changes a day – are further reasons for the lack of affective involvement of these youngsters. The affective neutrality of the staff gives a message to the children that they are not worthy of love. Despite some very positive outcomes, the study at Casa Franz Max, based on the efforts of a group of volunteers and one psychologist for one year, was not able to make any great impact on the young people's attachment disorder. Nevertheless, there can be no real doubt that a constant and secure care giver is the strongest need of the participants and others like them. This implies the need for a policy change in the staff attitude towards the residents. There needs to be a change from an objective, emotionally detached attitude towards a more 'therapeutic', emotionally involved one. The care given by the staff should be aimed at constructing a secure base for adult life by creating the opportunity for children to experience safe interpersonal relationships and develop a sense of self-efficacy and self-competence. If these youngsters have positive and safe relationships, they will learn from them, they will feel competent to try and get involved in other relationships that they feel that they can manage. The relationship between caregiver and a child or youngster, then, needs to become a model for the next relationship that will be formed after leaving the institution. Psychotherapy for attachment problems is a difficult process in relation to mentally disabled youngsters. The emotional involvement of a caregiver, and there are some who offer this, could be an 'alternative therapy' and a powerful one, especially because of how it is experienced by the child. Renata's words in her letter to a member of staff from the institution of residence illustrate what it means to her:

> All the time when you are at work I think of that day as beautiful, I don't get bored and I wish that day will stay still forever ... With you I feel safe, as if you were a mother who cares for her children. Then I don't care about anything else ... I think this is the relationship between us. *If I think better, I also deserve to be loved.*
>
> (Renata, 18 years old)

Many children and young people with learning disabilities still live in institutions in Romania. Many of these are not even officially registered. The great majority of children still living in institutions will soon be 18 and have to leave the protection service. So far there have been only feeble attempts at legal measures to protect their rights after living in the institutions.

With a strong Communist inheritance, the system of care and protection still needs changes. Disabled children and young people in Romania still have the problem of their fundamental rights not being recognized, a problem they share with all other disabled persons in Romania. Since 1997, the country has had a package of laws that are promoting human rights and adopting legal measures similar to those of other European countries. Many of the legal measures taken in this recent period are extremely useful, but as yet are not reflected in the operation of the key institutions or in the attitudes of many people working in the system. Consequently, some of the potential benefits of the legislation for disabled youngsters have yet to be realized. Because the conditions in the large Romanian institutions have now changed, the problems of hygiene, meeting children's basic needs or those of sustained ill-treatment are no longer the priorities they once were. The great challenge for the care system now is the provision of emotionally nourishing care and rehabilitation, and the prevention of social exclusion during childhood and ultimately an independent adult life. Maternal assistants are being trained to provide care to smaller children, but no measures are yet in place for older children. Warm, supportive and constant relationships with staff members are crucial for those young people too. Otherwise, disabled youngsters from institutions will continue to be ill-served by the very system which is set up to protect them.

References

Inclusion Europe (2002) *Human Right of Persons with Intellectual Disability: Country Report.* Available online at www.inclusion-europe.org. Accessed 28 November 2007.
UNICEF (2005) *Situatia abandonului in Romania.* Available online at www.unicef.org. Accessed 28 November 2007.

Useful websites

www.anph.ro – The National Authority for Persons with Handicap
www.copii.ro – The National Authority for Protection of Children's Rights

Notes

1 The relevant data show that the protection system in Romania offers no alternative services for mentally retarded persons other than institutionalization.
2 UNICEF (2004) *Child Care System Reform in Romania.* pp.24–7. Available online at www.unicef.org. Accessed 28 November 2007.
3 Decree No. 770/1960.
4 Miroiu, M. (2004) *Drumul catre autonomie,* Iasi: Editura Polirom, p.207.
5 Law 3/1970.
6 This idea is reflected in a song sung by many of the street children today: 'We were raised in orphanages, not by parents, but by the state.'
7 UNICEF (2004), op. cit. p.11.
8 Gunnar, M. and Morison, S. (2001) 'Salivary cortisol levels in children adopted from Romanian orphanages', *Development and Psychopathology,* 13, 612.
9 Law 18/1990.
10 National Agency for Child Protection and Adoption (2002) *Protectia copilului intre rezultate obtinute si prioritati de viitor.* p.7. Available online at www.copii.ro. Accessed 28 November 2007.
11 National Authority for Protection of Children's Rights (2005) *Drepturile omului si protectia copilului: Ghid de buna practica.* p.2. Available online at www.copii.ro. Accessed 28 November 2007.
12 Ordinance 137/2000 and Ordinance 102/1999.
13 National Authority for Protection of Children's Rights (2005), op. cit., p.12.
14 Ibid., p.47.
15 Howe, D. and Brandon, M. (1999) *Attachment Theory, Child Maltreatment and Family Support: A Practice and Assessment Model.* London: MacMillan Press, p.13.
16 Ibid. p.25; Zeenah, C. (1996) 'Beyond insecurity: A re-conceptualization of attachment disorders of infancy', *Journal of Consulting and Clinical Psychology,* 64, 1, 42–52.

17 Ainsworth, M.D.S., Bleher, M., Aters, E. and Wall, S. (1978) *Patterns of Attachment: A Psychological Study of the Strange Situation.* Hillsdale, NJ: Lawrence Erlbaum.

18 Bartholomew, K. and Horowitz, L.M.(1991) 'Attachment styles among young adults: A test of four-category model', *Journal of Personality and Social Psychology,* 61: 226–44.

19 Howe, D. and Brandon, M. (1999) op. cit.

13 The classification of newborn children
Consequences for survival

Jónína Einarsdóttir

Introduction

In this chapter I will be concerned with the classification of newborns and its consequences in two distinct social settings. The first one refers to anthropological fieldwork I conducted in 1993–1998 in Biombo region in Guinea-Bissau.[1] The second setting is Iceland where I conducted fieldwork on ethical questions concerning treatment and eventual end-of-life decisions for infants with a birth weight less than 1,000 g and the implications of their births on the daily lives of the families involved.[2] I will examine how certain infants are classified as non-humans in Biombo region, Guinea-Bissau, and unviable in Iceland, as well as the consequences these classifications may have for the infants concerned.

I will begin with a short overview of anthropological literature on the classification of newborns and infanticide, and then I will present my findings on children classified as non-humans in Biombo. Thereafter I examine the classification of preterm infants as unviable in neonatal intensive care units, and I will be concerned in particular with practices related to their treatment in the Nordic countries. Next, I will present data from my research in Iceland on parents' views on whether and when expensive intensive care treatment should be given to seriously ill infants who are born extremely prematurely. As the requisite for treatment is live birth, I will finally explore how advancements in the treatment of extremely preterm infants have contributed to a revision of definitions of reproductive concepts such as live birth, foetal death and stillbirth. I will end the chapter with some conclusions.

Classifications of newborns and infanticide

The anthropological literature indicates that the attribution of status to newborns, such as social membership, personhood or humanness, varies between societies.[3] The consequences for an infant may also vary but are likely to be significant in view of the fact that an infant not yet classified as a member of society, a person or a human being may be subjected to a particular treatment or even be killed. Examination of the anthropological literature shows that the criteria for belonging vary across time and between societies. In some societies, the importance of the right fatherhood of an infant has been documented as essential for its social membership.[4] In others a formal naming or a particular ceremony is the very event that gives an infant such a status.[5] For the Chewong of the Malay Peninsular, conceptions of humanity and personhood are seen as fused but their achievement is related to acquisition of knowledge.[6] The Punan Bah of Central Borneo attribute a human status to an infant when an ancestor spirit has taken a permanent residence in its body, which occurs when the infant is able to turn its body or has got its first teeth.[7] Shortly thereafter an infant will be given a name and from then on it is considered to be a person. According to Scheper-Hughes,[8] display of individual personality and human characteristics are crucial for an infant's gradual achievement of humanness in the shanty towns of North East Brazil, and only when an infant has a personal name is it considered fully to be a human being.

Most historians maintain that the frequency of infanticide in the earlier history of Western societies was high but there are disagreements on that point.[9] With the advent of Christianity newborns were conceptualized as having human souls and killing them became criminalized by law. While the practice declined in frequency, infanticide continued throughout the centuries.[10] Infanticide has been and still is practised worldwide. It is everywhere a sensitive issue, and the practice is characterized by concealment. For a comparative approach, there are few detailed descriptions of infanticide and important information is often missing.

Researchers have come to varied conclusions while explaining the practice.[11] Scheper-Hughes[12] argues for instance that in societies where destitute mothers give birth under adverse conditions passive infanticide and selective neglect are survival strategies. She concludes: 'I have no doubt ... that the local culture is organized to defend women against the psychological ravaging of grief, I assume that the culture is quite successful in doing so'.[13] In contrast, the primatologist Hrdy maintains that infanticide is an adaptive reproductive strategy applied by mothers who have evolved 'to trade off quantity for quality'.[14] Hrdy treats human nature as primarily biological and characterized by innate responses, with intellectual reasoning, religion and moral considerations playing limited function. She is, however, aware of certain exceptions to normal innate responses to the birth of an unviable infant such as 'the many modern mothers' who 'throw themselves utterly and wholeheartedly into care of babies unlikely to survive'.[15] Hrdy holds that these 'modern mothers' are misled by ethics, and in such cases social and cultural circumstances must be considered to explain their behaviour. In contrast, according to Hrdy, mothers from other parts of the world, free from such ethical concerns, seem to act in response to their nature, and thus eliminate infants unlikely to enhance human survival.

In Biombo, Guinea-Bissau certain infants are suspected to be born without human souls as a spirit has taken place in their body; thus they are referred to as spirit children (in Guinean Creole, *iran*). Let us examine the fate of these infants and their mothers' reactions to their birth.

Non-human children

Biombo region, a flat swampy marshland, is in everyday language named Papel Land. The population, at the time of fieldwork approximately 62,000 inhabitants, is largely agricultural. Almost three-quarters are Papel and I have estimated that at least 90 per cent adhere to local religions, mainly Papel but also Balanta. Christian converts are approximately 5 per cent and there is a small minority of Muslims living in the region. Malnutrition among children is widespread and a well-conducted study carried out in 1990–1995 shows that the Biombo region had the highest mortality rate among children under five years of age in Guinea-Bissau.[16] Of the ethnic groups, the Papel had the highest child mortality: 337 out of every 1,000 children died before they had reached five years of age.

The Papel, who reside in Biombo, practise their religion according to what they refer to as the original law. They believe in reincarnation which means that human souls circulate through births and deaths between this world and the 'other' world. Each soul reborn in an infant carries with it some personal characteristics and physical appearance may even be attributed to the former bearer of the soul. The Papel trace their kinship through maternal family lines which means that children belong to their maternal family. Inheritance is also matrilineal, which implies that upon a man's death his sister's son will inherit his material goods and position. A child has the family name of the father, who first takes up the maternal family name when he inherits his mother-brother. Otherwise, name-giving is informal and without a ritual ceremony.

The position of Papel newborns generally appears to be fairly secure. They belong to their mothers' lineage, their individual personalities are recognized and there is no requirement of ritual name-giving to acquire personhood or social membership. This does not however apply to all newborns. At times people begin to wonder if a particular infant may have been born without a human soul.[17] A pregnant woman may become penetrated by a spirit when washing clothes or fetching water from a spring-water well. The spirit can enter the foetus in her womb and replace the human soul, thus at birth a child without a human soul will be born. Such an infant is either somehow abnormal or does not develop normally during the first months of life. Thus, little by little, people start to speculate about the child's true nature.

Infants who become suspected of being non-human have a wide range of physical or behavioural anomalies or functional impairments. This group includes some, but not all, children who are disabled as well as some whom we would not regard as disabled. They are typically described as boneless, pale and listless, with weird eyes and frothing mouths. Descriptions of particular infants indicate that they are commonly paralysed but with a normal bodily shape; they cannot sit, walk or reach for things when they grow older. Others are described as having severe malformation. Minor disparities such as being too long, too small or having too big a head may however also indicate a non-human status, as well as an unusual colour or minor bodily impairments. Some of the suspected infants are said to exhibit peculiar behaviour such as leaving the bed at night or moving under the bed in search of eggs. Some survive with hardly any food while others suckle their mother's breast all the time. These infants are considered to be dangerous, even life threatening, to their maternal lineage and in particular, to the mother. If the mother breastfeeds a non-human child she is believed to continue giving birth to non-human children.

Notwithstanding the wide range of physical problems and anomalies described above, infants are not classified as non-humans with a sole reference to their anomaly. As they are considered to be dangerous for their maternal lineage, and especially for the mother, it is important to verify the true nature of suspected children. There are two procedures to identify the true nature of infants suspected of being non-human, and both correspond to what in anthropological literature is referred to as infanticide. First, they can be 'taken to the sea' by elderly maternal relatives and the infant and a calabash (the gourd of the baobab tree), with particular items such as an egg and distilled alcohol, are put on the beach. If the child is non-human, it will drink the egg and disappear with the other items into the sea and thereby the spirit will return to where it came from, its true home. Since colonial time, the law prohibits 'taking children to the sea'. The second alternative is to take the infant to a ritual specialist who makes an offer and asks for help from a spirit to identify the true nature of the infant. The specialist will define a test period, normally seven days, during which food will be arranged for the child, as the mother has to stop breastfeeding. Survival after the trial period is an indication of the human nature of the infant, which will be returned to its mother.

How do mothers react to the suggestion that their infants might be non-human? Mothers (and fathers who, however, do not have a say as the infant belongs to the lineage of the mother), and sometimes others, tend to argue for another interpretation of their child's condition. For them it is important to be able to construct a clear and consistent argument. Mothers are also reluctant to stop breastfeeding the child knowing that it is unlikely to survive without the breast milk. The hope for cure is evident and it encourages mothers to seek a solution to their child's problem. Thus, children suspected of being non-human are taken to a variety of health care alternatives before being taken to the sea or to a ritual specialist. The identification procedure is not faultless either. Sometimes the result of the test performed to identify the nature of an infant is questioned, and thus a child's death or survival can be explained differently.

After a seemingly successful identification procedure, new evidence may later give rise to new interpretations. Yet, anxious maternal relatives may be more concerned with restoration of social order through extinction of an eventual non-human child than with a strictly performed verification procedure. Evidently, interests are conflicting and the actors interpret events differently in their attempts to advance their cases.

When a suspected child dies the mother grieves, despite proscriptions to the contrary. She is likely to challenge the way the test was performed, but most likely without calling into question the very existence of non-human children. Obviously, for an infant to become classified as non-human is not a favourable situation. In addition, for those involved such classification contributes to ambiguity, disagreements and anguish. How can one be sure?

I maintain that the procedures described above to classify infants suspected to be non-humans in Biombo should be interpreted as an attempt to restore social order through alleviation of danger rather than being seen as a rational reproductive strategy.[18] The classificatory system applied explains and directs action, and as such helps humans to deal with perceived deviance. I argue that it is misleading to conceive of the procedures as a rational reproductive strategy, or as killing (conscious or unconscious) of 'lowered-viability infants'. Some of the children suspected of belonging to the category of non-human children in Biombo are not unviable: they may be slightly anomalous but are nevertheless healthy. At the same time, there are many surviving disabled children in the community, some of them severely impaired, who never become suspected of being non-humans. Their impairment is interpreted differently and their humanness is never questioned. In Biombo, truly human children are not killed, despite severe disability. To kill such children would be classified as a murder, an immoral and dangerous act.

When infants die in Biombo, which is far too common an event, maternal grief is evident. Children's deaths are always considered to be bad deaths, in contrast to the deaths of old people who die when God calls on them. Children's deaths are seen to be avoidable. In other words, there are no fatal diseases. According to the local etiological classification of diseases there are no fatal diseases as such; children die because of human shortcomings. Diseases are thought to be curable if they are diagnosed correctly and treated adequately and quickly. It is thus my interpretation that *per definition* there are no unviable infants in Biombo.[19] For a comparative approach let us look at classificatory systems and treatment procedures for infants suspected to be unviable in Iceland, a country that has one of the lowest infant mortality rates in the world. Are there any unviable infants in Iceland? In such a case, what criteria are used to assign a child into that category?

Unviable infants

In most societies there are children who are classified as unviable at birth, for instance extremely premature infants. Due to advances in treatment options and new medicines for preterm infants their chances of survival have increased considerably in the last decades. Nonetheless preterm birth is the principal cause of infant mortality in western Europe and the United States. While more than 70 per cent of infants with birth weights between 501–1000 g survive, almost one-tenth of these children endure serious intra-cerebral haemorrhage and nearly half of them have some severe neonatal complication, of which cerebral palsy, blindness, deafness and severe hypotonia are the most common.[20] Consequently, it is heavily debated whether and when expensive intensive care treatment should be given to infants who are born extremely preterm.

Are there infants who should be denied treatment due to their lack of viability or prospects for serious disability in the future? In short, within moral philosophy there are three main approaches to this question.[21]

According to the first one, newborns do not automatically have an individual right to live. The philosopher Singer[22] maintains that infants lack characteristics such as rationality, autonomy and self-consciousness which are crucial for such a right. 'Killing them, therefore, cannot be equated with killing normal human beings, or any other self-conscious beings.' Singer emphasizes that in this respect, he is not making a distinction between a disabled or non-disabled infant.

The second view on the rightness of end-of-life decisions may best be represented by the Catholic Church which argues that human life is sacred and everything should be done to preserve it.

According to the third argument human life should be maintained only when life is considered to be a better alternative than death. However, it has turned out to be difficult to predict the outcome for individual infants and there are disagreements on which criteria should be used.[23] As yet, there is no agreement on who should take the final decision and to what extent parents should be involved in the decision-making.

Tyson and Stoll[24] argue for 'evidence-based ethics' which would allow decision-making free from social context. They assume that 'good ethics begins with good facts' and argue that treatment should be opted for when 'the benefits outweigh the burdens'.[25] They suggest that infants born with birth weight less than a predefined limit based on probability of survival and high risk of impairment should not get treatment and parents should not be allowed to demand one. Likewise, parents should not be allowed to demand termination of treatment for infants with birth weight over a certain limit. This implies that girls will be treated with a lower birth weight than boys as they have a better chance of survival than boys. According to Tyson and Stoll, parents should be given a role in decision-making concerning their infant's eventual non-treatment only if the infant has a birth weight between the established limits.

Between and within the Nordic countries management routines of end-of-life decisions in neonatal intensive care units seem to vary. In Sweden, end-of-life decisions for extremely preterm infants have been heavily debated, even in the mass media.[26] Considering the different opinions that have been expressed by key professionals on the rightness of withholding and/or withdrawing treatment, it is reasonable to assume that the practice varies within neonatal intensive care units in the country. The law gives parents the right to make treatment decisions on behalf of their child but only if they are deemed able to take the child's best interests into consideration. According to Götlind,[27] who conducted fieldwork in a Swedish neonatal intensive care unit, staff opinion became streamlined during a 'wait-until-certain' period that allowed the neonatologists to represent their decision as founded on reliable knowledge and unanimity. Thereafter, parents' responses were crucial for final decisions. However, a parental request to withdraw or withhold a treatment from a child judged to be viable by medical staff would not be upheld.

At a conference with the title Limits for the Treatment of Prematurely Born Infants, held in 1998 in Norway, it was agreed not to use certain gestational age as a criterion for treatment decisions.[28] Decisions whether to start treatment at birth and continue treatment should rest on ethical considerations of the parents and the different health professionals involved. Important questions about parental participation were not outlined in any detail. However, it was stated that parents should take part in the decision-making process while the physician should have the final responsibility, which seems to reflect practice. A study found that parents took part in end-of-life decisions for 98 per cent of preterm infants who died in a Norwegian neonatal intensive care unit.[29]

The term 'vitality', or lack thereof, is frequently used as a criterion for assigning an infant to a category of not demonstrating enough 'will to live' at birth, with the result that treatment is withheld. Brinchmann and Nortvedt[30] found that an assessment of the child's vitality was an important criterion for a treatment decision in relation to preterm infants whose situation was uncertain. Evaluation of vitality was based on objective and subjective elements, as well as a judgement of the child's personality and temperament. As such, medical staff described vitality as 'a specific ability or characteristic, or a will to come out of a hopeless situation'.[31] However, not all physicians agree with vitality as a criterion for treatment decisions, arguing it is far too subjective, in addition to the fact that there are infants who appear to be lifeless at birth who nonetheless respond positively to treatment.

Greisen[32] underlines that Danish law gives the physician the final responsibility for treatment decisions while the parents should be fully informed and they must consent to any treatment decision. In urgent situations the physician is obliged to treat. According to Greisen, neonatal intensive care units in Denmark as of 2004 use conservative treatment for infants born before 26 weeks' gestational age which means that they are not given active life-sustaining treatment. Withholding or withdrawal of treatment from children is permitted by law if treatment can be expected only to prolong the process of dying. However, future disability and expected low quality of life is not a lawful cause for withholding or withdrawing of treatment. In cases where there is no consensus on a treatment the physician must get consent for his opinion from the child welfare board of the municipality, seemingly an uncommon event as Greisen does not recognize any such case. In recent years it has become more complicated not to step up life support when the infant has lived for some days. Greisen stresses that parents should by fully informed and he describes his own procedure as follows:

> I always try to express that we do not wish to support the life of very ill babies to the bitter end. If the baby's condition is poor at birth or if complications arise, the parents will be informed, and withholding or withdrawal of intensive care will be considered to avoid unnecessary suffering. Parents almost always express appreciation of this. I listen for an opening to discuss the risk of handicap. The parents may have had personal experience of handicap with family or friends. Usually, the parents agree that some forms of handicap may be worse than death, but some forms of handicap are quite acceptable.[33]

The Danish approach described by Greisen has certain similarities with the Dutch practices for treatment of preterm infants described by Vermeulen,[34] who maintains: 'The medical policy of the Dutch ward can be characterized as "statistical" or "categorical". On the basis of statistics about life chances and disability rates, treatment for some children is considered futile and cruel.'[35] This practice, as well as the Danish one described by Greisen, correspond quite closely with the so-called 'evidence-based ethics' as presented by Tyson and Stoll.[36]

Should parents have the right to request or refuse lifesaving treatment for their preterm infants? What chances of survival and probabilities of impairment are acceptable? Within bioethics and moral philosophy there are varied opinions on parents' participation in decision-making about the continuation of life-sustaining treatment for their severely ill or disabled children.[37] These opinions reflect assumptions about human nature. Some argue that parents should not be involved in end-of-life decisions for their children because they are emotionally involved. On one hand, parents are assumed to want to keep the child irrespective of the severity of its situation and suffering. On the other hand, parents are assumed not to want a disabled child and thus to be likely to demand withdrawal or withholding of treatment. Further, many underline parents' lack of medical knowledge to make an informed decision. Finally, some argue that the parents exclusively should make end-of-life decisions for their children, as they have to live with the outcome.

Let us now turn to the experiences and thoughts of parents of preterm infants born in Iceland with a birth weight of 1,000 g or less. How do they perceive their situations and think of their roles in treatment decisions?

Preterm birth in Iceland

The Icelandic population of approximately 300,000 inhabitants, has one of the lowest infant mortality rates in the world. There are approximately 10–15 infants born annually with a birth weight of 1,000 g or less and probabilities of disability and survival for this group of preterm children are comparable with other Nordic and western European countries.[38]

In the present study, prospective and retrospective groups of preterm infants with birth weight less than 1,000 g were identified for the research. Children in the prospective group were born in the period 1 September 2001 to 31 August 2002, and children in the retrospective group were born from 1 September 1998 to 31 August 2001. Fieldwork was conducted in a neonatal intensive care unit, day care centres, treatment facilities and through visits to the homes of the children. Parents, family members, and professionals were interviewed. The presentation given in this chapter is based mainly on discussions with 22 mothers and 19 fathers of these preterm infants.

Preterm birth and the first encounter

Preterm birth, in particular one that occurs before 30 gestational weeks, has little in common with the ideal birth so frequently romanticized in current literature on natural births. The parents who participated in the study could almost all recall the first signs of trouble in pregnancy that later resulted in the premature births of their children. Either the mothers had stayed in hospital for some days or weeks or else they had been rushed in. Information given to them by hospital staff stressed the importance of delaying the birth for as long as possible. The risk that the infant would not survive the birth was made clear and they were informed that the first days after delivery were the most dangerous ones. Uncertainty was underlined. Some parents were informed that the decision about initiation of treatment would be taken first after birth depending on the condition of the infant. No parents expressed their wish not to resuscitate the infant and all expressed their hope that the infant would survive, irrespective of the circumstances of pregnancy. Parents were informed that girls had better chances of survival than boys.

Most of the parents remembered when they entered the neonatal intensive care unit to see their newborn infants for the first time. Frequently the parents went together. However, several fathers were the first to see the infants because the mothers were too sick to visit the unit. Some of these fathers admitted that they had almost taken for granted that their infants would die, thus they were far more preoccupied with the health of their wives. At times, they even admitted to have consciously given better news back to their wives than was justified so as not to make them worry too much. Indeed, some of the mothers were aware of this. Staff members always congratulated parents on their newborns, regardless of the severity of the children's health, something parents interpreted as an optimistic sign. However, a few found it strange, considering the severity of the situation.

The most common remark about the appearance of the infant concerned the size, frequently followed by comments about all the technical apparatus to which the baby was attached. Comparison with a pack of margarine was common. Many found it a miracle their infants were alive and some parents admitted they had put their faith in God. Many mothers and fathers stressed that their infants were beautiful, but contradictory statements were sometimes given. A father said his twins were really 'cute' but also 'foetus-like' and in fact 'not so beautiful'. The mother of the same twins said they were 'healthy-looking'. A few parents said they found their infants somewhat alien and not so human-like, more like a bird, chicken, ET or a foetus. Several commented on their own surprise over the completeness of their infants' bodies. They took time to check details – counting toes and fingers. A mother explained how she examined her infant: 'My baby was so tiny and almost transparent. I looked at the fingers and ears and everything. The only thing I could do was to look and hope.'

For many parents it was a victory that their children had survived the first hours after birth. Some parents stressed their infants were 'chubby', 'bigger than others', or had 'a strong will'; others felt their newborns were vulnerable, helpless, and even more like a stillborn or almost dead. All the parents hoped for survival and cure independent of their conceptions about the physical appearance of the child and independent of circumstances of pregnancy. Faith in the medical sciences was evident. At the same time many mentioned having prayed to God for help.

What life is worth living?

Is it ever ethically acceptable to withhold lifesaving treatment from a premature infant? Almost all of the parents responded to this question with an affirmation that there were cases that would justify such a decision. Only one parent, a father, maintained that whatever the situation, nobody had the right to take such a decision, either for her- or himself, a child or an adult. He stressed that this opinion was not based on religion as he considered himself to be an atheist. Rather, according to his understanding, 'It is money, not respect for human life' that is the ultimate reason behind end-of-life decisions.

It was more difficult for some of the parents to clarify the conditions that would allow an end-of-life decision than to have an opinion about its general rightness. Criteria mentioned by parents tended to be related to quality of life. If an infant had 'no life' it would be better to withdraw treatment than let the infant suffer, many said. 'No life' referred to a life through postponement of inevitable death for a short period of time through painful treatment. 'No life' was also a question of life without crucial qualities, such as an ability to take part in human communication. Most of the parents stressed that it was not a question of whether the child would become disabled, rather what kind and how serious the disability. However, as long there was hope, suffering alone was not a sufficient criterion for withdrawal of treatment.

Assessment of quality of life turned out to be a tricky criterion for withdrawal of lifesaving treatment. Having an experience of living with a severely disabled person could result in both refusal and acceptance of quality of life as a valid argument for withdrawal of lifesaving treatment. Who could judge what life was worth living? Some parents wondered 'what kind of life' was awaiting a child with severe impairment, while others argued that it was not up to them to decide what kind of life was worth living.

During the first days and weeks after birth disability was not the most important issue, for most parents. Survival was what mattered. Considerations about disability emerged later. After discharge from the hospital, a few parents began to wonder why they had not been better informed about the risk of disability. Such information would not have changed their opinion about the survival of the child; nonetheless it would have been good to be prepared. On the other hand, some of the parents acknowledged that they had not wanted to know more about all possible future impairments, as they did not want to be worried about something that might never happen. 'When the problem is there, you tackle it.'

Who should take end-of-life decisions?

Almost all the parents agreed that life-sustaining treatment of extremely premature infants should not be withheld without parental involvement in that decision. Yet 'to be involved' or 'to take part in a decision' did not mean the same thing to all parents. For a few, taking part appeared to be synonymous with having knowledge about the issues; for others it meant having the final word.

Both mothers and fathers argued that they should take part in treatment decisions for their children. Of course, most parents were not trained in medical issues, and they felt that the physicians should inform them. That was their role: to inform parents about 'the facts of the case'. Many parents were unaware of disagreement among medical staff about 'the facts' that often characterizes decisions on the treatment of prematurely born infants due to difficulties in predicting their future prospects. Parents repeatedly expressed their confidence in the professionalism of the staff at the unit and admired their devotion to their work. However, nurses were not assumed to take part in treatment decisions, as it was the responsibility of the neonatologists. Parents commonly argued that decisions about withdrawal should not be taken without parental consent. However a joint agreement was preferable and, indeed, if the physicians would say there was nothing they could do they would accept that.

Few of the parents were aware of both the uncertainty that characterizes future prospects of premature babies and the disagreements among professionals about what to do in particular cases. A father highlighted different views and methods in 'explaining things' and a mother argued that the most important issue was how the physicians would 'present the information'. Most parents were aware of their right to be informed about all medical aspects that concerned their infant, and most of them were of the opinion that they got all available information. Only one father maintained that parents should not be involved at all in end-of-life decisions for their children. He meant that shielding parents from difficult information could be acceptable and argued that if the infant 'will be nothing, only institutional food, and if that is obvious, then the physicians should take a decision and you do not have to know too much about it ... of course one should first try to give treatment'. He based his opinion on the experience of friends whose infant was severely disabled from birth, not his own experience of having a preterm infant.

Only one father maintained that whatever the situation, parents should decide the fate of their children. Considering that a pregnant woman was allowed to have an abortion for a foetus with Down's syndrome, it would be logical that she could decide whether to keep a severely impaired newborn alive. This father had decided that his child should be given all available treatment, despite repeated medical warnings about extremely serious disability. 'Parents are not experts except emotionally', he argued, and that was a reason enough for their right to take part in treatment decisions. Most parents, however, found it difficult to give an unambiguous answer to the question of whether parents should demand withdrawal of care without the consent of medical specialists. A mother argued that withdrawal of treatment was unacceptable without the consent of parents. On the other hand, parents should not have the right to decide to withdraw treatment against the advice of medical staff, and indeed, parents who could not accept having severely disabled children should not have children. Some parents expressed their disapproval of parents who did not want to raise a disabled child. Others expressed their understanding.

In short, almost all the parents who participated in the study agreed that it was justifiable to withdraw or withhold treatment from dying preterm infants or when a severe future disability was predicted. Criteria most commonly mentioned for such a decision were 'no life' or inability to take part in human communication. It should be the work of specialists to judge if the infant was viable and worthy of treatment, many argued. At the same time, most, but not all, of the parents were unaware of disagreements among professionals about end-of-life decisions and the difficulty in assessing future outcome. However, whatever the future prospects for an extremely preterm infant the precondition for treatment at birth is essentially to be classified as 'born alive'.

Live birth

At first glance it appears an easy task to define what is live birth. Let us scrutinize the issue. According to the World Health Organization (WHO), the conventional definition of live birth refers to

> the complete expulsion or extraction from its mother of a product of conception, irrespective of the duration of the pregnancy, which, after such separation, breathes or shows any other evidence of life – e.g. beating of the heart, pulsation of the umbilical cord or definite movement of voluntary muscles – whether or not the umbilical cord has been cut or the placenta is attached. Each product of such a birth is considered live born.[39]

This definition of live birth is however not always practical and easy to follow. Increased chances of survival of infants born extremely prematurely have resulted in revised definitions of concepts related to birth outcome. As Greisen points out, 'beating of the heart, pulsation of the cord or even gasping may be seen in births earlier than 20 weeks' gestation, and the radical stance of giving all possible life support is probably not taken in any society'.[40] Greisen highlights that the proportion of infants who are classified dead at birth are considerably higher at 22, 23, 24 and 25 weeks' gestational age compared with those at 26 and 27 weeks' gestation, and suggests that the reason for this difference is more likely to be socially rather than biologically grounded.[41] Obviously, to be registered as having died an infant must first have been classified as having been born alive. Stanton illustrates this point clearly:

> Live-born babies who die early might be misclassified as stillbirths and vice versa for several reasons: lack of knowledge; lack of careful assessment for signs of life; avoidance of blame, extra work, or audit review for the birth attendant; or reasons of perceived gain or loss for the family. For example, the registration of a live birth could encumber the family with funeral arrangements and costs, and the physician with extensive paperwork, whereas a stillbirth requires no funeral and less paperwork – differences that may promote misclassification towards stillbirths.[42]

Stillbirths and deaths that occur during the first seven days of life (that is 0–6 days) – so-called early neonatal deaths – used to be, and sometimes still are, grouped together under the term perinatal deaths. Definitions of perinatal mortality have varied vastly[43] and thus there is an absence of comparative statistics even within Europe.[44] Advances in intensive neonatal treatment which have contributed to survival at 23 weeks have prompted changes in the definition of foetal death. Thus, according to WHO's latest recommendation, the perinatal period begins at the gestational age of 22 completed weeks (154 days) and lasts until seven days after birth. Stillbirths (or foetal deaths) refer to deaths prior to the complete expulsion or extraction from its mother of a product of conception, irrespective of the duration of pregnancy.[45] On the other hand, for international comparison WHO defines stillbirth (or late foetal death) as death occurring at least 28 weeks of gestation or 1,000 g birth weight or more.[46]

Disregarding evidence of life as the criterion for live birth has long been practised in Western medical care. In the 1970s and earlier, extremely prematurely born infants, with birth weights of 1,000 g or less, were routinely classified as either stillbirth or miscarriage, and limited efforts were made to save their lives. In a description of his first day of work in a neonatal intensive care unit in a New York hospital in 1969, a neonatologist illustrates the point.[47] To his surprise, a boy with a birth weight of 1,000 g and a gestational age of 28 weeks was put aside, in line with practice 'throughout the country'. He was told that all such babies died: they were unviable.

Conclusion

In this chapter I have discussed classifications of newborns in a global context. As case studies, I have paid particular attention to classification of infants as being non-humans in Biombo, Guinea-Bissau, and as unviable in Iceland. These classifications emerge in particular societies at a particular time, but nonetheless they have some similarities and distinctions.

In both settings, experts have their role in assigning the infants to categories while laypeople may influence the outcome. In both cases, the classifications described can have serious, even fatal, consequences for the infants involved. The categorizations are also contested by those involved in both settings, and their accuracy questioned. Yet, the legitimacy of the categories seems to be generally accepted. Both the classificatory systems are ambiguous, and they create tension and anxiety for those engaged in the process. The so-called evidence-based ethical aims to reduce ambiguity and measurable features such as birth weight and gestational age are proposed as criteria for making treatment decisions about preterm infants. Unmistakably, the definitions of concepts such as stillborn, foetal death and live birth originate at a particular time within a particular context. These concepts have been shaped by access to technology that has contributed to increased survival of preterm infants.

262 *Jónína Einarsdóttir*

Systematic discrimination in relation to disabled people is well documented. Jenkins[48] maintains that the classification of those who are incompetent is characterized by two themes. First, the division between humans and non-humans is emphasized, and second, 'it becomes a moral imperative' to be normal which is underpinned by the notion of 'the way things ought to be'. Both themes underlie the classifications of newborns documented in this chapter. Attribution of self-consciousness, personhood, humanness, membership and even competence may be crucial for a newborn when it concerns her or his right to life.

Acknowledgments

The Research Council of Iceland (RANNIS) funded the research on which this article is based. The Centre for Child Health Services in Reykjavík and the Institute of Anthropology, University of Iceland were guest institutions for the research project. The Icelandic Data Protection Authority and the Ethics Committee of the National University Hospital in Reykjavik granted requested ethical permissions. Parents and professionals who participated in the study are all gratefully acknowledged.

Notes

1 Einarsdóttir, J. (2004) *Tired of Weeping: Mother Love, Child Death, and Poverty in Guinea-Bissau*, (2nd edn). Madison, Wisconsin: University of Wisconsin Press.
2 Einarsdóttir, J. (2006) 'Child survival in affluence and poverty: Ethics and fieldwork experiences from Iceland and Guinea-Bissau', *Field Methods*, 18, 2, 189–204.
3 Einarsdóttir (2004), op. cit. pp.139–145.
4 Legesse, A. (1973) *Gada: Three Approaches to the Study of African Society*. New York: Free Press; Oboler, R.S. (1985) *Women, Power, and Economic Change: The Nandi of Kenya*. Stanford: Stanford University Press.
5 Alford, R.D. (1988) *Naming and Identity: A Cross-Cultural Study of Personal Naming Practices*. New Haven: HRAF Press.
6 Howell, S. (1989) 'From child to human: Chewong concepts of self', in G. Jahoda and I.M. Lewis (eds) *Acquiring Culture: Cross Cultural Studies in Child Development*. London: Routledge, pp.147–168.
7 Nicolaisen, I. (1995) 'Persons and nonpersons: Disability among the Punan Bah of Central Borneo', in B. Ingstad and S.R. Whyte (eds) *Disability and Culture*. Berkeley: University of California Press, pp.38–55.
8 Scheper-Hughes, N. (1992) *Death Without Weeping: The Violence of Everyday Life in Brazil*. Berkeley: University of California Press.
9 De Mause, L. (1974) 'The evolution of childhood', in L. de Mause (ed.) *The History of Childhood*. New York: Harper Torchbooks, pp.1–73; Cunningham, H. (1995) *Children and Childhood in Western Society since 1500*. London: Longman.
10 Hobbs, C.J. and Wynne, J.M. (1996) 'Child abuse and sudden infant death', *Child Abuse Review*, 5, 155–169; Hoffer, P.C. and Hull, N.E.H. (1981) *Murdering Mothers: Infanticide in England and New England 1558–1803*. New York: New York University Press; Meyer, C.L., Oberman, M., White, K., Rone, M., Batra, P. and Proano, T.C. (2001) *Mothers who Kill their Children: Understanding the Acts of*

Moms from Susan Smith to the 'Prom Mom'. New York and London: New York University Press; Schulte, R. (1984) 'Infanticide in rural Bavaria in the nineteenth century', in H. Medick and D.W. Sabean (eds) *Interest and Emotion: Essays on the Study of Family and Kinship.* Cambridge: Cambridge University Press, pp.77–102.

11 Einarsdóttir, J. (2005) 'Restoration of social order through the extinction of non-human children', in V. Steffen, R. Jenkins and H. Jessen (eds) *Managing Uncertainty: Ethnographic Studies of Illness, Risk and the Struggles of Control.* Copenhagen: Museum Tusculanum Press, pp.31–51.

12 Scheper-Hughes (1992), op. cit.

13 Scheper-Hughes (1992), op. cit. p.430.

14 Hrdy, S.B. (1999) *Mother Nature: A History of Mothers, Infants, and Natural Selection.* New York, Pantheon Books, p.10.

15 Ibid., pp.459–460.

16 Aaby, P., Gomes, J., Høj, L. and Sandström, A. (1997) *Estudo de Saúde de Mulheres em Idade Fertil e os Seus Filhos: Dados de 1990–1995.* Bissau, UNICEF/Projecto de Saúde de Bandim, Bissau.

17 See Einarsdóttir (2004), op. cit. pp. 162–173.

18 For a more detailed discussion, see Einarsdóttir (2005), op. cit.

19 See Einarsdóttir (2004) op. cit. pp.133–137.

20 Greene, M.F. (2002) 'Outcomes of very low birth weight in young adults', *New England Journal of Medicine,* 346, pp.146–148.

21 Árnason, V. (1997) *Siðfræði lífs og dauða: Erfiðar ákvarðanir í heilbrigðiskerfinu.* Reykjavík: Rannsóknastofnun í siðfræði, Háskóli Íslands.

22 Singer, P. (1993) *Practical Ethics.* Cambridge: Cambridge University Press, p.182.

23 Ambalavanan, N., Baibergenova, A., Carlo, W.A., Saigal, S., Schmidt, B. and Thorpe, K.E. (2006) 'Early prediction of poor outcome in extremely low birth weight infants by classification tree analysis', *Journal of Pediatrics,* 148, 434–438; Bharti, B. and Bharti, S. (2005) 'A review of the Apgar score indicated that contextualization was required within the contemporary perinatal and neonatal care framework in different settings', *Journal of Clinical Epidemiology,* 58, 121–129; Eriksson, M., Brodin, L., Finnström, O. and Schollin, J. (2002) 'Can severity-of-illness indices for neonatal intensive care predict outcome at 4 years of age?' *Acta Paediatrica,* 91, 1093–1100; Savage, T.A. and Kavanaugh, K. (2004) 'Resuscitation of the extremely preterm infant: A perspective from the social model of disability', *Newborn and Infant Nursing Reviews,* 4, 2, 114–120.

24 Tyson, J.E. and Stoll, B.J. (2003) 'Evidence-based ethics and the care and outcome of extremely premature infants', *Clinics in Perinatology,* 30, 2, 363–387.

25 Ibid., p.366.

26 Götlind, K. (2002) *Värderingskonflikter i praktiken. Hantering av ambivalens vid en neonatal intensivvårdsavdelning* (Dilemmas in practice: Handling of ambivalence in a neonatal intensive care unit). Department of Sociology, Uppsala, Uppsala University/Förlag AB Gondolin, pp.15–16.

27 Ibid., p.252.

28 Brinchmann, B.S. and Vik, T. (2005) 'Parents' involvement in life-and-death decisions in neonatal intensive care: Norwegian attitudes', *Newborn and Infant Nursing Reviews,* 5, 2, 77–81.

29 Ibid., p.78.

30 Brinchmann, B.S. and Nortvedt, P. (2001) 'Ethical decision making in neonatal units: The normative significance of vitality', *Medicine, Health Care and Philosophy,* 4, 193–200.

31 Ibid., p.196.

32 Greisen, G. (2004) 'Managing births at the limit of viability: The Danish experience', *Seminars in Fetal and Neonatal Medicine, Preterm Birth: Advances in Prevention and Management*, 9, 453–457.

33 Ibid., p.455.

34 Vermeulen, E. (2004) 'Dealing with doubt: Making decisions in a neonatal ward in The Netherlands', *Social Science* and *Medicine*, 59, 10, 2071–2085.

35 See also Walther, F.J. (2005) 'Withholding treatment, withdrawing treatment, and palliative care in the neonatal intensive care unit', *Early Human Development, Neonatal Update*, 81, 12, 965–972.

36 Tyson and Stoll (2003), op. cit.

37 Árnason (1997) op. cit.; Beauchamp, T.L. and Childress, J.F. (1994) *Principles of Biomedical Ethics*. New York: Oxford University Press; Rachels, J. (1993) *The Elements of Moral Philosophy*. New York: McGraw-Hill, Inc.

38 Georgsdóttir, I. and Dagbjartsson, A. (2003) 'Litlir fyrirburar á Íslandi: Lífslíkur og fötlun, *Læknablaðið*, 89, 299–302; Georgsdóttir, I., Sæmundsen, E., Leósdóttir, F., Símonardóttir, I., Egilsson, S.Þ. and Dagbjartsson, A. (2004) 'Litlir fyrirburar á Íslandi: Niðurstöður þroskamælinga við fimm ára aldur', *Læknablaðið*, 90, 747–754; Georgsdóttir, I., Sæmundsen, E., Símonardóttir, I., Halldórsson, J.G., Egilson, S.Þ., Leósdóttir, F., Ingvarsdóttir, B., Sindrason, E. and Dagbjartsson, A. (2003) 'Litlir fyrirburar á Íslandi: Heilsufar og þroski', *Læknablaðið*, 89, 575–581.

39 WHO (2006a) *Appendix: Glossary of Terms*. Geneva, World Health Organization. Available online at http://www.who.int/healthinfo/statistics/indunder5 mortality/en/ (Accessed 15 December 2006).

40 Greisen (2004),op. cit. p.453.

41 Greisen (2004), op. cit. p.455.

42 Stanton, C., Lawn, J.E., Rahman, H., Wilczynska-Ketende, K. and Hill, K. (2006) 'Stillbirth rates: Delivering estimates in 190 countries', *Lancet*, 367, 9521, 1487.

43 For instance, Buitendijk *et al.* (2003) found that Sweden and Denmark do not register deaths before 28 weeks, Italy before 180 days and the UK before 24 weeks of gestation. Buitendijk, S., Zeitlin, J., Cuttini, M., Langhoff-Roos, J. and Bottu, J. (2003) 'Indicators of fetal and infant health outcomes', *European Journal of Obstetrics & Gynecology and Reproductive Biology*, 111, S66–S77.

44 Stanton *et al.* (2006) op. cit, pp.1487–1488.

45 WHO (2006b) *Neonatal and Perinatal Mortality: Country, Regional and Global Estimates*. Geneva, World Health Organization, p.6.

46 Ibid, pp.44–45.

47 Solomon, S.D. (1995) 'Suffer the little children', *Technology Review*, 98, 3, 42–52.

48 Jenkins, R. (1998) 'Towards a social model of (in)competence', in R. Jenkins (ed.) *Questions of Competence: Culture, Classification and Intellectual Disability*. Cambridge: Cambridge University Press, pp.1–24.

Index